Customer
Information
Control
Systems
for microcomputers

Joseph J. Le Bert

McGraw-Hill Publishing Company

New York St. Louis San Francisco Auckland Bogotá
Caracas Hamburg Lisbon London Madrid Mexico
Milan Montreal New Delhi Oklahoma City
Paris San Juan São Paulo Singapore
Sydney Tokyo Toronto

Library of Congress Cataloging-in-Publication Data

Le Bert, Joseph J.
  CICS for microcomputers.

  Rev. ed. of: Customer information control systems
made easy. c1986.
  Bibliography: p.
  Includes index.
  1. CICS (Computer system) I. Le Bert, Joseph J.
Customer information control systems made easy.
II. Title.
QA76.76.T45 1989   005.4'3   88-27137
ISBN 0-07-036968-2

1234567890 DOC/DOC 89432109

ISBN 0-07-036968-2

*The editors for this book were Theron Shreve and Lucy Mullins, the
designer was Naomi Auerbach, and the production supervisor was Richard
A. Ausburn. It was set in Century Schoolbook. It was composed by the
McGraw-Hill Publishing Company Professional Reference Division
composition unit.*

Printed and bound by R. R. Donnelley & Sons Company.

An excerpt from Form 3270 Information Display System Layout Sheet
(GX27-2951) is reprinted by permission from International Business
Machines Corporation and is used in the following figures: 2-1 through
2-10, 6-3, 13-1, 14-1, and 15-1.

Screen images displayed in appendixes E, F, and G are reprinted by
permission respectively from Realia, Inc.; Micro Focus, Innovative
Solutions, and Phaser Systems, Inc.; and Triangle Software Company.

*For more information about other McGraw-Hill materials,
call 1-800-2-MCGRAW in the United States. In other
countries, call your nearest McGraw-Hill office.*

*To my wife, Maryann, who encouraged me,
and to my children, Joseph, Dorothy, and Jean,
who inspired me.*

CONTENTS

PREFACE

CICS for Microcomputers is for you if you wish to gain a strong foundation in COBOL command-level CICS (Customer Information Control Systems) design, coding, and concepts. CICS which was originally available only on IBM mainframe computers can now be executed on microcomputers using software that makes it *highly* compatible with mainframe CICS. All program examples in this text were translated, compiled, and debugged on an IBM PC/XT using CICS software available from Realia, Inc.; Micro Focus; and Triangle Software Company. The programs ran exactly as intended with only minor *design* modifications. They should be equally compatible with any additional microcomputer CICS software that becomes available. The vendors supply screen generators that make the creation of basic mapping support (BMS) code easy, and they have debugging tools that are easy to use. These tools consist of interactive source code debuggers and a microcomputer version of the mainframe's execution diagnostic facility (EDF). Application programmers, system analysts, and project leaders should find *CICS for Microcomputers* easy to read, as well as an ideal reference book. It can be used as a textbook in a one-semester course for information processing, business, and computer science majors. Familiarity with COBOL, 3270 terminals or microcomputer monitors, data processing concepts, and the DOS operating system is the only prerequisite to understanding this book. Knowledge of the mainframe's virtual storage access methods (VSAM) or the microcomputer's indexed sequential access methods (ISAM) is helpful but not required. The use of ISAM in CICS application programs is similar in a microcomputer environment to the use of VSAM on mainframes.

The original intent in preparing this book was to substantially rewrite parts of my text *CICS Made Easy* in order to reflect differences between the use of CICS on a mainframe and on a micro. The main differences that exist are due to restrictions of the DOS operating system that prevent multitasking and multiterminal support. The OS/2 operating system will eliminate some of these restrictions and should make microcomputer CICS even more compatible with its mainframe counterpart. The use of program function keys on a micro simulates the use of the corresponding keys on a mainframe. For instance, F1 is used in place of PF1, and Ctrl-End might be used to erase to the end of a field. The stated objective of software vendors currently marketing CICS for microcomputer use is to achieve as high a level of compatibility with mainframe CICS as possible. With this objective in mind it was decided that this book would contain most of the material presented in *CICS Made Easy*. That book was written for mainframe computer users. Consult the CICS user's guide for your microcomputer software to note any minor differences that are due mainly to the lack of multitasking and multiterminal support.

A new chapter has been added that describes the color attributes which are likely to be used in a microcomputer environment. A second new chapter was added that gives a brief introduction to additional commands and concepts that are supported by microcomputer CICS software. This latter chapter also discusses numeric editing considerations and contains code for a flexible edit module that should satisfy most of your editing needs. That module was developed and tested using Micro Focus's PC-CICS but should work equally well using Realia's Real-CICS or Triangle's CICS/pc; it will also work on a mainframe computer. Several appendixes have been added that should be of interest to both current and potential microcomputer users of CICS software. The ease of program development, simulation, and testing on a micro should improve productivity and the quality of CICS systems. System prototyping prior to starting detailed system design and program development should become commonplace. Personnel trained in the mainframe use of CICS will likely use CICS on micros, while those who learn CICS on a micro may want to use it on a mainframe. Most mainframe command-level COBOL CICS applications that access only VSAM files can be run using existing microcomputer software with *no* changes required.

Training costs and employees' learning curves should be reduced as those new to CICS are able to use the theory they learn immediately on a micro without the fear of *crashing* a mainframe system. Ambitious employees may be encouraged and motivated to improve their CICS skills on their own microcomputers. The quality of design and programming is likely to improve, and the number of persons knowledgeable in CICS is sure to expand rapidly. This will increase the supply of individuals who are able to implement the transition of a mainframe system to a more flexible interactive microcomputer system.

Extensive use of CICS on microcomputers is expected for both program development and testing. The ability to transport CICS code between mainframes and micros with little or no change required will increase the appeal of microcomputer development and testing. Any mainframe programmer who has *crashed* a CICS test region due to a bug in his or her program will appreciate the use of micros for testing. When a mainframe CICS region crashes, *all* users of that region are disabled and are unable to proceed until technical support personnel restart CICS. Data processing managers and technical support personnel, who are under pressure to bring up a crashed region, will feel a sense of relief as testing and debugging shifts to micros. The ability to translate and compile programs without being placed at the bottom of the list of a mainframe queue AWAITING EXECUTION will please programmers and make them more productive. The ability to easily print screen images should be welcomed by designers and programmers who do not have ready access to a nearby printer. Technical support personnel will be able to respond more easily to requests for program control table (PCT), processing program table (PPT), and file control table (FCT) entries. These entries will have been pretested and can be presented to the systems programming group as a unit instead of having to be submitted as individual entries when they are needed.

Online systems which send, receive, and process data via a terminal are here to stay and will soon exceed the number of batch systems in many companies. CICS makes it easy for a programmer to code instructions that facilitate online functions. The more you learn about CICS, the better prepared you will be to play a significant role in the transition from batch to online systems.

This book takes a very simple nuts-and-bolts approach toward CICS commands and concepts. It does not attempt to convey every detail of CICS; many of these details are confusing to the beginner. I believe that once you master the material in this book, you will be prepared to develop and maintain most CICS programs. The initial foundation gained from this book will provide you with the knowledge and confidence to pursue advanced studies in CICS. You will not be overwhelmed with terminology at the start — only those terms and concepts which will actually be used are introduced as needed. A person unfamiliar with CICS will benefit most from this book by reading it from start to finish. Experienced CICS programmers can read those chapters which cover the material that they wish to review.

CICS for Microcomputers illustrates techniques and concepts through numerous simple examples and programs. Designers and programmers using this text should become productive very quickly. The programs in the examples employ a simple structured programming style which eliminates most GO TO's without confusing you with numerous nested IF statements. The examples can serve as models for future programs and should result in increased programmer productivity.

Maintenance should be reduced because most of the program code is reusable. If you have a good model to begin with, it should comprise as much as 80 percent of the code required for similar programs. It follows that if you start each program with a substantial percent of its code pretested, program development should be quicker and easier.

Many CICS concepts and examples in the text are associated with COBOL commands and techniques with which you are familiar. The best way to learn anything is through examples and use; you will master these principles quite easily by using them when writing and testing your own programs.

Chapter 1 defines a typical CICS system as viewed by a user and introduces basic terms and concepts.

Chapter 2 is devoted to designing maps which are easy to work with. Map design and conversational flow from screen to screen play an important role in the success or failure of an online system. Several map design guidelines are presented to make your screen design more effective.

Pseudoconversational programming, a technique which minimizes computer main storage requirements, is explained in Chap. 3 and is used for all programs throughout the text. System and programming documentation standards, discussed in Chap. 4, are essential to the success of a CICS system. Emphasis has been placed on those standards and documentation methods which are most effective and easiest to create and maintain.

Chapter 5 presents short easy-to-understand programs which build a foundation for the more comprehensive programs introduced in later chapters.

Chapter 6 on basic mapping support (BMS) explains how assembler language macros are coded in order to create maps: BMS maps are included with program examples. Chapter 7 is devoted to the use of assembled BMS maps. It is easy to create BMS maps when you have models to use for new maps, but their use can cause much difficulty if you do not understand certain fundamentals. Map attribute usage and its relation to physical and symbolic maps are covered extensively. You will probably use a map generator for creating your own BMS maps, but it is important to understand the basic BMS entries.

Program control commands, covered in Chap. 8, aid in the design of programs which communicate with one another. They are necessary in order to design effective systems and to develop efficient programming techniques. Chapter 11 on file control presents and explains all the commands that you are likely to use. File control is easier in CICS programs than is the case in a batch environment.

Chapters 9, 10, 12, 13, 14, 15, and 17 are devoted, with complete examples, to the following programs, respectively: menu, linked, inquiry, addition, change, deletion, and browse. Commands and concepts which have been presented are discussed on a section-by-section basis. All programs function as a part of a simplified system, enabling you to see the relation of the parts to the whole. This should prepare designers for new system development. High-quality work is more important than ever in online systems because it is difficult to conceal poor design and programming in an online environment.

Temporary storage, for which creative programmers will find many applications, is covered in Chap. 16. Several paging techniques, which can be coded with or without using temporary storage, are discussed. The browse program uses temporary storage queues for its paging routines. Routines used to accomplish forward and backward paging are presented. Methods for resetting a browse starting point and for returning a selection to an invoking program are also explained.

Chapter 18 on debugging and testing concentrates on the execution diagnostic facility which is available with all command-level CICS mainframe systems. Appendix G explains microcomputer software that simulates the use of mainframe EDF. Techniques are explained that can decrease the amount of time required to debug CICS programs.

Chapter 19 explains the use of color and other attribute extensions that are likely to be used for microcomputer CICS systems because of the availability of color monitors. The use of these attributes with CICS is the same on microcomputers as on mainframe computers.

Chapter 20 gives a brief introduction to additional CICS commands and concepts that are available to microcomputer users. The FORMATTIME command is covered in more detail, and possible applications of its use are explained. This chapter discusses numeric editing and contains code for a flexible module that should satisfy most of your editing needs.

Appendix C briefly reviews some basic DOS commands and concepts, such as the use of batch files, which may be helpful in a microcomputer environment.

Appendix D presents more detail on the following CICS tables: PCT, PPT, and FCT. This material should be helpful to applications programmers who may need to become more familiar with the basic entries in these tables in order to use CICS in a microcomputer environment.

Appendix E highlights the features of Realia's RealCICS software, App. F that of Micro Focus's PC-CICS, and App. G that of Triangle Software Company's CICS/pc. These companies are working to improve the early releases of their software which already provide an impressive simulation of mainframe CICS. Each company's stated goal is to make the software as compatible with mainframe CICS as is possible within the constraints of the microcomputer's operating system. The companies also provide some easy-to-use development and testing tools which should increase overall CICS development and maintenance productivity.

Appendix H contains the source code for the DEMO system's initialization screen. This program will also initialize the common work area (CWA) for the software which supports this feature. Appendix I contains complete BMS maps for program examples in this text that do not include the full code for their maps. Appendix J is a quick reference to CICS command formats and to the chapter in which they are explained.

Online systems have been around for many years. The extent of their application over the next few years should far exceed all that has been done in the past. Without knowledgeable and competent data processing personnel and users, this transition will not occur smoothly. I hope that this book will be successful in preparing you for the role you will play in putting your company on line.

Joseph J. Le Bert

ACKNOWLEDGMENTS

CICS for Microcomputers contains much information gathered through experience and contact with knowledgeable associates. I am grateful for the help obtained from the numerous proofreaders of my original CICS text, *CICS Made Easy.* I would like to thank the highly professional personnel at Micro Focus; Realia, Inc.; and Triangle Software Company for assisting me in evaluating their CICS software for this book. Most of all I want to thank my wife Maryann and children Joseph R., Dorothy, and Jean for their patience and understanding for the countless times that I was home but not with them.

1

THE USER'S VIEW
OF A CICS SYSTEM

CICS (Customer Information Control System) is basically an IBM teleprocessing monitor that makes it easy to send, receive, and process data through interaction with a terminal that consists of a display unit or cathode-ray tube (CRT) and a keyboard. CICS runs on IBM and IBM-compatible mainframe and microcomputer systems and provides an interface between application programs and the computer's operating system. CICS application programmers use command-level Cobol to code easy-to-use instructions into their programs. These commands facilitate accessing and updating online database files, data entry, and display of data and other information on the CRT. Users of CICS can transmit data from their terminals to the system where the data is processed and then sent back to the user.

Hands-on experience is important when learning one's way around a new system. Since I cannot take each of you to a terminal for a demonstration, this book uses pictures called "maps" on simulated 3270 terminal screens to illustrate CICS.

CICS, like most of data processing, has a jargon all its own: the required terms will be explained as they arise. Familiarize yourself with your terminal keyboard; most are similar to typewriter keyboards, with some models containing additional keys that are used in combination with a primary key.

Terminal Keyboard Usage

The terminal keyboard keys referred to in this book are those found on a 3270 keyboard. Microcomputer CICS software simulates the use of these keys by using keys on the micro's keyboard.

Attention IDentifier (AID) Keys

1. ENTER—This is the most commonly used key; it is usually pressed in order to effect the transfer of data from a terminal into a program. A

program can test if this key was pressed in order to control the flow of its logic.

2. CLEAR—I use this key to terminate a session on the terminal. When the terminal operator is finished, the CLEAR key is pressed causing the program to display the message SESSION COMPLETED. This is a programmer-defined action, not a standard function.

3. PFXX—Program function (PF) keys transfer data from a terminal into a program. They are signals or switches set external to the program by keys on the terminal keyboard. PF keys can be used by a program to control the sequence of its logic. There are up to 24 PF keys, designated as PF1 through PF24.

4. PAX—Program attention (PA) keys are similar to PF keys, but they do not transfer data from a terminal into a program as the ENTER and PF keys do. There are three PA keys: PA1, PA2, and PA3.

Miscellaneous Keys

1. ALT—The ALTernate or shift key is used on some keyboards in conjunction with the CLEAR, PF, or PA keys in much the same fashion as the shift key is used on a typewriter.

2. TAB—The TAB key is used to position the cursor to a specific location on the screen. It moves the cursor across the terminal screen in a left-to-right, top-to-bottom sequence, stopping at designated fields.

3. EOF—The erase-to-End-of-Field (EOF) key will erase data in a specific field on the screen, from the point of the cursor position to the end of the field.

Screen Format

Screens for the 3270 terminals used for examples in this book consist of 24 lines and 80 columns. The screen is a grid in which line 1, column 1 is referred to as screen position 1; line 1, column 2 as position 2; line 2, column 1 as position 81; line 3, column 1 as position 161, etc. Screens for 3270 terminals contain a total of 1920 positions (24 lines by 80 columns). Screen position 1920 represents line 24, column 80. Figure 1-1 shows the format used for all 3270 screen illustrations presented in this book.

Screen Classifications

Most examples in this book will be based on a simplified purchasing system. Menu programs will be discussed as will be vendor file inquiry and maintenance programs. Maintenance programs will be presented for vendor file additions, changes, and deletions. A vendor file browse program will illustrate how to scroll backward and forward through a file. You may encounter combined maintenance programs which perform all maintenance and inquiry functions. I prefer individual maintenance programs, one for each function, and I employ this approach

1...5...10...15...20...25...30...35...40...45...50...55...60...65...70...75...80

Figure 1-1   Screen Layout for 3270 Terminal.

for program examples. Your installation standards and system requirements will determine which approach you will take.

Screens used by CICS programs usually fall into one of the following categories. They are discussed in more detail later in this chapter.

1. Menu or submenu screens are selection displays used to make a choice in order to initiate a desired function. Figure 1-2 is an example of a menu screen. A submenu, shown in Fig. 1-4, takes one of the functions shown on a menu and breaks it down into subfunctions.

2. Control screens are used by the terminal operator in order to enter a record key which is used in inquiry and maintenance functions. The key entered on the control screen is used to format the detail screen, which is usually displayed next by the program. Figure 1-5 is an example of a control screen.

3. Detail screens are used to display or to facilitate the entry of data into a program during inquiry and maintenance functions. At the completion of the inquiry or maintenance function, control is passed back to the control screen. Figures 1-6 through 1-10 are typical detail screens.

4. Browse screens permit the terminal operator to view many occurrences of similar data, for instance, to scroll through a vendor file, as shown in Fig. 1-11.

The above screens are the types used by examples in this book; they are not the only types of screens you will encounter. Some designers do not use control screens; they prefer to enter the key directly on the detail screen. I prefer to use control screens and will employ them as appropriate in all programs in this book. The method you employ in your design may be determined by standards

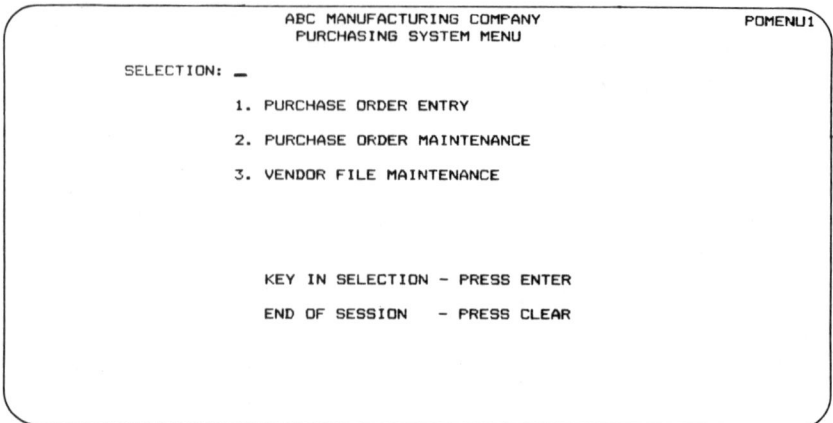

Figure 1-2   Purchasing System Menu Screen.

in effect at your installation. CICS commands and concepts are basically the same regardless of the screen design you use.

Types of CICS Systems

Most companies have two types of CICS systems, a test system and a production system.

Test System

The test system is used for development and enhancement of new and existing systems and programs. Test files contain fewer records than will actually be contained on the production system file, but they are typical of the kind expected to be on the production file. Do not rush programs through the test system without thoroughly testing them. It is difficult to explain to knowledgeable users why a program moved from the test system to the production system is not working properly.

Production System

Systems and programs which have been thoroughly tested and are error-free (hopefully) are put into the production system. This system is used for day-to-day online operations. Errors in design or programming not caught by the test system before programs are promoted to the production system can be a source of embarrassment to the data processing department.

Promotion from Test to Production

Moving or copying a program from the test to production system is often referred to as *promotion*. The interaction between the user and the system is the same for the test and production systems. This book assumes that the user utilizes the test system until convinced that a program is error-free, then signs off on the program and authorizes its promotion to the production system.

User Involvement

One major advantage of CICS is that users or user-interface personnel are required to get heavily involved in the development and testing of a system. High-quality work is essential, because, once a program is promoted, it may be accessed by users all across the country. The image of a system, or the reputation of data processing, is not enhanced if the system fails to function as expected. Batch systems, in which all data is grouped and entered into an input file before a program is run, sometimes encounter an abnormal termination (ABEND). The error can be fixed and the program rerun without the user ever knowing that a problem had existed. Depending on the system, an ABEND of an online program could trigger calls from users all across the country. The frequently heard complaint, "There is never time to do it right the first time, but always time to correct it" should never be said of the work of the online designer/programmer.

Getting on the CICS System

The procedure for logging on to a CICS system is generally similar from one installation to another. Screens displayed by the system during the log-on/sign-on procedure are not illustrated here because the procedure varies somewhat from one installation to another. To log on to the CICS system, the terminal operator presses the CLEAR key in order to clear the screen and set the cursor at position 1; keys in TESTCICS, PRODCICS, or a similar entry; then presses ENTER to get connected to the requested CICS system. An indicative message such as TEST CICS SYSTEM will be returned on the screen. Clear the screen and you are ready to sign on to CICS. Key in CSSN in screen positions 1 through 4 and press ENTER; a screen will be displayed requiring the entry of the operator's name and password (assigned by each installation). Key in these entries, which may not be displayed, and then press ENTER. A message indicating that the sign-on is complete will be displayed if the name and password keyed in match entries in the installation's sign-on table (SNT); otherwise, an error message will be displayed. Error messages usually appear when the terminal operator keys in a name or password incorrectly; if this occurs, the operator just clears the screen and enters CSSN again. The sign-on/sign-off procedure requirements for microcomputer implementations of CICS may vary somewhat. Consult your User's Guide for the appropriate procedure.

Summary of Sign-on Procedure

1. Clear the screen.
2. Key proper entry such as TESTCICS and press ENTER.
3. Clear the screen.

4. Key in CSSN.

5. Key in your name and password and press ENTER.

6. Clear the screen.

Initiating a CICS Transaction

The terminal screen is now clear, and you are ready to key in a TRANS-action IDentifier (TRANSID). The TRANSID is used as a key to search a CICS table in order to determine which program to access. Most installations have many TRANSIDs which a terminal operator can enter. A TRANSID is a one- to four-character code (usually four) which is keyed into screen positions 1 through 4 in order to start a CICS session when an AID key, generally ENTER, is pressed. This book defines a *session* as the period of time between entering a TRANSID and the point at which the terminal operator presses the CLEAR key to end the session. A session may consist of one or several programs being executed. There may be one or several sessions between the time you sign on to the CICS system and the time you log off.

Logging off CICS

When all sessions have been completed, a terminal operator is usually required to log off. This is accomplished by clearing the screen, keying CSSF LOGOFF, or a similar entry, and pressing ENTER.

Typical CICS Session

Sign on to CICS and clear the screen; you are now ready to start a session. Key in the TRANSID POMU and press ENTER; this TRANSID initiates the program which displays the purchasing system menu map illustrated in Fig. 1-2. A map is a formatted screen identified in this book by the mapname in the upper-right corner of the screen (POMENU1 in Fig. 1-2). Maps will be explained thoroughly in future chapters.

Purchasing System Menu

Menu programs have as their primary purpose the display of two or more options on a screen from which the one desired can be selected. Typically, a selection number or letter is keyed in and ENTER is pressed to start the program associated with the selection.

The purchasing system menu (Fig. 1-2) lists three selections, numbered 1, 2, and 3. The terminal operator should enter the selection number at the cursor, which will be positioned to the right of SELECTION: (shown by an underscore in Fig. 1-2).

Erroneous Menu Entries

What would happen if the terminal operator:

1. Entered a character other than a 1, 2, or 3?
2. Pressed the CLEAR key?
3. Pressed an invalid AID key, such as a PA or PF key?
4. Pressed ENTER without keying in a selection?

The following list explains what would happen in each instance.

1. Figure 1-3 illustrates what happens if a 4 or any other invalid character is entered. A message is displayed at the bottom of the screen which is brighter than the rest of the screen's constants and data. Messages are usually displayed in a conversational fashion, notifying the operator of action taken or required. Generally map line 24 is reserved for operator-notification messages. Some applications may require more than one message line at the bottom of a map, perhaps lines 23 and 24.

2. For examples in this book, when the CLEAR key is pressed the screen will be cleared, then the message SESSION COMPLETED will be displayed starting at position 1 of the screen.

3. Pressing an invalid AID key would result in a programmer-defined highlighted message being displayed at the bottom of the screen. The message displayed on line 24 of the menu screen in examples in this book is;

ENTER AND CLEAR KEYS ARE ONLY VALID KEYS — PLEASE TRY AGAIN

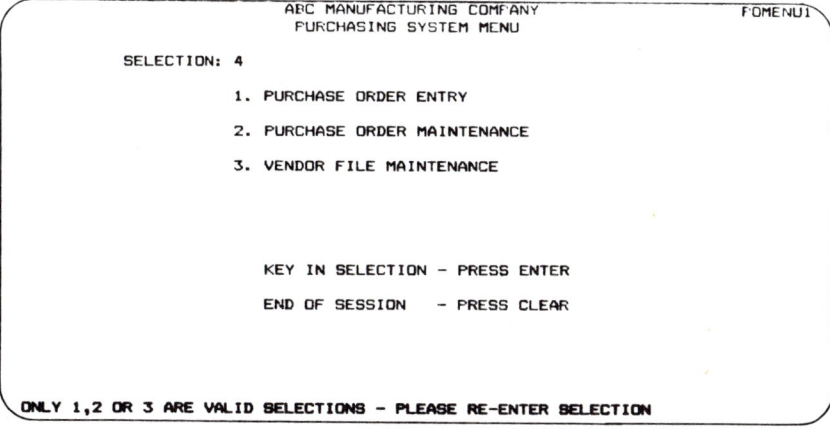

Figure 1-3 **Invalid Entry on Menu Screen.**

4. If ENTER is pressed without keying in a selection, the following highlighted message would appear on line 24 of the menu screen.

NO SELECTION WAS MADE — PLEASE ENTER SELECTION CODE

Valid Operator Menu Selection

Normally the terminal operator will make a valid selection and press ENTER, causing a transfer of control to the selected program. The system could be designed to display a default selection, perhaps a 1 next to SELECTION:. For our example, the terminal operator keys in a 3 next to SELECTION: and presses ENTER, causing the display shown in Fig. 1-4, the vendor file maintenance submenu screen. If the operator entered a 1 on this screen and pressed ENTER, the vendor file inquiry control screen shown in Fig. 1-5 would be displayed. The submenu shown in Fig. 1-4 could have been combined with the purchasing system menu shown in Fig. 1-2. I just want to point out options you have when designing a system. Sometimes a primary menu will have so many entries that there will not be room to include submenu fields for all items.

The cursor in Fig. 1-5 is located at the first position of the vendor code entry field, ready for the terminal operator to key in a code. The terminal operator could key in a code, for example, X-9234-1, and press the ENTER key in order to display the vendor file inquiry detail screen shown in Fig. 1-6. The message section at the bottom of the control screen (see Fig. 1-5) could show, depending on the key pressed, the following messages:

INVALID KEY PRESSED — PLEASE TRY AGAIN
VENDOR CODE MUST BE ENTERED — PLEASE KEY IN
VENDOR CODE FORMAT MUST BE: A-9999-9 — PLEASE REENTER
VENDOR RECORD NOT ON FILE

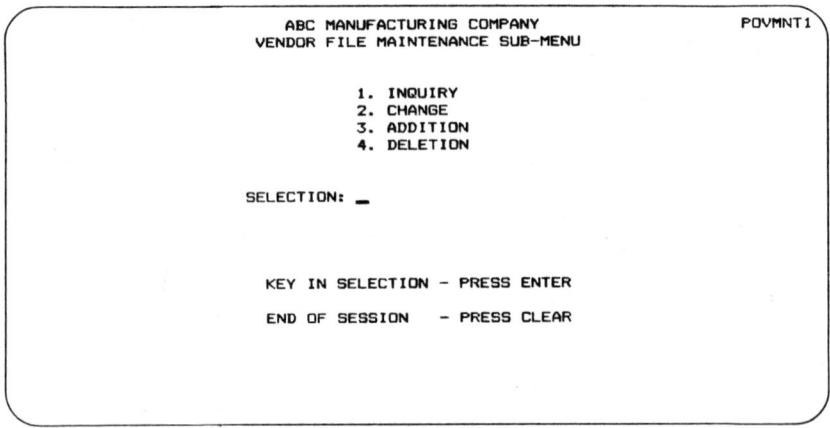

Figure 1-4 Vendor File Maintenance Submenu Screen.

```
DATE: 01/23/86            ABC MANUFACTURING COMPANY            POVMIQ1
TIME: 10.31.22            VENDOR FILE INQUIRY CONTROL



                   VENDOR CODE: X - 9234 -1



            1. FOR VENDOR FILE INQUIRY - PRESS ENTER

            2. TO BROWSE VENDOR FILE    - PRESS PF4

            3. TO RETURN TO MENU        - PRESS PF5

            4. TO END SESSION           - PRESS CLEAR
```

Figure 1-5   Vendor File Inquiry Control Screen.

Ending a Session

All programs in this book will end a CICS session by having the terminal operator press the CLEAR key. The screen will be cleared and the message SESSION COMPLETED displayed starting in position 1 of the screen.

A session could be terminated by leaving a cleared screen, but this sometimes leaves the terminal operator wondering if the session was ended properly. Displaying SESSION COMPLETED leaves no doubt. It is more positive. Programs can be written to end a session based on any designated AID key being pressed.

```
DATE: 01/23/86            ABC MANUFACTURING COMPANY            POVMIQ2
TIME: 10.32.41            VENDOR FILE INQUIRY

VENDOR CODE: X-9234-1
          NAME: XYZ INDUSTRIAL SUPPLIES    PHONE:   ( 412 ) 555 - 1000
                                           CONTACT: BILL O'BRIEN

ADDRESS - STREET: 555 MAIN STREET          DOLLARS COMMITTED:    $1,675.00
          CITY: PITTSBURGH
         STATE: PA PENNSYLVANIA
           ZIP: 15260

TO ATTENTION OF: MARY MASSI



          1. RETURN TO INQUIRY CONTROL SCREEN    - PRESS ENTER
          2. RETURN TO MENU                       - PRESS PF5
          3. END OF SESSION                       - PRESS CLEAR
```

Figure 1-6   Vendor File Inquiry Detail Screen.

Inquiry Function

An online inquiry function refers to the act of displaying an inquiry screen which shows data contained on an individual record. If the terminal operator presses the ENTER key and the code entered in Fig. 1-5 is on the vendor file, the map named POVMIQ2 shown in Fig. 1-6 will be displayed. The map shows all significant fields in the vendor master record for vendor code X-9234-1. Remember, I am using simplified examples—your vendor master record would most likely have additional or different fields. The user can view all fields on the vendor file inquiry detail screen but cannot modify any fields on this screen. (Some systems have been designed to combine inquiry and changes.) The ability to view the current file status on line has limited the number of batch reports needed by users. Batch reports only reflect the status of a file at some point in the past. The inquiry map in Fig. 1-6 prompts you for the desired action with its instructions at the lower part of the screen. The only message likely to be displayed would appear only if an invalid key was pressed. It might read: INVALID KEY PRESSED—PLEASE TRY AGAIN. After an inquiry, the user could return to the inquiry control screen (mapname POVMIQ1, see Fig. 1-5) for entry of another code. Depending upon the AID key pressed, the program could also return to the vendor file maintenance submenu or end the session.

The inquiry function is not actually a maintenance function, but I like to include it on a maintenance control map. Some designers allow the entry of record keys on detail screens and eliminate control screens. I generally prefer to have keys entered on a control screen.

Maintenance Functions

File maintenance functions refer to the act of adding, changing, or deleting an individual record. Additions, changes, and deletions are maintenance functions which can be performed using an online system. Two types of online systems are:

1. Online real time system—In a real time system, the file being maintained is updated immediately when the change is entered by the operator.

2. Online data entry—Data is entered online but does not change a master file immediately. It is accumulated throughout the day and run through a batch program at night in order to perform file updating.

All transactions in this book will use a real time system. This system allows the user to see immediately the results of any changes made to a file, and to make corrections if required.

Permitting users to make maintenance changes directly to a file, or to enter transactions which later affect the data in that file, places the responsibility for file integrity on the user. Systems may have many users, entering data at various locations, and some files are constantly being updated. Most online files are dynamic, constantly being added to, changed, and deleted from. Online systems are usually more accurate than batch systems because

1. Transactions are usually entered by persons familiar with the input data, so there is less chance of interpretation errors.

2. Data can be updated in the desired files immediately. It is not necessary to wait until later that evening or for several days.

3. Data-entry errors are often caught by the user and corrected immediately.

4. Online systems can have many program edit checks built into them. For instance, if a vendor does not exist or is entered incorrectly, the system would detect the error and prompt the user to make a correction immediately.

Additions

Additions involve adding a new record to an existing file. On a vendor file addition control screen, similar to the inquiry control screen in Fig. 1-5, you could key in the vendor to be added and press ENTER to display the addition detail screen. The map in Fig. 1-7 would be displayed, showing the fields with underlines, into which the terminal operator will enter the required data. The underlines are not normally displayed and are only shown here to illustrate the fields and their size. The system assumes that all fields except CONTACT: and TO ATTENTION OF: require data to be entered. A program can edit each required field before it is entered into the file as an addition. Some fields need only to be checked for the presence of data. Other fields may be required to be numeric, have a valid state code, or perhaps contain a valid zip code.

Entering data on a screen. When a map such as that shown in Fig. 1-7 is displayed, the cursor is normally positioned at the first data-entry field (NAME). Pressing the TAB key will cause the cursor to move across the screen from left to right, top to bottom, stopping at the beginning of each data-entry field. After

```
  DATE: 01/23/86            ABC MANUFACTURING COMPANY                 POVMAD2
  TIME: 10.35.38               VENDOR FILE ADDITION

  VENDOR CODE: A-0100-1
         NAME: _____        PHONE:   ( ___ ) ___ - ____
                                            CONTACT: _____

  ADDRESS - STREET: _____
             CITY: _____
            STATE: __
              ZIP: _____

  TO ATTENTION OF: _____



         1. ADDITIONS, KEY-IN REQUIRED DATA      - PRESS ENTER
         2. RETURN TO ADDITION CONTROL SCREEN    - PRESS PF3
         3. RETURN TO MENU                       - PRESS PF5
         4. END OF SESSION                       - PRESS CLEAR
```

Figure 1-7 Vendor File Additions Detail Screen.

we tab to the last field, pressing the TAB key again will position the cursor at the start of the first field to be entered. Fields of fixed length, such as the PHONE, STATE, and ZIP, when completely entered, cause the cursor to skip automatically to the next field to be entered. Remember the cursor moves left to right, top to bottom when you enter data (i.e., from NAME, to PHONE, to CONTACT, to STREET, to CITY, etc.).

Data-entry error indicators.   A programmer has several methods to indicate data-entry errors. Each technique listed below displays an indicative message on line 24 of the screen and positions the cursor at the first field in error.

1. Display field identifiers at a brighter intensity than those of correctly entered fields. Field identifiers as used here refer to the descriptions preceding each data-entry field, such as NAME, PHONE, and CONTACT (see Fig 1-8).
2. Display the erroneous data field itself at a brighter intensity than correctly entered fields. This method has the drawback that if failure to key in an entry is the error, there is no data to highlight. Some users of this method move asterisks to a nonentry field.
3. Display one or more messages at the bottom of the screen without any highlighting of error fields or field identifiers. The drawback to this method is that when multiple errors occur, it is not always practical to display all error messages at once.

This book will use the first technique, that of brightening all erroneous field identifiers and positioning the cursor at the start of the first incorrect field. A highlighted message will be displayed at the bottom of the screen, notifying the terminal operator to PLEASE CORRECT HIGHLIGHTED FIELDS.

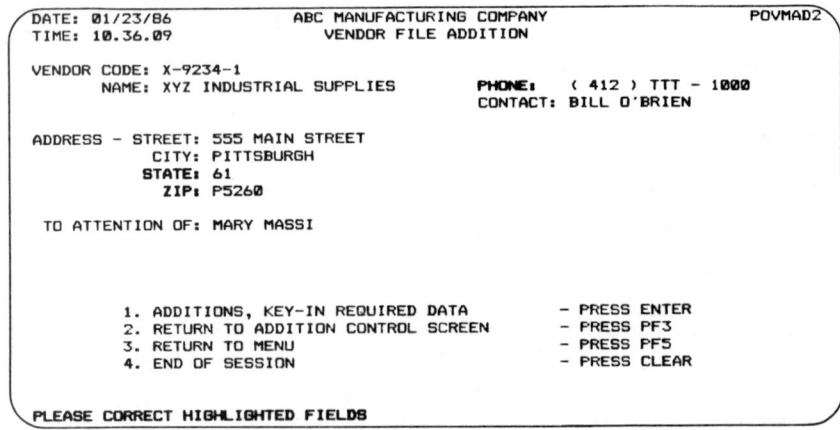

```
DATE: 01/23/86              ABC MANUFACTURING COMPANY                    POVMAD2
TIME: 10.36.09                  VENDOR FILE ADDITION

VENDOR CODE: X-9234-1
        NAME: XYZ INDUSTRIAL SUPPLIES        PHONE:  ( 412 ) TTT - 1000
                                             CONTACT: BILL O'BRIEN

ADDRESS - STREET: 555 MAIN STREET
            CITY: PITTSBURGH
           STATE: 61
             ZIP: P5260

TO ATTENTION OF: MARY MASSI



        1. ADDITIONS, KEY-IN REQUIRED DATA        - PRESS ENTER
        2. RETURN TO ADDITION CONTROL SCREEN      - PRESS PF3
        3. RETURN TO MENU                         - PRESS PF5
        4. END OF SESSION                         - PRESS CLEAR


 PLEASE CORRECT HIGHLIGHTED FIELDS
```

Figure 1-8   Errors on Vendor File Additions Detail Screen.

Key in all required data on the screen (see Fig. 1-7), and following the instructions at the bottom of the map, press ENTER to record the addition. Assume three fields were entered incorrectly. The field identifiers of the three fields would be brightened and the message PLEASE CORRECT HIGHLIGHTED FIELDS would be displayed at the bottom of the screen as shown in Fig. 1-8.

If only two of the three errors were corrected and you pressed ENTER again, only the field identifier of the one remaining incorrect item would be highlighted. The two corrected fields will now have their field identifiers displayed at a normal intensity. The same notification message will be displayed at the bottom of the screen.

When the final error is resolved and the operator presses ENTER, the record will be added to the file and the addition control screen will be displayed. The indicative message displayed at the bottom of the control screen will be RECORD SUCCESSFULLY ADDED. The terminal operator could now perform an inquiry against the new record to see if it was added correctly. The change or delete function could be initiated if the addition was incorrect.

When entering data, sometimes an error cannot be resolved or it is decided not to add the record. If this occurs, the terminal operator has several options, as shown by the instructions at the bottom of the screen in Fig. 1-8:

1. Return to the control screen.

2. Return to the menu.

3. End the session.

Changes

In data processing there is only one thing that you can be sure of—changes! Change is a certainty; therefore, all systems, programs, files, etc. should be designed with built-in flexibility. The vendor file has an associated change function which enables a user to change any field in the record, except for vendor code and dollars committed.

After adding a vendor record, you may realize that some of the data was entered incorrectly, or that it requires a change. The vendor code would be entered on a control screen and ENTER pressed in order to display the change detail screen. The system would then display the change detail map shown in Fig. 1-9. The spaces before and after area code and other fields are actually occupied by screen attribute characters, which are discussed in Chaps. 2 and 6. The cursor would initially be located at the first position of the vendor NAME field. Press TAB to position the cursor at the start of any field requiring a change, then enter the new data. You can alter as many fields as required on the changes screen. When all changes have been entered, the instructions at the bottom of the screen direct you to press ENTER to record the change(s). The change control screen will display the notification CHANGE COMPLETED SUCCESSFULLY in the message section at the bottom of the screen, if no errors were detected. The message PLEASE CORRECT HIGHLIGHTED FIELDS would continue to appear at the bottom of the change detail screen until the

```
DATE: 01/23/86              ABC MANUFACTURING COMPANY              POVMCH2
TIME: 10.44.59                 VENDOR FILE CHANGES

VENDOR CODE: A-0100-1
        NAME: AA INDUSTRIAL SUPPLIES        PHONE:   ( 301 ) 555 - 1000
                                            CONTACT: JOHN SIMPSON OR H. JONES

ADDRESS - STREET: 555 HUDSON STREET
            CITY: NEWARK
           STATE: NJ NEW JERSEY
             ZIP: 07102

TO ATTENTION OF: PAUL ANDERSON



        1. CHANGES, KEY-IN NEW DATA           - PRESS ENTER
        2. RETURN TO CHANGES CONTROL SCREEN   - PRESS PF3
        3. RETURN TO MENU                     - PRESS PF5
        4. END OF SESSION                     - PRESS CLEAR
```

Figure 1-9 Vendor File Changes Detail Screen.

changes were made correctly or the function was ended by pressing one of the other AID keys.

Deletions

Records are sometimes added in error or become obsolete over a period of time. These records may be purged or deleted by a batch program or can be deleted on-line. Our system allows the online deletion of records from the vendor master file.

The code of the vendor to be deleted is entered on a control screen and ENTER is pressed to display the delete detail screen. The vendor deletion detail screen (Fig. 1-10) will be displayed. The first instruction at the lower part of

```
DATE: 01/23/86              ABC MANUFACTURING COMPANY              POVMDL2
TIME: 10.48.23                 VENDOR FILE DELETION

VENDOR CODE: A-0100-1
        NAME: AA INDUSTRIAL SUPPLIES        PHONE:   ( 301 ) 555 - 1000
                                            CONTACT: JOHN SIMPSON OR H. JONES

ADDRESS - STREET: 555 HUDSON STREET
            CITY: NEWARK
           STATE: NJ NEW JERSEY
             ZIP: 07102

TO ATTENTION OF: PAUL ANDERSON



        1. DELETIONS VERIFY DATA BEFORE DELETING   - PRESS ENTER
        2. RETURN TO DELETION CONTROL SCREEN       - PRESS PF3
        3. RETURN TO MENU                          - PRESS PF5
        4. END OF SESSION                          - PRESS CLEAR
```

Figure 1-10 Vendor File Deletions Detail Screen.

the screen directs you to verify data before deleting. When the data has been checked to verify that you have the right record, press ENTER to finalize the delete. The next display would be that of the delete control screen with the message RECORD DELETED SUCCESSFULLY displayed at the bottom of the screen.

Browse Function

The browse function, like the inquiry function, is not a maintenance function, but it is often helpful to include it on a control screen as shown in Fig. 1-5.

A browse is a sequential search of a file, starting at the key passed to the browse program. For example, if you wanted to search the vendor file for a code beginning with S, you would enter one character, an S, in the vendor code entry field on the control screen (see Fig. 1-5) and press PF4 to start the browse function. The browse will display the vendor file browse map shown in Fig. 1-11. Since you entered only one character, the browse starts its sequential search with the first vendor record beginning with an S. If you were searching for a vendor named Smith Brothers Parts, which is near the middle of the S records, it wouldn't be advisable to start your browse at the beginning of the S records. You would have to read half of the S records before reaching the one which is desired. This would not only be a waste of time, since sequential file searches are slow, but it would also tie up computer resources by requiring numerous unnecessary file reads. Try to limit the scope of browse searches. Limit your search by trial and error. For instance, when searching for Smith, enter S-5 as the first two characters on the control screen (see Fig. 1-5) before initiating the browse (S-5000-0 should be near the middle of the S records). If S-5 is much greater than or less than the code of the desired vendor, reset the browse. Key in a new start browse code, a full or partial code on the bottom of the vendor file

```
DATE: 01/23/86          ABC MANUFACTURING COMPANY              FOVMBR1
TIME: 10.51.37               VENDOR FILE BROWSE
   VENDOR CD VENDOR NAME            STREET            CITY / STATE
01 S-0010-1 SABER SAWS & TOOLS      106 MULBERRY STREET  NEWARK        NJ
02 S-0020-1 SACRET CEMENT PRODUCTS  23 RIVER DRIVE       SCRANTON      PA
03 S-0030-1 SADLER SCRAP STEEL      1103 ESSEX STREET    PITTSBURGH    PA
04 S-0035-1 SADOR DISCOUNT EQUIPMENT 310 E MAIN AVENUE   CLEVELAND     OH
05 S-0040-1 SAFETY GLASS INSTALLERS 11 HUDSON STREET     JERSEY CITY   NJ
06 S-0050-1 SAFEWAY INDUSTRIAL TOOLS 48 BROADWAY         NEW HAVEN     CT
07 S-0060-1 SAKSON BROTHERS CHEMICALS 454 JUNCTION BLVD  PATERSON      NJ
08 S-0065-1 SALE ITEM PAINTS        1610 BLEEKER STREET  NEW YORK      NY
09 S-0070-1 SALVAGE METALS          34 UNION AVENUE      YOUNGSTOWN    OH
10 S-0070-2 SALVAGE METALS          88 BROAD STREET      BETHLEHEM     PA
11 S-0080-1 SAMPSON STEEL INC.      754 AVON STREET      PHILADELPHIA  PA
12 S-0090-1 SANDOR INDUSTRIAL ACIDS 101 MONROE STREET    HARTFORD      CT
13 S-0095-1 SANITARY CLEANSERS      33 EASTON DRIVE      SYRACUSE      NY
14 S-0100-1 SANDRA RESINS           2300 BELT PARKWAY    BUFFALO       NY
15 S-0065-1 SANTOR CHEMICALS        1000 ERIE BLVD       NEW YORK      NY
         : SELECTION
         RESET VENDOR CODE:
1. PF1  - FWD     4. PF3  - KEY IN SELECTION - RETURN TO CALLING PROGRAM
2. PF2  - BWD     5. PF4  - KEY IN RESET VENDOR CODE (FULL OR PARTIAL CODE)
3. PF5  - MENU    6. CLEAR - END OF SESSION
```

Figure 1-11 Vendor File Browse Screen.

browse map (Fig. 1-11), next to the field identifier RESET VENDOR CODE:, and press PF4. For instance, try S-4, S-6, S-45, or S-55. Partial key searches of a file are referred to as *generic* searches.

After displaying a full map of vendor browse data, the terminal operator has several options corresponding to the instructions at the bottom of Fig. 1-11.

1. Press PF1, which is commonly used for forward paging, in order to display the next page of sequential vendor browse data. The display of succeeding pages of data can be continued by pressing PF1. The browse process of paging forward and backward is often referred to as *scrolling*.

2. Press PF2, which is commonly used for backward paging, to display the previous page of data. Normally you are required to scroll forward and save succeeding pages before you can page backward.

3. Return to the vendor file maintenance submenu (see Fig. 1-4).

4. Key in a selection, from 01 to 15, and return with the selected vendor to the program which initiated the browse. Some systems may be designed to have a program pass control to a browse program in order to select a code and return it to the invoking program.

5. Enter a full or partial vendor code to reset the browse, then press PF4 to continue the browse from the point of the reset code.

6. Press CLEAR to end the session.

SUMMARY

The illustrations in this chapter are typical of online functions you are likely to encounter or to design into new applications at your installation. Your company may have some variations to the material presented in this chapter, but the concepts will be basically the same. Most installations will have a sign-on procedure, start transactions with a four-character TRANSID, and display and receive maps. You will most likely have a menu program and the following functions: additions, changes, deletions, and inquiries. A browse function, which should be tailored to your accessing and file structure requirements, will probably be present in many systems.

Online systems, unlike batch systems, make it difficult to cover up poor design and programming errors. It is in the best interest of both the user and the programmer/analyst to work closely in the design and testing stages of all systems. High-quality work is more important than ever in an online environment. It can only be achieved by substantial cooperation between users and system designers. Poor design will cause more problems than any other factor in an online system. The challenge presented by online systems should be *"do it right the first time!"*

2

DESIGNING
USER-FRIENDLY MAPS

The design of user-friendly maps requires user involvement. Users have to live with the screens and the system, while data processing personnel only maintain the system. Almost any concept the user can define and convey to a programmer/analyst can be implemented. The best in-house systems (not packages) and their associated screens are developed through close cooperation and coordination between users and data processing personnel.

Data processing in its simplest form has always consisted of receiving input, processing the data, and creating some form of output. CICS is no different, although the sequence is slightly different. Generally, after initiating a transaction by entering a TRANSID, the first thing you get is output, in the form of a map, displayed on a terminal. Next, you key information on the screen and enter the input into the system, which then processes it. The design of maps, which are the major source of input and output in a CICS system, is the subject of this chapter. Later chapters will explain the coding required to generate the maps.

Designing Maps

Maps define formatted screens which are users' input and output in an online environment. The map is the user's primary aid when conveying to data processing the input and output of a system. The map is used to send information to and receive data from a screen. Users will view some maps repeatedly throughout the day. Therefore, it is in their best interest to make sure they understand the map and feel comfortable with its format. Obtain or design a form similar to Fig. 2-1, which will be used to paint a picture of a map corresponding to a terminal screen and containing 80 columns and 24 lines. Figure 2-2 shows the basic map format I recommend. Many terminals have nearby printers that can

IBM

3270 Information Display System
Layout Sheet

Panel ID

Subj.

Job No.

Sheet ____ of ____

Originated by

Date

COLUMN

ROW

Figure 2-1 3270 Map Layout Form.

reproduce a screen image by pressing a designated key on the terminal keyboard. It is often important for future reference to know the date and time when map images were printed. I recommend putting date and time on detail and browse maps. They are optional on menu maps and control screens. These different types of maps were discussed under "Screen Classifications" in Chap. 1.

The mapname should be put on all maps; I find the upper-right-hand corner a convenient location for this. Users often have questions or recommendations pertaining to the system; it is easier to identify the map in question if it can be referred to by a common name. Occasionally a program will come to an ABEND; it is easier to identify where the problem occurred if the map which triggered the ABEND can be identified. The center of the first line of the map is a good location for company name or system name, and the map title should be centered on the second line. The last line of the map (line 24) is generally reserved for program-generated user-notification messages.

The area between the two heading lines and the message line contains the body of the map and user instructions. There are no rules for this part of the map, but the body of the map should precede the instructions. This is the area of the map where a user and an analyst can express their creativity and their good design skills. A series of maps helps develop the picture a user receives of a system. This picture can be pleasing, neutral, or irritating. How can a map be irritating? Anything which is difficult to understand, cumbersome to work

Figure 2-2 Basic Map Screen Format.

with, and causes frustration to a user is a source of irritation. Poorly planned and designed maps, as well as the sequence of map appearance in a system, can be a major irritant. Since users have to live and work with a system's screens, they should help design maps which are pleasing and logical.

I usually design and redesign a map several times before showing it to a user. The user usually offers suggestions which necessitate a few additional map alterations. This communication between screen designer and user, before programming begins, minimizes the number of changes required after a program has been written.

Map Design Guidelines

When designing maps, as in most areas of data processing, an important consideration should be, "keep it simple and straightforward" (KISS). Some guidelines I like to apply when designing a map are

1. Balance the data to be displayed. Don't cramp it all to the left and top of the map. You have 80 columns and 21 lines plus 2 header lines and a message line; don't be reluctant to use them.

2. Put date and time on detail maps.

3. Depending on company standards, display company, department, or system name, centered on line 1 of the map.

4. Always include mapname in the upper-right corner of each map.

5. Give the map a title centered on line 2 of the map.

6. Start the body of the map on line 3 or lower.

7. Indicate display-only variable data (such as date and time) by Z's and data-entry fields by X's.

8. Follow the body with instructions which will guide the terminal operator to perform the required function.

9. Number instructions when there are three or more options from which to choose.

10. Generally locate operator-notification and action-required messages on line 24 of the map. A notification message between the body and instructions is sometimes an asset, usually on control maps.

11. Brighten all messages so that they will stand out from the rest of the map.

12. Highlight the field identifiers of items which are entered incorrectly.

13. Strive for consistency of format for similar functions on different maps.

14. Reserve column 1 of all lines for map attributes (see "Map Attributes" later in this chapter). Attributes can be set in column 80 of the preceding line if you wish to display or enter data starting at column 1, but this is awkward and can lead to errors.

Consistency in Map Design

A map which is similar from one program to another is easier to reproduce and modify for new programs. Maps can be generated much more quickly for new programs if a skeleton map exists which is similar to the new map. Consistency will enable a programmer/analyst to design a prototype of a new system within a reasonable period of time using existing systems as models. Maps can generally be classified into types which have many similarities. Maps discussed in Chap. 1 which possess similarities from one system to another are

1. Menus

2. Control maps

3. Detail maps

4. Browse maps

I like to show the field identifiers for date and time. Your installation may just want to display the date and time without descriptions. Either method is acceptable, but when possible always place them in the same location on all maps. *Always* place the mapname in the same location for all maps.

Map Attributes

Each field on a map has an attribute associated with it. A field, as a user perceives it, is any displayed data or any location on a map at which data can be entered. In reality all literals, field identifiers, displayed data, and data-entry locations are map fields. Figure 2-3 shows a menu map for the purchasing system; this is the map used to format the screen shown in Fig. 1-2. There are several fields on this map, but only one in which the terminal operator is permitted to enter data—the SELECTION field.

The common attributes you should be familiar with are

1. ASKIP (Automatic SKIP)—The cursor skips over fields with this attribute.

2. UNPROT (UNPROTected)—A field the cursor will stop at so that the terminal operator can enter data.

3. BRT (BRighTer intensity)—A field displayed at a brighter intensity than normal. A BRT field may be referred to as a *highlighted* or *high-intensity* field. Messages and field identifiers of erroneous entries are highlighted in this book.

4. NORM (NORMal intensity)—The usual display for fields. When errors are corrected, their field identifiers are changed from BRT to NORM.

Figure 2-3 Purchasing System Menu Map.

5. DRK (DaRK intensity)—This field cannot be seen and is generally used for a password field. It is sometimes used to darken a message field on a subsequent display of the screen, when the message no longer applies.

Each attribute occupies one position on the map and controls the field which immediately follows it. All field attributes in Fig. 2-3 are defined as ASKIP, NORM initially, except the attribute for the entry of the selection. The attribute for the selection entry is UNPROT in order to allow for the entry of the selection number by the terminal operator. The UNPROT attribute occupies the screen position between SELECTION and the field to be entered (shown on the map by an X). The UNPROT attribute occupies screen location line 4, column 22; it is not visible, but it is there. An attribute immediately follows the SELECTION field; it is ASKIP and is located at screen location line 4, column 24. Without this ASKIP attribute, there would be nothing to stop the entry of data by the terminal operator. This attribute limits the operator to one digit of entry data. An ASKIP attribute following an UNPROT field is sometimes referred to as a *stopper* attribute. If there was another UNPROT field on the map, the cursor would skip to the start of that field when it encountered the ASKIP attribute. The cursor never stops at an ASKIP field. When designing a screen, just keep in mind that each UNPROT field is immediately preceded by and followed by an attribute, each of which occupies one position on the screen. ASKIP fields have only a preceding attribute which skips past the field until the next unprotected field is encountered. Note that the message line starts at line 24, column 2 because column 1 is occupied by an ASKIP attribute. A program can change this attribute from ASKIP,NORM to ASKIP,BRT to ASKIP,DRK and back again in order to highlight and "erase" messages by brightening and darkening them.

Screen or map size is 80 columns by 24 lines and contains 1920 available positions for characters and attributes. The two heading lines plus the message line take up 3 lines, or 240 of the available positions, leaving 21 lines or 1680 positions for the body and instructions of your map. Twenty-one lines are usually sufficient space for display and entry information and for instructions to the terminal operator. Two or more maps can be used in cases where one map is insufficient for a required function.

Map Body and Instructions

The body of the map is the most important part of the display screen and therefore requires the most planning; it is the area in which the designer can best express creativity. Users of the most complicated and advanced system, even if it performs every function imaginable, will think the system is poorly designed if it is difficult to understand and cumbersome to use.

The body of the purchasing system menu (see Fig. 2-3) is typical of that used for a menu program. Most menus will have more than three selections which may be indicated by numbers and/or letters. On a menu with numerous entries, you may display two or more entries per line if necessary. The operator will normally key in the number or letter and press ENTER.

The instruction section of a menu map is usually rather simple, generally consisting of two entries:

KEY IN SELECTION — PRESS ENTER

END OF SESSION   — PRESS CLEAR

I do not usually number fewer than three instructions on a map, although you may choose to do so. There is no reason a map must have instructions numbered, but doing so sometimes helps a user to remember the options by association.

Designing the Control Map

The heading and message lines of the control map are similar to those of the menu and all of the maps in this book. Date and time are the basic differences on the heading lines for the vendor file inquiry control map shown in Fig. 2-4.

Body of the Control Map

The body of a control map is generally brief, usually consisting of one or more entries which are concatenated (joined together) to develop a key for the

Figure 2-4 Vendor File Inquiry Control Map.

record which is to be acted upon. Figure 2-4 has just one item in the body, the vendor code. I like to have codes entered in a format to which the user is accustomed—for example, one alphabetic character followed by a four-digit sequence number and a one-digit location number. The vendor code and its associated attributes could be laid out in several different ways, as shown in Fig. 2-5. Use the structure with which the system's users are most comfortable.

Entering Data into a Key Field

Figure 2-5 shows four different ways a user can enter data into a field. The X's, indicating where data would be entered, do not actually appear on the control screen.

① Shows the field to be entered with the edit characters displayed on the screen. The cursor is initially positioned after the first UNPROT attribute to allow entry of the first character in the vendor code. After entering the first character, the ASKIP attribute causes the cursor to move to the right of the next UNPROT attribute. After the fourth digit is entered, the cursor skips to the right of the last UNPROT attribute to enable entry of the last vendor code digit. For all fields, the trailing ASKIP attribute is called a stopper attribute.

Figure 2-5 Key Field Entry Techniques.

② Leave a space between significant groupings of characters to be entered. The space actually contains an UNPROT attribute which causes the cursor to skip over the space to the start of the next significant entry field.

③ Enter the code without any editing characters displayed or implied by a space. This method becomes less effective when the size of the field to be entered increases.

④ Enter the edit characters (dashes,—) along with the key characters. This method involves additional keying (the dashes), and in general seems to cause the most problems; avoid it if possible.

Since there are many methods of entering data into a field on a terminal, understanding the various options will enable you to be more effective in your map design.

Instructions on the Control Map

Control maps are often dominated by instructions, and the vendor file inquiry control map in Fig. 2-4 is no exception. The instructions occupy the area between vendor code and the message line at the bottom of the map. Why display instructions on a map when they can be placed in a user's manual? They do occupy screen space and result in more data being transmitted to the screen, but I believe it is easier for the user to read instructions from a screen. This book is concerned with reducing maintenance and making the user and programmer more productive. It is not overly concerned with computer efficiencies and does not attempt to minimize terminal response time. I prefer to let new technology address that area.

Instructions on a control map generally list a number of functions which prompt the operator to press the appropriate key in order to invoke the desired function.

Messages Displayed on the Control Map

Normally, when a programmer writes a program, checks are made for all anticipated conditions which could create a problem, and a message is displayed notifying the terminal operator of the condition. The experienced CICS programmer/analyst who has dealt with users has an instinct for the type of messages which should be displayed. Users or user-interface personnel, when testing a system, will often offer suggestions for making the messages more meaningful. A professional programmer/analyst expects this kind of feedback from a user. Alterations of this type are not difficult to make. User representatives and data processing personnel realize that many of the messages displayed notify the terminal operator that an incorrect entry has been made. Nobody likes to be corrected in an abusive fashion or in a way that will make he or she feel foolish, so the professional will use care to soften messages. A word like "please" as part of messages of this type is usually an effective softener.

Detail Maps

A detail map is one which is displayed as a result of an entry made on a control map. Common detail map types are

1. Inquiries
2. Additions
3. Changes
4. Deletions

Inquiry Map

The inquiry detail map shown in Fig. 2-6 contains data found on the vendor master record. All attributes on the inquiry map are ASKIP,NORM. The only attribute which changes on this map is the message attribute, which can change from ASKIP,NORM to ASKIP,BRT when an error message is displayed.

The body of the report displays information from the vendor master record for the code entered on the control map. The instructions prompt you for action after viewing the map.

Figure 2-6 Vendor File Inquiry Detail Map.

```
IBM              3270 Information Display System          Panel ID            Subjs
 ®                        Layout Sheet                    Job No.      Sheet
                                                          Originated by  Date    of

                                         COLUMN
01  DATE: ZZ/ZZ/ZZ            ABC MANUFACTURING COMPANY                    P.O.V.MADZ
02  TIME: ZZ.ZZ.ZZ            VENDOR FILE ADDITION
04  VENDOR CODE: Z-ZZZZZ-Z
05       NAME: X            X          PHONE: ( XXX ) XXX - XXXX
06                                     CONTACT: X                        X
08  ADDRESS - STREET: X      X
09            CITY: X        X
10           STATE: XX Z     Z
11             ZIP: XXXXX
12                                                                             480
13  TO ATTENTION OF: X       X                                                 960
18     1. ADDITIONS, KEY IN REQUIRED DATA        - PRESS ENTER
19     2. RETURN TO ADDITION CONTROL SCREEN      - PRESS P.F.3
20     3. RETURN TO MENU                         - PRESS P.F.5
21     4. END OF SESSION                         - PRESS CLEAR
```

Figure 2-7 Vendor File Addition Detail Map.

Addition Map

Figure 2-7 shows the format of the vendor file addition detail map. Unlike the inquiry map, all variable field attributes in the body of this map with the exception of vendor code are UNPROT. Vendor code cannot be changed, since its attribute is ASKIP,NORM. It can only be entered on the control screen.

The body of the map contains fields into which new data can be entered. The ENTER key is then pressed to effect the addition. The design of this part of the addition map must be closely coordinated with the user, since the entry of data must flow smoothly. The layout of data should correspond closely with the format of the source document used for adding a new vendor. Plan the layout of the data fields carefully; for instance, it would be awkward to put PHONE on the same line as VENDOR CODE. Remember, the cursor moves from left to right, top to bottom, stopping at UNPROT fields and skipping over ASKIP fields. Placing PHONE, which is an UNPROT field, on the same line as VENDOR CODE, an ASKIP field, would position the cursor at the first UNPROT field, which is PHONE. This seems illogical for two reasons: first, it is backward to enter the phone number before keying in the vendor's name; second, it seems more logical to have the cursor positioned initially on the left side of the screen.

Another illogical and awkward situation would arise if the fields PHONE and CONTACT were moved down opposite STREET and CITY. The terminal operator would in this case enter STREET, then PHONE, followed by CITY,

CONTACT, and STATE. On a full screen, a better alternative than breaking up an address entry in this fashion would be to design the screen with the entire address on the same line. For example,

```
STREET                    CITY                    STATE   ZIP
XXXXXXXXXXXXXXXXXX XXXXXXXXXXXXXXXXX   XX    XXXXX
```

When a field is entered erroneously or inadvertently missed, the field identifier describing that field should have its attribute changed to ASKIP,BRT, which highlights the description. Field identifiers should be restored to ASKIP,NORM after their corresponding fields have been corrected and should no longer display brightly. The brightening of field identifiers is accompanied by the highlighting and display of the message field containing the message PLEASE CORRECT HIGHLIGHTED FIELDS (see Fig. 1-8).

Change Map

The vendor file change map layout is shown in Fig. 2-8. Upon the initial send of a change map, the existing record's data is displayed. Each variable data

Figure 2-8 Vendor File Change Detail Map.

attribute in the body of this map is UNPROT,NORM, except for vendor code, which is ASKIP,NORM.

Changes can be keyed in over the existing data that is displayed or the terminal operator can press the EOF key to clear the field before entering the new data. The TAB key can be used to skip over fields which do not require changes. The ENTER key is pressed to update the record with the altered data. Do *not* put data in different locations on the various maintenance maps. Terminal operators become more easily accustomed to a system if similar fields are located in the same relative positions on all inquiry and maintenance screens.

Deletion Map

The deletion detail map is shown in Fig. 2-9. The fields displayed all have attributes of ASKIP,NORM. The purpose of displaying a record before deleting it is to give the terminal operator a chance to verify that the record is the proper one to be deleted before pressing ENTER. The operator could exercise one of the other options listed in the instructions if he or she did not want to delete the record. I recommend *always* displaying a record for operator verification before deleting; it takes a little longer, but the additional check is worth performing.

Figure 2-9 Vendor File Deletion Detail Map.

IBM ® 3270 Information Display System Layout Sheet

Panel ID   Subjs

Job No.   Sheet

Originated by   Date   of

COLUMN

```
      1-10      11-20     21-30     31-40     41-50     51-60     61-70     71-80
01  DATE: ZZ/ZZ/ZZ              ABC MANUFACTURING COMPANY                        POVMBR.
02  TIME: ZZ/ZZ.ZZ              VENDOR FILE BROWSE
03     VENDOR CD VENDOR NAME              STREET              CITY V STATE
04  01 Z-ZZZZ-Z ZZZZZZZZZZZZZZZZZZZZZZZZZZZZ ZZZZZZZZZZZZZZZZZZZZZ ZZZZZZZZZZZZZZZZZZZZZZZ
05  02 Z    Z Z              Z Z              Z Z              Z
06  03 Z    Z Z              Z Z              Z Z              Z
07  04 Z    Z Z              Z Z              Z Z              Z
08  05 Z    Z Z              Z Z              Z Z              Z
09  06 Z    Z Z              Z Z              Z Z              Z
10  07 Z    Z Z              Z Z              Z Z              Z
11  08 Z    Z Z              Z Z              Z Z              Z
12  09 Z    Z Z              Z Z              Z Z              Z
13  10 Z    Z Z              Z Z              Z Z              Z
14  11 Z    Z Z              Z Z              Z Z              Z
15  12 Z    Z Z              Z Z              Z Z              Z
16  13 Z    Z Z              Z Z              Z Z              Z
17  14 Z    Z Z              Z Z              Z Z              Z
18  15 Z-ZZZZ-Z ZZZZZZZZZZZZZZZZZZZZZZZZZZZZ ZZZZZZZZZZZZZZZZZZZZZ ZZZZZZZZZZZZZZZZZZZZZZZ
19  XX : SELECTION
20     RESET VENDOR CODE: XXXXXX
21  1. FWD  -PF1      4. KEY IN SELECTION  - PF6
22  2. BWD  -PF2      5. KEY IN RESET VENDOR - PF7
23  3. MENU -PF5      6. END OF SESSION  - CLEAR
24  Z                                                                            Z
```

Figure 2-10 Vendor File Browse Map.

Browse Map

The browse map, shown in Fig. 2-10, contains many of the characteristics found in the other maps discussed. The headings and message lines have the same format and occupy the same line numbers as the other maps. The body follows the headings and precedes the map instructions.

The attributes for this map are all ASKIP, NORM, except for those on lines 19 and 20, the SELECTION and RESET VENDOR CODE data-entry fields, which are UNPROT. The message line attribute can be changed to brighten or darken the message.

SUMMARY

The design of user-friendly maps is best achieved through communication between users and data processing personnel. Users know their systems best and should work closely with programmer/analysts to ensure that maps and systems are designed to suit their requirements. Terminal operators frequently display and work with certain screens throughout the day. They must understand and feel comfortable with those formatted screens.

Maps can usually be broken down into header, body, instructions, and message sections. The location of certain items should be consistent from map to map.

Design maps so that they are pleasing or neutral but never irritating to work with.

Map attributes determine how screen fields are viewed and acted upon. Screen fields can be skipped over or stopped at in order to have a user enter data. These fields can be displayed at a normal or bright intensity. They can also be darkened so that they are not seen by the user. A basic understanding of map attributes will make the user more effective in working with data processing personnel in the development of maps.

Menu maps, control maps, and detail maps occur in most systems. Detail maps take many forms and cover such functions as inquiry, add, change, and delete. Browse programs are part of many systems. A professional constructs all map messages with the terminal operator's feelings in mind;—messages are often softened with words such as "please."

3

BACKGROUND TERMINOLOGY
AND CONSIDERATIONS

Required CICS terminology and other background considerations will be introduced in this chapter. The CICS command format is presented, and pseudoconversational and conversational programming are discussed. CICS tables covered are the program-control table (PCT) and the processing program table (PPT). Multitasking and multithreading are introduced, and their use is made clear through an example. Program considerations and restrictions are discussed. System and program security for online systems is covered.

CICS programmers usually refer to the display of a map as a *send* of the map. A CICS program issues a SEND MAP command in order to display various types of maps such as menu, control, or detail maps. The design of the system will determine the types of maps to be used and the sequence in which they are to appear. The map sent will usually require data to be entered and/or an AID key to be pressed in order to initiate the receive of the map.

A CICS program obtains the information entered by a terminal operator when an AID key is pressed. The AID keys consist of ENTER, PF, CLEAR, and PA; normally only the first three AID keys are used. A CICS program issues a RECEIVE MAP command in order to initiate the action requested by the terminal operator. The action indicated by the AID key pressed will determine the type of processing to be performed.

Pseudoconversational Programming

CICS allows many users to be logged on to and to use CICS concurrently. Computer main-storage size is finite. If there are numerous users running transactions demanding main storage, a short-on-storage condition could occur, causing delays.

Pseudoconversational programming is a coding technique which results in a program being loaded into main storage when required and released when it is no longer active. For instance, when a map is displayed and the program is waiting for a user's response, the program can be released from main storage and reloaded when needed (when the user responds). CICS loads and releases application programs from main storage automatically. High-use programs are often defined as main-storage resident, and the system keeps them in main storage. Tables and maps, which are considered programs by CICS, are usually controlled by a program. Generally, when using the pseudoconversational technique of processing, pressing an AID key causes a program to be loaded if it is not already in main storage. When a program is finished with a logical segment of processing, it normally sends a map, saves required data, and returns control to CICS. This allows the release of the program from main storage if storage is needed by other programs. When an AID key is pressed, the program will be loaded into main storage if necessary, saved data will be restored, and processing will continue. Pseudoconversational programming techniques should be used whenever possible, and all program examples in this book use this technique. Pseudoconversational programming techniques are the responsibility of the application programmer.

Conversational Programming

Conversational programming is a coding technique which results in a program being loaded into and remaining in main storage until a user is finished working with the program. The program is not released from main storage when not active, as in pseudoconversational programming. For instance, a conversational program will display a map and remain in main storage while waiting for a user's response.

Conversational programming techniques usually involve the send of a map with the program remaining in main storage while the terminal operator is entering data. Unless an AID key is pressed to end the session, the program will send another map and await the terminal operator's reply, remaining all the while in main storage. The conversational technique appears the same from a terminal operator's perspective as pseudoconversational programming. Sometimes the conversational technique causes main-storage utilization problems. This occurs for many reasons such as getting a telephone call, taking a break, or engaging in conversation after starting a session. The user is generally not aware of this situation, and it is the responsibility of the programmer/analyst to design and write programs which minimize the impact of this condition. Practical applications of conversational programming are very limited and will not be covered in this book. Pseudoconversational programming is widely used and will be addressed; it eliminates many of the problems which occur when using conversational programming.

Master Terminal Commands

Master terminal commands can be issued by a programmer or a designated master terminal operator (MTO) in order to perform many functions including:

1. Place the latest load library address of a program, table, or map into the PPT (discussed later in this chapter).

2. Monitor tasks which are running (discussed later in this chapter).

3. Terminate a task.

4. Enable, disable, or inquire as to the status of programs, transactions, or files (data sets). Files can also be opened or closed.

5. Put a terminal out of service.

Master terminal commands may be entered on a cleared screen by keying in CSMT followed by the required entries. CEMT, an enhanced version of the master terminal command CSMT, is a prompting transaction which allows abbreviated keywords to be entered. Just key in CEMT and press ENTER. You can enter PRO for program, TRAN for transaction, DAT for data set, etc. Master terminal commands do not apply to the use of CICS on a microcomputer.

CICS Tables

Many tables are used by CICS. A few are of direct interest to the application programmer, and only they are discussed. A user initiates a compiled CICS program by clearing the screen and keying in a four-character TRANSID which directs CICS to start a program at that terminal. It is necessary to identify the TRANSID and program to CICS and to tie them together. This is accomplished by means of two tables that are very important to the CICS programmer.

Program-Control Table

The basic function of the PCT is to tie together the TRANSID entered by the terminal operator with the program name. TRANSID and PROGRAM are the PCT entries of most interest to a programmer. The terminal operator enters a TRANSID in order to start a transaction, then the TRANSID is matched against the PCT to determine if it is a valid entry. A TRANSID not in the PCT will cause an invalid TRANSID message to be displayed on the terminal. A match on TRANSID will use the associated program name to search the PPT for a match on PROGRAM. The program is loaded into main storage if it is not a main-storage resident program or already in main storage.

Processing Program Table

The PPT contains entries such as

1. Program name, language, and size

2. The main-storage address of the program (if it has been loaded)

3. A task use counter (discussed later in this chapter)

4. The load library address of the program which is to be loaded into main storage

5. An indicator as to whether the program is a main-storage resident (usually high-use) program

A PPT entry is used to locate programs which are to be loaded into main storage and is required for each program, map, and table used by the CICS system. When CICS is started up, the PPT is initialized with the address of the load module for all programs, maps, and tables. When a program is changed and compiled or assembled after CICS has been started up, it is necessary to refresh the address of the load module in the PPT. This is a normal occurrence on the test system. The new load module address can be placed into the PPT by one of the following master terminal transactions entered on a cleared screen.

```
          CSMT NEW, PGRMID=progname
                      or
          CEMT SET PRO (progname) NEW
```

Both tables contain additional entries which are usually maintained by the systems programming staff. For simplicity, assume the tables contain information of only direct importance to the applications programmer. Additional entries are discussed in App. D.

```
    PCT Entries            PPT Entries
    TRANSID  = RECV        PROGRAM = RECEIVEP
    PROGRAM = RECEIVEP     PGMLANG = COBOL
```

Clear the screen, key in the TRANSID RECV, and press ENTER. CICS finds the TRANSID RECV and the program name RECEIVEP in the PCT. The PCT ties the transaction to the PPT entry RECEIVEP. The PPT entry is used to locate the associated program's load module and to load it into main storage.

CICS application programmers should obtain several PCT and PPT entries through their manager and the systems programming department. These entries can be used for testing new programs until a permanent entry is assigned. All examples in this book use the following table and entries shown in Fig. 3-1 [CICS program tables and file control table (FCT) entries will be discussed later in the book].

Maps, which are generated by an assembler program, will be discussed in more detail in Chaps. 6 and 7. Maps and tables do not have TRANSIDs; they are controlled by CICS programs. The program language for all PPT entries will

* * * PCT * * * TRANSID	Program	PPT Program	PPT Map	PPT Tables	FCT DATASET
DSPL	DISPLAYP	DISPLAYP			
RECV	RECEIVEP	RECEIVEP			
POMU	POMENUPM	POMENUPM	POMENU1		
POVM	POVMAINT	POVMAINT	POVMNT1		
		JRNLPOST		T053JRSQ	JOURNAL1
POVI	POVMINQY	POVMINQY	POVMIQ1 POVMIQ2	T037LOAD	VENDMAST
POVC	POVMCHGE	POVMCHGE	POVMCH1 POVMCH2	T037LOAD	VENDMAST
POVA	POVMADDN	POVMADDN	POVMAD1 POVMAD2	T037LOAD	VENDMAST
POVD	POVMDLET	POVMDLET	POVMDL1 POVMDL2	T037LOAD	VENDMAST
POVB	POVMBROW	POVMBROW	POVMBR1		VENDMAST

Program	Description
DISPLAYP	Displays message CICS IS EASY
RECEIVEP	Receives and sends social security number
POMENUPM	Purchasing system menu
POVMAINT	Vendor file maintenance submenu
JRNLPOST	Journal file updating
POVMINQY	Vendor file inquiry
POVMCHGE	Vendor file changes
POVMADDN	Vendor file additions
POVMDLET	Vendor file deletions
POVMBROW	Vendor file browse

Figure 3-1 CICS Table Entries Used in this Book.

be PGMLANG=COBOL for all programs.

Multiple PCT Entries

Multiple PCT entries are permitted to refer to the same program, but multiple programs cannot be associated with the same PCT entry.

	Valid		Invalid
PCT	**PPT**	**PCT**	**PPT**
POVA	POVMADDN	POVA	POVMADDN
POVB	POVMADDN	POVA	POVMDLET

CICS Command Format

CICS commands have the general format

```
EXEC CICS function
            option 1 (argument 1)
            option 2 (argument 2)
                    .
                    .
                    .

END-EXEC.
```

Function may be commands such as

```
SEND
RECEIVE
RETURN
HANDLE CONDITION
```

Options and arguments may be

```
FROM     (WS-OUTPUT)
INTO     (WS-INPUT)
LENGTH   (WS-LENGTH)
ERASE
```

Options have no required sequence but must be used under the corresponding function. Many options are available for some CICS commands, but only a few may actually be required. Only options required to illustrate selected functions will be presented.

Task

A task is created for each executed TRANSID which is recognized by CICS (found in the PCT). A task can include one or several programs. A task continues until a program returns control to CICS or issues a RETURN command in a pseudoconversational program. CICS's ability to handle multiple tasks simultaneously is called *multitasking*. Different tasks can concurrently access the same program's load module which is resident in main storage; this is referred to as *multithreading*. Since a single load module in main storage may be accessed by several tasks, a program cannot have its procedure division instructions modified during a specific task. Each task obtains main storage for its unique copy of a program's working storage. Programs should be written so that their working storage is kept as small as possible. Keep constants, literals, and messages in the program's procedure division when practical. Multitasking and multithreading do not apply to a microcomputer environment.

CICS Multitasking and Multithreading

Figure 3-2 and the following table illustrate how multitasking and multithreading might utilize main storage. Four users at different terminals have entered the

	PCT			PPT Table Entries		
				Main		Load
				Storage	Use	Library
TRANSID	Program		Program	Address	Counter	Address
DSPL	DISPLAYP		DISPLAYP	2000	4	10500
RECV	RECEIVEP		RECEIVEP	3000	3	25600

Figure 3-2 CICS Multitasking and Multithreading.

```
┌──────────────────────────────────────────────────────────────────────────
│   INQ TAS
│   STATUS:   RESULTS - OVERTYPE TO MODIFY
│     TAS(00311)  TRA(DSPL)  FAC(T022)  ACT  SHO  TER
│     TAS(00314)  TRA(RECV)  FAC(T014)  ACT  SHO  TER
│     TAS(00316)  TRA(RECV)  FAC(T031)  ACT  SHO  TER
│     TAS(00317)  TRA(DSPL)  FAC(T005)  ACT  SHO  TER
│     TAS(00322)  TRA(DSPL)  FAC(T017)  ACT  SHO  TER
│     TAS(00325)  TRA(RECV)  FAC(T003)  ACT  SHO  TER
│     TAS(00328)  TRA(DSPL)  FAC(T027)  ACT  SHO  TER
│
│                      .
│                      .
│                      .
│
│
│
│
│
│
│     RESPONSE: NORMAL                      TIME:  10.16.27   DATE 86.023
│
│    PF: 1 HELP        3 END                7 SBH 8 SFH 9 MSG 10 SB 11  SF
└──────────────────────────────────────────────────────────────────────────
```

Figure 3-3   CEMT Master Terminal Display for a Task.

TRANSID DSPL and three other users have entered the TRANSID RECV, starting seven different tasks. The initial task for each TRANSID resulted in the corresponding program in the PCT obtaining the associated program's load library address for each program from the PPT. The load module was then loaded into main storage and its main-storage address moved into the PPT.

Each task for both programs obtained a copy of its own unique working storage in main storage as shown, and one was added to the program's PPT use counter. As each task completes, its use counter in the PPT is decreased by one, and its working storage can be released from main storage. When the use counter is reduced to zero, as all tasks accessing a program complete, a program may be released from main storage (if it is not defined as a resident program in the PPT) if main storage is required for another task.

Either of the following master terminal transactions will give the status of all tasks active in the CICS partition or region.

```
┌─────────────────────────┐
│                         │
│        CSMT TAS         │
│           or            │
│       CEMT INQ TAS      │
│                         │
└─────────────────────────┘
```

Entering CEMT INQ TAS at the time the tasks shown in Fig. 3-2 were active would produce a display similar to that shown in Fig. 3-3. CEMT lists all tasks active in the CICS region showing:

1. TAS (XXXXX)—TASK number

2. TRA (XXXX) —TRANSID entered

3. FAC (XXXX) —FACility, terminal at which the task was entered

4. ACT or SUS   —ACTive or SUSpended task

5. SHO or LON   —SHOrt or LONg running task

6. TER   —TERminal

Program Considerations and Restrictions

A CICS programmer needs to be aware of certain considerations and restrictions when writing programs.

Considerations

1. Must eventually return control to CICS.

2. Cannot modify procedure division instructions because CICS programs may be shared by many tasks.

3. Can modify working storage since a unique copy of working storage is created for each task.

Restrictions

1. FILE SECTION, OPEN, CLOSE, and non-CICS READ and WRITE statements are not permitted because file management is handled by CICS.

2. Many Cobol features must be avoided such as internal sorts, use of special registers, ACCEPT, DISPLAY, EXHIBIT, TRACE, STOP RUN, and GOBACK. (STOP RUN and GOBACK are sometimes included in CICS programs in order to eliminate a compiler diagnostic but are *never* executed.)

System and Program Security

Security is a major concern in the design of some online systems such as payroll and a consideration in others. The design of security techniques can be implemented at the system and/or program level. There are many security techniques that an installation can utilize. Some may require extensive user interaction; others may be less obvious to a terminal operator. The discussion that follows applies to mainframe computers; however, security should also be considered for production systems that are run on microcomputers.

System Security

System security is important when there are applications which are restricted to certain terminals. For instance, if payroll is online, it would not be wise to allow access to these programs from every terminal in the system. Likewise, it may be necessary to limit the access or update of certain files to specific terminals. A current trend which I foresee will continue and expand is that of permitting customers and vendors to gain access to files and records, allowing them to monitor and update those files. Much as travel agents are able to access airline databases, delete stock (seats), and write out orders (tickets), I expect most major companies to partake in similar activities. A customer will be permitted to inquire as to how much stock of certain items is available for immediate delivery, then delete the stock by placing an order. Vendors will be permitted to monitor purchase orders against your files in order to determine what you actually received. Obviously it is advisable to limit customer and vendor access to certain transactions and files.

There are many software systems on the market which can restrict the use of specified transactions, programs, and files to designated terminals. Other security restrictions are possible, such as having the system restrict a terminal to certain operators and limit the time of day which a terminal can be used.

Program Security

Once the system's security has been passed and the customer or vendor is into your transaction, accessing your files, you obviously want to restrict access to specific items or purchase orders. The safest way to restrict access is by having each program check against a table of terminal identifiers and allowable passwords (see "Passwords" in Chap. 4). The table could contain authorized items, such as purchase orders and other record keys which are valid for customers or vendors to access at their terminals. A customer or vendor trying to access an item or purchase order on your system might get into your program, but an unauthorized message could be displayed if the item or purchase order was not in the table.

A situation which often occurs is that an authorized user signs on to CICS and leaves the terminal before signing off. Unauthorized personnel could use the vacated terminal. Programming techniques, not discussed in this book, are available which will force a program to terminate if an AID key is not pressed within a predetermined time interval. This technique is not often used and would be restricted to extremely sensitive transactions. A user who displays information on a terminal while on the phone with a customer would not want to be logged off CICS in the middle of a conversation.

Many of the techniques used by system security software could be coded into individual programs. Selected programs could contain routines to check a password against tables or files in order to determine file, record, transaction, program, and terminal authorization. Logic could be coded to permit or prohibit access between certain dates and times and on specified days of the week. Security violations can be written out to a file and be printed by category by a batch program. An audible alarm could be sounded at the violating terminal. All of these checks require additional program code and make programs less efficient and more complicated. Let your system security software handle as many of these checks as possible, if your installation has such software.

Program security, if planned properly and implemented correctly, can run very smoothly; if not, all types of security problems will occur. Some day, access to a system by persons outside of a company will be just as widespread as current access by company employees. This should be a major growth area for CICS usage in the years to come.

Summary

Pseudoconversational programming is a technique used to minimize computer main-storage requirements. An understanding of the advantage of this technique as opposed to conversational programming is needed in order to develop efficient systems.

The PCT and PPT were discussed. Task initiation and termination and their effects on PPT entries were covered. An example illustrated how multitasking and multithreading function. Master terminal transactions which refresh the load module address of a program in the PPT and those which list all active tasks in a CICS partition or region were discussed. CICS program considerations and restrictions were listed.

The trend toward allowing customers and vendors to access company programs and files through CICS transactions presents certain security considerations in the design of a system. Security should not be an excuse to prevent customer and vendor access to your system, but should present a challenge to plan your security system with care. Demand for system access by users has grown within companies; it will expand even further to include access by users outside the company. Companies which ignore this demand will find themselves at a competitive disadvantage in the future.

4

SYSTEM AND PROGRAMMING DOCUMENTATION STANDARDS

Standards are uniform methods of performing required functions. A standard should serve a definite purpose. The problem with standards is that few people agree about what is beneficial, and many consider documentation a wasted effort. Two excellent books which promote program standards—*How to Design and Develop COBOL Programs* and *The COBOL Programmer's Handbook*—are listed in the Bibliography. The creation and maintenance of standards often require more time than the task they support; if not kept up to date, they become useless and can actually create problems. Most data processing personnel agree that certain standards are necessary, but the fewer the better. This chapter covers what I consider to be the most worthwhile standards for use in an online environment; many can be applied also to batch systems.

System Design Standards

The best design tool and standard is perhaps one of the easiest to create and maintain—the system structure chart. A system structure chart should show at a glance the scope of a system; it should be simple, yet comprehensive. I like to work with a structure chart that shows the major functions of a system, including related PCT and PPT entries.

Structure Charts

Figure 4-1 illustrates a system structure chart which diagrams the entire purchasing system. The PCT entry, which is also referred to as the TRANSID, is shown above each block. The top section of each block contains the PPT entry; it is the program's name. Each block contains a description of the associated program. This type of structure chart requires a minimal amount of effort to

Figure 4-1 Purchasing System Structure Chart.

create and maintain, yet is an excellent planning tool and shows the scope of a project at a glance.

Once the system structure chart has been established, it is often advantageous to draw subsystem structure charts as shown in Fig. 4-2. The format of a subsystem structure chart is identical to that of a regular system structure chart. The value of both charts is twofold: they help the designer plan what functions should be contained in a system, and they also provide a picture of the scope of a system, making it easy to explain to others.

The subsystem structure chart shown in Fig. 4-2 is the structure which will be used for programs in the text. POVMAINT, referred to as the menu program, will be discussed in Chap. 9. The inquiry program POVMINQY, additions program POVMADDN, change program POVMCHGE, delete program POVMDLET, and browse program POVMBROW will be discussed in Chaps. 12, 13, 14, 15, and 17, respectively.

Figure 4-2 Vendor File Maintenance Menu—Subsystem Structure Chart.

Programming Standards

Program standards generally are time-consuming to create and often require considerable effort to maintain. Even in the best-documented installations, the programmer/analyst who has to maintain a program seldom uses standards as more than a general guideline as to what function a program should perform. Programs contain a tremendous amount of detail, and that detail is seldom completely and correctly reflected in program documentation. The best place for program documentation is in the program itself, by using meaningful comments. Program structure charts, program comments, and style of programming all help to determine how easy or difficult a program will be to maintain. The use of standard file layouts and of standard program routines can greatly aid the programmer in the initial writing and in future maintenance of a program. Program documentation is more of an art than a science. This chapter covers many of the techniques I employ to make a program self-documenting and easy to maintain.

Program Structure Charts

A well-designed program structure chart informs the person viewing the chart what the major functions of a program include. The structure chart for a menu program (Fig. 4-3) is rather straightforward and varies little from menu program to menu program. Fig. 4-3 lists the program section prefix at the top of each block; this prefix is usually attached to the description inside the block to form program section names. I generally prefix my mainline section with AA00 and the levels under it as B000, C000, etc. The next sublevel, if one exists, might be C100, C200, C300, etc.; sub-sublevels would be numbered C110, C120, C130, followed by C111, C112, etc., for even lower levels. If a program cannot be covered by this structure, it is probably too complicated and should be analyzed for a simpler design. I find it easier to maintain several simple programs, each of which performs one function, than one large program which performs many functions. The program structure chart, if well thought out, can be an excellent tool for the initial design and future maintenance of a program. The more functions a program contains, the more beneficial a program structure chart will be to a programmer/analyst. I like to include the program's structure as comments at the start of the procedure division of each program. I believe this technique is easier to maintain than is the block structure chart. See the menu program example in Chap. 9 for an illustration of how this is done.

Program Comments

The first place a programmer generally looks when maintaining an existing program is at the latest Cobol source program listing; often this is the only place. Time spent making this listing as readable as possible is well worth the effort. Write every program as if you will have to go through it from beginning to end 6 months after it has been written, explaining to another programmer/analyst what it is doing. You would most likely use meaningful

Figure 4-3   Purchasing System Menu—Program Structure Chart.

program labels which describe the function of each routine. You would include comments in the program, detailing the function of more complicated routines and clarifying others. Write all programs with ample comments; they will most likely be used as models for other programs.

Keep Programs Short and Simple

I prefer to keep programs short and simple, isolating functions into several simple programs instead of writing one large program. Maintenance functions, against the same file, usually have many common routines and use similar maps. Many designers have a tendency to put all maintenance functions into a single program. I prefer a separate program for each major function. This approach creates more PCT and PPT entry requirements for TRANSIDs, programs, and maps, but each program will be easier to write and to maintain. The trend toward sharing access to certain files and programs with customers and vendors is made easier when functions such as additions, changes, deletions, and inquiries are put into separate programs. For example, a customer may have access to inquiry and change functions, but not to add or delete functions. When each function in a system has a separate program, security is more easily maintained. Because of the trend toward sharing access to files with others outside the installation, programs should be designed to be as simple and flexible as possible. Keep it simple and straightforward—with change being inevitable, you'll be glad you did.

Different Levels of Menus

A system can be designed with many levels of menus. The purchasing system defined in Figs. 4-1 and 4-2 has two levels of menus. One menu can be displayed by entering the TRANSID POMU and the other by entering the TRANSID POVM. A system could be designed to start all installation transactions through a master menu, possibly with a TRANSID of MENU. The terminal operator could enter MENU to display the master menu, make a selection to display the purchasing system menu, make another selection to display the vendor file maintenance menu, and finally, make a selection to display an inquiry map. I am sure that you would find it cumbersome to be required to display three menus prior to the display of an inquiry map. Many systems do not require a user to go through three menus to reach an inquiry screen. The advantages of multimenus are that a user has fewer TRANSIDs to remember, and there are some security advantages to this approach. A system can be designed requiring that all programs be started by a main menu or to allow programs to be started by entering a TRANSID. The purchasing system is designed so that a program can be initiated indirectly by a menu or directly by keying the proper TRANSID. For instance, a user can key in MENU, POMU, POVM, POVI, etc. to initiate the desired function. Your installation's security requirements and design philosophy will determine which approach you will take regarding system menus. Figure 4-4 illustrates the level of menus;—any of the shown TRANSIDs will lead to the vendor file inquiry.

Passwords

Passwords provide a system with a certain degree of security because they can be used to limit system access to specific users. Personnel at a location where terminals are located must assume some responsibility for monitoring access to the system. System or program security can limit access based on specific passwords but cannot actually monitor *who* enters an authorized password. Each location should be responsible for who uses a terminal. Some users at a given location may know the passwords of other employees. Unauthorized personnel could gain access to the system by using these passwords. Passwords aid system security, but they are not foolproof. At best, passwords can restrict users at specific terminals to certain transactions, programs, or files.

Password requirements should be limited; continuous entering of passwords can make a system's operation cumbersome. Keying in of passwords, which are normally entered into nondisplay (DRK attribute) fields, should be limited to sign-on and to initial transaction entry screens. Carried to the ultimate, every display of a map could require the entry of a password, but the nuisance factor involved would far outweigh any security advantage gained. Passwords

Figure 4-4 Levels of Menus.

are a necessary part of many systems, but you must plan carefully where to use them.

Message File

The use of a message file may be considered if a system is going to be adapted for use in several countries. The key to this type of a file would probably be a four-character number, the file data being the message to be displayed on the message line (line 24) of the map. A programmer would move the key of the message to be displayed to the appropriate program area, read the message file, and then move the file's message to line 24 of the map. The advantage of a message file is that the messages could be translated into the language of the country using the system. The disadvantages are that each program contains unique messages, and that a message file can grow very large. Since a read of the message file is required to fetch the proper message, program usage and maintenance of such a file can be cumbersome. It is often difficult to find an appropriate predefined message for many program conditions. When no message exists, a new message must be added to the file. Other programmer/analysts should be notified of new messages and their codes so that they will not use the same codes or create duplicate or similar messages. It is not uncommon for a program to contain dozens of messages. I recommend avoiding the use of a message file.

Program Tables

The use of tables, like the certainty of change, is inevitable in most systems. Three types of tables are commonly used, those which are

1. Defined in the program itself
2. Loaded into main storage as needed
3. Set up on a VSAM file

Tables Defined in a Program

Tables can be coded directly in a program or may be set up in a source code library, then copied into a program when it is compiled. A change to this type of table always requires programs which use the table to be recompiled. Limit the use of such tables to those which are short and unlikely to change often; otherwise you will design ongoing maintenance into your system.

Tables Loaded into Main Storage

Tables can be created and stored in a load library so that they can be loaded into main storage by a program as required, then released when the program is finished with the table. This type of table requires a PPT entry; it is the type used for large tables and for those requiring frequent maintenance. This kind of table requires an amount of main storage equal to the size of the table; it should be released, to free main storage, as soon as it is no longer needed by a program. Maintenance of such a table requires the creation of a new table load module and may require program maintenance. The table itself does require maintenance; changes can be time-consuming and the possibility of error is great on large-volume changes.

VSAM Table Files

Virtual storage access method (VSAM) is a technique for accessing and updating files randomly. An individual or general purpose VSAM file can be set up to handle each table required by the system. An advantage of individual VSAM table files is that the table can be set up to be the exact size required by the table's key plus its data. The disadvantages of individual table files are that each table has to be maintained separately and each table requires a FCT entry. A general purpose table requires only one FCT entry and can be maintained by a single program, although several programs could be used. This type of table is easy to create and maintain but has the disadvantage of wasting disk space. A general purpose table would require the key field size to be set to the largest key in the file. For instance, a table's key might consist of a four-character prefix, followed by the key itself, and then the data in the table. A two-digit state code would require the same key size as a 15-position key. The file could be set up with variable-length records so that less space would be wasted in the data portion of the file. I recommend the creation and use of a general purpose table file because it is easy to work with, flexible, and facilitates table maintenance. A general purpose file, once created, can be maintained on line by a single program or by several customized programs.

Summary

Standards should be developed with consideration given to the future maintenance of the documentation to support the standards. A worthwhile standard is the system structure chart, which shows at a glance the scope of a system. Subsystem structure charts should be used to break complicated systems into simpler segments.

Program standards should include a program structure chart; it helps a programmer/analyst design a program and serves as documentation once the program is written. Consider coding your program structure chart at the start of the procedure division to supplement or replace the block structure chart.

Keep programs simple and straightforward; they will be easier to design and maintain and will be more flexible and easier to modify. This will become more important as the trend toward sharing files with customers and vendors expands.

Programs can be designed so that they can be started only by a menu program or by individual TRANSIDs. Passwords are a necessary part of any system, but they are no guarantee that unauthorized access to a system will be prevented. Consider the creation of a general purpose VSAM table file which can be easily maintained on line.

BASIC PROGRAM EXAMPLES

CICS, as perceived by the applications programmer, is a collection of commands interspersed in a Cobol program. CICS commands provide the ability to send and receive terminal messages, read and write files, and perform other functions. The easiest way to learn CICS is through examples used to establish concepts the creative programmer can apply to real-life situations. Simple programs are covered here, and new commands are explained as encountered.

Send a Message to a Terminal

The program DISPLAYP shown in Fig. 5-1 is initiated by the TRANSID DSPL which is entered on a cleared screen. That's all there is to writing a CICS program which displays the message CICS IS EASY on the screen. Two commands were introduced in this program—the SEND command and the RETURN command.

SEND Command

```
EXEC CICS SEND
          FROM    (WS-MESSAGE)
          LENGTH (12)
END-EXEC.
```

The SEND command, as used in Fig. 5-1, is very similar in concept to the DISPLAY statement used in Cobol batch processing programs. WS-MESSAGE is the same as a working-storage message would be in a batch Cobol

```
0001 IDENTIFICATION DIVISION.
0002*
0003 PROGRAM-ID. DISPLAYP.
0004*
0005 REMARKS.
0006*
0007*************************************************************
0008*    THIS PROGRAM ILLUSTRATES CICS SEND AND RETURN COMMANDS.   *
0009*    A MESSAGE 'CICS IS EASY' IS DISPLAYED ON THE CRT.         *
0010*************************************************************
0011*
0012 ENVIRONMENT DIVISION.
0013*
0014 DATA DIVISION.
0015*
0016 WORKING-STORAGE SECTION.
0017*
0018 01  WS-MESSAGE           PIC X(12)     VALUE 'CICS IS EASY'.
0019*
0020 LINKAGE SECTION.
0021*
0022*
0023 PROCEDURE DIVISION.
0024*
0025* SEND CRT MESSAGE
0026     EXEC CICS SEND
0027            FROM   (WS-MESSAGE)
0028            LENGTH (12)
0029     END-EXEC.
0030*
0031* RETURN TO CICS
0032     EXEC CICS RETURN
0033     END-EXEC.
```

Figure 5-1 Program Illustrating SEND and RETURN Commands.

program. CICS requires a program to specify the length of the message being sent.

RETURN Command

```
EXEC CICS RETURN
END-EXEC.
```

The RETURN command, conceptually much like the GOBACK command in Cobol, returns control to CICS.

Compiling a CICS Program

Most data processing installations have standard procedures set up for translating and compiling CICS programs and placing the compiled output in the appropriate CICS load library.

All CICS commands begin with EXEC CICS. The translator recognizes this and breaks down CICS commands into call statements and prints a list of the original source program. The translated source data is then passed through a Cobol compiler which prints a second listing showing CICS commands

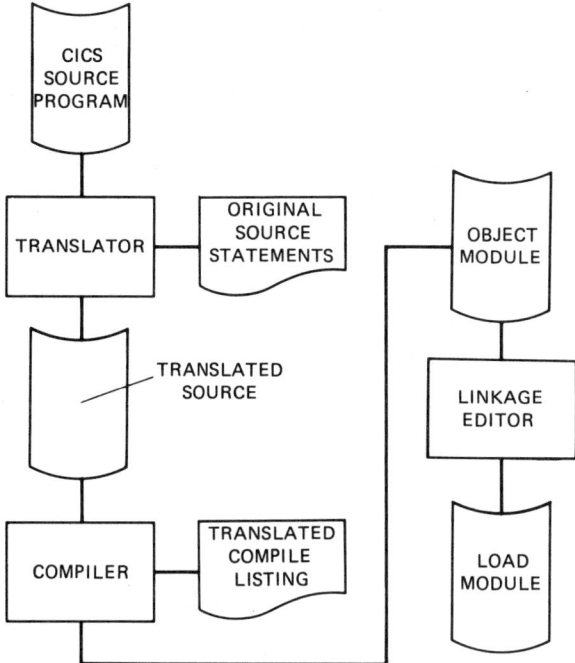

Figure 5-2 CICS Compile Procedure.

translated into move-and-call statements. Additional code is also placed into the program by the compiler. The object module created is "link-edited" to produce a load module. Figure 5-2 illustrates the CICS compile procedure.

The translated version of the program would be similar to that shown in Fig. 5-3. A look at this version shows a field called DFHEIVAR in working storage. DFHEIVAR's subfields are copied into a program by the translator and used to hold call parameters employed by the translated version of CICS commands. CICS commands for send and return are commented out (*), and calls are generated by the translator for CICS commands, using DFHEIVAR subfields. These fields are similar to the fields shown at the top of page 57.

Translator call fields are copied into a program by the translator in order to set up Calls which effect CICS commands. These fields are of no direct interest to the application programmer and are only mentioned so that you will recognize them when they appear in your program.

The translator generates, in the linkage section, fields named DFHEIBLK, the execute interface block (EIB) (see App. A-1), and DFHCOMMAREA, the communication area. CICS creates a new version of the EIB, with its updated values, for program use each time a new task is initiated.

```
0001 IDENTIFICATION DIVISION.
0002*
0003 PROGRAM-ID. DISPLAYP.
0004*
0005 REMARKS.
0006*
0007********************************************************************
0008*            TRANSLATED VERSION OF SAMPLE PROGRAM              *
0009*       THIS PROGRAM ILLUSTRATES CICS SEND AND RETURN COMMANDS *
0010*  THAT HAVE BEEN ALTERED AS THE FIRST STEP OF CHANGING SOURCE *
0011*  CODE INTO COMPUTER USABLE INSTRUCTIONS.                     *
0012*     A MESSAGE 'CICS IS EASY' IS DISPLAYED ON THE CRT.        *
0013********************************************************************
0014*
0015 ENVIRONMENT DIVISION.
0016*
0017 DATA DIVISION.
0018*
0019 WORKING-STORAGE SECTION.
0020*
0021 01  WS-MESSAGE             PIC X(12)     VALUE 'CICS IS EASY'.
0022*
0023 01  DFHEIVAR   COPY   DFHEIVAR
0024*
0025*
0026 LINKAGE SECTION.
0027*
0028 01  DFHEIBLK  COPY  DFHEIBLK.
0029*       (see Appendix A-1)
0030*
0031 01  DFHCOMMAREA           PIC X.
0032*
0033 PROCEDURE DIVISION USING DFHEIBLK DFHCOMMAREA.
0034*
0035* SEND CRT MESSAGE
0036*    EXEC CICS SEND
0037*            FROM   (WS-MESSAGE)
0038*            LENGTH (12)
0039*    END-EXEC.
0040     MOVE 12 TO DFHEIV11 MOVE '             TO DFHEIV0
0041     CALL 'DFHEI1' USING DFHEIV0 DFHEIV99 DFHEIV98 WS-MESSAGE
0042     DFHEIV11.
0043*
0044* RETURN TO CICS
0045*    EXEC CICS RETURN
0046*    END-EXEC.
0047     MOVE '          ' TO DFHEIV0 CALL 'DFHEI1' USING DFHEIV0.
```

Figure 5-3 Translated CICS Program.

The application programmer need not be overly concerned with how the translator works; no further illustrations will be presented for the translated version of programs.

Running a Compiled Program

Once a program compiles without error, it is ready for execution (if it has the appropriate PCT and PPT entries). Refresh the PPT program address by entering CSMT NEW,PGRMID=DISPLAYP. Clear the screen to set the cursor at POS=(01,01) on the screen. Key in the TRANSID DSPL and press ENTER. The following will appear starting at POS=(01,01) of the screen:

DSPLCICS IS EASY

```
01  DFHEIVAR COPY DFHEIVAR.
    02 DFHEIV0          PIC X(26).
    02 DFHEIV1          PIC X(8).
    02 DFHEIV2          PIC X(8).
    02 DFHEIV3          PIC X(8).
    02 DFHEIV4          PIC X(6).
    02 DFHEIV5          PIC X(4).
    02 DFHEIV6          PIC X(4).
    02 DFHEIV7          PIC X(2).
    02 DFHEIV8          PIC X(2).
    02 DFHEIV9          PIC X(1).
    02 DFHEIV10         PIC S9(7)          COMP-3.
    02 DFHEIV11         PIC S9(4)          COMP.
    02 DFHEIV12         PIC S9(4)          COMP.
    02 DFHEIV13         PIC S9(4)          COMP.
    02 DFHEIV14         PIC S9(4)          COMP.
    02 DFHEIV15         PIC S9(4)          COMP.
    02 DFHEIV16         PIC S9(9)          COMP.
    02 DFHEIV17         PIC X(4).
    02 DFHEIV18         PIC X(4).
    02 DFHEIV19         PIC X(4).
    02 DFHEIV97         PIC S9(7)  COMP-3  VALUE ZERO.
    02 DFHEIV98         PIC S9(4)  COMP    VALUE ZERO.
    02 DFHEIV99         PIC X(1)           VALUE SPACE.
```

To display the message without DSPL, that is

CICS IS EASY

An ERASE option must be added to the SEND command:

```
EXEC CICS SEND
         FROM     (WS-MESSAGE)
         LENGTH (12)
         ERASE
END-EXEC.
```

ERASE will clear the screen and position the cursor at line 1, column 1 of the screen prior to the send. The sequence of the options following a command is not fixed. For instance, ERASE is specified last but will result in the screen's being cleared before information is sent to it.

Receive a Message

Now that you know how to send a message to the terminal, let's see how you might receive data entered by an operator. The program in Fig. 5-4 will

```
0001 IDENTIFICATION DIVISION.
0002*
0003 PROGRAM-ID. RECEIVEP.
0004*
0005 REMARKS.
0006*
0007*****************************************************************
0008*        THIS PROGRAM ILLUSTRATES THE CICS RECEIVE COMMAND      *
0009*        SOCIAL SECURITY NUMBER IS ENTERED AND THEN DISPLAYED    *
0010*        IN A DIFFERENT FORMAT                                   *
0011*****************************************************************
0012*
0013 ENVIRONMENT DIVISION.
0014*
0015 DATA DIVISION.
0016*
0017 WORKING-STORAGE  SECTION.
0018*
0019 01  WS-INPUT.
0020     05  WS-TRANSID                PIC X(4).
0021     05  FILLER                    PIC X.
0022     05  WS-INPUT-SOC-SEC-NO        PIC X(9)    VALUE ALL 'X'.
0023*
0024 01  WS-OUTPUT.
0025     05  FILLER                    PIC X(25)    VALUE
0026         'SOCIAL SECURITY NUMBER = '.
0027     05  WS-OUTPUT-SOC-SEC-NO       PIC X(9).
0028*
0029 01  WS-LENGTH                     PIC S9(4)    COMP.
0030*
0031*
0032 LINKAGE SECTION.
0033*
0034*
0035 PROCEDURE DIVISION.
0036*
0037 AA00-MAINLINE  SECTION.
0038*
0039     PERFORM B000-RECEIVE-INPUT.
0040     PERFORM C000-SEND-OUTPUT.
0041*
0042* RETURN TO CICS
0043     EXEC CICS RETURN
0044     END-EXEC.
0045 B000-RECEIVE-INPUT  SECTION.
0046     MOVE 14  TO  WS-LENGTH.
0047*
0048     EXEC CICS RECEIVE
0049               INTO   (WS-INPUT)
0050               LENGTH (WS-LENGTH)
0051     END-EXEC.
0052*
0053     MOVE WS-INPUT-SOC-SEC-NO  TO  WS-OUTPUT-SOC-SEC-NO.
0054*
0055 B000-EXIT.
0056     EXIT.
0057*
0058 C000-SEND-OUTPUT  SECTION.
0059     EXEC CICS SEND
0060               FROM   (WS-OUTPUT)
0061               LENGTH (34)
0062               ERASE
0063     END-EXEC.
0064*
0065 C000-EXIT.
0066     EXIT.
```

Figure 5-4 Program Illustrating CICS RECEIVE Command.

receive a social security number and send a message using that number. The operator keys in the TRANSID RECV, a space, and then a nine-digit social security number. The program will receive the data entered and display the message

SOCIAL SECURITY NUMBER = 999999999.

RECV 999999999   (Keyed in on first screen)

SOCIAL SECURITY NUMBER = 999999999   (Displayed on
                                         next screen)

The program in Fig. 5-4 illustrates several new CICS concepts plus the RECEIVE command. This program will receive the input message, which consists of the TRANSID, a blank, and social security number. It will then display a message containing the social security number. The new command introduced is RECEIVE. The program receives the input message, including the TRANSID. Note that the RECEIVE's length option is specified with an argument WS-LENGTH, which must be defined in working storage as a binary halfword. LENGTH can be hard-coded in the SEND command [i.e., LENGTH (34)]. You always receive *into* and *send* from. Basically that's all there is to the SEND and RECEIVE commands, but there are a few additional considerations when using the RECEIVE command.

The input field entered may be shorter than the specified working-storage length parameter WS-LENGTH. For instance, if only the first eight positions of a social security number were keyed in, what would happen? WS-LENGTH would be set to 13 instead of the expected 14 (TRANSID + space + social security number), and the displayed message would show an X as the last digit of the social security number. Characters keyed in are received from left to right in the input area WS-INPUT.

The input field keyed in may be greater than WS-LENGTH. What will occur if the social security number is keyed in as 10 digits in error? WS-LENGTH will be set to 15 instead of the anticipated 14 characters. Unfortunately, the output message will not display the 10-digit social security number. The program will come to an ABEND. You could probably get around this condition by making WS-INPUT-SOC-SEC-NO several digits longer than required and by adjusting WS-LENGTH accordingly, but there is a better way to handle this and similar anticipated or unexpected occurrences.

HANDLE CONDITION Commands

There is a CICS command which will handle various anticipated or unexpected CICS conditions: the CICS HANDLE CONDITION. An example of this command is

```
EXEC CICS HANDLE CONDITION
          ERROR  (ERROR-MESSAGE)
END-EXEC.
```

The ERROR option directs a program to transfer control to ERROR-MESSAGE if any unanticipated events occur which cause an ABEND. The program will transfer control to the paragraph named ERROR-MESSAGE which can display a message and cause a normal program termination. The HANDLE CONDITION command must be executed prior to the condition being encountered. CICS debugging aids, which assist CICS programmers in determining the cause of errors, will be discussed in Chap. 18.

CICS programmers can usually anticipate and handle most conditions which occur in a program. There is an option of the HANDLE CONDITION command called LENGERR which can be used to check for a length-error condition. LENGERR and other conditions which can be provided for will take precedence over the ERROR option.

```
EXEC CICS HANDLE CONDITION
          LENGERR (LENGTH-ERROR)
          ERROR    (ERROR-MESSAGE)
END-EXEC.
```

This handle condition will cause the program to branch to the paragraph named LENGTH-ERROR if the input data is longer than the anticipated working-storage length of 14.

The programmer could make the above handle condition into two separate statements as follows:

```
EXEC CICS HANDLE CONDITION
          ERROR(ERROR-MESSAGE)
END-EXEC.

EXEC CICS HANDLE CONDITION
          LENGERR (LENGTH-ERROR)
END-EXEC.
```

To make it easier for the programmer to recover from unanticipated problems, omit the ERROR option on the HANDLE CONDITION function and let the program ABEND. A program might be updating several files when an ABEND occurs. CICS has the ability to dynamically back out file updates when an ABEND occurs. The ERROR condition would prevent this back-out. Unless the program made provision for a back-out in the error message routine, files

```
0001 B000-RECEIVE-INPUT   SECTION.
0002*
0003* HANDLE LENGTH ERRORS
0004      EXEC CICS HANDLE CONDITION
0005              LENGERR (B000-LENGTH-ERROR)
0006      END-EXEC.
0007*
0008      MOVE 14  TO  WS-LENGTH.
0009*
0010      EXEC CICS RECEIVE
0011              INTO  (WS-INPUT)
0012              LENGTH (WS-LENGTH)
0013      END-EXEC.
0014*
0015      MOVE WS-INPUT-SOC-SEC-NO  TO  WS-OUTPUT-SOC-SEC-NO.
0016*
0017      GO TO  B000-EXIT.
0018*
0019 B000-LENGTH-ERROR.
0020      MOVE 'TOO MANY DIGITS ENTERED, PLEASE CLEAR SCREEN AND TRY AGAIN'
0021          TO  WS-OUTPUT.
0022*
0023 B000-EXIT.
0024      EXIT.
```

Figure 5-5 HANDLE CONDITION Command Illustration.

could get out of sync. When you maintain programs written by others, you will most likely encounter the ERROR condition. Just remember that a specific check for a condition such as LENGERR will supersede the ERROR condition if both conditions are coded.

Figure 5-5 illustrates how the procedure division of the sample program in Fig. 5-4 would appear if the HANDLE CONDITION command was added. Program examples in future chapters will contain techniques for eliminating GO TOs from similar conditions.

Note that in paragraph C000-SEND-OUTPUT, the LENGTH option is specified with a length of 58; this is to allow for the length of the larger error message. The working-storage area WS-OUTPUT in Fig. 5-4 would have a FILLER PIC X(24) added after WS-OUTPUT-SOC-SEC-NO to make the field 58 positions long.

If the operator forgot and entered dashes as part of social security number as follows:

RECV 150-22-3333

A length error would be detected because the input length would now be 16 instead of the expected length of 14. The following message would be displayed:

TOO MANY DIGITS ENTERED, PLEASE CLEAR SCREEN AND TRY AGAIN

instead of the anticipated message

SOCIAL SECURITY NUMBER = 150223333

The program could have had two separate SEND commands; one for displaying social security number and one for the length-error message. The advantage of this technique would be the ability to eliminate ERASE from the length-error send. Without ERASE, the send would keep the original entry on the screen for verification by the terminal operator. The message would be displayed from the last recognized position of the cursor as follows:

RECV 150-22-3333TOO MANY DIGITS ENTERED, PLEASE CLEAR SCREEN AND TRY AGAIN

Cursor positioning will be discussed in greater detail later in this chapter.

General Information about Handle Conditions

1. Up to 12 conditions can be handled by one command.

2. The last command encountered takes precedence when prior commands list the same option.

3. To turn off an option, list the option without an argument.

In Fig. 5-6, any length errors in HANDLE-PARAGRAPH-1 would cause a transfer of control to LENGERR-PARAGRAPH-1. Length errors in HANDLE-PARAGRAPH-2 would cause a branch to LENGERR-PARAGRAPH-2. HANDLE-PARAGRAPH-3 would turn off the LENGERR condition causing the program to default to the ERROR condition and to be directed to the paragraph ERROR-MESSAGE if a LENGERR condition occurred. If a length error occurred after HANDLE-PARAGRAPH-3 turned off the LENGERR condition and if the HANDLE ERROR condition was absent, the program would ABEND.

Cursor Position (EIBCPOSN)

CICS programs have the ability to check what the position of the cursor was when an AID key was pressed to initiate a receive. EIBCPOSN, a field in the EIB, can be tested to determine the line and column at which the cursor was positioned. The program in Fig. 5-5 could have replaced

```
      EXEC CICS HANDLE CONDITION
               LENGERR (B000-LENGTH-ERROR)
      END-EXEC.

         by

   IF EIBCPOSN  IS GREATER THAN 14
         MOVE 'TOO MANY DIGITS ENTERED, PLEASE CLEAR SCREEN
—          ' AND TRY AGAIN' TO WS-OUTPUT
         GO TO  B000-EXIT.
```

```
PROCEDURE DIVISION.

    EXEC CICS HANDLE CONDITION
              ERROR (ERROR-MESSAGE)
    END-EXEC.
       .
       .
       .
HANDLE-PARAGRAPH-1.
    EXEC CICS HANDLE CONDITION
              LENGERR (LENGERR-PARAGRAPH-1)
    END-EXEC.
       .
       .
       .
HANDLE-PARAGRAPH-2.
    EXEC CICS HANDLE CONDITION
              LENGERR (LENGERR-PARAGRAPH-2)
    END-EXEC.
       .
       .
       .
HANDLE-PARAGRAPH-3.
    EXEC CICS HANDLE CONDITION
              LENGERR
    END-EXEC.
       .
       .
       .
```

Figure 5-6 HANDLE CONDITION Command Priorities.

The HANDLE CONDITION command is removed and replaced by the EIBCPOSN check which should precede the receive, otherwise LENGERR could occur on the receive, causing an ABEND. In this case, the paragraph B000-LENGTH-ERROR could be eliminated.

When developing applications and writing programs, it is sometimes beneficial to know the line and column at which the cursor is positioned. The cursor position for line 1, column 1 is 0; for line 2, column 1, 80; for line 3, column 1, 160; etc. The last allowable cursor position is 1918. A programmer can determine the value of EIBCPOSN for any line and column by subtracting 1 from line number, multiplying that result by 80, and adding column number minus 1. For example,

> Line 3, column 1
> $(3-1) \times 80 + (1-1) = 160 = $ EIBCPOSN
>
> Line 11, column 10
> $(11-1) \times 80 + (10-1) = 809 = $ EIBCPOSN

The technique of cursor positioning is sometimes used in order to select an item, if the cursor is placed next to that item, prior to pressing a designated AID key. Positioning the cursor anywhere on a line could be used as a signal to delete the record displayed on that line when a designated AID key is pressed.

SUMMARY

Simplified program examples were used to present the following commands—SEND, RECEIVE, RETURN, and HANDLE CONDITION. The CICS compiler and translator were discussed and a sample program was presented in order to illustrate how the translator breaks down CICS commands.

This chapter was intended to give you an indication of how easy the use of CICS commands will be with practice. Future chapters will build on this basic knowledge by introducing more involved program examples.

6

BASIC MAPPING SUPPORT

Proper design of maps is essential to the success of a CICS system. This discussion of basic mapping support (BMS) will be limited to what you need to know in order to create usable maps; it will not cover every option and possibility. BMS maps, which are collections of assembler language macros, can create problems if not properly understood; Chap. 7 will present examples which should help to eliminate most difficulties you may encounter. The theory presented in this chapter will make more sense when it is used with the commands presented in Chap. 7.

The SEND command examples in Chap. 5 were introduced to aid in the presentation of important concepts; in reality, most terminal communication is performed through the use of maps. A map is basically an assembler program which formats terminal screens and controls the transfer of data between a terminal and CICS programs.

Map Types

The BMS map is run through an assembler program twice in order to produce two maps; the physical map and the symbolic map. A macro is an instruction which generates additional code when it is passed through an assembler program. Macros generate many statements when the BMS map is assembled; these statements result in instructions which aid in controlling physical and symbolic maps.

Physical Maps

Physical maps are assembly language programs which are created and placed in a load library. Physical maps control screen alignment plus the sending and receiving of constants and data to and from a terminal.

Symbolic Maps

Symbolic maps define map fields used to store variable data referenced in a Cobol program. They may be placed by BMS into a copy library and included in the Cobol program at compile time.

Format and Structure

Figure 6-1 defines a skeleton BMS map which should aid you in understanding the format and structure of a BMS map. When BMS maps are assembled, the macros are expanded. The application programmer is generally not interested

```
1...5...10...15...20...25...30...35...40...45...50...55...60...65...70..
         PRINT NOGEN
mapset   DFHMSD TYPE=MAP,                                              X
         CTRL=(FREEKB,FRSET),                                         X
         LANG=COBOL,                                                  X
         MODE=INOUT,                                                  X
         TERM=3270,                                                   X
         TIOAPFX=YES
*
mapnam1  DFHMDI LINE=01,                                              X
         COLUMN=01,                                                   X
         SIZE=(24,80)
*
field1   DFHMDF POS=(   ,   ),                                        X
         ATTRB=(attr1,attr2,...),                                     X
         LENGTH=99,                                                   X
         INITIAL='Map Constants'
*
         DFHMDF POS=(   ,   ),                                        X
         ATTRB=(attr1,attr2,...),                                     X
         LENGTH=99,                                                   X
         INITIAL='Map Constants'
*
field2   DFHMDF POS=(   ,   ),                                        X
         ATTRB=(attr1,attr2,...),                                     X
         LENGTH=99
*
         .
         .
         .
*
fieldN   DFHMDF POS=(   ,   ),                                        X
         ATTRB=(attr1,attr2,...),                                     X
         LENGTH=99
*
*
mapnam2  DFHMDI
         .
         .
         .
*
field1   DFHMDF
         .
         .
         .
*
fieldN   DFHMDF
         .
         .
         .
*
         DFHMSD TYPE=FINAL
         END
```

Figure 6-1 BMS Map Structure.

in the listing of expanded macros. Including the statement PRINT NOGEN at the beginning of the BMS map will suppress the listing of expanded macros.

BMS Format Rules

The basic format of a BMS entry is

[Label][Macro]operand=(parameter 1, [parameter 2,...]),   X

Some of the rules BMS maps follow are

1. PRINT NOGEN starts in the same column as the mapset definition (DFHMSD) macro, usually column 10.
2. Mapset, mapname(s), and field name(s) start in column 1, begin with an alphabetic character, and are seven or fewer characters in length.
3. Macros such as DFHMSD, map definition for individual maps (DFHMDI) and map definition for fields (DFHMDF) usually begin in column 10 and are followed by operands and parameters.
4. Macros should be followed by one space and then an operand plus parameters such as TYPE=MAP,.
5. Additional continuation operands must start in column 16, as does CTRL=(FREEKB,FRSET),.
6. If an operand is to be continued from one line to the next, it must be followed by a comma and have a continuation character (usually an X) in column 72. Parameters plus a comma must end at column 71 or sooner. An operand to be continued must be followed by a comma; otherwise the assembler assumes it is the last operand and ignores additional operands and parameters until it encounters the next macro.
7. END usually starts in the same column as the preceding DFHMSD TYPE=FINAL macro; it signals the end of a map.
8. Multiple parameters for the same operand are enclosed in parentheses, such as CTRL=(FREEKB,FRSET).
9. The operands for all macros can be set up as shown in Fig. 6-1 or can be strung across a couple of lines, such as

```
mapset    DFHMSD TYPE=MAP,CTRL=(FREEKB,FRSET),        X
                 LANG=COBOL,MODE=INOUT,                X
                 TERM=3270,TIOAPFX=YES
```

I recommend placing one operand per line for ease of maintenance and readability.

10. The sequence of operands is free-form.

11. An asterisk in column 1 defines the line as a comment line; its use as shown in Fig. 6-1 improves readability.

Map Structure

The BMS map structure shown in Fig. 6-1 consists of the DFHMSD, DFHMDI, and DFHMDF macros.

Mapset definition macro (DFHMSD). DFHMSD macros vary little from map to map within an installation; usually mapset name is the only difference. All maps in this book use identical DFHMSD operands and parameters; only mapset changes from map to map. This macro applies to all individual maps within a mapset; it occurs only as the first and last macro in a BMS map. Mapset is the name assigned to the BMS map.

Most installations have standards for assigning mapset names. The name assigned to mapset *must* be supported by a PPT entry; it is the label used in a SEND MAP (mapset) command, which will be discussed in the next chapter. Mapset name will be included in the physical map's load module. The DFHMSD macro follows mapset name and is preceded and followed by a space.

$$TYPE = \begin{cases} MAP \\ DSECT \\ FINAL \end{cases}$$

This operand may use one of the first two parameters listed above for the first DFHMSD macro. A BMS map is assembled twice in order to create two maps: a physical map and a symbolic map. When defined as TYPE=MAP, the physical map is created, and when TYPE=DSECT, the symbolic map is generated. Application programmers refer to the symbolic map as a DSECT. A proc or standard JCL generally handles the creation of both maps. Usually only one job is submitted and BMS ignores the operands not required for each individual map. Always assemble both maps at the same time, otherwise the physical and symbolic maps may become out of sync. Every BMS map ends with a DFHMSD TYPE=FINAL macro, followed on the last line by END.

CTRL=(FREEKB,FRSET)

The CTRL operand can contain several parameters. The most common are FREEKB, FRSET, and ALARM.

- FREEKB—This parameter FREEs the KeyBoard and permits the entry of data when a map is sent to the screen; this parameter is usually included.

- FRSET—Resets FSET attributes to OFF before the send of a map; modified data tags (MDTs), part of the attribute which were on, will be turned off.

This concept will be explained later in the chapter, under FSET. (When ON, FSET attributes result in the transfer of data from the screen into the program.)

• ALARM—Sounds an audible alarm or beep at a terminal when a map is sent.

LANG=COBOL

This statement defines the language of the source program in which the map will be used. It would only be modified if the map were to be used in a non-Cobol program. This entry generates the proper symbolic map.

MODE=INOUT

Specifies that the map will be used for both input and output operations and generates input and output symbolic map labels.

• =IN—generates an input symbolic map only

• =OUT—generates an output symbolic map only

I recommend using MODE=INOUT for all maps because it is required if you use symbolic cursor positioning, which is discussed in Chap. 7.

TERM=3270

Defines the type of terminal this map will be used with.

TIOAPFX=YES

Always include this parameter; it generates a 12-byte filler at the beginning of the symbolic map in order to skip over control characters. Failure to include this operand would cause the map to be misaligned when it is sent.

Mapset definition of individual maps (DFHMDI). DFHMDI macros, like DFHMSD macros, differ little from map to map within an installation; usually mapname is the only difference. All maps in this book use the same DFHMDI operands and parameters; only mapname varies from map to map. A mapset can have several maps associated with it as shown in Fig. 6-l; each map would have its own mapname, DFHMDI, and DFHMDF macros.

Mapname

This is the name assigned to individual maps within a mapset. This label is used in the SEND (mapname) command, which will be discussed in Chap. 7. Mapname is stored along with mapset in the physical map load module. The DFHMDI macro follows mapname and is preceded and followed by a space.

LINE=01, COLUMN=01, SIZE=(24,80)

These operands and parameters specify that the map starts at line 01, column 01 and is to be displayed on a screen 24 lines deep by 80 columns wide.

Map definition for fields (DFHMDF). DFHMDF macros, unlike DFHMSD and DFHMDI macros, vary considerably from map to map. Each field to be displayed or received through a map must be defined by a DFHMDF macro. The basic structure of the field macro is shown in Fig. 6-2; only the most commonly used operands and parameters will be discussed.

Field name

Every map field name which is to be referenced in a program must have a one- to seven-character name; this name supplies the symbolic map with a field name label. The DFHMDF macro follows field name and is preceded and followed by a space.

POS=

This refers to the position of the attribute immediately preceding a field; it is usually defined as a two-digit line and column number.

ATTRB=

This defines the attribute characteristics of a field. All attributes take up 1 byte immediately preceding the field defined. ASKIP, UNPROT, and PROT attributes define how the cursor will react to a field; they are mutually exclusive.

• ASKIP—The cursor will automatically skip over this field and stop at the next UNPROT field encountered. Remember that the cursor moves left to right, top to bottom; when it reaches the end of the map, it starts at the beginning

```
field name     DFHMDF POS=(line,column),

                        ⎧ ASKIP           ⎧ NORM
               ATTRB= ⎨ UNPROT,   NUM, ⎨ BRT,   FSET, IC,
                        ⎩ PROT            ⎩ DRK

               LENGTH=99,   (01 thru 256)

               INITIAL='Map Constants',

               PICIN='Edit Mask',

               PICOUT='Edit Mask',

               OCCURS=Number of Occurrences
```

Figure 6-2 DFHMDF—Macro Format.

of the map again. I usually use ASKIP as a stopper field following UNPROT fields, to skip to the next UNPROT field.

- UNPROT—The cursor will stop at the first position of each UNPROT field (just to the right of the attribute) in order to allow for the entry of data. An UNPROT field should be followed by a stopper field (ASKIP or PROT), otherwise the entry of data would be permitted to continue until the next ASKIP or PROT field was encountered.

- PROT—Data cannot be entered into a PROT field. PROT is commonly used as a stopper field following an UNPROT field, when it is important to know if too many digits were entered into a field. PROT will stop movement of the cursor in this case, whereas ASKIP would skip to the next UNPROT field and allow the entry of the excess characters into that field. PROT could also be defined for map constant fields since the cursor will bypass PROT fields and stop at the next UNPROT field. *Note*: ASKIP and PROT attributes are often used interchangeably. The major difference occurs when they are used at the end of an UNPROT field as a stopper field. PROT will stop data entry, while ASKIP will skip to the next UNPROT field and allow the continued entry of data.

- NUM—Data entered into a numeric field will be right-justified, and unfilled positions to the left will be filled with zeros. Fields not defined as NUM are left-justified and filled with spaces to the right of the last significant character entered. Unless a keyboard numeric lock feature is installed, it is possible to enter nonnumeric data into a NUM field. For instance if "A " was entered into a NUM field, it would be received as 000A. I recommend editing all input data.

- NORM—A field with this attribute is displayed at normal intensity.

- BRT—A field with bright intensity is highlighted to stand out on a screen. I normally brighten field identifiers of items which were entered incorrectly, position the cursor at the start of the first field in error, and brighten error and operator-notification messages.

- DRK—Fields with dark intensity are usually used for passwords or for information that an onlooker is not permitted to view, since data entered into a dark field cannot be seen. Dark fields are sometimes used to store data in unused positions of the screen in order to pass information to the same program or among different programs.

- FSET—When the terminal operator keys data into a field, an MDT is turned on which causes entered data to be received into a program. Fields without the MDT on are not transmitted to a program. Specifying FSET in the BMS or symbolic map will turn on the MDT. This returns data in a map field to the program on a RECEIVE MAP command, even if the operator did not key data into the field. Sometimes data sent to a screen, perhaps from a file which was read, is needed upon a succeeding receive of the map. FSET fields are turned off *before* the map is sent when FRSET is specified on the CTRL operand of the DFHMSD macro; the map being displayed then controls FSET attributes. This concept is very important and will be discussed in detail in Chap. 7.

• IC—The Insert Cursor (IC), part of an attribute, places the cursor at the first position of the map field which contains IC. Normally only the first UNPROT field on a map would contain IC; if specified for more than one field, the *last* field specified with IC would be the field at which the cursor would stop. Using symbolic cursor positioning, which will be discussed in the next chapter, the cursor would be positioned at the *first* field if multiple fields were set. The cursor will be positioned at screen position line 1, column 1 if IC is not specified and symbolic cursor positioning is not used. IC could be defined for an ASKIP or PROT field but no data could be entered into the field; this is normally not done.

ASKIP,NORM is the default if **ATTRB=** is not defined and UN-PROT,NORM is the default if only NUMeric and/or IC is specified.

LENGTH=field length

The valid values are 1 to 256 (characters).

INITIAL='map constants'

This gives an initial value to a constant or variable field. The DFHMDF macro should be assigned a field name if the field contents or its display intensity attribute is to be modified. INITIAL generally defines map constants which will only be displayed at a predetermined intensity, and the macro does not require a field name in this case. If the map constant exceeds one line, continue the constant to column 71 of the first line, put an X in column 72, then on the next line continue the constant starting at column 16. Quotation marks should only occur at the beginning and at the end of the map constant. The characters ' and &, if used within an initial value, must be repeated twice. For example,

'O"Rourke && Sons' displays O'Rourke & Sons. The length of the constant is 15, not 17, because the extra characters do not take up any additional space on the map.

If the number of characters defined by INITIAL exceeds the value set by the length parameter, the excess characters are truncated when the map is sent.

PICIN='edit mask'

Input symbolic map fields will be assigned a picture of X unless the PICIN (PICture IN) operand defines the picture differently. For example,

> PICIN='999999'

PICOUT='edit mask'

Output symbolic map fields will be assigned a picture of X unless the PICOUT (PICture OUT) operand defines the picture differently. For example,

> PICOUT='$ZZ,ZZZ.99'

OCCURS=number of occurrences

This generates a symbolic map OCCURS clause for the defined number of occurrences. This clause is most commonly used with map fields to be indexed, such as in a browse display. For example,

```
MAPDESC DFHMDF POS=(09,01),        X
                ATTRB=ASKIP,       X
                LENGTH=79,         X
                OCCURS=14
```

The above would generate 14 lines of 79 characters, each with an ASKIP attribute in column 1 of each line. A programmer could then move a 79-character working-storage field to each MAPDESCO (map-index) line.

BMS Map for a Menu

Figure 6-3 shows the vendor file maintenance submenu map and Fig. 6-4, the BMS map used to format the screen.

The first macro (DFHMSD) in Fig. 6-4 ① has a label POVMNT1, the mapset name, which must be defined in the PPT. The rest of the operands and parameters are identical to those shown in Fig. 6-1.

The second macro (DFHMDI) ② is shown with a mapname of MAPPOVM; the rest of the macro is the same as shown in Fig. 6-1. Several DFHMDI macros can be defined in one mapset. I generally limit each mapset to one map.

The last macro, DFHMSD TYPE=FINAL, followed by END ⑦ is standard for all maps. Other maps in this book will not refer to the last two entries or to the mapset and mapname macros; only mapset and mapname labels will vary from map to map.

DFHMDF Macro Usage

Figure 6-4 demonstrates the use of many of the DFHMDF parameters discussed, and a comparison with Fig. 6-3 should make the defining of BMS macros easy to understand.

③ a. Defines a map-constant field ABC MANUFACTURING COMPANY with a preceding ASKIP attribute in line 1, column 27; it is 25 characters long.

Figure 6-3 Vendor File Maintenance Submenu Map.

b. The option ATTRB=ASKIP could be omitted since it is the default; I like to include the ATTRB operand for all map fields.

c. No label is shown in columns 1 to 7; therefore no symbolic map entry will be generated. Constant fields which may be displayed with varying intensity (BRT, NORM, or DRK) require a label in order to generate a symbolic map field name.

d. LENGTH must correspond to INITIAL=map constant size.

④ a. Defines the field into which the terminal operator will make a selection. A symbolic map field name will be generated since this macro has a field name MSELECT.

b. The attribute preceding the field starts at line 11, column 34; it is one character long.

c. The attribute UNPROT will cause the cursor to stop at a field for data entry, and IC will cause the cursor to be positioned initially at the start of the field (not at the attribute) when the physical map is sent (Chap. 7 will explain this technique). This is the only UNPROT field on this map. IC alone could be entered in the ATTRB field since, in this case, UNPROT would be the default. Chapter 7 will explain symbolic cursor positioning, which allows the program to override IC on a send which includes the symbolic map.

```
          PRINT NOGEN
POVMNT1   DFHMSD TYPE=MAP,                                              X
              CTRL=(FREEKB,FRSET),                                      X
              LANG=COBOL,                           ①                   X
              MODE=INOUT,                                               X
              TERM=3270,                                                X
              TIOAPFX=YES
*
MAPPOVM   DFHMDI LINE=01,                                               X
              COLUMN=01,                      ②                         X
              SIZE=(24,80)
*
          DFHMDF POS=(01,27),                                           X
              ATTRB=ASKIP,                                              X
              LENGTH=25,                                  ③             X
              INITIAL='ABC MANUFACTURING COMPANY'
*
          DFHMDF POS=(01,72),                                           X
              ATTRB=ASKIP,                                              X
              LENGTH=07,                                                X
              INITIAL='POVMNT1'
*
          DFHMDF POS=(02,24),                                           X
              ATTRB=ASKIP,                                              X
              LENGTH=32,                                                X
              INITIAL='VENDOR FILE MAINTENANCE SUB-MENU'
*
          DFHMDF POS=(05,34),                                           X
              ATTRB=ASKIP,                                              X
              LENGTH=10,                                                X
              INITIAL='1. INQUIRY'
*
          DFHMDF POS=(06,34),                                           X
              ATTRB=ASKIP,                                              X
              LENGTH=09,                                                X
              INITIAL='2. CHANGE'
*
          DFHMDF POS=(07,34),                                           X
              ATTRB=ASKIP,                                              X
              LENGTH=11,                                                X
              INITIAL='3. ADDITION'
*
          DFHMDF POS=(08,34),                                           X
              ATTRB=ASKIP,                                              X
              LENGTH=11,                                                X
              INITIAL='4. DELETION'
*
          DFHMDF POS=(09,34),                                           X
              ATTRB=ASKIP,                                              X
              LENGTH=09,                                                X
              INITIAL='5. BROWSE'
*
          DFHMDF POS=(11,23),                                           X
              ATTRB=ASKIP,                                              X
              LENGTH=10,                                                X
              INITIAL='SELECTION:'
*
MSELECT   DFHMDF POS=(11,34),                                           X
              ATTRB=(UNPROT,IC),          ④                             X
              LENGTH=01
*
          DFHMDF POS=(11,36),                                           X
              ATTRB=PROT,              ⑤                                X
              LENGTH=01
*
          DFHMDF POS=(16,25),                                           X
              ATTRB=ASKIP,                                              X
              LENGTH=30,                                                X
              INITIAL='KEY IN SELECTION - PRESS ENTER'
*
          DFHMDF POS=(18,25),                                           X
              ATTRB=ASKIP,                                              X
              LENGTH=30,                                                X
              INITIAL='END OF SESSION   - PRESS CLEAR'
*
MAPMESG   DFHMDF POS=(24,01),                                           X
              ATTRB=ASKIP,              ⑥                               X
              LENGTH=79
*
          DFHMSD TYPE=FINAL          ⑦
          END
```

Figure 6-4 BMS Map for Vendor File Maintenance Submenu.

d. INITIAL is often omitted for UNPROT fields unless it is desired to assign an initial default value to the field. For instance, if INQUIRY was selected much more frequently than any other item on the vendor file maintenance submenu, the DFHMDF macro would be defined as follows:

```
MSELECT DFHMDF POS=(11,34),                    X
              ATTRB=(UNPROT,FSET,IC),          X
              LENGTH=01,                        X
              INITIAL='1'
```

Note: ATTRB= now contains FSET to turn on the MDT so that when the terminal operator presses ENTER, the selection of 1 will be received by the program as if the operator had entered a 1, turning on the MDT.

⑤ a. Defines a 1-byte stopper field with an attribute of PROT; without this stopper field, the terminal operator could continue entering data into the SELECTION field. An attempt to enter more than one digit into the SELECTION field will cause the cursor to stop, the keyboard to lock, and require the terminal operator to press RESET in order to continue.

b. Generally if more than one UNPROT field exists on a map, the stopper field will contain an ATTRB=ASKIP so that when one field is entered the cursor will skip to the next UNPROT field. Setting all stopper attributes to PROT would require the terminal operator to press the TAB key each time a data field was completely filled.

⑥ a. A symbolic map field name will be generated since a field name MAPMESG is included in this field.

b. ASKIP attribute preceding this field is in line 24, column 1.

c. This field will often have its intensity changed by the program to ASKIP,BRT when operator-notification or error messages are displayed.

d. This field is sometimes defined with an initial value and ATTRB=(ASKIP,DRK), defined so that the message does not display until a program changes the attribute to ASKIP,BRT. I prefer not to assign an initial value to message fields and to let the program select the message to be displayed.

Refresh the PPT When a Map Changes

The PPT should be refreshed with the latest load library address of the physical map when it is reassembled; failure to do so can lead to unpredictable results. A map is considered a program by CICS and the PPT is updated by:

```
CSMT NEW,PGRMID=mapset
or
CEMT SET PRO (mapset) NEW
```

A program almost always changes when a symbolic map is altered. Make sure the BMS map is assembled correctly before compiling the changed program to ensure that the program will have the latest version of the BMS-generated symbolic map (unless you employ user-friendly symbolic maps, discussed later in this chapter). After the program has been compiled, refresh its address in the PPT

```
CSMT NEW,PGRMID=program
or
CEMT SET PRO (program) NEW
```

Command-Level Interpreter

The format of a physical map can be checked by using the command-level interpreter (CECI). CECI, a transaction identifier, initiates the command level interpreter, which is a CICS application program. CECI is a translator supplied with CICS which is useful for checking the syntax and execution of many CICS commands. The operator can clear the screen, key in CECI, and press the ENTER key in order to display a list of CICS commands. Commands can be syntax-checked and executed from this list. The complete command can be keyed in when CECI is entered, if you know the syntax and want to see the results of the execution of the command. If you do not know the syntax, just key in CECI and press ENTER and the system will prompt you for other entries.

The command-level interpreter is useful for testing new or changed BMS physical maps for format and entry of UNPROT fields. You just have to key in the following and press ENTER.

CECI SEND MAP (mapset) ERASE

The above command will display the same physical map that the SEND command in a program would. This allows you to test your physical map before it is used in a program. The microcomputer's equivalent to CECI for the send of a map is discussed in Apps. E, F, and G.

The Generated Symbolic Map

The symbolic map generated by the BMS map in Fig. 6-4 would look similar to the map in Fig. 6-5. Blank (*) lines, comments, and alignment are included to improve readability; they are not found in the actual symbolic map which

```
0001******************************************************************
0002*             SYMBOLIC MAP FOR MAPSET 'POVMNT1'              *
0003*     COMMENTS AND ASTERISKS ARE NOT GENERATED BY BMS        *
0004*       - THEY ARE INSERTED TO IMPROVE READABILITY           *
0005******************************************************************
0006*
0007 01  MAPPOVMI.
0008     02  FILLER              PIC X(12).
0009*
0010     02  MSELECTL            PIC S9(4)    COMP.
0011     02  MSELECTF            PIC X.
0012      02  FILLER  REDEFINES  MSELECTF.
0013         03  MSELECTA        PIC X.
0014     02  MSELECTI            PIC X.
0015*
0016     02  MAPMESGL            PIC S9(4)    COMP.
0017     02  MAPMESGF            PIC X.
0018      02  FILLER  REDEFINES  MAPMESGF.
0019         03  MAPMESGA        PIC X.
0020     02  MAPMESGI            PIC X(79).
0021*
0022 01  MAPPOVMO  REDEFINES  MAPPOVMI.
0023     02  FILLER              PIC X(12).
0024*
0025     02  FILLER              PIC X(3).
0026     02  MSELECTO            PIC X.
0027*
0028     02  FILLER              PIC X(3).
0029     02  MAPMESGO            PIC X(79).
```

Figure 6-5 Symbolic Map Generated by BMS Map in Fig. 6-4.

would be generated. The symbolic map could be copied into a program by using the following COPY statement.

01 MAPPOVMI COPY POVMNT1.

Most symbolic maps will usually contain more fields than shown in Fig. 6-5, but the format of the generated symbolic map will always be the same. The first 12 bytes of the Cobol symbolic map consist of a FILLER PIC X(12). Variable fields in a map will be generated with an input (I) suffix and an output (O) suffix (such as MSELECTI and MSELECTO).

The input map MAPPOVMI contains various types of fields:

- L suffix (length field)—This field contains the length of the input field keyed in on the map by a terminal operator when the program receives the map. By moving a -1 to the length field, before issuing a SEND MAP command, the cursor is positioned at the start of that field on the screen. This is referred to as *symbolic cursor positioning* and is discussed in Chap. 7.

- F suffix (flag byte)—This field can be used by the application programmer during input procedures to test if the terminal operator has cleared a field using the EOF key on the terminal. The flag byte would contain hexadecimal 80 (X'80') if EOF had been pressed; otherwise it would equal X'00' (low-values).

- Map redefinition of this field

- A suffix (attribute field)—This field may be used during output procedures (see SEND MAP discussed in Chap. 7) to override the attribute field defined in the BMS map.

• I suffix (input field)—This field contains the data entered by the terminal operator and received into the program (see RECEIVE MAP, discussed in Chap. 7).

• Map redefinition of this field.

• O suffix (output field)—This field is used to hold the output field for operations requiring the send of a map.

A close look at the symbolic map shows that the F (flag) and A (attribute) fields share the same storage location as do I (input) and O (output) fields. The main determinant of how these fields are referenced is whether we are receiving a map (F and I) or sending a map (A and O).

The last line of the map is usually reserved for messages sent to the terminal operator regarding conditions which may require action such as keying data into a certain field or notification of error conditions. Figure 6-5 labels this field MAPMESGO.

Creating User-Friendly Symbolic Maps

The symbolic map created by BMS is difficult to read and cumbersome to work with. Depending on your installation's standards, you may wish to create a more readable map. All Cobol symbolic maps have the same format as shown in Fig. 6-5:

1. A 12-byte filler at the beginning of the map

2. A 2-byte length field PIC S9(4) COMP for each field

3. An attribute or flag byte for each field

4. A data field for input and output

Figure 6-6 shows a user-friendly symbolic map equivalent to that shown in Fig. 6-5. All examples in this book will employ user-friendly symbolic maps. See Chap. 19 for color attribute considerations.

```
0001*****************************************************************
0002*                   USER FRIENDLY MENU SYMBOLIC MAP              *
0003*****************************************************************
0004*
0005 01  MPM-MENU-MAP.
0006     05  FILLER              PIC X(12).
0007*
0008     05  MPM-L-SELECTION     PIC S9(4)      COMP.
0009     05  MPM-A-SELECTION     PIC X.
0010     05  MPM-D-SELECTION     PIC X.
0011*
0012     05  MPM-L-MESSAGE       PIC S9(4)      COMP.
0013     05  MPM-A-MESSAGE       PIC X(4).
0014     05  MPM-D-MESSAGE       PIC X(79).
```

Figure 6-6 User-Friendly Menu Symbolic Map.

SUMMARY

The creation of BMS maps, once the technique is understood, is one of the most easily utilized facets of CICS. There are two types of maps: physical maps and symbolic maps. Physical maps control map alignment and constant data on a map, while the symbolic map defines variable data. Format and structure of a BMS map was discussed, along with a detailed presentation of the DFHMSD, DFHMDI, and DFHMDF macros. BMS map attributes were discussed in detail. A simple BMS menu map was used in examples to show how it related to a screen layout and how the macros discussed were used. The command-level interpreter (CECI), which is used for checking syntax and executing CICS commands, was discussed.

A sample generated symbolic map was presented, showing how it related to the BMS map. Each field in the symbolic map was discussed, and it was shown how user-friendly symbolic maps could be created.

Most programmers I have spoken to agree that after they create a few BMS maps, the techniques given here are easy to understand and to utilize. Concentrate on the field definitions; you will find the other macros similar for most maps. More maps will be created and used in succeeding chapters. Chapter 7 will discuss the practical use of the material covered in this chapter.

7

USING ASSEMBLED BMS MAPS

Cobol CICS command-level programs are generally compiled after the BMS map has been assembled. The BMS-generated symbolic map or its user-friendly counterpart is included in the program. The symbolic map may be copied from a copy library or coded directly into the program's working-storage or linkage section. Maps are either sent from or received into working storage or the linkage section of a program. This book will define its maps in working storage where they are commonly found. Conceptually, there is little difference in mapping regardless of where the map is located.

This chapter covers the SEND MAP and RECEIVE MAP commands, the use of map attributes, and cursor positioning on the map. I consider this chapter the key to mastering CICS; reread it until you thoroughly understand all concepts presented. It has been my experience that a large percentage of programming difficulty is caused by a lack of understanding of the function which map attributes perform in pseudoconversational programming.

Send Map Command

The SEND MAP command can be issued to send the physical and/or symbolic map in order to format a terminal screen. The format of the SEND MAP command is as follows; only the options you are most likely to encounter are listed.

```
EXEC CICS SEND
        MAP        (mapname)
        MAPSET     (mapset)
        FROM       (WS-MAP-AREA)
        [MAPONLY / DATAONLY]
        [ERASE /   ERASEAUP]
        [CURSOR]
        [FREEKB]
        [FRSET]
        [ALARM]
END-EXEC.
```

FREEKB, FRSET, and ALARM can be specified on the send of a map, but because I define only one map per mapset, these options, when desired, are included in the BMS map. All three options perform the same function as described under the DFHMSD CTRL= option in Chap. 6. This book will include FREEKB and FRSET in the BMS map for all examples and *not* on the SEND command. I do not use the ALARM parameter in this book.

- MAP (mapname)—The mapname from the BMS map DFHMDI label.

- MAPSET (mapset)—The mapset from the BMS map DFHMSD label; this is the PPT entry.

- FROM (WS-MAP-AREA)—A programmer-defined working-storage area from which the symbolic map is sent.

- MAPONLY—Only the physical map is to be sent.

- DATAONLY—Only the symbolic map is to be sent.

- ERASE—Clears the screen before sending the map. This option would not be used with DATAONLY because the symbolic map's data would be sent to a screen which had no constant data displayed.

- ERASEAUP—Erases all UNPROT fields; it is used only with a send of DATAONLY. ASKIP or PROT fields such as constants and message fields would not be erased by this option.

- CURSOR—This option is used with symbolic cursor positioning (discussed later in this chapter) in order to place the cursor at the start of the required field.

Types of Send Commands

The SEND MAP command is similar to the send of a message as presented in Chap. 5. There are three command types frequently selected when using the SEND MAP command: SEND MAP AND DATA, SEND MAP DATAONLY, and SEND MAP MAPONLY. The application programmer must thoroughly understand these command types in order to design and use maps properly in CICS programs.

SEND MAP AND DATA

The format of this send is

```
EXEC CICS SEND
          MAP      (mapname)
          MAPSET (mapset)
          [FROM    (WS-MAP-AREA)]
          ERASE
          [CURSOR]
END-EXEC.
```

This option will send both physical and symbolic maps, which will be merged together on the screen. Always specify ERASE with this option of SEND MAP AND DATA in order to clear the screen prior to the send. CURSOR is used with symbolic cursor positioning to set the cursor to the proper location on the screen. If CURSOR is not included on this send, the BMS map controls cursor positioning. Use this send if there is variable data on the initial send; for instance, date and time.

When FROM is omitted, the program sends its map from the working-storage symbolic map, which is generated by BMS and copied into the program at compile time. With FROM specified, the program will send its symbolic map's data from the programmer-created user-friendly symbolic map which is placed in the working-storage area WS-MAP-AREA.

SEND MAP MAPONLY

The format of this send is

```
EXEC CICS SEND
          MAP      (mapname)
          MAPSET  (mapset)
          ERASE
          MAPONLY
END-EXEC.
```

It sends only the physical map and is generally used for the initial send of a map when there is no variable data to be sent to the screen. MAPONLY is also used to send informative or help screens which do not require an operator to enter data. Help screens are, in a sense, online instructions which supplement user guides. MAPONLY is usually sent only once in a program, to a cleared screen. The cursor position for this option is determined by the BMS map IC attribute. The cursor would be set at screen POS=(01,01) if the BMS map did not specify an IC attribute.

SEND MAP DATAONLY

The format of this send is

```
EXEC CICS SEND
        MAP        (mapname)
        MAPSET     (mapset)
        [FROM      (WS-MAP-AREA)]
        DATAONLY
        [CURSOR]
END-EXEC.
```

It sends the symbolic map. This send is generally used after the physical map has been sent by one of the previously described SEND MAP commands. Only variable data has to be sent when the physical map is showing on the screen. This format of the SEND MAP command is generally used to send error and operator messages, as well as to highlight fields which contain errors. Do not specify ERASE with this option of the send, otherwise you will display a screen which contains only the variable data from the symbolic map.

Symbolic Cursor Positioning

Cursor positioning can be controlled by specifying IC in an attribute field on the BMS map and then issuing a send which includes the physical map (not DATAONLY). This method works fine if the cursor is always located at the same position, which is often not the case. On an addition or change map, a variety of fields may be entered incorrectly, and it may be desirable to position the cursor at the first field in error. Symbolic cursor positioning provides this facility. The cursor will be positioned at the start of the designated field and will override IC if specified in the BMS map. For example,

MOVE −1 TO mapfldL.

This places the cursor at the start of the map field. Sometimes multiple errors are encountered when a map's fields are edited. A −1 is moved to the length field of each item incorrectly entered. If more than one length field contains a −1, the first such field encountered controls the cursor position. The cursor is set at the start of that field when a SEND MAP command is issued.

To use symbolic cursor positioning:

1. The BMS map must specify MODE=INOUT on the DFHMSD macro.

2. CURSOR must be specified on a SEND MAP command which includes the symbolic map (not MAPONLY).

3. The program must move −1 to the symbolic map length field of the item at which the CURSOR is to be positioned, prior to issuing a SEND MAP command. If CURSOR is not specified on a DATAONLY send, the cursor will be set at POS=(01,01).

SEND MAP Transaction ABEND

During the execution of a SEND MAP command, an unanticipated condition sometimes occurs, causing a program to come to an ABEND. A message will be displayed on the screen such as:

TRANSACTION TTTT ABEND APCT IN PROGRAM MMMMMMM HH:MM:SS
TTTT = Transaction ID
APCT = ABEND Code
MMMMMMM = Program Name (mapset)
HH:MM:SS = Time of ABEND

The ABEND code APCT will be displayed if the map has not been defined in the PPT or if the map has been disabled.

Disabling a Program

Programs, maps, and tables are occasionally disabled by the use of the master terminal commands CEMT or CSMT in order to prevent the access of problem modules. A program is also disabled if no load module is found when the CICS system is started up. This condition will lead to an APCT ABEND for maps which are sent and a PGMIDERR handle condition for programs and tables which a program attempts to bring into main storage.

Low-Values Are Not Transmitted

Low-values are the characters of least value known to the computer system; they are represented by hexadecimal zeros (X'00'). Low-values are not transmitted between a program and a terminal when a map is sent or received; therefore, it is good practice to initialize symbolic maps. A program should initialize the symbolic map to low-values prior to a receive of a map and prior to formatting the map with data to be sent. A map formatted with spaces would result in the transmission of those spaces during a send operation, resulting in unnecessary traffic over transmission lines. Sometimes a field such as a message which has been displayed on the screen has to be blanked out on a subsequent send of the map. Moving low-values to the field to be blanked out will not eliminate the display of a field because low-values are not transmitted. Move spaces to any symbolic map fields which are to be blanked out by the SEND MAP command since spaces *are* transmitted.

RECEIVE MAP Command

The following RECEIVE MAP command facilitates the receive of the symbolic map into working storage.

```
EXEC CICS RECEIVE
        MAP      (mapname)
        MAPSET (mapset)
        [INTO     (WS-MAP-AREA)]
END-EXEC.
```

The program can receive the map into the working-storage area generated for the symbolic map by BMS. This area is copied into the program at compile time from a copy library. The program can also receive the map *into* a user-friendly symbolic map in working storage (WS-MAP-AREA) which can be defined by the programmer. Remember to initialize the symbolic map's working storage to low-values before issuing the RECEIVE MAP command. All fields which contain significant data (not low-values) will be received into the symbolic map when the RECEIVE MAP command is issued, provided that their MDTs are turned on (see "FSET" in Chap. 6). Remember, data may appear on the screen and *not* be returned to the program on a RECEIVE MAP command if the MDT for the field is turned off.

Map Attributes

It has been my experience that misuse of map attributes and of MDTs causes more confusion and program errors than does any other area of CICS application programming. Attributes control individual map fields on the screen. The terminal operator is given the ability to automatically skip over a field (ASKIP) or to enter data into an unprotected field (UNPROT), or is prevented from entering data into a protected field (PROT). The BMS map or program can determine the intensity at which a map field will display: BRT, NORM or DRK. A field can be received as alphanumeric data (left-justified, padded with spaces) or numeric (NUM) data (right-justified, padded with zeroes). The cursor can be set by specifying IC in the BMS map or through program symbolic cursor positioning. Specifying FSET for a field in the BMS or symbolic map will turn on its MDT when the map is sent. Symbolic map attributes override BMS map attributes. The terminal operator turns on the MDT when a map field is keyed into. Including FRSET in the CTRL operand of the BMS map's DFHMSD macro causes all MDTs to be turned off before a map is sent. The combination of all the above considerations causes the best of programmers much grief.

Standard Attribute Characters

CICS has available a list of standard attribute characters in the form of a copy book called DFHBMSCA. The standard attribute control list is a set of standard control characters used by CICS, which can be copied into a program. Many data processing departments create their own list of the more commonly used attribute characters, assigning more meaningful labels.

```
01  DFHBMSCA  COPY  DFHBMSCA.
    02  DFHBMPEM      PIC X    VALUE ' '.
    02  DFHBMPNL      PIC X    VALUE ' '.
    02  DFHBMASK      PIC X    VALUE '0'.
    02  DFHBMUNP      PIC X    VALUE ' '.
    02  DFHBMUNN      PIC X    VALUE '&'.
    02  DFHBMPRO      PIC X    VALUE '–'.
    02  DFHBMBRY      PIC X    VALUE 'H'.
    02  DFHBMDAR      PIC X    VALUE ')'.
    02  DFHBMFSE      PIC X    VALUE 'A'.
    02  DFHBMPRF      PIC X    VALUE '/'.
    02  DFHBMASF      PIC X    VALUE '1'.
    02  DFHBMASB      PIC X    VALUE '8'.
```

DFHBMSCA fields all begin with DFHBM..., and the last three characters are not very descriptive. These fields do not cover many of the attribute configurations required by the application programmer. The programmer may move the attribute character directly to the symbolic map prior to issuing a SEND MAP command. Illustrated below is the alignment of the more commonly used attribute names found in the list above (DFHBMSCA) and in App. B (STWSATTR).

DFHBMSCA	Descriptive	Value
DFHBMASK	ASKIP-NORM	'0'.
DFHBMUNP	UNPROT-NORM	SPACE.
DFHBMUNN	UNPROT-NUM	'&'.
DFHBMBRY	UNPROT-BRT	'H'.
DFHBMFSE	UNPROT-FSET	'A'.
DFHBMASF	ASKIP-FSET	'1'.
DFHBMASB	ASKIP-BRT	'8'.

The application programmer may move any of the equivalent characters, shown above, during execution of an application program, to the symbolic map's attribute field. For example,

```
MOVE DFHBMASB  TO   mapfldA.
MOVE ASKIP-BRT  TO      "
MOVE '8'        TO      "
```

This book will use the attribute characters shown in App. B for all program examples. You should be aware of DFHBMSCA characters, since you may encounter them in programs which you have to maintain. I recommend using a list of characters similar to STWSATTR and making it a standard copy library member at your installation.

Changing Map Attributes

Changing the map attributes frequently causes confusion because it is often not understood how physical and symbolic maps interact. Figure 7-1 represents the interaction of the physical and symbolic maps.

Physical Map Strings

Physical maps can be visualized as a string of data consisting of control characters, a data length field, an attribute byte, and a data field. The control characters (CC) direct the positioning of data on the screen. Length (L suffix) fields determine the length of the data to be sent, as specified on the BMS map. The attribute field (A suffix) contains the attribute specified in the BMS map. The data field (D suffix) contains the *initial* value given to a field in the BMS map. If no initial value was specified, then the data field contains low-values and no data is transmitted on a send of only the physical map.

My interpretation of the physical map data string as shown in Fig. 7-1 contains three different prefix characters: C for constant, F for field, and S for stopper field. The circled physical and symbolic map letters and numbers relate to the corresponding items on the screen.

Physical map character prefix. The constant prefix C pertains to BMS map fields which are defined without a DFHMDF macro field name; therefore no symbolic map entry is generated. The screen constant ABC MANUFACTURING COMPANY ⒷB is defined without a field name in the BMS map; therefore no symbolic map entry is generated. The BMS map would normally define this field with an attribute Ⓐ of ASKIP or ASKIP,BRT, and the program could not change the attribute because no symbolic map field is generated. The constant ADDRESS: Ⓓ and its attribute Ⓒ would follow this same pattern.

Physical map field prefix. The F prefix represents items which were defined in the BMS map with a field name; these fields generate corresponding symbolic map entries. The attribute ① for the constant VENDOR CODE: ② would generally be set to ASKIP in the BMS map and could be turned on to ASKIP,BRT

Figure 7-1 Physical Map and Symbolic Map Interaction.

through the symbolic map if the field was not entered correctly. The constant NAME: ⑥ and its attribute ⑤ would be used in a similar fashion. The attribute of a field, which contains a symbolic map entry, can be changed each time a map is sent. The attribute ③ for the data ④ to be keyed in for VENDOR CODE would most likely be UNPROT. Data-entry fields ⑧ and ⑩ would also be likely to have UNPROT attributes. The attributes ③, ⑦, and ⑨ could have some combination of UNPROT, such as UNPROT,BRT, or UNPROT,FSET.

Field ⑫ and its attribute ⑪ define the message field; this field is usually defined in the BMS map with an attribute of ASKIP. Sometimes a program detects an error condition or wants to display an operator-notification message. To highlight the message, the program sends the map with the attribute of the appropriate field in the symbolic map changed to ASKIP,BRT. The BMS map can set an initial value for the message field by defining its attribute as ATTRB=(ASKIP,DRK). When the appropriate program condition is encountered, the program highlights the message field (making it visible) by sending the symbolic map with the message field's attribute changed to ASKIP,BRT. The message can be erased on a subsequent send by changing the attribute back to ASKIP,DRK.

Physical map stopper field prefix. Stopper fields are shown with a prefix of S. Like constants, they are usually defined without a BMS map field name. The primary purpose of stopper fields is to limit the size of the preceding UNPROT data-entry field. Stopper fields (S1), (S2), and (S3) serve this purpose; they are defined in the physical map with attributes of ASKIP or PROT.

Physical Map Interaction with Symbolic Map

Figure 7-1 shows the symbolic map as a data string in which its F prefix has a one-to-one correspondence with the physical map fields. This is to be expected since these are the items which were defined with field names on the BMS map. It is important to understand how the three types of SEND MAP commands handle attributes and data fields.

SEND ONLY physical map. The SEND MAP MAPONLY command erases the screen before the send and transmits the constants and attributes defined in the BMS map to the screen. The symbolic map is never used with a MAPONLY send, therefore no variable data is transmitted. This book will refer to input data and attributes as being received from the screen and to symbolic map output data and attributes as being sent to the screen.

SEND both physical and symbolic maps. The SEND MAP AND DATA command erases the screen before sending the combined physical and symbolic maps. Visualize the physical map in Fig. 7-1 as initially being sent to the screen, then as being overlaid by corresponding attribute and data fields from the symbolic map. Remember, if the symbolic map contains low-values in any attribute or data field, then no transmission will take place for those items. On a SEND MAP AND DATA command, the physical map BMS-defined attribute will take effect if the symbolic map attribute contains low-values. When the symbolic map contains a significant attribute, it will override the physical map attribute.

SEND ONLY Symbolic Map. The SEND MAP DATAONLY command does not normally erase the screen before sending only the symbolic map. Prior to this send, one of the other two SEND MAP commands would have been executed. The prior send would have formatted the screen with constants from the BMS map and with attributes from the BMS map and/or symbolic map. The SEND

MAP AND DATA command could have sent data from the symbolic map. Once again, visualize the existing data and attributes on the screen as being overlaid by the symbolic map's data and attributes.

Manipulating MDTs

An ON MDT, which is part of the attribute byte, causes data on the screen to be returned to the program when a map is received. MDTs can be turned on by

1. Specifying FSET as part of the attribute on the BMS map, then issuing a send which includes the physical map. Do not overlay the BMS map's attribute with the symbolic map's attribute on a send of map and data. Symbolic map attributes equal to low-values will *not* overlay the BMS attributes. For example,

```
ATTRB=(ASKIP,FSET),
```

2. Moving a standard attribute which contains FSET to the symbolic map's attribute before issuing a send which includes the symbolic map, such as

```
MOVE UNPROT-FSET TO mapfldA
```

3. Keying data into an UNPROT field on the screen. Entering data into a field always turns its MDT on.

FRSET

Specifying FRSET in the BMS map (or on the SEND MAP command) will cause all MDTs on the screen to be turned off prior to sending a map. This will require the physical map field attribute or the symbolic override to control the MDT status of an attribute. An operator could key data into a field, turning on its MDT. A receive of the map and a subsequent send of the map would turn the MDT off if CTRL=FRSET was specified in the DFHMSD macro of the BMS map. If CTRL=FRSET was not specified, the MDTs would remain on.

Confusion often results when data appearing on the screen is not received into the program because its MDT is not turned on. I recommend specifying the appropriate attributes in the BMS map and in the symbolic map so that they will be properly set prior to a send. For instance, if the terminal operator enters data into a field, the MDT will be turned on. Let's suppose that the program, when it receives the map, detects an error on a different field and resends the map with an error message. The MDTs of all fields are turned off prior to the

SEND MAP Options	Type of Map Sent		**** Attribute Sent to Screen ****		
	Symbolic	Physical	Physical Map Only	Symbolic Map Attribute Field Contains	
				Attribute	Low Values
MAP and Data	S	P		SYM	BMS
MAPONLY		P	BMS		
DATAONLY	S			SYM	Screen

Figure 7-2   Attribute Usage Summary.

send because FRSET was specified. Correctly entered fields will not be received into the program on a subsequent receive map, even though they appear on the screen, because their MDTs have been turned off. The programmer can ensure that required fields will be returned by moving the UNPROT,FSET attribute to the appropriate symbolic map field before issuing the send. Once a field has been keyed in and verified, you may not want the operator to be allowed to change it, but it must be returned to the program on a subsequent receive. Including the attributes ASKIP,FSET in the symbolic map prior to issuing a send will ensure that the field will be returned to the program on a subsequent receive. With practice, the use of attributes and the manner in which FRSET works should become clear.

Attribute Usage Summary

Figure 7-2 and the following outlines summarize the more common attribute considerations. Control of attribute fields depends upon the type of SEND MAP command:

1. MAP AND DATA (specify ERASE)

   a. Symbolic map attributes will override the physical map attributes defined by the BMS map.

   b. Low-values in an attribute field will cause the BMS map attribute to be sent to the screen.

2. MAPONLY (specify ERASE)

   The BMS-map-defined attributes will be sent to the screen.

3. DATAONLY (omit ERASE)

   a. Attributes in the symbolic map will override existing screen attributes.

   b. Low-values in an attribute field will not change the existing attributes on the screen.

MDTs can be turned on in an attribute field by

1. The BMS map FSET parameter

2. The terminal operator's keying data into a field

3. Moving a program-defined FSET-containing attribute to a field before a send which includes the symbolic map.

Specifying FRSET in CTRL=(FREEKB,FRSET) of the BMS map DFHMSD macro turns off the attribute MDTs of all fields on the screen prior to the send of the map to the screen.

RECEIVE MAP Considerations

The RECEIVE MAP command, as presented earlier in the chapter, is easy to understand and use. However, there are additional considerations when a map is received.

1. The length of the data keyed into a map field will be received as the result of executing a RECEIVE MAP command.

2. A MAPFAIL condition will occur if no data is received from the map; if this condition is not properly handled, a program ABEND will occur.

3. The AID key pressed by the terminal operator can be tested and acted upon in several different ways.

Length Field on Map Receive

When a map is received, the symbolic map length field can be tested for two conditions:

1. If data were entered into a field

2. If the required number of characters were entered

Length field indicative of data entry. Many programs test if the symbolic map length field is greater than zero. A positive value is an indication that the terminal operator entered data into the field. For example,

```
IF mapfldL    IS GREATER THAN    ZERO
   MOVE mapfldI    TO    WS-INPUT-DATA.
```

Here, mapfldL represents a map length field and mapfldI an input field.

Monitoring number of characters entered. Sometimes a program must know the exact number of characters keyed in, for example, when a field requires a specific number of characters or digits.

MAPFAIL Conditions

A MAPFAIL, indicating that no characters were passed from the screen on a RECEIVE MAP command, occurs when

1. The CLEAR key is pressed.

2. PA1, PA2, or PA3 is pressed.

3. Any other AID key is pressed without data having been entered on the screen, and no map fields had been FSET.

MAPFAIL, which can cause a program ABEND if not provided for, can be controlled by

1. Issuing an IGNORE CONDITION MAPFAIL command before the receive. This command states that if a MAPFAIL occurs on a receive of a map, ignore the condition and continue processing. For example,

```
EXEC CICS IGNORE CONDITION
            MAPFAIL
END-EXEC.
```

2. Issuing a HANDLE CONDITION MAPFAIL before the receive. For example,

```
EXEC CICS HANDLE CONDITION
            MAPFAIL (C100-MAPFAIL)
END-EXEC.
```

This HANDLE CONDITION command directs that if a MAPFAIL occurs, then control is to be transferred to paragraph C100-MAPFAIL.

3. Coding a 1-byte BMS map field with an attribute of ASKIP,DRK,FSET so that at least 1 byte of data is always returned on a receive. If you specify FRSET in the BMS map, the MDTs are turned off before a SEND MAP command. If this method is ·employed, it is best to standardize the byte location on the screen at a position not likely to be used.

4. Executing the HANDLE AID command, discussed later in this chapter, in order to direct control to the proper routines if the CLEAR or PA key is pressed. PA keys can be handled by the ANYKEY option.

5. Testing data-entry AID keys (see below) in order to direct control to the proper routines if the CLEAR or a PA key is pressed.

It seems more logical to send a message to the terminal operator indicating that no data was keyed in (when data is required) than it is to send a message indicating that an invalid entry was made. There are situations when a receive without data having been entered is valid: for example, pressing a PF key to end an inquiry and return to a control screen. MAPFAIL sounds complicated, but it is easy to control in your program; examples which follow should help to clarify the required techniques.

Testing Data-Entry AID Keys

When the terminal operator presses an AID key, an indicator is stored in the EIB field EIBAID. The AID fields in DFHAID (see App. A-3) can be copied into working storage. They are compared against EIBAID to determine which AID key was pressed in order to determine the flow of program logic.

Valid AID keys are ENTER; CLEAR; PF1 through PF24; PA1, PA2, and PA3; and ANYKEY. DFHAID fields are DFHENTER; DFHCLEAR; DFHPF1 through DFHPF24; and DFHPA1, DFHPA2, and DFHPA3.

Options for testing EIBAID.   EIBAID can be tested in three ways:

1. Compare EIBAID against one of the DFHAID fields. For instance, to test if the AID key PF1 was pressed, code

```
IF EIBAID = DFHPF1
```

2. Execute a HANDLE AID command; for example

```
EXEC CICS HANDLE AID
    PF1 (C100-EXIT)
```

3. Test EIBAID against its actual value (see App. A-3); for example,

```
IF EIBAID = 1
```

Testing EIBAID fields against DFHAID fields.   Unlike the CICS-supplied list of standard attributes, the DFHAID fields are often used in application programs. Copy DFHAID (which is supplied with CICS) into the working-storage section of your program.

```
0001 C100-RECEIVE-CONTROL-MAP   SECTION.
0002*
0003     MOVE LOW-VALUES  TO  VM-CONTROL-MAP.
0004*
0005     IF EIBAID  =   DFHENTER    OR
0006                    DFHPF1      OR
0007                    DFHPF2      OR
0008                    DFHPF3      OR
0009                    DFHPF4
0010          MOVE 'F'  TO  STATUS-OF-RECEIVE
0011*
0012          EXEC CICS HANDLE CONDITION
0013                    MAPFAIL (C100-EXIT)
0014          END-EXEC
0015*
0016          EXEC CICS RECEIVE
0017                    MAP    ('MAPPOVC')
0018                    MAPSET ('POVMNT1')
0019                    INTO   (VM-CONTROL-MAP)
0020          END-EXEC
0021*
0022          MOVE 'G'  TO  STATUS-OF-RECEIVE
0023     ELSE
0024         IF EIBAID  =  DFHCLEAR
0025            PERFORM C110-END-SESSION
0026         ELSE
0027         IF EIBAID  =  DFHPF5
0028            PERFORM C120-TRANSFER-XCTL-TO-MENU
0029         ELSE
0030            MOVE 'I'        TO  STATUS-OF-RECEIVE
0031            MOVE 'INVALID KEY PRESSED - PLEASE TRY AGAIN'
0032                            TO  MVC-D-MESSAGE
0033            MOVE ASKIP-BRT  TO  MVC-A-MESSAGE.
0034*
0035 C100-EXIT.
0036     EXIT.
```

Figure 7-3   Illustration of EIBAID Usage.

Any AID key pressed by the terminal operator can be tested and acted upon as soon as the program is entered. These checks can be made at the beginning of the main line of a program, before or after a receive, or almost any place in the program. For ease of maintenance, I recommend being consistent regarding where you check EIBAID against DFHAID fields. I prefer to keep these checks in the RECEIVE MAP section of my program whenever possible.

EIBAID remains unchanged throughout a program and a task until another AID key is pressed. It can be tested and used as a switch throughout the program or task. An AID key pressed prior to a receive in one program can be tested by another program in the same task [i.e., a program XCTLed or linked to (see Chap. 8, "Program Control")].

Figure 7-3 illustrates typical usage of DFHAID fields. AID keys for ENTER, PF1, PF2, PF3, and PF4 are valid data-entry keys in this example. The program will receive the map and continue processing if any of the keys are pressed. Prior to the receive, an F is moved to STATUS-OF-RECEIVE, indicating a MAPFAIL condition. If a MAPFAIL does *not* occur on the receive, a G is moved to STATUS-OF-RECEIVE after the receive is completed. STATUS-OF-RECEIVE can be tested by the routine which performed C100-RECEIVE-CONTROL-MAP.

Other valid AID keys which could have been pressed are CLEAR and PF5. All other keys would cause an I to be moved to STATUS-OF-RECEIVE and an INVALID KEY PRESSED message to be moved to the map message field.

HANDLE AID command. The HANDLE AID command is similar to the HANDLE CONDITION command discussed in Chap. 5 in format and in transfer of control. HANDLE AID is invoked upon the receive of a map. If you use this technique, I recommend placing the command in your RECEIVE MAP program section. Its basic format is

```
EXEC CICS HANDLE AID
            AID KEY   (program-paragraph)
                .
                .
                .
     END-EXEC.
```

HANDLE AID considerations. The applications programmer must be aware of the following when writing a program:

1. Up to 12 AID keys can be specified on one command. Use two or more commands if required.

2. The last AID command encountered takes precedence and overrides AID keys which were specified in prior commands.

3. ANYKEY should be included to cover any key not specifically mentioned.

4. A specified AID key will override ANYKEY.

5. If ENTER is not specified in the HANDLE AID command, control will pass to the statement which follows the RECEIVE MAP command. ENTER is not included in ANYKEY.

6. AID keys listed in a HANDLE AID command without a paragraph name will fall through to the statement following a RECEIVE MAP command.

7. HANDLE AID commands take precedence over commands such as HANDLE CONDITION MAPFAIL.

HANDLE AID illustration. Figure 7-4 illustrates the use of the HANDLE AID command; it performs the same functions as the example in Fig. 7-3. AID keys ENTER, PF1, PF2, PF3, and PF4 are valid data-entry keys. Unless there is a MAPFAIL on the receive, the program will fall through to the statement following the receive. Pressing the CLEAR key always causes a MAPFAIL to occur, but since HANDLE AID takes precedence over HANDLE CONDITION, MAPFAIL will be overridden by the transfer of control to C100-END-OF-SESSION. A MAPFAIL would direct control to C100-MAPFAIL.

```
0001 C100-RECEIVE-CONTROL-MAP   SECTION.
0002*
0003      MOVE LOW-VALUES  TO  VM-CONTROL-MAP.
0004*
0005      EXEC CICS HANDLE AID
0006           PF1
0007           PF2
0008           PF3
0009           PF4
0010           PF5     (C100-RETURN-TO-MENU)
0011           CLEAR   (C100-END-OF-SESSION)
0012           ANYKEY  (C100-INVALID-KEY)
0013      END-EXEC.
0014*
0015      EXEC CICS HANDLE CONDITION
0016           MAPFAIL (C100-MAPFAIL)
0017      END-EXEC.
0018*
0019      EXEC CICS RECEIVE
0020           MAP     ('MAPPOVC')
0021           MAPSET  ('POVMNT1')
0022           INTO    (VM-CONTROL-MAP)
0023      END-EXEC.
0024*
0025      MOVE 'G'  TO  STATUS-OF-RECEIVE.
0026*
0027* WILL REACH THIS POINT IF PF1, PF2, PF3, PF4 OR ENTER KEY PRESSED
0028*      AND DATA WAS ENTERED - OTHERWISE A MAPFAIL OCCURS
0029* PF5, CLEAR AND OTHER KEYS PASS CONTROL TO INDICATED PARAGRAPHS
0030*
0031      GO TO  C100-EXIT.
0032*
0033 C100-RETURN-TO-MENU.
0034*
0035      PERFORM C120-TRANSFER-XCTL-TO-MENU.
0036*
0037* PRECEDING PERFORM DOES NOT RETURN - IT TRANSFERS CONTROL TO MENU
0038*
0039 C100-END-SESSION.
0040*
0041      PERFORM C110-END-SESSION.
0042*
0043* PRECEDING PERFORM DOES NOT RETURN - CONTROL IS RETURNED TO CICS
0044*
0045 C100-INVALID-KEY.
0046      MOVE 'I'       TO  STATUS-OF-RECEIVE.
0047      MOVE 'INVALID KEY PRESSED - PLEASE TRY AGAIN'
0048               TO  MVC-D-MESSAGE.
0049      MOVE ASKIP-BRT  TO  MVC-A-MESSAGE.
0050      GO TO  C100-EXIT.
0051*
0052 C100-MAPFAIL.
0053      MOVE 'F'  TO  STATUS-OF-RECEIVE.
0054*
0055 C100-EXIT.
0056      EXIT.
```

Figure 7-4 Illustration of HANDLE AID Command.

PF5 is the only other valid AID key; it would override a **MAPFAIL** and transfer control to C100-RETURN-TO-MENU. For any unspecified AID key, except ENTER, ANYKEY will direct control to C100-INVALID-KEY.

Testing EIBAID against its value. Testing EIBAID against its actual value would be handled in an identical fashion to comparing EIBAID against DFHAID fields. The only difference would be that instead of using DFHAID fields, the actual value would be used (see Fig. 7-3 for similarities).

```
IF EIBAID = QUOTE      OR
            1          OR
            2          OR
            3          OR
            4
   MOVE 'F'  TO   STATUS-OF-RECEIVE
```

SUMMARY

This chapter is the key to understanding CICS; once you master the concepts presented, CICS will be easy. Three types of SEND MAP commands were covered: SEND MAP AND DATA, SEND MAP MAPONLY, and SEND MAP DATAONLY. Symbolic cursor positioning, a technique for positioning the cursor at any field on a map, was discussed. The reasons for moving low-values to a symbolic map were explained, and the RECEIVE MAP command was introduced.

Map attributes were thoroughly explained. It was shown how you could set up a standard attribute list in your source library and how to use this list to interactively change map attributes. An illustration showed how the physical and symbolic maps interact to display data and constants and to modify map attributes. A chart was presented showing the interaction between the physical and symbolic maps and the effect of this interaction on map attributes.

MDT manipulation was discussed. It was shown how the return of data to a program occurs. The effect of FRSET on MDTs was also explained.

Considerations for the receive of a map were detailed. The functions of the AID keys, map length, and MAPFAIL were explained. Examples were presented showing two program methods for handling program AID keys: comparing EIBAID against DFHAID fields and using the HANDLE AID command.

I cannot emphasize the importance of this chapter strongly enough. Reread it now *and* again when you finish the book and are ready to start using some of the concepts you have learned.

8

PROGRAM CONTROL

Program-control commands facilitate returning control to the CICS system; passing control from one program to another; and loading and releasing programs, tables, and maps to or from main storage. An understanding of program logical levels is required in order to follow the flow of program control. A communications area is used to pass data from one program to another when using program-control commands. These commands include

1. RETURN—Return control to CICS or to an invoking program (see "LINK" below).
2. XCTL—Transfer control to another program without returning. This is conceptually similar to a GO TO statement in a Cobol program.
3. LINK—Pass control to another program which returns control to the invoking program, after performing its logic. This command is similar in concept to a PERFORM command in a Cobol program.
4. LOAD—Access and load a table, program, or map into main storage.
5. RELEASE—When a table, program, or map is no longer required, this command releases it from main storage.

Program Logical Levels

Programs of the type presented in Chap. 5 are basically started by keying in a TRANSID and pressing an AID key. CICS, which is shown at level 0 in Fig. 8-1, then passes control to the program associated with the TRANS-ID. A program initiated by CICS is considered to be at the highest logical level, level 1. (A program's logical level refers to its executing sequence relative to the CICS system, which is by definition at level zero.) When a

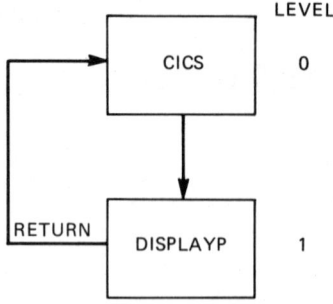

Figure 8-1 Single Program Logical Levels.

RETURN command is issued in the level 1 program, control is returned to CICS.

Transactions such as those represented in Fig. 8-1 are not as common as systems of programs which communicate with one another. Menu programs are commonly started by a TRANSID. The menu program then transfers control (XCTL) to another program at the same logical level as itself. The program transferred to can either end the session by returning to CICS or can transfer control back to the menu program. The menu program can then either return to CICS or transfer control to another program.

Programs at level 1 can always return to CICS. A program can transfer control to any program at the same level, including a program which has directly or indirectly transferred control to itself. Figure 8-2 shows this interaction.

Often a menu program will transfer control to a submenu at the same logical level. POVMAINT, a submenu program, will transfer control to individual inquiry, maintenance, and browse functions. A program to which control is transferred is always at the same logical level as the transferring program. Figure 8-3 illustrates how POMENUPM at level 1 can transfer control to three programs: POVMAINT, POMAINTN, and POENTRY1. POVMAINT

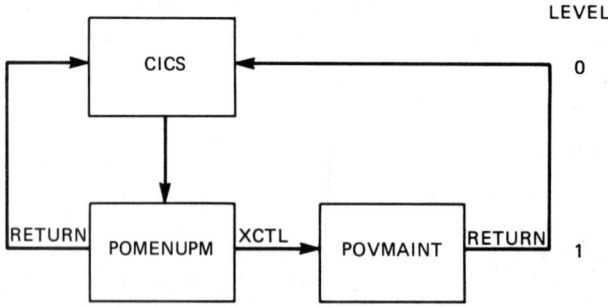

Figure 8-2 Menu Program Logical Levels.

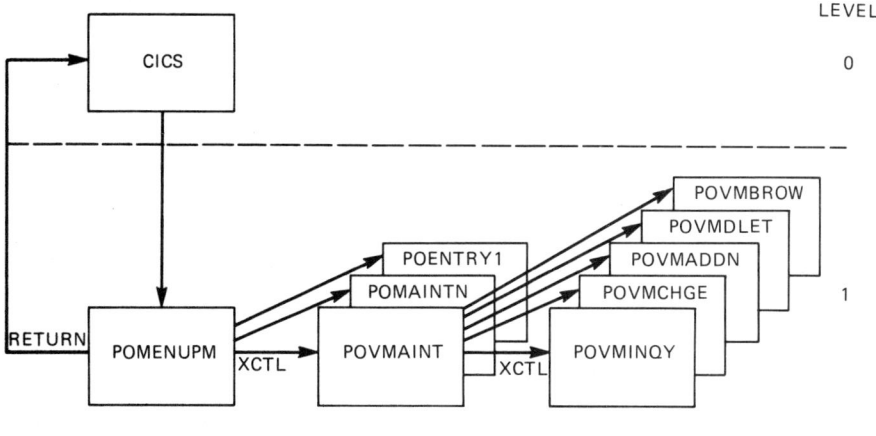

Figure 8-3 Multimenu Logical Levels—All are XCTLed to.

is shown transferring control to one of five programs, all at the same logical level. Any program shown in Fig. 8-3 at logical level 1 can return control to CICS. Each program at level 1 could be written so that it could transfer control to any other program shown at the same level. By definition, an XCTLed-to program is at the same logical level as the invoking program.

Normally an XCTLed-to program is not intended to immediately transfer control back to the invoking program. XCTL can be considered an absolute transfer of control to another program, with an option to return. Often system development requires an unconditional return from a program to which control has been passed. A change program, prior to changing a record, might write a before-journal record, and, following the change, write an after-journal record. A common program is often employed to handle such postings; our system calls this program JRNLPOST. Figure 8-4 shows how a linked program would appear at a lower logical level than the linking program.

POMENUPM is initiated by keying in the TRANSID POMU. Vendor file maintenance is selected and POMENUPM XCTLs to POVMAINT. POV-MAINT displays its submenu and the change function is selected, resulting in an XCTL to POVMCHGE. POMENUPM, POVMAINT, and POVMCHGE are all at the same logical level, level 1. The change program, POVMCHGE, needs to record the before-and-after image of all changes. This type of logic is commonly handled by a linked program. A linked program, JRNLPOST level 2, is always at a lower logical level than the invoking program, POVMCHGE level 1. When a RETURN command is issued in the linked program, control is passed back to the invoking program at the next sequential instruction following the LINK command.

The logical level structure shown in Fig. 8-4 is generally sufficient to handle most design and programming situations you will encounter. Keep your logical level structure design simple and modular; it will make maintenance easier.

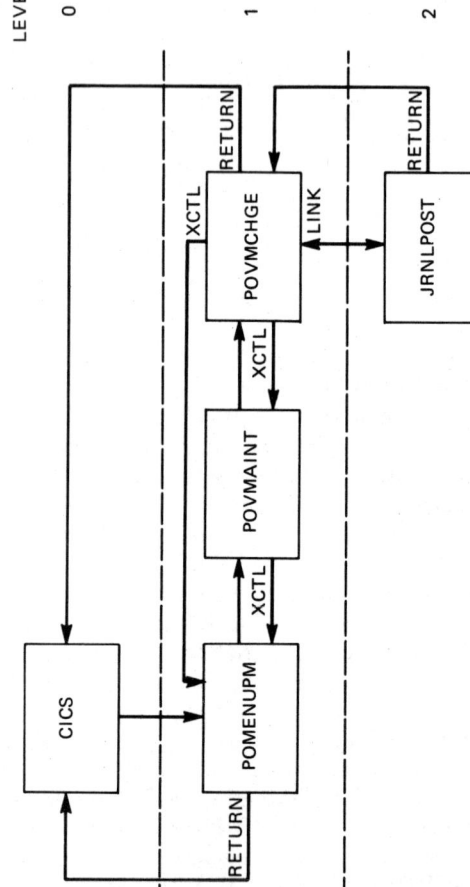

Figure 8-4 Logical Levels with LINKed-to Program.

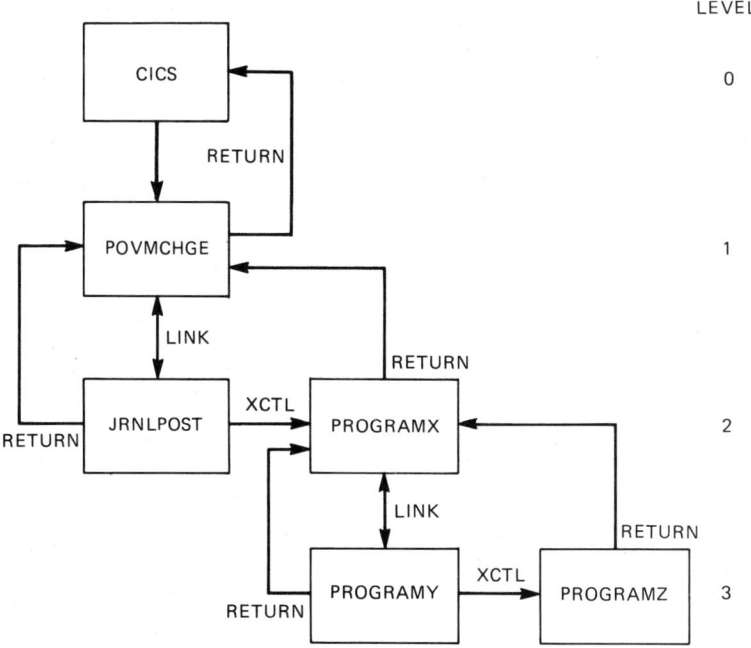

Figure 8-5 Extended Logical Level Structure.

Occasionally, a situation may arise which requires a more complicated logical level structure. Keep in mind that if a program links to another program, the linked program is always at a lower logical level. A RETURN command issued in any program at the next lower level always returns to the linking program at the next higher logical level.

Figure 8-5 illustrates how an extended logical level structure would function. POVMGHGE could be initiated by entering the TRANSID POVC. POVMCHGE then links to JRNLPOST. After the link to JRNLPOST, several paths could be followed:

1. JRNLPOST could issue a RETURN command, which would pass control up to the next higher logical level, back to POVMCHGE.

2. JRNLPOST might XCTL to PROGRAMX. If PROGRAMX issues a RETURN command, control is passed up to the next higher logical level, program POVMCHGE.

3. PROGRAMX could link to PROGRAMY, which could return to PROGRAMX or XCTL to PROGRAMZ. A RETURN command issued in PROGRAMZ would pass control up to PROGRAMX. When PROGRAMX issues a RETURN command, control is passed up to the next higher logical level, to POVMCHGE.

Task Number Considerations

Each time a new transaction is initiated, a task number is assigned to the task. The task number assigned is stored in the EIB field EIBTASKN. The task number remains unchanged until a RETURN command is issued at the highest logical level, level 1.

Communications Area

A communications area (COMMAREA) is a field in working storage used for passing data from one program to another. The COMMAREA can have its length defined in working storage as a halfword binary value, thus limiting the size of COMMAREA to a maximum size of 32,768 bytes. This is not a problem, since data passed in a COMMAREA is generally small in size, often less than 100 bytes. When COMMAREA is passed to another program, the receiving program retrieves the passed data in a linkage-section field called DFHCOMMAREA.

COMMAREA can be passed between programs by using the RETURN, XCTL, and LINK commands. The COMMAREA is specified for the above commands as follows:

```
EXEC CICS ...
        [PROGRAM   (WS-PROGRAM-NAME)]
        [TRANSID   (TRID)]
        COMMAREA (WS-COMMAREA)
        LENGTH    (WS-CA-LENGTH)      or LENGTH (15)
END-EXEC.
```

- WS-PROGRAM-NAME—The name of a linked or XCTLed-to program. Program name would not be included on a RETURN. WS-PROGRAM-NAME, or your label, could be defined in working storage as PIC X (8), or it could be hard-coded as PROGRAM ('POVMCHGE').
- TRID—The TRANSID of the next transaction to be initiated at a terminal. It is only specified on a RETURN command with a TRANSID, discussed later in this chapter.
- WS-COMMAREA—This is a data field in working storage (you can refer to this communications area by any appropriate name).
- WS-CA-LENGTH (or your label)—If this option is used, it must be defined in working storage as a halfword binary value. I prefer to include the actual length in the LENGTH option, i.e., LENGTH (15).

The program to which control is passed receives the data transferred in a linkage-section field called DFHCOMMAREA. DFHCOMMAREA should, whenever possible, be the same length as the passed data. Sometimes data of various types and lengths is passed to a program. *Avoid this if possible*: the results are unpredictable if DFHCOMMAREA is defined as being longer than the passed data *and* if your program accesses DFHCOMMAREA fields which have not been passed. You will minimize problems if the passed COMMAREA length is equal to the length of DFHCOMMAREA in the linkage section of the invoked program.

The invoked program can access passed data directly in the subfields of DFHCOMMAREA or move DFHCOMMAREA to a working-storage field. A program can determine if data has been passed to it by testing an EIB field called EIBCALEN. EIBCALEN contains the length of the COMMAREA passed by the initiating program.

EIBCALEN, the COMMAREA length, is often referred to as a *first-time switch*. A program initiated by entering a TRANSID, or one which is invoked by another program without a COMMAREA being passed to it, will have an EIBCALEN equal to 0. Subsequent entries into the program can return with a COMMAREA of length 1; COMMAREA is not required to contain any significant data. This is done so that EIBCALEN will equal the length of the COMMAREA or 1, and not 0, as it does upon initial entry. Statements similar to the following are commonly found in the main line of CICS programs:

```
IF EIBCALEN = ZERO
      PERFORM (FIRST-TIME-PROCESSING)
ELSE
      MOVE DFHCOMMAREA TO WS-COMMAREA
      PERFORM (SECOND-TIME-PROCESSING).
```

COMMAREA is sometimes used as a first-time switch or to direct the flow of program logic in pseudoconversational programs. Often a value will be moved to a WS-COMMAREA subfield; I call this field CA-SWITCH, before issuing a return to a program. The subfield will be tested upon a subsequent reentry into the program in order to determine program flow. For example,

```
IF EIBCALEN = 0
      PERFORM (FIRST-TIME-PROCESSING)
ELSE
      MOVE DFHCOMMAREA TO WS-COMMAREA
      IF CA-SWITCH = 2
            PERFORM (SECOND-TIME-PROCESSING)
      ELSE
      IF CA-SWITCH = 3
            PERFORM (THIRD-TIME-PROCESSING)
      ELSE
      IF CA-SWITCH = 4
            .
            .
            .
```

Some of these techniques will be employed in program examples in future chapters. As you work with the COMMAREA concept, you will find that it is easy to understand and master.

RETURN Command

The RETURN command, as used in the programs in Chap. 5, returned control to CICS and terminated a transaction. Most CICS systems and programs are not that simple. A program is usually initiated by a TRANSID, XCTL, or LINK command. The initiated program often sends a map upon which the terminal operator enters data. The program then executes a return to itself in order to receive and process the map's data. If invalid data has been entered, the program sends an error message, allows the terminal operator to correct the data, and issues a return to itself.

The format of the RETURN command used in previous examples to return to CICS was

```
EXEC CICS RETURN
END-EXEC.
```

This format, when issued at the highest logical level, will always terminate a task and return control to CICS. It is also the format executed at a lower logical level to return control to an invoking program which had issued a LINK command.

Return with a TRANSID

The format of the RETURN command as used in pseudoconversational programming is

```
EXEC CICS RETURN
         TRANSID    ('TRAN')
         COMMAREA (WS-COMMAREA)
         LENGTH     (WS-CA-LENGTH)
END-EXEC.
```

This format can only be issued in a program returning to CICS from the highest logical level, level 1. Using this format in a lower-logical-level program will result in the INVREQ (INValid REQuest) handle condition being invoked. Never use this option in a linked program or in programs at or below the logical level of the linked program.

This format of the RETURN command returns control back to CICS and ends the task. The program associated with the TRANSID in the RETURN command is initiated when an AID key is pressed. It is the RETURN command used to set a first-time switch. A return is issued with a one-character WS-COMMAREA and a length of 1. EIBCALEN will equal 1 when an AID key is pressed to initiate the program again. The first time the program was initiated, EIBCALEN should have been equal to 0 in order to use EIBCALEN as a first-time switch.

COMMAREA can be used to return a variety of switches and/or data to a program. A program may send a map, receive the map, and store data from the map or program in COMMAREA. When this format of the RETURN command is executed and the program is reentered, DFHCOMMAREA will contain the data returned in COMMAREA.

Transactions which are accessed frequently may use COMMAREA to store "valid" map data. If errors occur which necessitate the resend and receive of the map, the valid data saved in COMMAREA need not be retransmitted to or from the map. This is an advanced technique which will not be covered in this book.

A RETURN command with a TRANSID can be used to initiate a new program associated with the TRANSID which differs from the one which issued the return. You could design a system so that one program would send a map, then issue a return with a TRANSID in order to initiate a different program. The new program could receive and process the map and, when finished, either return with a TRANSID, which will initiate the send program again, or end the session. This technique has the advantage of using less main storage because it is more modular. I do not, however, recommend this technique because I find systems using this method more difficult to maintain. It is more logical to send and receive a map in the same program.

XCTL Command

The XCTL command is used to pass control to a program at the same logical level. Transfer is made by releasing the current program and loading the new program into main storage. Programs can be written to transfer control to another program and have the new program in turn transfer control back to the original program. This type of processing is common when a menu program transfers control to a selected program. The new program processes in the pseudoconversational mode and, when finished, transfers control back to the menu.

The format of the XCTL command is

```
EXEC CICS XCTL
          PROGRAM    (WS-PROGRAM-NAME)
          [COMMAREA (WS-COMMAREA)]
          [LENGTH     (WS-CA-LENGTH)]
     END-EXEC.
```

An XCTL command can be executed with or without COMMAREA and length being specified:

1. A program invoked without COMMAREA and LENGTH being specified on an XCTL command is similar in its initial entry to that of a program which is started by entering a TRANSID, in that EIBCALEN will equal zero.

2. If COMMAREA and LENGTH are specified on the XCTL command, EIB-CALEN of the new program will be equal to the length of the COMMAREA passed to it. DFHCOMMAREA in the new program will contain the data passed from the COMMAREA of the initiating program.

The program initiated by the XCTL command can have data of varying lengths passed to it from the COMMAREA of different programs. Try to avoid this in your system design; when possible, keep the passing program's COMM-AREA the same length as the invoked program's DFHCOMMAREA. If your program attempts to access data in the linkage-section field DFHCOMMAREA which is longer than the length of the COMMAREA passed, the results are unpredictable.

The handle condition PGMIDERR (ProGraM IDentification ERRor) will occur if the XCTLed-to program is not in the PPT or if it has been disabled. I generally do not check for this condition; it should not normally occur.

LINK Command

The LINK command is similar in format to the XCTL command; however, its function is much different. A LINK command passes control to a program at a lower logical level, with the intent of returning. A RETURN command issued in a program at the next lower logical level will return to the next sequential instruction in the invoking program, immediately following the LINK command. Linking to a program is costly in terms of computer system resources which are tied up. A LINK command holds the linking program in main storage as well as the linked-to program. Figure 8-5 shows how a link could require several programs to be in main storage simultaneously. Avoid using the LINK command unless absolutely necessary because it requires more main storage and results in slower response time.

The format of the LINK command is

```
EXEC CICS LINK
        PROGRAM    (WS-PROGRAM-NAME)
        [COMMAREA (WS-COMMAREA)]
        [LENGTH    (WS-CA-LENGTH)]
END-EXEC.
```

A program which links to another program generally passes a COMM-AREA to the invoked program. There are other methods of passing data.

Actually, the address of WS-COMMAREA in the issuing program is passed to the linked program. The data passed in COMMAREA is accessed under DFHCOMMAREA in the invoked program. Any data changes made under DFHCOMMAREA in the linked program will be available under WS-COMMAREA when control is returned to the invoking program (refer to Fig. 8-5 for the following). If POVMCHGE passed a COMMAREA to JRNL-POST via a LINK command, DFHCOMMAREA in JRNLPOST would in effect point to the same address and data as WS-COMMAREA in the invoking program POVMCHGE. If JRNLPOST with COMMAREA (DFH-COMMAREA) XCTLed to PROGRAMX, DFHCOMMAREA in PROGRAMX would point to the same WS-COMMAREA in POVMCHGE. Any changes made under DFHCOMMAREA in PROGRAMX would be reflected under WS-COMMAREA in POVMCHGE, when PROGRAMX issued a RETURN command to POVMCHGE. If JRNLPOST XCTLed to PROGRAMX with COMMAREA (WS-NEW-COMMAREA), only changes made by JRNLPOST would be reflected in WS-COMMAREA of POVMCHGE when PROGRAMX issued a RETURN command. An additional new copy of COMMAREA, containing the data passed from WS-NEW-COMMAREA, would be created, and this new copy of COMMAREA would be received in DFHCOMMAREA of PROGRAMX.

When a program which has issued a LINK command is returned to, then working storage, all handle aids, handle conditions, etc., except possibly, COMMAREA, are restored to their status prior to the issue of the LINK command.

The handle condition PGMIDERR will occur if the linked-to program is not in the PPT or if it has been disabled. I generally do not check for this condition; it should not normally occur.

LOAD Command

The LOAD command is used to access and load a table, map, or program into main storage. It can be used to load program tables such as a state code table, a sales force table, or a cost table into main storage. The table accessed is addressed through a linkage-section pointer called base locator for linkage or BLL cells. The format of the LOAD command is

```
        EXEC CICS LOAD
                PROGRAM (name)
                SET        (BLL-pointer)
                HOLD
        END-EXEC.
```

- name—Name of the table, map, or program which is to be loaded into main storage.

- BLL-pointer—Pointer which is set to the address of the loaded program.

- HOLD—Indicates that the program is to be held in main storage, even after the task is terminated. The program will be deleted from main storage only when a RELEASE command is executed in the current or in a future task.

Chapter 10 will illustrate the load of a highly used table which is defined in the PPT as a main-storage resident table. The use of BLL-pointers for setting addressability to a table will be demonstrated.

The handle condition PGMIDERR will occur if the program to be loaded is not in the PPT or if it has been disabled. I generally do not check for this condition; it should not normally occur.

RELEASE Command

This command is issued in order to release a table, program, or map from main storage. A RELEASE command should be issued in order to free main storage as soon as the program loaded is no longer required. The format of the RELEASE command is

```
        EXEC CICS RELEASE
                    PROGRAM (name)
        END-EXEC.
```

[(name) is the name of the table, map, or program which is to be released from main storage.]

This command must be executed in order to release programs which are loaded with the HOLD option. The program loaded will be automatically released when the task is completed if hold was not specified on the LOAD command. Load tables as close as possible to their point of use; then release them as soon as they are no longer required.

The handle condition PGMIDERR can occur if the program to be released is not in the PPT or if it has been disabled. I generally do not check for this condition; it should not normally occur.

SUMMARY

An understanding of program-control commands is essential for the design of good systems and the development of efficient programming techniques. Program-control commands aid in the design of programs which communicate with one another. Communication between programs is implemented through a communications area called COMMAREA. COMMAREA passes data to the same or to another program, which receives that data in a linkage-section field called DFHCOMMAREA.

The program-control commands RETURN, XCTL, LINK, LOAD, and RE-LEASE were discussed in detail. Several diagrams were presented to convey the concept of program logical levels. EIBCALEN (COMMAREA length), often referred to as a first-time switch, was discussed, and examples of its use were included.

Program-control commands sound complicated but are reasonably easy to master. Examples in succeeding chapters should clarify their usage.

9

THE MENU PROGRAM

You have learned many important CICS concepts and commands. Practical application programs will help you pull together the theory which you have been reading. The purchase order menu program and the vendor file maintenance menu programs are similar; this chapter discusses the latter. Concepts such as pseudoconversational programming and the communications area are discussed. SEND MAP, RECEIVE MAP, and MAPFAIL commands will be used as well as the program-control commands RETURN, RETURN with a TRANSID, XCTL, and LINK.

The standard attention identifier list (DFHAID) will be used as a comparison with the EIB field EIBAID in order to determine the AID key pressed by the terminal operator. EIB fields as well as translator call fields (DFHEIVAR, see p. 57) will be copied into the linkage and working-storage sections, respectively, for all programs at compile time. COPY statements generated by the translator will accomplish this. EIB fields such as EIBCALEN are used and discussed. DFHEIVAR fields are used by the translator and are not of direct importance to the application programmer.

This chapter lays the foundation for sample programs in succeeding chapters. The explanation of the example presented is more thorough than those in following chapters, which will only detail new commands and concepts as they are encountered.

Most installations have one or more menu programs. Their basic function is to initiate other programs. A terminal operator keys in a TRANSID and presses ENTER to display a menu screen. A selection is keyed in and ENTER is pressed in order to effect the transfer of control to the chosen program.

Often a main menu cannot accommodate all the required functions. This is not the case in the purchase order system; I just want to show how it would be done. A selection of 3 entered on the purchasing system menu (Fig. 2-3) would display the submenu shown by the screen layout in Fig. 6-3.

The vendor file maintenance menu subsystem structure chart was illustrated in Fig. 4-2, and a program structure chart, which is similar for most menu programs, in Fig. 4-3. This program contains an equivalent structure chart in the form of comments at the start of the procedure division. The BMS map was shown in Fig. 6-4 and its BMS-generated symbolic map in Fig. 6-5. The user-friendly symbolic map used by this program was shown in Fig. 6-6.

Vendor File Maintenance Submenu

Figure 9-1 presents the vendor file maintenance menu program. The remarks in your CICS programs should contain sufficient information to enable someone unfamiliar with the program to understand its basic function. Be brief yet thorough; the REMARKS section of a program and a program's comments are among the first references for a maintenance programmer. Include just enough comments to make the intent of the program clear to someone unfamiliar with it. Write all of your programs as if you will have to explain them to your co-workers. All programs should be written with ease of understanding and future change in mind. Write them as if you or your fellow workers will have to make changes in them 6 months from today. You will! I like to include in the remarks the program title, the method of program initiation, and the basic program functions.

I generally start the working-storage section with the program name, i.e., POVMAINT, and if the program

1. Displays a message to end a session, the literal SESSION COMPLETED.
2. Does not end a session, for instance, a linked program—the program name and the literal START OF WS, i.e., JRNLPOST—START OF WS.

I like to end a program's working storage with a literal followed by the program's name (i.e., END WS POVMAINT). These literals often help in program debugging.

Try to be consistent from program to program in your label names. Give them meaningful names. Use your source code library to store working-storage and procedure division code that is used in more than one program. BMS-generated symbolic maps are usually copied into working storage. User-friendly symbolic maps can either be copied or hard-coded in the program's working storage.

Working-Storage Section

It is good practice to keep working storage as small as possible, since each task obtains its own unique copy of this section. Avoid unnecessarily storing literals and messages in this section; instead hard-code them in the procedure division. Fields used in this program and their meaning are as follows:

- WS-CRT-MESSAGE—Contains the literal SESSION COMPLETED, which is displayed when a program at the highest logical level returns to CICS.

Figure 9-1 Vendor File Maintenance Submenu Program.

```
000100 IDENTIFICATION DIVISION.
000200 PROGRAM-ID. POVMAINT.
000300 REMARKS.
000400***********************************************************************
000500*    VENDOR FILE MAINTENANCE SUB MENU - STARTED BY TRANSID 'POVM' *
000600*         OR BY ANOTHER MENU     PROGRAM FUNCTIONS:               *
000700*     A) SEND MENU SCREEN                                         *
000800*     B) RECEIVE MENU MAP AND DEPENDING ON SELECTION - XCTL TO:*
000900*        1) INQUIRY        2) CHANGE         3) ADD              *
001000*        4) DELETE         5) BROWSE                             *
001100***********************************************************************
001200 ENVIRONMENT DIVISION.
001300 DATA DIVISION.
001400*
001500 WORKING-STORAGE SECTION.
001600*
001700 01   WS-PROGRAM-FIELDS.
001800      05   FILLER           PIC X(8)     VALUE 'POVMAINT'.
001900      05   WS-CRT-MESSAGE   PIC X(17)    VALUE 'SESSION COMPLETED'.
002000      05   WS-XCTL-PROGRAM  PIC X(8)     VALUE SPACES.
002100      05   WS-COMMAREA      PIC X        VALUE SPACE.
002200*
002300 01   MPM-MENU-MAP.
002400      05   FILLER              PIC X(12).
002500      05   MPM-L-SELECTION     PIC S9(4)     COMP.
002600      05   MPM-A-SELECTION     PIC X.
002700      05   MPM-D-SELECTION     PIC X.
002800      05   MPM-L-MESSAGE       PIC S9(4)     COMP.
002900      05   MPM-A-MESSAGE       PIC X.
003000      05   MPM-D-MESSAGE       PIC X(79).
003100*
003200*01   WS-STATUS-FIELDS.
003300      COPY   STWSSTAT.
003400*01   ATTRIBUTE-LIST.
003500      COPY   STWSATTR.
003600*
003700      COPY   DFHAID.
003800*
003900      COPY   DFHBMSCA.
004000*
004100 01   END-OF-WORKING-STORAGE    PIC X(15)   VALUE 'END WS POVMAINT'.
004200*
004300 LINKAGE SECTION.
004400*
004500 01   DFHCOMMAREA       PIC X.
004600*
004700 PROCEDURE DIVISION.
004800***********************************************************************
004900*            PROGRAM STRUCTURE IS:                                *
005000*               AA00-MAINLINE                                     *
005100*                  B000-SEND-MAPONLY                              *
005200*                  C000-PROCESSING                               *
005300*                     C100-RECEIVE-MAP                           *
005400*                        C110-END-SESSION                        *
005500*                     C200-EDIT-MAP-SELECTION                    *
005600*                     C300-TRANSFER-CONTROL                      *
005700*                     C400-SEND-MAP-DATAONLY                     *
005800***********************************************************************
005900
006000 AA00-MAINLINE  SECTION.
006100*
006200      IF EIBCALEN  =  ZERO
006300          PERFORM B000-SEND-MAPONLY
006400      ELSE
006500          PERFORM C000-PROCESSING.
006600*
006700      EXEC CICS RETURN
006800            TRANSID   ('POVM')
006900            COMMAREA  (WS-COMMAREA)
007000            LENGTH    (1)
007100      END-EXEC.
007200*
007300*
007400 B000-SEND-MAPONLY   SECTION.
007500***********************************************************************
007600*            SEND MAPONLY - PHYSICAL MAP                          *
007700*            PERFORMED FROM:  AA00-MAINLINE                       *
007800*    ONLY PERFORMED ONCE, UPON INITIAL ENTRY WHEN EIBCALEN = 0   *
007900***********************************************************************
008000*
008100      EXEC CICS SEND
```

Figure 9-1 *(Continued)*

```
008200                     MAP      ('MAPPOVM')
008300                     MAPSET ('POVMNT1')
008400                     MAPONLY
008500                     ERASE
008600         END-EXEC.
008700*
008800     B000-EXIT.
008900         EXIT.
009000*
009100*
009200 C000-PROCESSING  SECTION.
009300******************************************************************
009400*                    MAIN PROCESSING MODULE                      *
009500*                 PERFORMED FROM:   AA00-MAINLINE                 *
009600*  RECEIVE AND PROCESS SELECTION SCREEN - IF VALID RECEIVE, AND   *
009700*    SELECTION - TRANSFER CONTROL TO SELECTED PROGRAM ELSE        *
009800*       SEND MAP MESSAGE DEPENDING ON STATUS:                     *
009900*    1) STATUS-OF-RECEIVE    = 'I'   INVALID KEY PRESSED          *
010000*    2) STATUS-OF-RECIEVE    = 'F'   MAPFAIL - NO SELECTION MADE  *
010100*    3) STATUS-OF-SELECTION  = 'E'   INVALID SELECTION KEYED-IN   *
010200******************************************************************
010300*
010400         PERFORM C100-RECEIVE-MAP.
010500         IF GOOD-RECEIVE
010600            PERFORM C200-EDIT-MAP-SELECTION
010700            IF VALID-SELECTION
010800               PERFORM C300-TRANSFER-CONTROL
010900            ELSE
011000               PERFORM C400-SEND-MAP-DATAONLY
011100         ELSE
011200            IF STATUS-OF-RECEIVE  = 'F'
011300               MOVE 'NO SELECTION WAS MADE - PLEASE ENTER SELECTION'
011400                              TO   MPM-D-MESSAGE
011500               MOVE ASKIP-BRT  TO   MPM-A-MESSAGE
011600               PERFORM C400-SEND-MAP-DATAONLY
011700            ELSE
011800               PERFORM C400-SEND-MAP-DATAONLY.
011900*
012000 C000-EXIT.
012100         EXIT.
012200*
012300*
012400 C100-RECEIVE-MAP  SECTION.
012500******************************************************************
012600*             PERFORMED FROM:   C000-PROCESSING                   *
012700*          ONLY ENTER AND CLEAR KEYS ARE VALID                    *
012800*        OTHER CONDITIONS CHANGE STATUS-OF-RECEIVE                *
012900*  GOOD-RECEIVE = 'G'    INVALID-KEY = 'I'    MAPFAIL = 'F'   *
013000******************************************************************
013100*
013200         IF EIBAID = DFHENTER
013300            MOVE 'F' TO STATUS-OF-RECEIVE
013400*
013500            EXEC CICS HANDLE CONDITION
013600                    MAPFAIL (C100-EXIT)
013700            END-EXEC
013800*
013900            EXEC CICS RECEIVE
014000                    MAP      ('MAPPOVM')
014100                    MAPSET ('POVMNT1')
014200                    INTO    (MPM-MENU-MAP)
014300            END-EXEC
014400*
014500            MOVE 'G'  TO  STATUS-OF-RECEIVE
014600         ELSE
014700            IF EIBAID = DFHCLEAR
014800               PERFORM C110-END-SESSION
014900            ELSE
015000               MOVE 'I'  TO  STATUS-OF-RECEIVE
015100               MOVE 'ENTER AND CLEAR KEYS ARE ONLY VALID KEYS - PLEA
015200-                'SE TRY AGAIN'   TO  MPM-D-MESSAGE
015300               MOVE ASKIP-BRT  TO  MPM-A-MESSAGE
015400               MOVE UNPROT-FSET  TO  MPM-A-SELECTION.
015500*
015600 C100-EXIT.
015700         EXIT.
015800*
```

Figure 9-1 *(Continued)*

```
015900*
016000 C110-END-SESSION  SECTION.
016100*****************************************************************
016200*              OPERATOR PRESSED CLEAR - END SESSION           *
016300*              PERFORMED FROM:  C100-RECEIVE-MAP              *
016400*****************************************************************
016500*
016600     EXEC CICS SEND
016700              FROM    (WS-CRT-MESSAGE)
016800              LENGTH (17)
016900              ERASE
017000     END-EXEC.
017100*
017200     EXEC CICS RETURN
017300     END-EXEC.
017400*
017500 C110-EXIT.
017600     EXIT.
017700*
017800*
017900 C200-EDIT-MAP-SELECTION  SECTION.
018000*****************************************************************
018100*           EDIT SELECTION MADE BY THE CRT OPERATOR         ***
018200*              PERFORMED FROM:  C000-PROCESSING             ***
018300*****************************************************************
018400*
018500     MOVE 'G'  TO  STATUS-OF-SELECTION.
018600*
018700     IF MPM-D-SELECTION =  '1'  MOVE 'POVMINQY' TO WS-XCTL-PROGRAM
018800        ELSE
018900     IF MPM-D-SELECTION =  '2'  MOVE 'POVMCHGE' TO WS-XCTL-PROGRAM
019000        ELSE
019100     IF MPM-D-SELECTION =  '3'  MOVE 'POVMADDN' TO WS-XCTL-PROGRAM
019200        ELSE
019300     IF MPM-D-SELECTION =  '4'  MOVE 'POVMDLET' TO WS-XCTL-PROGRAM
019400        ELSE
019500     IF MPM-D-SELECTION =  '5'  MOVE 'POVMBROW' TO WS-XCTL-PROGRAM
019600        ELSE
019700        MOVE 'E'     TO  STATUS-OF-SELECTION
019800        MOVE 'INVALID SELECTION - PLEASE RE-ENTER YOUR SELECTION'
019900                     TO  MPM-D-MESSAGE
020000        MOVE ASKIP-BRT  TO  MPM-A-MESSAGE.
020100*
020200 C200-EXIT.
020300     EXIT.
020400*
020500*
020600 C300-TRANSFER-CONTROL  SECTION.
020700*****************************************************************
020800*          TRANSFER CONTROL 'XCTL' TO SELECTED PROGRAM       *
020900*              PERFORMED FROM:  C000-PROCESSING              *
021000*****************************************************************
021100*
021200     EXEC CICS XCTL
021300              PROGRAM (WS-XCTL-PROGRAM)
021400     END-EXEC.
021500*
021600 C300-EXIT.
021700     EXIT.
021800*
021900*
022000 C400-SEND-MAP-DATAONLY  SECTION.
022100*****************************************************************
022200*              SEND MAP DATAONLY - SYMBOLIC MAP             *
022300*              PERFORMED FROM:  C000-PROCESSING             *
022400*              WHEN INVALID CONDITIONS ARE DETECTED         *
022500*****************************************************************
022600*
022700     EXEC CICS SEND
022800              MAP      ('MAPPOVM')
022900              MAPSET   ('POVMNT1')
023000              FROM     (MPM-MENU-MAP)
023100              DATAONLY
023200     END-EXEC.
023300*
023400 C400-EXIT.
023500     EXIT.
```

- WS-XCTL-PROGRAM—Based on the selection made by the terminal operator, the program to be transferred to is moved to this field before a common XCTL command is executed.

- WS-COMMAREA—Communications area used to return with a COMMAREA and LENGTH. This is used as a first-time switch.

- MPM-MENU-MAP—Chapter 6 showed how to create user-friendly symbolic maps.

- WS-STATUS-FIELDS—Program status fields found in the copy library (see STWSSTAT in App. B). These fields contain the status of program functions such as RECEIVE MAP, SELECTION, EDIT, READ, WRITE, CHANGE, and DELETE RECORDS, etc.

- ATTRIBUTE-LIST—User-friendly standard attribute character list (see STWSATTR in App. B).

- DFHAID—AID fields (see App. A-3).

Linkage Section

The only field defined in this program's linkage section is DFHCOMMAREA (see Fig. 9-1). The translator automatically generates a 1-byte DFHCOMMAREA, even if it is not coded.

Procedure Division

The procedure division contains the program's logic and comments which assist the programmer who has to test and maintain the program.

Program comments and section-naming conventions. I recommend starting the procedure division with comments describing the program's structure. Use descriptive paragraph names, which should be the actual names used for program sections. I label my mainline section AA00-MAINLINE. All other section names begin with an alphabetic character followed by three digits and then a description of the function performed. I indent the program structure section name four spaces to reflect sections which are performed from a higher level section.

Sections which are performed or invoked from another section are listed following the literal PERFORMED FROM: or INVOKED BY:. The rest of the comment area for each section contains information which should aid somebody unfamiliar with the program to understand the intent of the section. Do not put unnecessary information in this area, just enough to clarify.

I strongly recommend using structured programming techniques. They aid in development, debugging, and maintenance. Keep your structured code straightforward and simple. KISS will make your job much easier.

AA00-MAINLINE. Many programs contain initial or first-entry processing logic which is performed only once. Succeeding entries into the program follow a different logic path.

Initial program entry. On initial entry into the vendor file maintenance menu program, EIBCALEN is equal to zero because the program is initiated either by entering the TRANSID POVM or by a transfer of control from the purchasing system menu (POMENUPM, see Fig. 2-3). EIBCALEN will always equal zero when a program is initiated by entering a TRANSID. Any program which transfers control to this program will do so without COMMAREA and LENGTH specified. This will result in EIBCALEN equaling zero on initial entry. Transferring control to this program with COMMAREA and LENGTH specified would require that the program be written differently. EIBCALEN would be greater than 0. This program could test a switch sent in the COMMAREA in order to determine program flow. It could test an EIB field EIBTRNID, the TRANSID, in order to determine how the program was initiated. The browse program in Chap. 17 will employ EIBTRNID.

When EIBCALEN equals 0, the program sends the vendor file maintenance submenu screen shown in Fig. 6-3 and returns to CICS with a TRANSID, COMMAREA, and LENGTH. Return with a TRANSID is the main technique used in pseudoconversational programming. This enables the terminal operator to initiate the next execution of the program by pressing an AID key instead of entering a TRANSID. Specifying an invalid TRANSID on a RETURN command would cause the task to ABEND with an INVALID TRANSACTION IDENTIFICATION message displayed on the screen. When a program returns with a TRANSID, the current task is terminated. The program can be released from main storage, unless the program is defined in the PPT as being main-storage resident, and storage can be used for other tasks. Each program obtains its unique copy of working storage, and when a task ends, this copy is released from main storage. Each time CICS initiates a program, working storage reverts to its initial values. For this reason a program cannot pass data from one task to another through working storage. You have so far learned two methods which can be used to transfer data between tasks: through a map and the COMMAREA. This program is not concerned with passing data through the COMMAREA. It only returns with a COMMAREA containing a space and a length of 1, in order to set EIBCALEN for succeeding entries into the program. This technique is referred to as using EIBCALEN as a first-time switch.

Second and succeeding program entries. The first entry into the program sent the initial map, MAPONLY, and returned to CICS with a TRANSID and a length of 1. On succeeding entries into the program, EIBCALEN will be equal to 1, and the program will perform C000-PROCESSING. If a RETURN command had been issued with TRANSID but without COMMAREA and LENGTH specified, EIBCALEN would equal 0 and the program would loop, performing B000-SEND-MAPONLY each time an AID key was pressed.

When a valid selection is made, control is transferred to the selected program. Invalid conditions such as pressing an invalid AID key, not entering a selection (MAPFAIL), and making an invalid selection will result in a DATAONLY map send and the execution of the return with TRANSID. The return with TRANSID, COMMAREA, and length after the send of the DATAONLY map allows the terminal operator to correct the map's data. The terminal operator reads the error message. A valid selection is keyed in. The operator presses the proper AID key (ENTER); then this program is initiated again. Upon reentry into the program, EIBCALEN equals 1 and the program will perform C000-PROCESSING again. This process is repeated as often as required until a correct selection is entered. Transfer of control will take place, or the terminal operator will press CLEAR to end the session.

An understanding of the technique presented in the menu program should aid you in learning pseudoconversational programming. Pseudoconversational programming basically involves the send of a map and the release of the program from main storage if storage is required for another task. The map can be received without having to enter a TRANSID again since the RETURN command is issued with a TRANSID. Then, if the map's data is valid, the required logic is performed. When invalid data is entered, the map is resent with an indicative message. This process continues until valid data is entered or the session is ended.

B000-SEND-MAPONLY. This section is performed only once, upon initial entry into the program, when EIBCALEN equals 0. The program specifies MAPONLY in the send because the initial map contains no variable data. Only the physical map, which contains constants, needs to be sent. Maps which contain variable data such as date and time will eliminate MAPONLY from the send and will send both map and data (physical and symbolic maps).

C000-PROCESSING. This section is executed for all entries into the program after the first time. EIBCALEN will *not* be equal to 0. Section functions are

1. Perform C100-RECEIVE-MAP—Receives the selection entered on the map.

2. Perform C200-EDIT-MAP-SELECTION—Validate the selection.

3. Perform C300-TRANSFER-CONTROL—Transfer control to the selected program if a valid selection was entered.

4. Perform C400-SEND-MAP-DATAONLY—Send only the symbolic map if any invalid conditions are encountered, such as:

    a. Invalid AID key pressed.

    b. MAPFAIL (encountered when no selection is entered).

    c. An invalid selection was entered.

C100-RECEIVE-MAP. The RECEIVE MAP section checks which AID key was pressed in order to determine a logic path to follow. The only valid AID keys are ENTER and CLEAR. Any other AID key pressed would result in an invalid key message displayed on the screen. I check which AID key was pressed by comparing the EIB field EIBAID against one of the attention identifier fields listed in App. A-3. Figure 7-4 showed an alternate method of testing which AID key was pressed; that method is used in the browse program in Chap. 17. EIBAID can be tested and used as a switch at any point in the program.

EIBAID equals DFHENTER. I move an F immediately to STATUS-OF-RECEIVE so that if a MAPFAIL occurs, the program can determine this condition by testing the status field. The HANDLE CONDITION MAPFAIL command is invoked on the receive of a map if no field is FSET. If the EOF key is pressed prior to a receive, MAPFAIL will not occur. If a MAPFAIL occurs on the receive of a map, control will pass to the section exit with an F in STATUS-OF-RECEIVE. On a good receive for which a selection has been entered, a G will be moved to STATUS-OF-RECEIVE.

The RECEIVE MAP command will receive the map into the working-storage area MPM-MENU-MAP. The flag (attribute) byte MPM-A-SELECTION can be tested for hexadecimal 80 (X'80') in order to determine if the EOF key had been pressed. In all other cases the flag byte will equal X'00' (low-values). The L suffix (length field) can be tested after a RECEIVE MAP command to determine if data has been keyed into a field. Its length will be greater than 0 if data has been entered.

EIBAID equals DFHCLEAR. If the CLEAR key is pressed, the program will perform C110-END-SESSION. The end-of-session section will send a message and return control to CICS. Any AID key(s) could have been programmed to perform this function.

EIBAID not equal to DFHENTER or DFHCLEAR. This program considers any AID key other than ENTER or CLEAR an invalid entry. An I is moved to STATUS-OF-RECEIVE and a message moved to the map output field MPM-D-MESSAGE. The attribute character ASKIP,BRT is moved to the map message attribute field MPM-A-MESSAGE. UNPROT,FSET is moved to the SELECTION field attribute MPM-A-SELECTION; otherwise the selection code would not be returned on a subsequent read of the map. The DFHMSD macro of the BMS map defines CTRL=(FREEKB,FRSET). FRSET turns off all MDTs before a map is sent. The selection would be displayed on the screen, but it would not be returned to the program when a RECEIVE MAP command was executed because its MDT was not on. Moving UNPROT,FSET to the attribute field prior to the SEND MAP DATAONLY command will turn the MDT on. This will result in the selection being returned as is if it is not changed.

C110-END-SESSION. The RECEIVE MAP section will perform the C110-END-SESSION when the terminal operator presses the CLEAR key. It will display the message SESSION COMPLETED. The length of the message (17) must be specified. ERASE clears the screen before the send. Since this program is at the highest logical level, the execution of the CICS RETURN command will return control to CICS. No TRANSID is specified on the RETURN command; therefore, if the terminal operator presses an AID key after the message is displayed, an invalid transaction message will appear on the screen.

C200-EDIT-MAP-SELECTION. The selection entered by the terminal operator will be edited in this section. The appropriate program will be moved to WS-XCTL-PROGRAM if the selection is valid. On an invalid selection, an E is placed in STATUS-OF-SELECTION. A message is then moved to the map's message field and ASKIP,BRT is moved to the map's field attribute. Unlike section C100-RECEIVE-MAP, it is *not* necessary to move UNPROT,FSET to the map's selection attribute. When an invalid selection is keyed in, it is not required to be returned on a subsequent receive of the map; the corrected selection should be entered. What do you think would happen if, after displaying the invalid selection message, the terminal operator pressed ENTER without keying in any selection? The invalid selection which was displayed on the screen would not be returned to the program since the send with FRSET turns off its MDT. Low-values would be returned. Section C000-PROCESSING would move NO SELECTION WAS MADE. . . to the message field and would resend the map. All the while, the invalid selection would be showing on the screen. The terminal operator might press the EOF key to erase the invalid entry and then press ENTER. This would *not* cause a MAPFAIL. Low-values would be transmitted on a RECEIVE MAP command, but the flag byte MPM-A-SELECTION would contain X'80'. In this case the selection would be treated as invalid by section C200-EDIT-MAP-SELECTION. The flag byte received would be equal to low-values (X'00') if EOF was not pressed or if a selection had been entered. The flag byte is not used often, but you may encounter it in programs which you have to maintain. Remember that the flag and attribute bytes occupy the same field. Also keep in mind that BMS map A and F suffix fields are shown only as A fields on user-friendly maps. BMS map suffix fields I and O are shown as data (D) fields on user-friendly symbolic maps.

C300-TRANSFER-CONTROL. After section C200-EDIT-MAP-SELECTION moves the selection program name to WS-XCTL-PROGRAM, this section immediately transfers control to the selected program. The new program will be loaded into main storage if necessary, and control will be transferred to that program. The menu program can be released from main storage, if it's not required by another task or if it's not defined in the PPT as a main-storage resident program. The EIB fields, task number (EIBTASKN), and TRANSID (EIB-TRNID) will remain unchanged in the new program until it issues a RETURN command at the highest logical level.

The handle condition PGMIDERR will be invoked if the program has not been defined in the PPT or if the program has been disabled. This condition generally occurs only during an initial test. I do not check for this condition; if it occurs, I let the program ABEND.

Programs initiated by this section will be entered with a communications area length (EIBCALEN) equal to 0. This program could transfer control with data, in which case the XCTL command would require the COMMAREA and LENGTH options.

C400-SEND-MAP-DATAONLY. This section is performed from C000-PROCESSING when an invalid condition has been detected, such as invalid key pressed, MAPFAIL, or an invalid selection. This send does not include the physical map. Only the symbolic map (DATAONLY) is sent. The physical map should have been previously sent by either a SEND MAP MAPONLY command or a SEND

MAP AND DATA command. Do not specify ERASE on the DATAONLY option of the SEND MAP command because you will display variable data on a screen which has no physical constants. When the FROM option is not specified on a SEND MAP command, the output symbolic map generated by BMS, MAPPOVMO in Fig. 6-5, is the default.

If CURSOR was specified in this SEND MAP DATAONLY command, -1 would have to be moved to one of the symbolic map length field's (L suffix). The cursor would be set at map POS=(01,01) if -1 was not moved to a length field when CURSOR was specified.

SUMMARY

The best way to learn most data processing concepts is through practice and by reference to practical examples. The menu program presented in this chapter is typical of most menu programs. Many of the commands and concepts discussed so far were illustrated in the menu program. Several suggestions for program documentation and standardization were presented. I recommend comments be included as part of the program's remarks in order to make the intent of the program clear to someone unfamiliar with the system. I showed how a section reference structure chart could be included at the start of the procedure division. Comments at the start of each section should show which sections performed or invoked this logic.

Structured programming techniques, when kept simple (KISS), make program development, debugging, and maintenance easier and will be used for all program examples. As you develop your program code, keep ease of maintenance and future reusability in mind. Program code which is used in one program is often reused in others. Do not reinvent a program each time you write one!

10

THE LINKED PROGRAM

When one program links to another, the original program remains and the linked program is loaded into main storage. Since linked programs tie-up more main storage, you should limit their use. The journal-posting program discussed in this chapter is a linked program. It utilizes the COMMAREA for passing data to the linked program and for returning data to the linking program.

A couple of new commands will be introduced—ASKTIME and the file control command WRITE, which will be covered in more detail in Chap. 11. BLL pointers will be presented and explained.

Many systems require the posting of audit records when transactions change the contents of a record. Rather than having each transaction write its own audit record, one program may be designated as a journal-posting program which writes audit records for several files. Journal program JRNLPOST (Fig. 10-2) is an example of a linked program. This program will post audit transactions for the following files: vendor master, purchase order master, and item master. Programs in this book will write a before-and/or after-record for the following file maintenance transactions: changes, additions, and deletions.

Linking Routine

An audit record can be written only for designated significant field changes or whenever any field in a record changes. *All* changes, additions, and deletions in the vendor master file maintenance programs will write an audit record. Change programs will write a before-and after-record, additions an after-record, and deletions a before-record.

Figure 10-1 contains the section of program code which will be used to invoke the journal-posting program JRNLPOST. The record layout for JOURNAL-RECORD can be found in the copy library [see App. B, JRNLRECD].

```
0001 E121-POST-JOURNAL-RECORD   SECTION.
0002******************************************************************
0003*    POST JOURNAL ENTRY - LINK TO JOURNAL PROGRAM 'JRNLPOST'    *
0004******************************************************************
0005*
0006     MOVE 'VM'                   TO   JR-PREFIX.
0007     MOVE VENDOR-MASTER-RECORD   TO   JR-RECORD-DATA.
0008     MOVE SPACES                 TO   JR-PASSWORD.
0009*
0010     EXEC CICS LINK
0011            PROGRAM    ('JRNLPOST')
0012            COMMAREA   (JOURNAL-RECORD)
0013            LENGTH     (524)
0014     END-EXEC.
0015*
0016 E121-EXIT.
0017     EXIT.
```

Figure 10-1   LINKing Program Section.

A B (before) is moved to JR-TYPE in JOURNAL-RECORD by maintenance programs immediately after reading a record for update and prior to a change or delete being executed. An A (after) is moved to JR-TYPE in JOURNAL-RECORD immediately after rewriting a changed record or after writing an added record to the vendor master file. Chapter 11 will discuss all file control commands. After moving an A or B to JR-TYPE, all maintenance programs perform E121-POST-JOURNAL-RECORD.

E121-POST-JOURNAL-RECORD

This section formats the journal record prior to executing a LINK command. Depending upon your installation's security requirements, a password might have to be entered on the maintenance screen or in a prior program. The password is then passed to the journal-posting program.

The LINK command invokes the program JRNLPOST, which is by definition at a lower logical level. The linking program remains in main storage while the linked program, if necessary, is loaded into main storage. Task number remains the same. JOURNAL-RECORD in COMMAREA and its length (524) are passed to JRNLPOST.

Journal-Posting Program

Figure 10-2 is the linked program JRNLPOST. The working-storage section contains the journal record layout which is found in App. B.

Linkage Section

DFHCOMMAREA is defined in the linkage section as a 524-byte field. This is the length passed by the invoking maintenance program. DFHCOMMAREA, which is moved to JOURNAL-RECORD upon entering the program, could contain subfields corresponding to JOURNAL-RECORD fields, if no data were required to be returned to the linking program. JRNLPOST issues a WRITE command from the journal record. Main storage of a record which is written from the linkage section is not available after a WRITE command is issued.

BLL Cells definition. BLL cells are pointers which must immediately follow DFHCOMMAREA in the linkage section. The filler following BLL-CELLS is automatically set to point to the BLL cell list itself. Each labeled 02 field under FILLER can be set to point to the corresponding 01 field which follows the BLL cell list. This program will set BLL-SEQ-TABLE-ADDRESS to point

---

Figure 10-2 LINKed Program JRNLPOST.

```
0001 IDENTIFICATION DIVISION.
0002 PROGRAM-ID. JRNLPOST.
0003 REMARKS.
0004************************************************************************
0005*                    JOURNAL POSTING PROGRAM                         *
0006*      POST A JOURNAL RECORD FOR ITEMS PASSED TO THIS PROGRAM        *
0007*          IN THE COMMAREA BY A LINK FROM ANOTHER PROGRAM.           *
0008************************************************************************
0009 ENVIRONMENT DIVISION.
0010 DATA DIVISION.
0011*
0012 WORKING-STORAGE SECTION.
0013*
0014 01   WS-PROGRAM-FIELDS.
0015      05  FILLER        PIC X(22)   VALUE 'JRNLPOST - START OF WS'.
0016*
0017 01   JOURNAL-RECORD   COPY   JRNLRECD.
0018*
0019 01   END-OF-WORKING-STORAGE   PIC X(15)   VALUE 'END WS JRNLPOST'.
0020*
0021 LINKAGE SECTION.
0022*
0023 01   DFHCOMMAREA            PIC X(524).
0024*
0025 01   BLL-CELLS.
0026      02  FILLER                PIC S9(8)   COMP.
0027      02  BLL-SEQ-TABLE-ADDRESS PIC S9(8)   COMP.
0028*
0029 01   T053-SEQUENCE-TABLE.
0030      05  T053-SEQUENCE-NUMBER  PIC S9(5)   COMP-3.
0031*
0032 PROCEDURE DIVISION.
0033************************************************************************
0034*               PROGRAM STRUCTURE IS:                                *
0035*                  AA00-MAINLINE                                      *
0036*                     B000-LOAD-SEQUENCE-TABLE                        *
0037*                     C000-FORMAT-JOURNAL-RECORD                      *
0038*                     D000-WRITE-JOURNAL-RECORD                       *
0039************************************************************************
0040*
0041 AA00-MAINLINE  SECTION.
0042*
0043*    SERVICE RELOAD BLL-CELLS.
0044*
0045     MOVE DFHCOMMAREA  TO   JOURNAL-RECORD.
0046*
0047     PERFORM B000-LOAD-SEQUENCE-TABLE.
0048*
0049     PERFORM C000-FORMAT-JOURNAL-RECORD.
0050*
0051     PERFORM D000-WRITE-JOURNAL-RECORD.
0052*
0053     MOVE JOURNAL-RECORD  TO  DFHCOMMAREA.
0054*
0055* RETURN TO LINKED FROM PROGRAM
0056     EXEC CICS RETURN
0057     END-EXEC.
0058*
```

Figure 10-2 (*Continued*)

```
0059 B000-LOAD-SEQUENCE-TABLE  SECTION.
0060***********************************************************
0061*        SET ADDRESS OF MAIN STORAGE RESIDENT TABLE       *
0062*              PERFORMED FROM:  AA00-MAINLINE              *
0063***********************************************************
0064*
0065     EXEC CICS LOAD
0066              PROGRAM ('T053JRSQ')
0067              SET    (BLL-SEQ-TABLE-ADDRESS)
0068     END-EXEC.
0069*
0070*    SERVICE RELOAD T053-SEQUENCE-TABLE.
0071*
0072 B000-EXIT.
0073     EXIT.
0074*
0075 C000-FORMAT-JOURNAL-RECORD  SECTION.
0076***********************************************************
0077*        FORMAT JOURNAL RECORD - PRIOR TO WRITING         *
0078*              PERFORMED FROM:  AA00-MAINLINE              *
0079***********************************************************
0080*
0081     MOVE T053-SEQUENCE-NUMBER  TO  JR-SEQUENCE-NUMBER.
0082     ADD 1                      TO  T053-SEQUENCE-NUMBER.
0083*
0084     EXEC CICS ASKTIME
0085     END-EXEC.
0086*
0087     MOVE EIBDATE   TO  JR-EIBDATE.
0088     MOVE EIBTIME   TO  JR-EIBTIME.
0089     MOVE EIBTRMID  TO  JR-EIBTRMID.
0090*
0091 C000-EXIT.
0092     EXIT.
0093*
0094 D000-WRITE-JOURNAL-RECORD  SECTION.
0095***********************************************************
0096*        ADD A 'BEFORE' OR 'AFTER' JOURNAL RECORD         *
0097*              PERFORMED FROM:  AA00-MAINLINE              *
0098*     INCLUDING SEQUENCE NUMBER AS PART OF KEY ELIMINATES  *
0099* POSSIBILITY OF DUPREC HANDLE CONDITION ON FOLLOWING WRITE *
0100***********************************************************
0101*
0102     EXEC CICS WRITE
0103              DATASET ('JOURNAL1')
0104              FROM    (JOURNAL-RECORD)
0105              RIDFLD  (JR-KEY)
0106     END-EXEC.
0107*
0108 D000-EXIT.
0109     EXIT.
```

to T053-SEQUENCE-TABLE. BLL-cell usage will be explained further as we examine the procedure division of JRNLPOST.

Procedure Division

The program structure is defined as comments at the start of the procedure division.

AA00-MAINLINE. The SERVICE RELOAD statement must be issued at the start of the program to ensure proper linkage-section addressability if your installation uses a Cobol compiler which has the optimization feature. The SERVICE RELOAD statement should be issued whenever the address of a BLL cell is changed. The SERVICE RELOAD statement is shown commented out at points in programs where it should be included if your installation uses the optimization feature.

DFHCOMMAREA, which contains the journal record data passed from the linking program, is moved to JOURNAL-RECORD. A sequence table is loaded. The journal record is then formatted and written to the journal file. JOURNAL-RECORD is then moved to DFHCOMMAREA and a RETURN command, without TRANSID, is executed in order to return to the higher-logical-level linking program. Control will return to the statement following the LINK command (E121-EXIT) in Fig. 10-1. Any JOURNAL-RECORD fields which were changed by JRNLPOST are available in the working-storage communications area, JOURNAL-RECORD, of the linking program, *not* in DFHCOMMAREA.

B000-LOAD-SEQUENCE-TABLE. The LOAD command sets a BLL address pointer to the journal sequence table (T053JRSQ), in the linkage section. BLL-SEQ-TABLE-ADDRESS will have addressability to T053-SEQUENCE-TABLE. T053-SEQUENCE-NUMBER can be referenced and changed. The sequence table is defined in the PPT as a main-storage resident table. For nonresident tables, it is good practice to release the table as soon as it is no longer required.

The PGMIDERR handle condition will be invoked if T053JRSQ is not in the PPT or is disabled.

BLL Cells usage. BLL cells are defined, as shown in the linkage section, as binary full words. Each BLL cell can address only 4096 bytes of main storage. If a table exceeds 4096 bytes, the additional positions must be addressed in multiples of 4096, even if fewer than 4096 additional bytes are needed. Figure 10-3 illustrates how this works. Table 2 requires 9606 bytes or two full blocks of 4096 plus one partial block. Three BLL cells are required to address this table as shown. The LOAD command addresses the first 4096 bytes; then 4096 is added to the first address in order to set the address pointer to the next 4096 bytes. Finally, 4096 is added to the second address to set the address pointer to the third block of 4096. I do not show service reloads in Fig. 10-3. If your system uses the optimization feature, you would have to issue three SERVICE RELOAD commands, one after the LOAD command and one after each add of 4096 which establishes addressability.

C000-FORMAT-JOURNAL-RECORD. This section formats the journal record prior to writing it. The journal record's data is passed in DFHCOMMAREA from the linking program. When a task is initiated, the EIB is established with initial values. In a long-running task, it may be desirable to refresh the value of certain EIB fields such as EIBDATE and EIBTIME. Most likely, EIBDATE won't change, but EIBTIME might. The ASKTIME command updates the fields EIBTIME and EIBDATE when it is issued. Its format is

```
                    ┌──────────────────────────────────────┐
                    │                                      │
                    │    EXEC CICS ASKTIME                 │
                    │    END-EXEC.                         │
                    │                                      │
                    └──────────────────────────────────────┘
```

See FORMATTIME in Chap. 20 for the ABSTIME option of ASKTIME.

The journal record's key consists of EIBDATE, EIBTIME, and a sequence number. The sequence number is obtained from the sequence table and is incremented by 1 each time it is used. Sequence number is needed as part of the key to ensure that no multiple record keys occur. It is possible for the same task to pass the identical date and time to this program. For instance, the before- and after-record posting of a changed record could occur in a program before time had a chance to change. The EIB TeRMinal IDentification (EIBTRMID) field is moved to the journal record as a data element for audit reporting.

The journal file can be closed off line and its data written to another file by a batch program. Journal-file records can be deleted, and the next day's processing can begin with an empty file. The "stripped" journal file can be used for audit reporting and saved if required.

D000-WRITE-JOURNAL-RECORD. The journal record formatted in section C000- FORMAT-JOURNAL-RECORD is written out to a file called JOURNAL1. The WRITE command will be covered in Chap. 11, "File Control."

```
0001 LINKAGE SECTION.
0002*
0003 01   DFHCOMMAREA                      PIC X.
0004*
0005 01   BLL-CELLS.
0006      02   BLL-CELLS-ADDRESS           PIC S9(8)    COMP.
0007      02   BLL-TABLE-1-ADDRESS         PIC S9(8)    COMP.
0008      02   BLL-TABLE-2-ADDRESS-1       PIC S9(8)    COMP.
0009      02   BLL-TABLE-2-ADDRESS-2       PIC S9(8)    COMP.
0010      02   BLL-TABLE-2-ADDRESS-3       PIC S9(8)    COMP.
0011      02   BLL-TABLE-3-ADDRESS         PIC S9(8)    COMP.
0012*
0013 01   TABLE-1                          PIC X(10).
0014*
0015 01   TABLE-2                          PIC X(9606).
0016*
0017 01   TABLE-3                          PIC X(4000).
0018*
0019*
0020 PROCEDURE DIVISION.
0021         .
0022         .
0023         .
0024      EXEC CICS LOAD
0025           PROGRAM ('T002BIGT')
0026           SET     (BLL-TABLE-2-ADDRESS-1)
0027      END-EXEC.
0028*
0029      ADD 4096  BLL-TABLE-2-ADDRESS-1
0030           GIVING BLL-TABLE-2-ADDRESS-2.
0031*
0032      ADD 4096  BLL-TABLE-2-ADDRESS-2
0033           GIVING BLL-TABLE-2-ADDRESS-3.
0034         .
0035         .
0036         .
```

Figure 10-3 Establishing BLL Addressability for Large Tables.

SUMMARY

Linked programs should be used only when necessary, since they tie up more main storage than do independent programs. The journal program was presented to show how the linked program is used when required. The LINK and ASKTIME commands were used and discussed. BLL cells were used, and an illustration showed how to establish addressability to large tables.

11

FILE CONTROL

File control seems to be one of the easier concepts for CICS programmers to understand, especially those who have worked on batch systems which use virtual storage access methods (VSAM). Knowledge of VSAM is helpful but not required in order to understand this chapter. You should be familiar with the concept of random access file processing in order to gain maximum benefit from the material presented.

This chapter addresses file control using VSAM key-sequenced data sets (VSAM KSDS), the file structure used for all examples in this book. A VSAM file used for CICS must have at least one record loaded to initialize the file, even if the single record is later deleted. Files are generally opened when CICS is initialized and closed when CICS is shut down; therefore, programs do not need to open or close files. Files must *never* be opened or closed in a CICS application program. The handle condition NOTOPEN will be invoked by most file control commands if a file is closed. You can test for this condition or allow the task to ABEND if a file is not open. I generally do not test for this condition because it should not normally occur.

All CICS files must be defined in a table called the file control table (FCT). Some FCT entries are: data set name, record size, and permissible file access and update functions. The FCT eliminates the need for programmers to define those entries contained in the table. The programmer generally needs only to specify data set name, key field, and the working-storage name of a record's I/O area. For program examples, all required entries are assumed to have been made in the FCT for files containing fixed-length records. VENDMAST and JOURNAL1 are the two files which will be used, and they permit the use of all file control commands required for examples in this book. The FCT is generally maintained by the system programming staff.

Opening and Closing Files

Files used by CICS are usually opened when CICS is started up by operations personnel at the beginning of the day. CICS files must be closed if they need to be changed by a batch program since they cannot be updated by both CICS and batch systems at the same time. Occasionally users on a test system get an indicative message that files have been closed; they are most likely needed by a batch program. Whenever practical, data processing gives notice to users before closing and reopening files.

File Control Commands

The most common options used with file control commands are discussed. The commands covered are

1. READ command—Read a file for inquiry or access without update intended.
2. READ FOR UPDATE—Read a file with the intent of changing and updating a record.
3. WRITE—Write a new record to a file.
4. REWRITE—Rewrite a record read for update.
5. UNLOCK—Release a record read for update if processing indicates that updating is not required.
6. DELETE—Remove a record from the file.
7. STARTBR—Establish a starting point for a browse (sequential reads against a file).
8. READNEXT—Read the next record after a STARTBR or after a prior READNEXT command.
9. READPREV—Read the preceding record after a STARTBR or after a prior READPREV command.
10. ENDBR—Terminate a browse function initiated by the STARTBR command.
11. RESETBR—End the previous browse and start a new browse.

Options Common to Many File Control Commands

- DATASET (FCT entry)—The FCT entry uses up to seven alphanumeric characters for disk operating systems (DOS) and up to eight alphanumeric characters for operating systems (OS). Examples in this book will use eight-character FCT names. FCT entry is enclosed in single quotes, for instance, DATASET ('VENDMAST').

- INTO (WS-RECORD-I-O-AREA) / FROM (WS-RECORD-I-O-AREA)—Program-defined working-storage area used to hold your program's input and/or output area.

- RIDFLD (WS-RECORD-KEY)—RIDFLD (Record IDentification FieLD) contains the key of the record to be operated upon. This field may be defined as part of the record's key or it may be defined separately in working storage.

READ Command

The READ command reads a record into a record area defined in working storage. After a successful read, the record's data is available in working storage.
The READ command format is

```
EXEC CICS READ
        DATASET (FCT entry)
        INTO    (WS-RECORD-I-O-AREA)
        RIDFLD  (WS-RECORD-KEY)
END-EXEC.
```

- Handle Conditions—Record NOT FouND (NOTFND) is the only handle condition I generally check for when using the READ command.

WRITE Command

The WRITE command writes a record *from* an area defined in working storage. The required data must be moved to the working-storage area of the record to be added, prior to issuing a WRITE command. When a write is successful, the record will have been added to the file.
The WRITE command format is

```
EXEC CICS WRITE
        DATASET (FCT entry)
        FROM    (WS-RECORD-I-O-AREA)
        RIDFLD  (WS-RECORD-KEY)
END-EXEC.
```

- Handle Conditions—Record already exists on the file [DUPlicate RECord (DUPREC)]is the only handle condition I generally check for when using the WRITE command. NOSPACE occurs when a file to which a record is being added is full.

READ FOR UPDATE Command

The READ FOR UPDATE version of the READ command reads a record into an area defined in working storage, with the intent of updating the record. Normally, fields to be updated will have new data moved into the I/O area of the record to be changed, before the record is rewritten (see REWRITE command below). After a successful read, the record's data is available in the working-storage area (WS-RECORD-I-O-AREA).

A record READ FOR UPDATE should be read as close to the UPDATE command as possible in order to prevent file lockout of other tasks. If it is determined that a record READ FOR UPDATE will not be rewritten, issue the UNLOCK command as soon as it is determined that the record will not be rewritten (see "Exclusive Control" below).

The format of the READ FOR UPDATE option of the READ command is identical to the regular READ command, except that the option UPDATE must be specified.

```
EXEC CICS READ
        DATASET (FCT entry)
        INTO      (WS-RECORD-I-O-AREA)
        RIDFLD    (WS-RECORD-KEY)
        UPDATE
END-EXEC.
```

• Handle Conditions—NOTFND is the only handle condition I generally check for when using the READ FOR UPDATE command.

REWRITE Command

The REWRITE command writes a record *from* an area defined in working storage. Prior to issuing a REWRITE command, the required data must be moved to the working-storage area of the record to be changed. When a rewrite is successful, the record's new data replaces the old data in the designated record. A rewrite will only be successful against a record which was found when read for update.

The REWRITE command format is

```
EXEC CICS REWRITE
        DATASET (FCT entry)
        FROM      (WS-RECORD-I-O-AREA)
END-EXEC.
```

• Handle Conditions—I do not test for any handle conditions on the rewrite. The handle condition INVREQ will occur if a rewrite is attempted against a record *not* read for update.

Exclusive Control

File control gives exclusive control to the control interval which contains a record read for update. A control interval is a block of records with sequentially adjacent keys. Exclusive control prevents reading of the same record, or any record in the control interval for update, until the record read for update has been rewritten. A lockout occurs when a task tries to read another record for update or attempts to add a record before a record read for update in the same control interval is rewritten, deleted, or unlocked. Sometimes it is determined that a record which was read for update will not be changed. When the programmer can determine the point at which a record will not need to be rewritten, exclusive control should be released by issuing the UNLOCK command. Rewriting or deleting a record read for update as well as terminating a task releases exclusive control of the control interval.

Release exclusive control of a record read for update before reading another record in the same file for update. Failure to do this could cause a lockout in the same program. It is good practice to read files which may be updated in the same sequence in all programs in order to prevent a lockout from occurring between two different tasks. Try to limit the number of programs which can directly update a file.

UNLOCK Command

The UNLOCK command should be used in programs which contain much processing, after it is known that a record will not be rewritten. Exclusive control is released by issuing the UNLOCK command.

The UNLOCK command format is

```
EXEC CICS UNLOCK
          DATASET (FCT entry)
END-EXEC.
```

DELETE Command

Although it is not necessary, I recommend reading a record for update prior to deletion. You might display the record in an inquiry format with a message DO YOU WISH TO DELETE THIS RECORD? To delete the record you might have the terminal operator key in YES and press a designated AID key or some similar action. The common practice is to write the record to a journal file which can be used later offline to print a batch-processing listing of transactions which updated the file. A record read prior to deletion must be read with the UPDATE option.

The format for the DELETE command when read first is

```
EXEC CICS DELETE
          DATASET (FCT entry)
END-EXEC.
```

Only the DATASET option is required when the file is read for update prior to issuing the DELETE command. If the record is *not* read prior to deletion, the RIDFLD option must be included as follows.

```
EXEC CICS DELETE
          DATASET (FCT entry)
          RIDFLD   (WS-RECORD-KEY)
END-EXEC.
```

You have to move the key of the record to be deleted to WS-RECORD-KEY prior to issuing the delete.

• Handle Conditions—I generally read a record first before deleting it and do not test for any handle conditions. INVREQ could occur on this delete if no previous read for update had been executed. NOTFND could occur for the delete without a preceding READ FOR UPDATE, if WS-RECORD-KEY was not on the file.

FILE BROWSE Commands and Considerations

Some applications require a program to start at a specified item in the file and then to display records sequentially beginning from that point. A record cannot be updated using browse commands; it must first be read for update. A vendor file could be in alphabetical sequence by vendor code prefix; assume the code is of the format A-9999-9, with the first character being A through Z. The next four digits could position the vendor alphabetically within the alphabetic prefix and the last digit might be used for vendor location. The terminal operator may want to search the file for vendors which have a name starting with the letter M. The browse could be initiated by entering vendor code M00000 or just M. The program would move the entered vendor code to WS-RECORD-KEY and issue the browse command to establish a position at that record, or at the first record with a greater key value.

STARTBR Command

The STARTBR (START BRowse) command sets the beginning position for a browse. The READNEXT and READPREV commands discussed below will read records sequentially, starting at the position established by the STARTBR command. *No record is read* by the STARTBR command; a starting point in the file is established for the first READNEXT or READPREV command.

The STARTBR command format is

```
EXEC CICS STARTBR
          DATASET (FCT entry)
          RIDFLD    (WS-RECORD-KEY)
          GTEQ
END-EXEC.
```

Low-values in RIDFLD will position the browse at the beginning of the file. High-values will position it at the end of the file.

- GTEQ—The Greater Than or EQual to (GTEQ) operand of the STARTBR command specifies that if the RIDFLD record key is not found, the browse is to set the file starting point at the next sequential record. EQUAL is assumed if GTEQ is not specified.

- Handle Conditions—NOTFND will occur if GTEQ is not specified and an exact hit is not made for the record in RIDFLD. NOTFND also occurs if GTEQ is included and the record specified in RIDFLD has a key which is greater than the last key in the file. INVREQ will occur if a STARTBR command is issued against a file not defined in the FCT with the browse option.

Browse Inefficiencies

Browse operations are inefficient because many records have to be read from a file. Limit a browse by providing the ability to reset its starting key. Files which are browsed frequently should have a larger file blocking factor in order to minimize the number of required file accesses. A browse against a file with a small blocking factor will be less efficient because a greater number of accesses will be required.

READNEXT Command

The format of the READNEXT command is similar to that of the READ command. The first time READNEXT is executed following a STARTBR command, the record retrieved is the record positioned at by the STARTBR command. Succeeding READNEXT executions retrieve records sequentially from that position in the file. WS-RECORD-KEY is updated with the entire record key each time a READNEXT command is executed. Records in the file could be skipped by changing WS-RECORD-KEY to a key greater than that of the last record read. This is called "skip sequential processing" and is not frequently used.

The READNEXT command format is

```
EXEC CICS READNEXT
        DATASET    (FCT entry)
        INTO       (WS-RECORD-I-O-AREA)
        RIDFLD     (WS-RECORD-KEY)
END-EXEC.
```

• Handle Conditions—ENDFILE occurs when the end of a file is reached. NOTFND may occur if, in the same task, WS-RECORD-KEY is set to a key lower than the last key read. If this occurs, the program should execute a RESETBR or an ENDBR command (discussed later in this chapter). INVREQ occurs if no preceding STARTBR command was executed.

Generic Search

A generic (partial key) search can be used with the STARTBR command. The generic search requires the move of the generic key to the first portion of WS-RECORD-KEY and the specification of the KEYLENGTH and GENERIC options on the STARTBR command.

The format of the STARTBR command with the GENERIC option is

```
EXEC CICS STARTBR
        DATASET    (FCT entry)
        RIDFLD     (WS-RECORD-KEY)
        GTEQ
        KEYLENGTH (GENERIC-KEY-LENGTH)
        GENERIC
END-EXEC.
```

• GTEQ—This operand specifies that if the RIDFLD record key is not found, the browse is to set the file starting point at the next sequential record.

• KEYLENGTH (GENERIC-KEY-LENGTH)—This is a working-storage entry defined as a halfword binary field. The length of the portion of the key to be searched for must be moved to this field prior to execution of the GENERIC option of the STARTBR command. A generic STARTBR command will establish position at the start of the file if KEYLENGTH (0) is specified.

- GENERIC—This statement must be included along with KEYLENGTH for a generic search.
- Handle Conditions—NOTFND will occur if GTEQ is omitted and an exact hit is not made for the record in RIDFLD. NOTFND also occurs if GTEQ is included and the record specified in RIDFLD contains a key greater than the last key in the file. INVREQ will occur if a STARTBR command is issued against a file not defined in the FCT with the browse option.

READPREV Command

The READPREV command functions similarly to the READNEXT command, following the execution of a STARTBR command. The first time READPREV is executed following a STARTBR command, the record retrieved is the record at which position was established by the STARTBR command. Succeeding READPREV executions retrieve records containing keys sequentially lower than the previous record. WS-RECORD-KEY is updated with the entire record key each time a READPREV command is executed. READPREV cannot be issued following a browse initiated with the GENERIC option of the STARTBR command. If a READNEXT command is followed by a READPREV command, the READPREV reads the same record read by the READNEXT. Issue another READPREV to read the desired record. Skip sequential processing cannot be used with a backward browse.

The READPREV command format is

```
EXEC CICS READPREV
          DATASET   (FCT entry)
          INTO      (WS-RECORD-I-O-AREA)
          RIDFLD    (WS-RECORD-KEY)
END-EXEC.
```

- Handle Conditions—ENDFILE occurs when the "beginning" of the file is reached. INVREQ occurs if no preceding STARTBR command was executed or if the STARTBR command had a GENERIC option specified. NOTFND will occur if an immediately preceding STARTBR did not get an EQUAL hit.

End Browse (ENDBR) Command

The ENDBR command is issued in order to terminate a browse. Executing a new STARTBR command against the same file in a task without having ended a previous browse will result in an INVREQ handle condition. Terminate all browses with the ENDBR command as soon as possible.

The ENDBR command format is

```
EXEC CICS ENDBR
            DATASET (FCT entry)
END-EXEC.
```

- Handle Conditions—INVREQ occurs if no preceding STARTBR command was executed.

Reset Browse (RESETBR) Command

The RESETBR command resets a browse to the original or to a new browse starting point. It has the same effect as an ENDBR command followed by a STARTBR command. RESETBR commands could be used to skip sequentially through a file.

The RESETBR command format is similar to STARTBR,

```
EXEC CICS RESETBR
            DATASET (FCT entry)
            RIDFLD   (WS-RECORD-KEY)
            GTEQ
END-EXEC.
```

Low-values in RIDFLD will position the browse at the beginning of the file. High-values will position it at the end of the file.

- GTEQ—This operand of the RESETBR command specifies that if the RID-FLD record key is not found, the browse is to set the file starting point at the next sequential record. EQUAL is assumed if GTEQ is not specified.

- Handle Conditions—NOTFND will occur if GTEQ is not specified and an exact hit is not made for the record in RIDFLD. NOTFND also occurs if GTEQ is included and if the record specified in RIDFLD has a key which is greater than the last key in the file. INVREQ will occur if a RESETBR command is issued against a file not defined in the FCT with the browse option.

SUMMARY

File control commands make it easy for the application programmer to read, write, and update files in a CICS system. The commands covered were READ, WRITE, REWRITE, UNLOCK, DELETE, STARTBR, READNEXT, READPREV, ENDBR, and RESETBR. Programmers who have an understanding of random-access methods generally master file control commands quickly. Exclusive control was discussed, and suggestions for preventing lockout were presented.

Program examples in succeeding chapters will cover many of the commands presented and make the use of file control commands easier to understand.

12

THE INQUIRY PROGRAM

An inquiry program is one of the first programs you should write after an online file is created. This is not a maintenance program, but I include it on many maintenance menus. Inquiries generally list most fields contained on the record being displayed. Inquiry and maintenance programs are helpful during the testing stage of a system and are usually necessary once the system is running in a production environment.

Control and detail maps are used for the inquiry program. The control map, shown in Fig. 2-4, requires the terminal operator to key in a vendor code and press ENTER in order to display the inquiry detail map. The operator also has the option of transferring control to the vendor file browse program, of returning to the vendor file maintenance submenu (see Fig. 6-3), or of ending the session. The vendor file inquiry detail map shown in Fig. 2-6 is displayed when the operator enters a vendor code on the control screen and then presses ENTER. The detail screen displays all fields contained on the vendor's record. The operator can view the vendor's data and then press ENTER in order to return to the control screen. The detail screen also permits the operator to return to the submenu or to end the session.

BMS Maps

Figures 12-1 and 12-2 show the BMS maps for the control and detail maps shown in Figs. 2-4 and 2-6, respectively. The DFHMSD and DFHMDI macros are the same as those on previous maps except for the mapset and mapname labels.

BMS Control Map

All control map fields have ASKIP attributes, except for vendor code, which is UNPROT. The first vendor code entry field, MCVCOD1, has IC specified as part of its attribute. This will result in the cursor being positioned under this field if the command-level interpreter (CECI, discussed in Chap. 6) is used to test the physical map. This program specifies CURSOR as part of its SEND MAP commands and uses symbolic cursor positioning. Stopper fields are not required following BMS map labels MCVCOD1 and MCVCOD2 because the following hyphens have ASKIP attributes. MCVCOD3 is followed by a stopper field, an unlabeled 1-byte ASKIP attribute in POS=(07,51).

BMS Detail Map

All inquiry detail map attributes are defined as ASKIP. All BMS maps could be generated with ASKIP attributes defined for every field. Programs can

Figure 12-1 Vendor File Inquiry BMS Control Map.

```
          PRINT NOGEN
POVMIQ1   DFHMSD TYPE=MAP,                                    X
                 CTRL=(FREEKB,FRSET),                         X
                 LANG=COBOL,                                  X
                 MODE=INOUT,                                  X
                 TERM=3270,                                   X
                 TIOAPFX=YES
*
MAPPOVC   DFHMDI LINE=01,                                     X
                 COLUMN=01,                                   X
                 SIZE=(24,80)
*
          DFHMDF POS=(01,01),                                 X
                 ATTRB=ASKIP,                                 X
                 LENGTH=05,                                   X
                 INITIAL='DATE:'
*
MCDATE    DFHMDF POS=(01,07),                                 X
                 ATTRB=ASKIP,                                 X
                 LENGTH=08
*
          DFHMDF POS=(01,27),                                 X
                 ATTRB=ASKIP,                                 X
                 LENGTH=25,                                   X
                 INITIAL='ABC MANUFACTURING COMPANY'
*
          DFHMDF POS=(01,72),                                 X
                 ATTRB=ASKIP,                                 X
                 LENGTH=07,                                   X
                 INITIAL='POVMIQ1'
*
          DFHMDF POS=(02,01),                                 X
                 ATTRB=ASKIP,                                 X
                 LENGTH=05,                                   X
                 INITIAL='TIME:'
*
MCTIME    DFHMDF POS=(02,07),                                 X
                 ATTRB=ASKIP,                                 X
                 LENGTH=08
*
          DFHMDF POS=(02,26),                                 X
                 ATTRB=ASKIP,                                 X
                 LENGTH=27,                                   X
                 INITIAL='VENDOR FILE INQUIRY CONTROL'
*
          DFHMDF POS=(07,25),                                 X
                 ATTRB=ASKIP,                                 X
                 LENGTH=12,                                   X
                 INITIAL='VENDOR CODE:'
*
MCVCOD1   DFHMDF POS=(07,38),                                 X
                 ATTRB=(UNPROT,IC),                           X
                 LENGTH=01
*
```

Figure 12-1 *(Continued)*

```
              DFHMDF POS=(07,40),                                    X
                     ATTRB=ASKIP,                                    X
                     LENGTH=01,                                      X
                     INITIAL='-'
*
MCVCOD2       DFHMDF POS=(07,42),                                    X
                     ATTRB=UNPROT,                                   X
                     LENGTH=04
*
              DFHMDF POS=(07,47),                                    X
                     ATTRB=ASKIP,                                    X
                     LENGTH=01,                                      X
                     INITIAL='-'
*
MCVCOD3       DFHMDF POS=(07,49),                                    X
                     ATTRB=UNPROT,                                   X
                     LENGTH=01
*
              DFHMDF POS=(07,51),                                    X
                     ATTRB=ASKIP,                                    X
                     LENGTH=01
*
              DFHMDF POS=(12,19),                                    X
                     ATTRB=ASKIP,                                    X
                     LENGTH=40,                                      X
                     INITIAL='1. FOR VENDOR FILE INQUIRY - PRESS ENTER'
*
              DFHMDF POS=(14,19),                                    X
                     ATTRB=ASKIP,                                    X
                     LENGTH=38,                                      X
                     INITIAL='2. TO BROWSE VENDOR FILE    - PRESS PF4'
*
              DFHMDF POS=(16,19),                                    X
                     ATTRB=ASKIP,                                    X
                     LENGTH=38,                                      X
                     INITIAL='3. TO RETURN TO MENU        - PRESS PF5'
*
              DFHMDF POS=(18,19),                                    X
                     ATTRB=ASKIP,                                    X
                     LENGTH=40,                                      X
                     INITIAL='4. TO END SESSION           - PRESS CLEAR'
*
MCMESSG       DFHMDF POS=(24,01),                                    X
                     ATTRB=ASKIP,                                    X
                     LENGTH=79
*
              DFHMSD TYPE=FINAL
              END
```

control attributes by modifying them prior to a send which includes the symbolic map. No IC attribute is defined on the BMS map because when the map is sent, the cursor is to be set at POS=(01,01). The cursor defaults to this position when the map is sent, unless CURSOR is specified on a send which includes the symbolic map, and −1 is moved to a map length field.

User-Friendly Symbolic Maps

User-friendly symbolic maps which correspond to the BMS-generated maps are shown in the copy library (App. B, members MAPVMCTL and MAPVDTL1). Each field defined on the BMS map has a corresponding user-friendly map field (see Chap. 6).

Figure 12-2   Vendor File Inquiry BMS Detail Map.

```
          PRINT NOGEN
POVMIQ2   DFHMSD TYPE=MAP,                                              X
                 CTRL=(FREEKB,FRSET),                                   X
                 LANG=COBOL,                                            X
                 MODE=INOUT,                                            X
                 TERM=3270,                                             X
                 TIOAPFX=YES
*
MAPPOVD   DFHMDI LINE=01,                                               X
                 COLUMN=01,                                             X
                 SIZE=(24,80)
*
          DFHMDF POS=(01,01),                                          X
                 ATTRB=ASKIP,                                          X
                 LENGTH=05,                                            X
                 INITIAL='DATE:'
*
MDDATE    DFHMDF POS=(01,07),                                          X
                 ATTRB=ASKIP,                                          X
                 LENGTH=08
*
          DFHMDF POS=(01,27),                                          X
                 ATTRB=ASKIP,                                          X
                 LENGTH=25,                                            X
                 INITIAL='ABC MANUFACTURING COMPANY'
*
          DFHMDF POS=(01,72),                                          X
                 ATTRB=ASKIP,                                          X
                 LENGTH=07,                                            X
                 INITIAL='POVMIQ2'
*
          DFHMDF POS=(02,01),                                          X
                 ATTRB=ASKIP,                                          X
                 LENGTH=05,                                            X
                 INITIAL='TIME:'
*
MDTIME    DFHMDF POS=(02,07),                                          X
                 ATTRB=ASKIP,                                          X
                 LENGTH=08
*
          DFHMDF POS=(02,30),                                          X
                 ATTRB=ASKIP,                                          X
                 LENGTH=19,                                            X
                 INITIAL='VENDOR FILE INQUIRY'
*
          DFHMDF POS=(04,01),                                          X
                 ATTRB=ASKIP,                                          X
                 LENGTH=12,                                            X
                 INITIAL='VENDOR CODE:'
*
MDVNDCD   DFHMDF POS=(04,14),                                          X
                 ATTRB=ASKIP,                                          X
                 LENGTH=08
*
          DFHMDF POS=(05,08),                                          X
                 ATTRB=ASKIP,                                          X
                 LENGTH=05,                                            X
                 INITIAL='NAME:'
*
MDVNDNM   DFHMDF POS=(05,14),                                          X
                 ATTRB=ASKIP,                                          X
                 LENGTH=25
*
          DFHMDF POS=(05,45),                                          X
                 ATTRB=ASKIP,                                          X
                 LENGTH=06,                                            X
                 INITIAL='PHONE:'
*
          DFHMDF POS=(05,54),                                          X
                 ATTRB=ASKIP,                                          X
                 LENGTH=01,                                            X
                 INITIAL='('
*
MDAREAC   DFHMDF POS=(05,56),                                          X
                 ATTRB=ASKIP,                                          X
                 LENGTH=03
*
          DFHMDF POS=(05,60),                                          X
                 ATTRB=ASKIP,                                          X
                 LENGTH=01,                                            X
                 INITIAL=')'
```

Figure 12-2 *(Continued)*

```
*
MDPHON1    DFHMDF POS=(05,62),                                          X
                  ATTRB=ASKIP,                                          X
                  LENGTH=03
*
           DFHMDF POS=(05,66),                                          X
                  ATTRB=ASKIP,                                          X
                  LENGTH=01,                                            X
                  INITIAL='-'
*
MDPHON2    DFHMDF POS=(05,68),                                          X
                  ATTRB=ASKIP,                                          X
                  LENGTH=04
*
           DFHMDF POS=(06,45),                                          X
                  ATTRB=ASKIP,                                          X
                  LENGTH=08,                                            X
                  INITIAL='CONTACT:'
*
MDCONTA    DFHMDF POS=(06,54),                                          X
                  ATTRB=ASKIP,                                          X
                  LENGTH=25
*
           DFHMDF POS=(08,01),                                          X
                  ATTRB=ASKIP,                                          X
                  LENGTH=17,                                            X
                  INITIAL='ADDRESS - STREET:'
*
MDSTRET    DFHMDF POS=(08,19),                                          X
                  ATTRB=ASKIP,                                          X
                  LENGTH=20
*
           DFHMDF POS=(08,45),                                          X
                  ATTRB=ASKIP,                                          X
                  LENGTH=18,                                            X
                  INITIAL='DOLLARS COMMITTED:'
*
MDDLRSC    DFHMDF POS=(08,64),                                          X
                  ATTRB=ASKIP,                                          X
                  LENGTH=15,                                            X
                  PICOUT='$$,$$$,$$$.99CR'
*
           DFHMDF POS=(09,13),                                          X
                  ATTRB=ASKIP,                                          X
                  LENGTH=05,                                            X
                  INITIAL='CITY:'
*
MDCITY     DFHMDF POS=(09,19),                                          X
                  ATTRB=ASKIP,                                          X
                  LENGTH=18
*
           DFHMDF POS=(10,12),                                          X
                  ATTRB=ASKIP,                                          X
                  LENGTH=06,                                            X
                  INITIAL='STATE:'
*
MDSTATE    DFHMDF POS=(10,19),                                          X
                  ATTRB=ASKIP,                                          X
                  LENGTH=02
*
MDSTANM    DFHMDF POS=(10,22),                                          X
                  ATTRB=ASKIP,                                          X
                  LENGTH=14
*
           DFHMDF POS=(11,14),                                          X
                  ATTRB=ASKIP,                                          X
                  LENGTH=04,                                            X
                  INITIAL='ZIP:'
*
MDZIP      DFHMDF POS(11,19),                                           X
                  ATTRB=ASKIP,                                          X
                  LENGTH=05
*
           DFHMDF POS=(13,02),                                          X
                  ATTRB=ASKIP,                                          X
                  LENGTH=16,                                            X
                  INITIAL='TO ATTENTION OF:'
```

Figure 12-2 *(Continued)*

```
*
MDATTOF    DFHMDF POS=(13,19),                                         X
                  ATTRB=ASKIP,                                        X
                  LENGTH=20
*

           DFHMDF POS=(18,10),                                         X
                  ATTRB=ASKIP,                                        X
                  LENGTH=56,                                           X
                  INITIAL='1. RETURN TO INQUIRY CONTROL SCREEN     - PRX
           ESS ENTER'
*
           DFHMDF POS=(19,10),                                         X
                  ATTRB=ASKIP,                                        X
                  LENGTH=54,                                           X
                  INITIAL='2. RETURN TO MENU                       - PRX
           ESS PF5'
*
           DFHMDF POS=(20,10),                                         X
                  ATTRB=ASKIP,                                        X
                  LENGTH=56,                                           X
                  INITIAL='3. END OF SESSION                       - PRX
           ESS CLEAR'
*
MDMESSG    DFHMDF POS=(24,01),                                         X
                  ATTRB=ASKIP,                                        X
                  LENGTH=79
*
           DFHMSD TYPE=FINAL
           END
```

Inquiry Program Source Code

The inquiry program source code shown in Fig. 12-3 follows the format used in previous examples. I will only discuss sections which contain new commands and concepts or those which need reinforcement.

Working-Storage Section

Copy library members, for all program examples, are found in the copy library (App. B). DFHAID can be found in App. A-3.

Linkage Section

The BLL cells in this program are used to establish addressability to two fields, the common work area (CWA) and state code table. The CWA is a system area common to all command-level CICS programs. It can be initialized by a system initiator program which is run on a daily basis. Member STLNKCWA in App. B contains a typical group of fields you might find in the CWA. The only CWA field that program examples in this book refer to is CWA-CURRENT-DATE. The CWA and state table will be discussed in more detail in the procedure division.

Procedure Division

The program structure for all sample programs is shown at the start of the procedure division. I find this format an acceptable and easier-to-maintain

Figure 12-3 Vendor File Inquiry Program Source Code.

```
000100 IDENTIFICATION DIVISION.
000200 PROGRAM-ID. POVMINQY.
000300 REMARKS.
000400************************************************************************
000500*              PURCHASING SYSTEM - VENDOR FILE INQUIRY               *
000600*       - STARTED BY PURCHASING SYSTEM SUB-MENU PROGRAM 'POVMAINT'   *
000700*             COULD ALSO BE STARTED BY TRANSID 'POVI'                *
000800************************************************************************
000900 ENVIRONMENT DIVISION.
001000 DATA DIVISION.
001100*
001200 WORKING-STORAGE  SECTION.
001300*
001400 01   WS-PROGRAM-FIELDS.
001500      05  FILLER           PIC X(8)      VALUE 'POVMINQY'.
001600      05  WS-CRT-MESSAGE   PIC X(17)     VALUE 'SESSION COMPLETED'.
001700*
001800*01  VENDOR-MASTER-RECORD
001900                           COPY    VENDMAST.
002000*01  WS-COMMAREA
002100                           COPY    POWSVMCA.
002200*01  WS-STATUS-FIELDS
002300                           COPY    STWSSTAT.
002400*01  VM-CONTROL-MAP
002500                           COPY    MAPVMCTL.
002600*01  VM-DETAIL-MAP
002700                           COPY    MAPVDTL1.
002800*01  WS-DATE-AND-TIME
002900                           COPY    STWSDTTM.
003000*01  WS-STATE-CODE-SEARCH-ENTRIES
003100                           COPY    STWST037.
003200*01  ATTRIBUTE-LIST
003300                           COPY    STWSATTR.
003400*01  DFHAID
003500                           COPY    DFHAID.
003600*
003700 01   END-OF-WORKING-STORAGE   PIC X(15)   VALUE 'END WS POVMINQY'.
003800*
003900 LINKAGE SECTION.
004000*
004100 01   DFHCOMMAREA                  PIC X(8).
004200*
004300 01   BLL-CELLS.
004400      05  FILLER                   PIC S9(8)    COMP.
004500      05  BLL-CWA-ADDRESS          PIC S9(8)    COMP.
004600      05  BLL-T037-STATE-TABLE-ADDRESS PIC S9(8)  COMP.
004700*
004800*01  CWA-DATA
004900                           COPY    STLNKCWA.
005000*01  T037-STATE-TABLE
005100                           COPY    T037STAT.
005200*
005300 PROCEDURE DIVISION.
005400************************************************************************
005500*        PROGRAM STRUCTURE IS:                                       *
005600*           AA00-MAINLINE                                            *
005700*              B000-INITIAL-ENTRY                                    *
005800*                 B100-SEND-CONTROL-MAP-AND-DATA                     *
005900*                    B110-GET-DATE-AND-TIME                          *
006000*                                                                    *
006100*              C000-PROCESS-CONTROL-MAP                              *
006200*                 C100-RECEIVE-CONTROL-MAP                           *
006300*                    C110-END-SESSION                                *
006400*                    C120-TRANSFER-XCTL-TO-MENU                      *
006500*                    C130-TRANSFER-XCTL-TO-BROWSE                    *
006600*                 C200-VERIFY-VENDOR-FORMAT                          *
006700*                 C400-VERIFY-VENDOR-FILE-STATUS                     *
006800*                    C410-READ-VENDOR-FILE                           *
006900*                 C500-SEND-DETAIL-MAP-AND-DATA                      *
007000*                    B110-GET-DATE-AND-TIME                          *
007100*                    C530-FORMAT-DETAIL-MAP                          *
007200*                       C531-GET-STATE-NAME                          *
007300*                 C600-SEND-CONTROL-MAP-DATAONLY                     *
007400*                                                                    *
007500*              D000-INQUIRY-PROCESSING                               *
007600*                 D100-RECEIVE-DETAIL-MAP                            *
007700*                    C110-END-SESSION                                *
```

Figure 12-3 *(Continued)*

```
007800*                        C120-TRANSFER-XCTL-TO-MENU              *
007900*                   B100-SEND-CONTROL-MAP-AND-DATA               *
008000*                   D200-SEND-DETAIL-MAP-DATAONLY                *
008100*****************************************************************
008200*
008300 AA00-MAINLINE  SECTION.
008400*
008500*     SERVICE RELOAD BLL-CELLS.
008600*
008700     IF EIBCALEN = 0
008800        PERFORM B000-INITIAL-ENTRY
008900     ELSE
009000        MOVE DFHCOMMAREA  TO  WS-COMMAREA
009100        IF CA-BROWSE
009200           MOVE SPACE        TO  CA-FUNCTION-CODE
009300           MOVE LOW-VALUES   TO  VM-CONTROL-MAP
009400           PERFORM C400-VERIFY-VENDOR-FILE-STATUS
009500           IF GOOD-VERIFY
009600              PERFORM C500-SEND-DETAIL-MAP-AND-DATA
009700           ELSE
009800              PERFORM B100-SEND-CONTROL-MAP-AND-DATA
009900        ELSE
010000           IF CA-RECEIVE-CTL-MAP
010100              PERFORM C000-PROCESS-CONTROL-MAP
010200           ELSE
010300              PERFORM D000-INQUIRY-PROCESSING.
010400*
010500     EXEC CICS RETURN
010600           TRANSID  ('POVI')
010700           COMMAREA (WS-COMMAREA)
010800           LENGTH   (8)
010900     END-EXEC.
011000*
011100 B000-INITIAL-ENTRY  SECTION.
011200*****************************************************************
011300*        INITIAL ENTRY INTO PROGRAM - ONLY EXECUTED ONCE·       *
011400*                PERFORMED FROM:  AA00-MAINLINE                  *
011500*****************************************************************
011600*
011700     MOVE LOW-VALUES  TO  VM-CONTROL-MAP.
011800     PERFORM B100-SEND-CONTROL-MAP-AND-DATA.
011900*
012000 B000-EXIT.
012100     EXIT.
012200*
012300 B100-SEND-CONTROL-MAP-AND-DATA  SECTION.
012400*****************************************************************
012500*        SEND CONTROL MAP - SYMBOLIC AND PHYSICAL MAPS          *
012600*            PERFORMED FROM:  B000-INITIAL-ENTRY                 *
012700*                             D000-INQUIRY-PROCESSING            *
012800*****************************************************************
012900*
013000     PERFORM B110-GET-DATE-AND-TIME.
013100     MOVE WS-CURRENT-DATE  TO  MVC-D-DATE.
013200     MOVE WS-MAP-TIME      TO  MVC-D-TIME.
013300*
013400     MOVE -1  TO  MVC-L-VEND-CD-1.
013500     MOVE '1' TO  CA-MAP-CONTROL.
013600*
013700     EXEC CICS SEND
013800           MAP     ('MAPPOVC')
013900           MAPSET  ('POVMIQ1')
014000           FROM    (VM-CONTROL-MAP)
014100           ERASE
014200           CURSOR
014300     END-EXEC.
014400*
014500 B100-EXIT.
014600     EXIT.
014700*
014800 B110-GET-DATE-AND-TIME  SECTION.
014900*****************************************************************
015000*        STPDDTTM - OBTAIN DATE FROM CWA AND FORMAT TIME        *
015100*            PERFORMED FROM:  B100-SEND-CONTROL-MAP-AND-DATA     *
015200*                             C500-SEND-DETAIL-MAP-AND-DATA      *
015300*****************************************************************
015400*
```

Figure 12-3 *(Continued)*

```
015500     COPY   STPDDTTM.
015600*
015700 B110-EXIT.
015800     EXIT.
015900*
016000 C000-PROCESS-CONTROL-MAP   SECTION.
016100*************************************************************
016200*          PERFORMED FROM: AA00-MAINLINE              *
016300*     PROCESS CONTROL MAP - IF VALID SEND DETAIL MAP  *
016400*        ELSE SEND CONTROL MAP WITH INVALID MESSAGE:  *
016500* 1) STATUS-OF-RECEIVE  =  'I'   INVALID KEY PRESSED  *
016600* 2) STATUS-OF-RECEIVE  =  'M'   MAPFAIL - NO DATA ENTERED *
016700* 3) STATUS-OF-FORMAT   =  'E'   INVALID VENDOR KEYED FORMAT *
016800* 4) STATUS-OF-VERIFY   =  'E'   VENDOR FILE STATUS ERROR   *
016900*************************************************************
017000*
017100     PERFORM C100-RECEIVE-CONTROL-MAP.
017200     IF GOOD-RECEIVE
017300        PERFORM C200-VERIFY-VENDOR-FORMAT
017400         IF VALID-FORMAT
017500            PERFORM C400-VERIFY-VENDOR-FILE-STATUS
017600             IF GOOD-VERIFY
017700                PERFORM C500-SEND-DETAIL-MAP-AND-DATA
017800             ELSE
017900                PERFORM C600-SEND-CONTROL-MAP-DATAONLY
018000         ELSE
018100            PERFORM C600-SEND-CONTROL-MAP-DATAONLY
018200     ELSE
018300         IF MAPFAIL-ON-RECEIVE
018400            MOVE 'VENDOR CODE MUST BE ENTERED - PLEASE KEY-IN'
018500                          TO MVC-D-MESSAGE
018600            MOVE ASKIP-BRT  TO MVC-A-MESSAGE
018700            PERFORM C600-SEND-CONTROL-MAP-DATAONLY
018800         ELSE
018900            PERFORM C600-SEND-CONTROL-MAP-DATAONLY.
019000*
019100 C000-EXIT.
019200     EXIT.
019300*
019400 C100-RECEIVE-CONTROL-MAP   SECTION.
019500*************************************************************
019600*          PERFORMED FROM: C000-PROCESS-CONTROL-MAP    *
019700*        ENTER IS ONLY VALID DATA ENTRY KEY           *
019800* CLEAR KEY - ENDS TERMINAL SESSION      PF5 - RETURNS TO MENU *
019900*                                        PF4 - XCTL TO BROWSE  *
020000*          ALL OTHER AID KEYS ARE INVALID             *
020100*    STATUS-OF-RECEIVE  =  'G'  =  GOOD RECEIVE       *
020200*                          'M'  =  MAPFAIL            *
020300*                          'I'  =  INVALID KEY PRESSED *
020400*************************************************************
020500*
020600     MOVE LOW-VALUES  TO VM-CONTROL-MAP.
020700*
020800     IF EIBAID  =  DFHENTER
020900        MOVE 'M'  TO  STATUS-OF-RECEIVE
021000*
021100        EXEC CICS HANDLE CONDITION
021200                  MAPFAIL (C100-EXIT)
021300        END-EXEC
021400*
021500        EXEC CICS RECEIVE
021600                MAP    ('MAPPOVC')
021700                MAPSET ('POVMIQ1')
021800                INTO   (VM-CONTROL-MAP)
021900        END-EXEC
022000*
022100        MOVE 'G'  TO  STATUS-OF-RECEIVE
022200     ELSE
022300         IF EIBAID  =  DFHCLEAR
022400            PERFORM C110-END-SESSION
022500         ELSE
022600         IF EIBAID  =  DFHPF5
022700            PERFORM C120-TRANSFER-XCTL-TO-MENU
022800         ELSE
022900         IF EIBAID  =  DFHPF4
023000            PERFORM C130-TRANSFER-XCTL-TO-BROWSE
023100         ELSE
023200            MOVE 'I'       TO  STATUS-OF-RECEIVE
```

Figure 12-3 *(Continued)*

```
023300               MOVE 'INVALID KEY PRESSED - PLEASE TRY AGAIN'
023400                    TO   MVC-D-MESSAGE
023500               MOVE ASKIP-BRT  TO  MVC-A-MESSAGE.
023600*
023700 C100-EXIT.
023800     EXIT.
023900*
024000 C110-END-SESSION  SECTION.
024100******************************************************************
024200*    CRT OPERATOR PRESSED CLEAR KEY TO END TERMINAL SESSION     *
024300*        PERFORMED FROM:  C100-RECEIVE-CONTROL-MAP              *
024400*                         D100-RECEIVE-DETAIL-MAP               *
024500******************************************************************
024600*·
024700     EXEC CICS SEND
024800               FROM   (WS-CRT-MESSAGE)
024900               LENGTH (17)
025000               ERASE
025100     END-EXEC.
025200*
025300     EXEC CICS RETURN
025400     END-EXEC.
025500*
025600 C110-EXIT.
025700     EXIT.
025800*
025900 C120-TRANSFER-XCTL-TO-MENU  SECTION.
026000******************************************************************
026100*        OPERATOR PRESSED PF5 TO RETURN TO MENU PROGRAM         *
026200*           PERFORMED FROM:  C100-RECEIVE-CONTROL-MAP           *
026300*                            D100-RECEIVE-DETAIL-MAP            *
026400******************************************************************
026500*
026600     EXEC CICS XCTL
026700               PROGRAM ('POVMAINT')
026800     END-EXEC.
026900*
027000 C120-EXIT.
027100     EXIT.
027200*
027300 C130-TRANSFER-XCTL-TO-BROWSE  SECTION.
027400******************************************************************
027500*        OPERATOR PRESSED PF4 TO TRANSFER CONTROL TO BROWSE     *
027600*           PERFORMED FROM:  C100-RECEIVE-CONTROL-MAP           *
027700******************************************************************
027800*
027900     MOVE LOW-VALUES  TO  WS-COMMAREA.
028000     MOVE 'I'         TO  CA-FUNCTION-CODE.
028100*
028200     EXEC CICS XCTL
028300               PROGRAM  ('POVMBROW')
028400               COMMAREA (WS-COMMAREA)
028500               LENGTH   (8)
028600     END-EXEC.
028700*
028800 C130-EXIT.
028900     EXIT.
029000*
029100 C200-VERIFY-VENDOR-FORMAT  SECTION.
029200******************************************************************
029300*        VERIFY FORMAT OF VENDOR CODE KEYED-IN = A-9999-9       *
029400*           PERFORMED FROM:  C000-PROCESS-CONTROL-MAP           *
029500*    IF VALID FORMAT - MOVE CODE TO WS-COMMAREA FIELDS (CA- )   *
029600******************************************************************
029700*
029800     IF (MVC-D-VEND-CD-1 IS  ALPHABETIC
029900               AND
030000        MVC-D-VEND-CD-1  IS NOT =  SPACE)
030100     AND
030200        MVC-D-VEND-CD-2  IS  NUMERIC
030300     AND
030400        MVC-D-VEND-CD-3  IS  NUMERIC
030500        MOVE MVC-D-VEND-CD-1  TO  CA-VEND-1
030600        MOVE MVC-D-VEND-CD-2  TO  CA-VEND-2
030700        MOVE MVC-D-VEND-CD-3  TO  CA-VEND-3
030800        MOVE 'G'              TO  STATUS-OF-FORMAT
030900     ELSE
031000        MOVE 'E'       TO  STATUS-OF-FORMAT
031100        MOVE 'VENDOR CODE FORMAT MUST BE: A-9999-9 - PLEASE RE-EN
031200-             'TER'    TO  MVC-D-MESSAGE
031300        MOVE ASKIP-BRT TO  MVC-A-MESSAGE.
031400*
031500 C200-EXIT.
031600     EXIT.
```

Figure 12-3 (Continued)

```
031700*
031800 C400-VERIFY-VENDOR-FILE-STATUS  SECTION.
031900****************************************************************
032000*          PERFORMED FROM:  C000-PROCESS-CONTROL-MAP         *
032100*            MUST BE A VENDOR RECORD FOR INQUIRIES            *
032200****************************************************************
032300*
032400     MOVE 'G'  TO  STATUS-OF-VERIFY.
032500*
032600     PERFORM C410-READ-VENDOR-FILE.
032700*
032800     IF RECORD-NOT-FOUND
032900         MOVE 'E'        TO   STATUS-OF-VERIFY
033000         MOVE 'VENDOR RECORD NOT ON FILE'
033100                         TO  MVC-D-MESSAGE
033200         MOVE ASKIP-BRT  TO  MVC-A-MESSAGE.
033300*
033400 C400-EXIT.
033500     EXIT.
033600*
033700 C410-READ-VENDOR-FILE  SECTION.
033800****************************************************************
033900*          PERFORMED FROM:  C400-VERIFY-VENDOR-FILE-STATUS    *
034000****************************************************************
034100*
034200     MOVE 'E'  TO  STATUS-OF-READ.
034300*
034400     EXEC CICS HANDLE CONDITION
034500               NOTFND  (C410-EXIT)
034600     END-EXEC.
034700*
034800     EXEC CICS READ
034900               DATASET ('VENDMAST')
035000               INTO    (VENDOR-MASTER-RECORD)
035100               RIDFLD  (CA-VENDOR-CODE)
035200     END-EXEC.
035300*
035400     MOVE 'G'  TO  STATUS-OF-READ.
035500*
035600 C410-EXIT.
035700     EXIT.
035800*
035900 C500-SEND-DETAIL-MAP-AND-DATA  SECTION.
036000****************************************************************
036100*        SEND DETAIL MAP - PHYSICAL AND SYMBOLIC MAPS         *
036200*          PERFORMED FROM:  C000-PROCESS-CONTROL-MAP          *
036300*   SENT WHEN ALL VALIDATION AND EDIT CONDITIONS HAVE BEEN MET *
036400****************************************************************
036500*
036600     MOVE LOW-VALUES  TO  VM-DETAIL-MAP.
036700*
036800     PERFORM B110-GET-DATE-AND-TIME.
036900     MOVE WS-CURRENT-DATE  TO  MVD-D-DATE.
037000     MOVE WS-MAP-TIME      TO  MVD-D-TIME.
037100*
037200     PERFORM C530-FORMAT-DETAIL-MAP.
037300*
037400     MOVE '2'  TO  CA-MAP-CONTROL.
037500*
037600     EXEC CICS SEND
037700               MAP     ('MAPPOVD')
037800               MAPSET  ('POVMIQ2')
037900               FROM    (VM-DETAIL-MAP)
038000               ERASE
038100     END-EXEC.
038200*
038300 C500-EXIT.
038400     EXIT.
038500*
038600 C530-FORMAT-DETAIL-MAP  SECTION.
038700****************************************************************
038800*          PERFORMED FROM:  C500-SEND-DETAIL-MAP-AND-DATA     *
038900****************************************************************
039000*
039100* FORMAT VENDOR CODE: A-9999-9   WS- FIELDS ARE AT END OF VENDMAST
039200     MOVE CA-VEND-1           TO  WS-VENDOR-CD-1.
039300     MOVE CA-VEND-2           TO  WS-VENDOR-CD-2.
039400     MOVE CA-VEND-3           TO  WS-VENDOR-CD-3.
039500     MOVE WS-VENDOR-CODE      TO  MVD-D-VENDOR-CODE.
039600*
039700     MOVE VM-AREA-CD          TO  MVD-D-PHONE-AREA-CD.
039800     MOVE VM-PHONE-1-3        TO  MVD-D-PHONE-1.
039900     MOVE VM-PHONE-4-7        TO  MVD-D-PHONE-2.
040000     MOVE VM-VENDOR-NAME      TO  MVD-D-VENDOR-NAME.
```

Figure 12-3 (*Continued*)

```
040100      MOVE VM-CONTACT            TO  MVD-D-CONTACT.
040200      MOVE VM-STREET-ADDRESS     TO  MVD-D-STREET.
040300      MOVE VM-CITY               TO  MVD-D-CITY.
040400      MOVE VM-STATE              TO  MVD-D-STATE-CODE.
040500*
040600      MOVE VM-STATE              TO  WS-STATE-CODE.
040700      PERFORM C531-GET-STATE-NAME.
040800      MOVE WS-STATE-NAME         TO  MVD-D-STATE-NAME.
040900*
041000      MOVE VM-ZIP-CODE           TO  MVD-D-ZIP-CODE.
041100      MOVE VM-TO-ATTN-OF         TO  MVD-D-ATTENTION-OF.
041200      MOVE VM-DOLLARS-COMMITTED  TO  MVD-D-DLRS-COMMITTED.
041300*
041400 C530-EXIT.
041500      EXIT.
041600*
041700 C531-GET-STATE-NAME   SECTION.
041800***************************************************************
041900*            LOAD AND SEARCH STATE CODE TABLE               *
042000*         PERFORMED FROM: C530-SEND-DETAIL-MAP-AND-DATA     *
042100***************************************************************
042200*
042300      COPY    STPDT037.
042400*
042500 C531-EXIT.
042600      EXIT.
042700*
042800 C600-SEND-CONTROL-MAP-DATAONLY  SECTION.
042900***************************************************************
043000*         SEND CONTROL MAP DATAONLY - SYMBOLIC MAP          *
043100*         PERFORMED FROM: C000-PROCESS-CONTROL-MAP          *
043200*               SENT FOR INVALID CONDITIONS                 *
043300***************************************************************
043400*
043500      MOVE '1' TO  CA-MAP-CONTROL.
043600      MOVE -1  TO  MVC-L-VEND-CD-1.
043700*
043800      MOVE UNPROT-FSET  TO  MVC-A-VEND-CD-1
043900                            MVC-A-VEND-CD-2
044000                            MVC-A-VEND-CD-3.
044100*
044200      EXEC CICS SEND
044300              MAP      ('MAPPOVC')
044400              MAPSET   ('POVMIQ1')
044500              FROM     (VM-CONTROL-MAP)
044600              DATAONLY
044700              CURSOR
044800      END-EXEC.
044900*
045000 C600-EXIT.
045100      EXIT.
045200*
045300 D000-INQUIRY-PROCESSING  SECTION.
045400***************************************************************
045500*              PERFORMED FROM:  AA00-MAINLINE                *
045600*      DETAIL MAP IS SENT IF AN INVALID KEY WAS PRESSED     *
045700***************************************************************
045800*
045900      PERFORM D100-RECEIVE-DETAIL-MAP.
046000*
046100      IF GOOD-RECEIVE
046200          PERFORM B100-SEND-CONTROL-MAP-AND-DATA
046300      ELSE
046400          PERFORM D200-SEND-DETAIL-MAP-DATAONLY.
046500*
046600 D000-EXIT.
046700      EXIT.
046800*
046900 D100-RECEIVE-DETAIL-MAP  SECTION.
047000***************************************************************
047100*         PERFORMED FROM:  D000-INQUIRY-PROCESSING           *
047200* ENTER - RETURN TO CONTROL SCREEN    CLEAR - ENDS SESSION   *
047300*                                     PF5   - RETURN TO MENU  *
047400*               ALL OTHER KEYS ARE INVALID                   *
047500*      STATUS-OF-RECEIVE  =  'G'  =  GOOD RECEIVE            *
047600*                            'I'  =  INVALID KEY PRESSED     *
047700***************************************************************
047800*
047900      MOVE LOW-VALUES  TO  VM-DETAIL-MAP.
048000*
048100      IF EIBAID  =  DFHENTER
048200*
```

Figure 12-3 *(Continued)*

```
048300              EXEC CICS IGNORE CONDITION
048400                        MAPFAIL
048500              END-EXEC
048600*
048700              EXEC CICS RECEIVE
048800                        MAP      ('MAPPOVD')
048900                        MAPSET   ('POVMIQ2')
049000                        INTO     (VM-DETAIL-MAP)
049100              END-EXEC
049200*
049300              MOVE 'G'  TO  STATUS-OF-RECEIVE
049400         ELSE
049500              IF EIBAID  =  DFHCLEAR
049600                  PERFORM C110-END-SESSION
049700              ELSE
049800              IF EIBAID  =  DFHPF5
049900                  PERFORM C120-TRANSFER-XCTL-TO-MENU
050000              ELSE
050100                  MOVE 'I'      TO  STATUS-OF-RECEIVE
050200                  MOVE 'INVALID KEY PRESSED - PLEASE TRY AGAIN'
050300                                TO  MVD-D-MESSAGE
050400                  MOVE ASKIP-BRT  TO  MVD-A-MESSAGE.
050500*
050600 D100-EXIT.
050700      EXIT.
050800*
050900 D200-SEND-DETAIL-MAP-DATAONLY  SECTION.
051000***********************************************************************
051100*        SEND DETAIL MAP DATA ONLY - SYMBOLIC MAP              *
051200*     PERFORMED FROM:  D000-INQUIRY-PROCESSING                 *
051300* SENT IF INVALID KEY IS PRESSED ON A RECEIVE OF THE DETAIL MAP *
051400***********************************************************************
051500*
051600      MOVE '2'  TO  CA-MAP-CONTROL.
051700*
051800      EXEC CICS SEND
051900                MAP      ('MAPPOVD')
052000                MAPSET   ('POVMIQ2')
052100                FROM     (VM-DETAIL-MAP)
052200                DATAONLY
052300      END-EXEC.
052400*
052500 D200-EXIT.
052600      EXIT.
```

substitute for a drawn block program structure chart. Even this form of the program structure chart requires maintenance. You might want to write a program which will generate the program structure and print it in this format. As you develop or enhance your standards, you will have to decide on the level of documentation you want to maintain.

AA00-MAINLINE.   This section is similar to that of previously discussed programs. On the first entry into the program, EIBCALEN is equal to 0 and the program performs B000-INITIAL-ENTRY. On succeeding entries EIBCALEN equals 8 (see the RETURN command) and DFHCOMMAREA will be moved to WS-COMMAREA. The contents of the COMMAREA field CA-MAP-CONTROL (see App. B, POWSVMCA) will be used as a switch to determine whether the program will receive the control or detail map. The program issues a RETURN command, with a TRANSID of POVI and a COMMAREA 8 bytes long. When the terminal operator presses an AID key, this program will be initiated again.

B100-SEND-CONTROL-MAP-AND-DATA.   Issues a PERFORM command to obtain date and time and then moves them to the control map. A 1 is moved to

CA-MAP-CONTROL. This is a signal on a subsequent entry into the program that the control map is to be received. A −1 is moved to the map's vendor code length field in order to set the cursor at the first position of that field on the SEND MAP command which contains the symbolic map and the CURSOR option.

B110-GET-DATE-AND-TIME. The get-date-and-time routine is found in the copy library (App. B, member STPDDTTM). Two new CICS commands are introduced: the ASSIGN and ADDRESS commands. The ASSIGN command allows a program to access values outside the program. The most commonly accessed value is the length of the CWA. The CWA, as mentioned earlier in the chapter, is an area used by the system to pass common data to a program. Before attempting to establish addressability and access CWA data, it is good practice to make sure the CWA is available to CICS. The copy library member used for the CWA should be the proper length.

```
EXEC CICS ASSIGN
          CWALENG (WS-CWA-LENGTH)
END-EXEC.
```

Execution of this command makes the length of the CWA available in a working-storage field WS-CWA-LENGTH, which must be defined as a halfword binary value.

The ADDRESS command is used to establish addressability to the CWA and other system areas. It is similar in effect to the LOAD command in that it sets the address so that the BLL cell points to the CWA. Once addressability has been established, the program can access all data defined in the CWA.

```
EXEC CICS ADDRESS
          CWA (BLL-CWA-ADDRESS)
END-EXEC.
```

The execution of this command will set the linkage-section pointer BLL-CWA-ADDRESS to the address of CWA-DATA and make the CWA data available to the program.

Time is obtained from the EIB field EIBTIME and formatted to HH.MM.SS.

C000-PROCESS-CONTROL-MAP. This section, which is similar for all maintenance functions, receives the control map, then verifies the format of vendor code. The status of the vendor file is checked to make sure a record is available to display; if so, a formatted detail map is sent. Invalid conditions, which prevent the display of the detail map, will result in the control map's being sent with an appropriate highlighted ASKIP,BRT message displayed.

C100-RECEIVE-CONTROL-MAP. This section receives the symbolic map into the working-storage area VM-CONTROL-MAP and can invoke the end-of-session or the transfer of control to the submenu or to the browse program.

C120-TRANSFER-XCTL-TO-MENU. This section transfers control back to the vendor file maintenance submenu, program POVMAINT (see Fig. 6-3).

C130-TRANSFER-XCTL-TO-BROWSE. This section transfers control to the vendor file browse program POVMBROW, which is discussed in Chap. 17. This program could pass an entered vendor code to POVMBROW. For simplicity, the code will be entered in the browse program. An I moved to CA-FUNCTION-CODE signals the browse program that control was transferred to POVMBROW by the inquiry program POVMINQY. This code will be used by the browse program to signal a return of control to POVMINQY if desired. The addition, change, and delete programs will, respectively, move an A, C, or D to CA-FUNCTION-CODE.

C200-VERIFY-VENDOR-FORMAT. This section verifies that the keyed-in vendor code is of the proper format A-9999-9. If the format is correct, the vendor code is moved to the working-storage area WS-COMMAREA; otherwise an error message and indicator are returned.

C400-VERIFY-VENDOR-FILE-STATUS. This section performs a read of the vendor file to make sure the vendor entered is on the file. If the vendor is not on the file, an error indicator is set and an error message returned.

C410-READ-VENDOR-FILE. In this section an E is moved immediately to STATUS-OF-READ, prior to executing the READ command for the vendor file. If the record is on the file, it is read into the working-storage area VENDOR-MASTER-RECORD, and a G is moved to STATUS-OF-READ. RIDFLD was set in section C200-VERIFY-VENDOR-FORMAT.

C500-SEND-DETAIL-MAP-AND-DATA. This section performs a format of the detail map and moves a 2 to CA-MAP-CONTROL, so that on a succeeding entry into this program the detail map will be received. Physical and symbolic maps are sent; the symbolic map is located in the working-storage area VM-DETAIL-MAP.

C530-FORMAT-DETAIL-MAP. This section moves vendor master file data to the appropriate map fields.

C531-GET-STATE-NAME. Logic for obtaining state name is found in the copy library (App. B, member STPDT037). This logic is included in the system in order to demonstrate the use of a nonresident table which is released from main storage as soon as it is no longer required.

```
EXEC CICS LOAD
          PROGRAM ('T037STAT')
          SET       (BLL-T037-STATE-TABLE-ADDRESS)
END-EXEC.
```

This LOAD command establishes addressability to the state code table. The state name obtained is moved to the working-storage field WS-STATE-NAME. If a state is not found, all * are moved to WS-STATE-NAME.

After the search of the state table is complete, the following command releases the state table from main storage.

```
EXEC CICS RELEASE
          PROGRAM ('T037STAT')
END-EXEC.
```

C600-SEND-CONTROL-MAP-DATAONLY. This is performed when an invalid condition occurs. UNPROT,FSET attributes are moved to the map's vendor code fields so that if vendor code was entered correctly, it will be returned on a subsequent receive of the map. FRSET on the BMS map's DFHMSD parameter turns off all MDTs prior to a send; −1 is moved to the symbolic map's length field. CURSOR is specified on the send in order to set the cursor at the first position of vendor code.

D100-RECEIVE-DETAIL-MAP. This section receives the detail map and, if the ENTER key was pressed, returns to the invoking section. The IGNORE command is used as follows:

```
EXEC CICS IGNORE CONDITION
          MAPFAIL
END-EXEC.
```

This command directs that if the specified condition (in this case MAPFAIL) occurs, the condition should be ignored. MAPFAIL is a common occurrence on many types of maps which do not require the entry of data. This command permits program logic to fall through to the MOVE command following the receive. The same result would be achieved on a MAPFAIL if a HANDLE CONDITION command directed control as follows:

```
        EXEC CICS   HANDLE CONDITION
                    MAPFAIL (D100-MOVE-G-TO-STATUS)
        END-EXEC.
                .
                .
                .
        D100-MOVE-G-TO-STATUS.
            MOVE 'G'    TO    STATUS-OF-RECEIVE.
```

If the CLEAR key or PF5 key is pressed, this section directs control to
C110-END-SESSION or C120-TRANSFER-XCTL-TO-MENU, respectively.
Any other key would result in an invalid key message being displayed on
the detail map.

D200-SEND-DETAIL-MAP-DATAONLY.   If an invalid key was pressed prior to the
receive of the detail map, this section sends the detail symbolic map only. A 2 is
moved to CA-MAP-CONTROL so that the mainline section AA00-MAINLINE
will direct control to the receive of the detail map on a subsequent entry into
this program.

SUMMARY

The inquiry program presented here can be used as a model for most inquiry
programs you will have to write. Several of the commands explained in preceding
chapters were used, and a few new commands introduced. The COMMAREA
contents were used in order to determine whether to receive the control or detail
map. The SEND MAP AND DATA command was used, as was the READ file
command. Other new commands presented were ASSIGN and ADDRESS. The
maintenance programs presented in the next three chapters are very similar in
format to the inquiry program.

13

THE ADDITION PROGRAM

After a file has been created and an inquiry program written to check the status of various fields, it is often necessary to make new additions to the file. The addition program is discussed in this chapter.

Control and detail maps are used for the addition program. The control map shown in Fig. 13-1 requires the terminal operator to key in a vendor code and to press ENTER in order to display the addition detail map. The operator also has the option of transferring control to the vendor file browse, returning to the vendor file maintenance submenu (see Fig. 6-3), or ending the session. The vendor file addition detail screen is defined by the map shown in Fig. 2-7. It is displayed when the operator keys in a vendor code on the control screen, which is not currently on the vendor file. The detail map shows as X's all fields which can be added to the vendor's record. This map permits the operator to key in the vendor's data and then press ENTER in order to add the record. The detail map gives an operator the option of returning to the addition control screen without adding the record, returning to the submenu, or ending the session.

BMS Maps

Figures 13-2 and 13-3 show the BMS maps for the control and detail maps shown in Figs. 13-1 and 2-7, respectively.

BMS Control Map

Only the differences between this map and the BMS control map for the inquiry program (see Fig. 12-1) are shown in Fig. 13-2. Keeping fields in the same position for similar maps makes the creation of new maps easy. An existing map serves as a model for others.

```
IBM                    3270 Information Display System
  ®                          Layout Sheet
```

Figure 13-1 Vendor File Additions Control Map.

BMS Detail Map

All addition detail map attributes could be defined as ASKIP. The program could then control the attributes by modifying them prior to a send which includes the symbolic map. I have defined data-entry fields as UNPROT because this makes the initial testing of the map's format easier. The data-entry fields can be checked by using the command-level interpreter (CECI) discussed in Chap. 6 to display the map and check its format. All UNPROT fields have either a trailing ASKIP field or a following stopper field to limit the size of the data-entry field. Fields which require data to be entered on an addition screen have field names assigned. For instance, NAME:, a required field, is assigned a field name MDCVMNM. This will result in a symbolic map label being generated when the BMS map is assembled. Include user-friendly symbolic map entries for all field identifiers of items which will be referenced. For instance, see user-friendly map label MVD-C-A-VENDOR-NAME for member MAPVDTL2 in App. B. The ·program has the ability to brighten and darken field identifiers as required when testing for the entry of valid data. No IC attribute is defined on this map because the program sets the cursor by moving −1 to the appropriate length field in the symbolic map. The map is then sent with CURSOR specified.

```
            PRINT NOGEN
POVMAD1     DFHMSD TYPE=MAP,                                            X
              .
              .
              .
            DFHMDF POS=(01,72),                                         X
                   ATTRB=ASKIP,                                         X
                   LENGTH=07,                                           X
                   INITIAL='POVMAD1'
              .
              .
              .
            DFHMDF POS=(02,25),                                         X
                   ATTRB=ASKIP,                                         X
                   LENGTH=29,                                           X
                   INITIAL='VENDOR FILE ADDITIONS CONTROL'
              .
              .
              .
            DFHMDF POS=(12,19),                                         X
                   ATTRB=ASKIP,                                         X
                   LENGTH=40,                                           X
                   INITIAL='1. TO ADD VENDOR RECORD    - PRESS ENTER'
              .
              .
              .
```

Figure 13-2   Vendor File Additions BMS Control Map.

User-Friendly Symbolic Maps

User-friendly symbolic maps created to correspond to generated BMS maps are shown in the copy library (App. B, members MAPVMCTL and MAPVDTL2). Note the inclusion of additional names for the field identifiers on the detail symbolic map. They are used by the addition program to highlight field identifiers of incorrectly entered items.

Addition Program Source Code

The addition program source code shown in Fig. 13-4 follows the format used in previous examples. I will discuss only sections which differ from previous examples.

Procedure Division

AA00-MAINLINE. This section is similar to that of the inquiry program in Chap. 12 except that the perform E000-ADDITION-PROCESSING replaces D000-INQUIRY-PROCESSING and TRANSID POVA replaces POVI.

C400-VERIFY-VENDOR-FILE-STATUS. This section performs a read of the vendor file to make sure that the vendor to be added is not already on the file. If the vendor is on the file, an error indicator is set and an error message is returned.

C410-READ-VENDOR-FILE. An E is moved immediately to STATUS-OF-READ prior to executing the READ command for the vendor file. If the record is on

Figure 13-3   Vendor File Additions BMS Detail Map.

```
           PRINT NOGEN
POVMAD2    DFHMSD TYPE=MAP,                                          X
                  CTRL=(FREEKB,FRSET),                               X
                  LANG=COBOL,                                        X
                  MODE=INOUT,                                        X
                  TERM=3270,                                         X
                  TIOAPFX=YES
*
MAPPOVD    DFHMDI LINE=01,                                           X
                  COLUMN=01,                                         X
                  SIZE=(24,80)
*
           DFHMDF POS=(01,01),                                       X
                  ATTRB=ASKIP,                                       X
                  LENGTH=05,                                         X
                  INITIAL='DATE: '
*
MDDATE     DFHMDF POS=(01,07),                                       X
                  ATTRB=ASKIP,                                       X
                  LENGTH=08
*
           DFHMDF POS=(01,27),                                       X
                  ATTRB=ASKIP,                                       X
                  LENGTH=25,                                         X
                  INITIAL='ABC MANUFACTURING COMPANY'
*
           DFHMDF POS=(01,72),                                       X
                  ATTRB=ASKIP,                                       X
                  LENGTH=07,                                         X
                  INITIAL='POVMAD2'
*
           DFHMDF POS=(02,01),                                       X
                  ATTRB=ASKIP,                                       X
                  LENGTH=05,                                         X
                  INITIAL='TIME: '
*
MDTIME     DFHMDF POS=(02,07),                                       X
                  ATTRB=ASKIP,                                       X
                  LENGTH=08
*
           DFHMDF POS=(02,30),                                       X
                  ATTRB=ASKIP,                                       X
                  LENGTH=20,                                         X
                  INITIAL='VENDOR FILE ADDITION'
*
           DFHMDF POS=(04,01),                                       X
                  ATTRB=ASKIP,                                       X
                  LENGTH=12,                                         X
                  INITIAL='VENDOR CODE: '
*
MDVNDCD    DFHMDF POS=(04,14),                                       X
                  ATTRB=ASKIP,                                       X
                  LENGTH=08
*
MDCVMNM    DFHMDF POS=(05,08),                                       X
                  ATTRB=ASKIP,                                       X
                  LENGTH=05,                                         X
                  INITIAL='NAME: '
*
MDVNDNM    DFHMDF POS=(05,14),                                       X
                  ATTRB=(UNPROT,IC)                                  X
                  LENGTH=25
*
           DFHMDF POS=(05,40),                                       X
                  ATTRB=ASKIP,                                       X
                  LENGTH=01
*
MDCPHON    DFHMDF POS=(05,45),                                       X
                  ATTRB=ASKIP,                                       X
                  LENGTH=06,                                         X
                  INITIAL='PHONE: '
*
           DFHMDF POS=(05,54),                                       X
                  ATTRB=ASKIP,                                       X
                  LENGTH=01,                                         X
                  INITIAL='('
*
MDAREAC    DFHMDF POS=(05,56),                                       X
                  ATTRB=UNPROT,                                      X
                  LENGTH=03
```

Figure 13-3 (*Continued*)

```
*
          DFHMDF POS=(05,60),                                    X
                 ATTRB=ASKIP,                                    X
                 LENGTH=01,                                      X
                 INITIAL=')'
*
MDPHON1   DFHMDF POS=(05,62),                                    X
                 ATTRB=UNPROT,                                   X
                 LENGTH=03
*
          DFHMDF POS=(05,66),                                    X
                 ATTRB=ASKIP,                                    X
                 LENGTH=01,                                      X
                 INITIAL='-'
*
MDPHON2   DFHMDF POS=(05,68),                                    X
                 ATTRB=UNPROT,                                   X
                 LENGTH=04
*
          DFHMDF POS=(05,73),                                    X
                 ATTRB=ASKIP,                                    X
                 LENGTH=01
*
          DFHMDF POS=(06,45),                                    X
                 ATTRB=ASKIP,                                    X
                 LENGTH=08,                                      X
                 INITIAL='CONTACT:'
*
MDCONTA   DFHMDF POS=(06,54),                                    X
                 ATTRB=UNPROT,                                   X
                 LENGTH=25
*
          DFHMDF POS=(06,80),                                    X
                 ATTRB=ASKIP,                                    X
                 LENGTH=01
*
MDCSTRT   DFHMDF POS=(08,01),                                    X
                 ATTRB=ASKIP,                                    X
                 LENGTH=17,                                      X
                 INITIAL='ADDRESS - STREET:'
*
MDSTRET   DFHMDF POS=(08,19),                                    X
                 ATTRB=UNPROT,                                   X
                 LENGTH=20
*
          DFHMDF POS=(08,40),                                    X
                 ATTRB=ASKIP,                                    X
                 LENGTH=01
*
MDCCITY   DFHMDF POS=(09,13),                                    X
                 ATTRB=ASKIP,                                    X
                 LENGTH=05,                                      X
                 INITIAL='CITY:'
*
MDCITY    DFHMDF POS=(09,19),                                    X
                 ATTRB=UNPROT,                                   X
                 LENGTH=18
*
          DFHMDF POS=(09,38),                                    X
                 ATTRB=ASKIP,                                    X
                 LENGTH=01
*
MDCSTAT   DFHMDF POS=(10,12),                                    X
                 ATTRB=ASKIP,                                    X
                 LENGTH=06,                                      X
                 INITIAL='STATE:'
*
MDSTATE   DFHMDF POS=(10,19),                                    X
                 ATTRB=UNPROT,                                   X
                 LENGTH=02
*
MDSTANM   DFHMDF POS=(10,22),                                    X
                 ATTRB=ASKIP,                                    X
                 LENGTH=14
*
```

Figure 13-3 *(Continued)*

```
MDCZIP     DFHMDF POS=(11,14),                                    X
           ATTRB=ASKIP,                                           X
           LENGTH=04,                                             X
           INITIAL='ZIP:'
*
MDZIP      DFHMDF POS(11,19),                                     X
           ATTRB=UNPROT,                                          X
           LENGTH=05
*
           DFHMDF POS=(11,25),                                    X
           ATTRB=ASKIP,                                           X
           LENGTH=01
*
           DFHMDF POS=(13,02),                                    X
           ATTRB=ASKIP,                                           X
           LENGTH=16,                                             X
           INITIAL='TO ATTENTION OF:'
*
MDATTOF    DFHMDF POS=(13,19),                                    X
           ATTRB=UNPROT,                                          X
           LENGTH=20
*
           DFHMDF POS=(13,40),                                    X
           ATTRB=ASKIP,                                           X
           LENGTH=01
*
           DFHMDF POS=(18,10),                                    X
           ATTRB=ASKIP,                                           X
           LENGTH=56,                                             X
           INITIAL='1. ADDITIONS, KEY IN REQUIRED DATA      - PRX
           ESS ENTER'
*
           DFHMDF POS=(19,10),                                    X
           ATTRB=ASKIP,                                           X
           LENGTH=54,                                             X
           INITIAL='2. RETURN TO ADDITION CONTROL SCREEN    - PRX
           ESS PF3'
*
           DFHMDF POS=(20,10),                                    X
           ATTRB=ASKIP,                                           X
           LENGTH=54,                                             X
           INITIAL='3. RETURN TO MENU                        - PRX
           ESS PF5'
*
           DFHMDF POS=(21,10),                                    X
           ATTRB=ASKIP,                                           X
           LENGTH=56,                                             X
           INITIAL='4. END OF SESSION                        - PRX
           ESS CLEAR'
*
MDMESSG    DFHMDF POS=(24,01),                                    X
           ATTRB=ASKIP,                                           X
           LENGTH=79
*
           DFHMSD TYPE=FINAL
           END
```

the file, it is read into the working-storage area VENDOR-MASTER-RECORD and a G is moved to STATUS-OF-READ. A vendor record should not be found for a record which is being added, and a record-found condition will be treated as an error in the invoking section (C400-VERIFY-VENDOR-FILE-STATUS).

C500-SEND-DETAIL-MAP-AND-DATA. This section is similar to that of the Inquiry program in Chap. 12. The differences are

1. Perform C520-SET-MAP-ATTRIBUTES.

Figure 13-4   Vendor File Addition Program Source Code.

```
000100 IDENTIFICATION DIVISION.
000200 PROGRAM-ID. POVMADDN.
000300 REMARKS.
000400***********************************************************************
000500*              PURCHASING SYSTEM - VENDOR FILE ADDITIONS              *
000600*       - STARTED BY PURCHASING SYSTEM SUB-MENU PROGRAM 'POVMAINT'    *
000700*            COULD ALSO BE STARTED BY TRANSID 'POVA'                  *
000800***********************************************************************
000900 ENVIRONMENT DIVISION.
001000 DATA DIVISION.
001100*
001200 WORKING-STORAGE  SECTION.
001300*
001400 01   WS-PROGRAM-FIELDS.
001500      05  FILLER            PIC X(8)      VALUE 'POVMADDN'.
001600      05  WS-CRT-MESSAGE    PIC X(17)     VALUE 'SESSION COMPLETED'.
001700*
001800*01   VENDOR-MASTER-RECORD
001900                                      COPY   VENDMAST.
002000*01   JOURNAL-RECORD
002100                                      COPY   JRNLRECD.
002200*01   WS-COMMAREA
002300                                      COPY   POWSVMCA.
002400*01   WS-STATUS-FIELDS
002500                                      COPY   STWSSTAT.
002600*01   VM-CONTROL-MAP
002700                                      COPY   MAPVMCTL.
002800*01   VM-DETAIL-MAP
002900                                      COPY   MAPVDTL2.
003000*01   WS-DATE-AND-TIME
003100                                      COPY   STWSDTTM.
003200*01   WS-STATE-CODE-SEARCH-ENTRIES
003300                                      COPY   STWST037.
003400*01   ATTRIBUTE-LIST
003500                                      COPY   STWSATTR.
003600*01   DFHAID
003700                                      COPY   DFHAID.
003800*
003900 01   END-OF-WORKING-STORAGE   PIC X(15)   VALUE 'END WS POVMADDN'.
004000*
004100 LINKAGE SECTION.
004200*
004300 01   DFHCOMMAREA                    PIC X(8).
004400*
004500 01   BLL-CELLS.
004600      05  FILLER                     PIC S9(8)   COMP.
004700      05  BLL-CWA-ADDRESS            PIC S9(8)   COMP.
004800      05  BLL-T037-STATE-TABLE-ADDRESS PIC S9(8) COMP.
004900*
005000*01   CWA-DATA
005100                     COPY   STLNKCWA.
005200*01   T037-STATE-TABLE
005300                     COPY   T037STAT.
005400
005500
005600 PROCEDURE DIVISION.
005700***********************************************************************
005800*     PROGRAM STRUCTURE IS:                                           *
005900*        AA00-MAINLINE                                                *
006000*          B000-INITIAL-ENTRY                                         *
006100*            B100-SEND-CONTROL-MAP-AND-DATA                           *
006200*              B110-GET-DATE-AND-TIME                                 *
006300*                                                                     *
006400*          C000-PROCESS-CONTROL-MAP                                   *
006500*            C100-RECEIVE-CONTROL-MAP                                 *
006600*              C110-END-SESSION                                       *
006700*              C120-TRANSFER-XCTL-TO-MENU                             *
006800*              C130-TRANSFER-XCTL-TO-BROWSE                           *
006900*            C200-VERIFY-VENDOR-FORMAT                                *
007000*            C400-VERIFY-VENDOR-FILE-STATUS                           *
007100*              C410-READ-VENDOR-FILE                                  *
007200*            C500-SEND-DETAIL-MAP-AND-DATA                            *
007300*              B110-GET-DATE-AND-TIME                                 *
007400*              C520-SET-MAP-ATTRIBUTES                                *
007500*              C530-FORMAT-DETAIL-MAP                                 *
007600*                C531-GET-STATE-NAME                                  *
007700*            C600-SEND-CONTROL-MAP-DATAONLY                           *
007800*                                                                     *
```

Figure 13-4 *(Continued)*

```
007900*              E000-ADDITION-PROCESSING                         *
008000*              D100-RECEIVE-DETAIL-MAP                          *
008100*                    C110-END-SESSION                           *
008200*                    C120-TRANSFER-XCTL-TO-MENU                 *
008300*              E100-ADD-VENDOR-RECORD                           *
008400*                 E110-EDIT-MAP-FORMAT-VM-RECORD                *
008500*                      C531-GET-STATE-NAME                      *
008600*                 E120-WRITE-VENDOR-RECORD                      *
008700*                      E121-POST-JOURNAL-RECORD                 *
008800*              B100-SEND-CONTROL-MAP-AND-DATA                   *
008900*              D200-SEND-DETAIL-MAP-DATAONLY                    *
009000*                 C520-SET-MAP-ATTRIBUTES                       *
009100*********************************************************************
009200*
009300 AA00-MAINLINE   SECTION.
009400*
009500*    SERVICE RELOAD BLL-CELLS.
009600*
009700      MOVE LOW-VALUES  TO  VM-CONTROL-MAP.
009800*
009900      IF EIBCALEN  =  0
010000          PERFORM B000-INITIAL-ENTRY
010100      ELSE
010200          MOVE DFHCOMMAREA  TO  WS-COMMAREA
010300          IF CA-BROWSE
010400              MOVE SPACE         TO  CA-FUNCTION-CODE
010500              MOVE LOW-VALUES   TO  VM-CONTROL-MAP
010600              PERFORM C400-VERIFY-VENDOR-FILE-STATUS
010700              IF GOOD-VERIFY
010800                  PERFORM C500-SEND-DETAIL-MAP-AND-DATA
010900              ELSE
011000                  PERFORM B100-SEND-CONTROL-MAP-AND-DATA
011100          ELSE
011200              IF CA-RECEIVE-CTL-MAP
011300                  PERFORM C000-PROCESS-CONTROL-MAP
011400              ELSE
011500                  PERFORM E000-ADDITION-PROCESSING.
011600*
011700      EXEC CICS RETURN
011800              TRANSID  ('POVA')
011900              COMMAREA (WS-COMMAREA)
012000              LENGTH   (8)
012100      END-EXEC.
012200*
012300 B000-INITIAL-ENTRY   SECTION.
012400*********************************************************************
012500*                PERFORMED FROM:   AA00-MAINLINE                 *
012600*********************************************************************
012700*
012800      MOVE LOW-VALUES  TO  VM-CONTROL-MAP.
012900      PERFORM B100-SEND-CONTROL-MAP-AND-DATA.
013000*
013100 B000-EXIT.
013200      EXIT.
013300*
013400 B100-SEND-CONTROL-MAP-AND-DATA   SECTION.
013500*********************************************************************
013600*           PERFORMED FROM:   B000-INITIAL-ENTRY                 *
013700*                             E000-ADDITION-PROCESSING           *
013800*********************************************************************
013900*
014000      PERFORM B110-GET-DATE-AND-TIME.
014100      MOVE WS-CURRENT-DATE  TO  MVC-D-DATE.
014200      MOVE WS-MAP-TIME      TO  MVC-D-TIME.
014300*
014400      MOVE -1  TO  MVC-L-VEND-CD-1.
014500      MOVE '1'  TO  CA-MAP-CONTROL.
014600*
014700      EXEC CICS SEND
014800              MAP      ('MAPPOVC')
014900              MAPSET ('POVMAD1')
015000              FROM    (VM-CONTROL-MAP)
015100              ERASE
015200              CURSOR
015300      END-EXEC.
015400*
015500 B100-EXIT.
015600      EXIT.
015700*
015800 B110-GET-DATE-AND-TIME   SECTION.
015900*********************************************************************
016000*        STPDDTTM - OBTAIN DATE FROM CWA AND FORMAT TIME         *
016100*           PERFORMED FROM:   B100-SEND-CONTROL-MAP-AND-DATA      *
```

Figure 13-4 (*Continued*)

```
016200*                              C500-SEND-DETAIL-MAP-AND-DATA           *
016300*****************************************************************
016400*
016500      COPY STPDDTTM.
016600*
016700 B110-EXIT.
016800      EXIT.
016900*
017000 C000-PROCESS-CONTROL-MAP  SECTION.
017100*****************************************************************
017200*         PERFORMED FROM:  AA00-MAINLINE                         *
017300*           PROCESS CONTROL MAP - IF VALID SEND DETAIL MAP       *
017400*           ELSE SEND CONTROL MAP WITH INVALID MESSAGE:          *
017500*    1) STATUS-OF-RECEIVE    =  'I'    INVALID KEY PRESSED       *
017600*    2) STATUS-OF-RECEIVE    =  'M'    MAPFAIL - NO DATA ENTERED *
017700*    3) STATUS-OF-FORMAT     =  'E'    INVALID VENDOR KEYED FORMAT *
017800*    4) STATUS-OF-VERIFY     =  'E'    VENDOR FILE STATUS ERROR  *
017900*****************************************************************
018000*
018100      PERFORM C100-RECEIVE-CONTROL-MAP.
018200      IF GOOD-RECEIVE
018300          PERFORM C200-VERIFY-VENDOR-FORMAT
018400          IF VALID-FORMAT
018500              PERFORM C400-VERIFY-VENDOR-FILE-STATUS
018600              IF GOOD-VERIFY
018700                  PERFORM C500-SEND-DETAIL-MAP-AND-DATA
018800              ELSE
018900                  PERFORM C600-SEND-CONTROL-MAP-DATAONLY
019000          ELSE
019100              PERFORM C600-SEND-CONTROL-MAP-DATAONLY
019200      ELSE
019300          IF MAPFAIL-ON-RECEIVE
019400              MOVE 'VENDOR CODE MUST BE ENTERED - PLEASE KEY-IN'
019500                                 TO MVC-D-MESSAGE
019600              MOVE ASKIP-BRT   TO MVC-A-MESSAGE
019700              PERFORM C600-SEND-CONTROL-MAP-DATAONLY
019800          ELSE
019900              PERFORM C600-SEND-CONTROL-MAP-DATAONLY.
020000*
020100 C000-EXIT.
020200      EXIT.
020300*
020400 C100-RECEIVE-CONTROL-MAP  SECTION.
020500*****************************************************************
020600*         PERFORMED FROM:  C000-PROCESS-CONTROL-MAP             *
020700*             ENTER IS ONLY VALID DATA ENTRY KEY               *
020800*   CLEAR KEY - ENDS TERMINAL SESSION     PF5 - RETURNS TO MENU *
020900*                                         PF4 - XCTL TO BROWSE  *
021000*             ALL OTHER AID KEYS ARE INVALID                   *
021100*         STATUS-OF-RECEIVE  =  'G'  =  GOOD RECEIVE           *
021200*                               'M'  =  MAPFAIL               *
021300*                               'I'  =  INVALID KEY PRESSED   *
021400*****************************************************************
021500*
021600      MOVE LOW-VALUES  TO  VM-CONTROL-MAP.
021700*
021800      IF EIBAID  =  DFHENTER
021900          MOVE 'M'  TO  STATUS-OF-RECEIVE
022000*
022100          EXEC CICS HANDLE CONDITION
022200                    MAPFAIL (C100-EXIT)
022300          END-EXEC
022400*
022500          EXEC CICS RECEIVE
022600                    MAP     ('MAPPOVC')
022700                    MAPSET  ('POVMAD1')
022800                    INTO    (VM-CONTROL-MAP)
022900          END-EXEC
023000*
023100          MOVE 'G'  TO  STATUS-OF-RECEIVE
023200      ELSE
023300          IF EIBAID  =  DFHCLEAR
023400              PERFORM C110-END-SESSION
023500          ELSE
023600          IF EIBAID  =  DFHPF5
023700              PERFORM C120-TRANSFER-XCTL-TO-MENU
023800          ELSE
023900          IF EIBAID  =  DFHPF4
024000              PERFORM C130-TRANSFER-XCTL-TO-BROWSE
024100          ELSE
024200              MOVE 'I'        TO  STATUS-OF-RECEIVE
024300              MOVE 'INVALID KEY PRESSED - PLEASE TRY AGAIN'
024400                              TO  MVC-D-MESSAGE
```

Figure 13-4 *(Continued)*

```
024500                MOVE ASKIP-BRT  TO  MVC-A-MESSAGE.
024600*
024700 C100-EXIT.
024800      EXIT..
024900*
025000 C110-END-SESSION , SECTION.
025100***************************************************************
025200*   CRT OPERATOR PRESSED CLEAR KEY TO END TERMINAL SESSION    *
025300*        PERFORMED FROM:  C100-RECEIVE-CONTROL-MAP            *
025400*                         D100-RECEIVE-DETAIL-MAP             *
025500***************************************************************
025600*
025700      EXEC CICS SEND
025800              FROM   (WS-CRT-MESSAGE)
025900              LENGTH (17)
026000              ERASE
026100      END-EXEC.
026200*
026300      EXEC CICS RETURN
026400      END-EXEC.
026500*
026600 C110-EXIT.
026700      EXIT.
026800*
026900 C120-TRANSFER-XCTL-TO-MENU  SECTION.
027000***************************************************************
027100*        OPERATOR PRESSED PF5 TO RETURN TO MENU PROGRAM       *
027200*        PERFORMED FROM:  C100-RECEIVE-CONTROL-MAP            *
027300*                         D100-RECEIVE-DETAIL-MAP             *
027400***************************************************************
027500*
027600      EXEC CICS XCTL
027700              PROGRAM ('POVMAINT')
027800      END-EXEC.
027900*
028000 C120-EXIT.
028100      EXIT.
028200*
028300 C130-TRANSFER-XCTL-TO-BROWSE  SECTION.
028400***************************************************************
028500*        OPERATOR PRESSED PF4 TO TRANSFER CONTROL TO BROWSE   *
028600*        PERFORMED FROM:  C100-RECEIVE-CONTROL-MAP            *
028700*                         D100-RECEIVE-DETAIL-MAP             *
028800***************************************************************
028900*
029000      MOVE LOW-VALUES  TO  WS-COMMAREA.
029100      MOVE 'A'         TO  CA-FUNCTION-CODE.
029200*
029300      EXEC CICS XCTL
029400              PROGRAM  ('POVMBROW')
029500              COMMAREA (WS-COMMAREA)
029600              LENGTH   (8)
029700      END-EXEC.
029800*
029900 C130-EXIT.
030000      EXIT.
030100*
030200 C200-VERIFY-VENDOR-FORMAT  SECTION.
030300***************************************************************
030400*         VERIFY FORMAT OF VENDOR CODE KEYED-IN = A-9999-9    *
030500*             PERFORMED FROM:  C000-PROCESS-CONTROL-MAP       *
030600*    IF VALID FORMAT - MOVE CODE TO WS-COMMAREA FIELDS (CA- ) *
030700***************************************************************
030800*
030900      IF (MVC-D-VEND-CD-1   IS  ALPHABETIC
031000            AND
031100         MVC-D-VEND-CD-1   IS NOT =  SPACE)
031200         AND
031300         MVC-D-VEND-CD-2   IS  NUMERIC
031400         AND
031500         MVC-D-VEND-CD-3   IS  NUMERIC
031600         MOVE MVC-D-VEND-CD-1  TO  CA-VEND-1
031700         MOVE MVC-D-VEND-CD-2  TO  CA-VEND-2
031800         MOVE MVC-D-VEND-CD-3  TO  CA-VEND-3
031900         MOVE 'G'              TO  STATUS-OF-FORMAT
032000      ELSE
032100         MOVE 'E'         TO  STATUS-OF-FORMAT
032200         MOVE 'VENDOR CODE FORMAT MUST BE: A-9999-9 - PLEASE RE-EN
032300-             'TER'   TO  MVC-D-MESSAGE
032400         MOVE ASKIP-BRT TO  MVC-A-MESSAGE.
032500*
032600 C200-EXIT.
032700 ·    EXIT.
```

Figure 13-4 *(Continued)*

```
032800*
032900 C400-VERIFY-VENDOR-FILE-STATUS  SECTION.
033000***********************************************************************
033100*             PERFORMED FROM:  C000-PROCESS-CONTROL-MAP           *
033200*             MUST NOT BE A VENDOR RECORD FOR ADDITIONS           *
033300***********************************************************************
033400*
033500      MOVE 'G' TO  STATUS-OF-VERIFY.
033600*
033700      PERFORM C410-READ-VENDOR-FILE.
033800*
033900      IF RECORD-NOT-FOUND
034000         NEXT SENTENCE
034100      ELSE
034200         MOVE 'E'          TO  STATUS-OF-VERIFY
034300         MOVE 'VENDOR TO BE ADDED IS ALREADY ON THE FILE'
034400                           TO  MVC-D-MESSAGE
034500         MOVE ASKIP-BRT    TO  MVC-A-MESSAGE.
034600*
034700 C400-EXIT.
034800      EXIT.
034900*
035000 C410-READ-VENDOR-FILE  SECTION.
035100***********************************************************************
035200*      PERFORMED FROM:  C400-VERIFY-VENDOR-FILE-STATUS           *
035300***********************************************************************
035400*
035500      MOVE 'E' TO  STATUS-OF-READ.
035600*
035700      EXEC CICS HANDLE CONDITION
035800               NOTFND  (C410-EXIT)
035900      END-EXEC.
036000*
036100      EXEC CICS READ
036200            DATASET ('VENDMAST')
036300            INTO    (VENDOR-MASTER-RECORD)
036400            RIDFLD  (CA-VENDOR-CODE)
036500      END-EXEC.
036600*
036700      MOVE 'G' TO  STATUS-OF-READ.
036800*
036900 C410-EXIT.
037000      EXIT.
037100*
037200 C500-SEND-DETAIL-MAP-AND-DATA  SECTION.
037300***********************************************************************
037400*       SEND DETAIL MAP - PHYSICAL AND SYMBOLIC MAPS             *
037500*       PERFORMED FROM:  C000-PROCESS-CONTROL-MAP                *
037600*  SENT WHEN ALL VALIDATION AND EDIT CONDITIONS HAVE BEEN MET    *
037700***********************************************************************
037800*
037900      MOVE LOW-VALUES  TO  VM-DETAIL-MAP.
038000*
038100      PERFORM B110-GET-DATE-AND-TIME.
038200      MOVE WS-CURRENT-DATE  TO  MVD-D-DATE.
038300      MOVE WS-MAP-TIME      TO  MVD-D-TIME.
038400*
038500      PERFORM C520-SET-MAP-ATTRIBUTES.
038600      PERFORM C530-FORMAT-DETAIL-MAP.
038700*
038800      MOVE -1   TO  MVD-L-VENDOR-NAME.
038900      MOVE '2'  TO  CA-MAP-CONTROL.
039000*
039100      EXEC CICS SEND
039200            MAP    ('MAPPOVD')
039300            MAPSET ('POVMAD2')
039400            FROM   (VM-DETAIL-MAP)
039500            ERASE
039600            CURSOR
039700      END-EXEC.
039800*
039900 C500-EXIT.
040000      EXIT.
040100*
040200 C520-SET-MAP-ATTRIBUTES  SECTION.
040300***********************************************************************
040400*       PERFORMED FROM:  C500-SEND-DETAIL-MAP-AND-DATA           *
040500*                        D200-SEND-DETAIL-MAP-DATAONLY           *
040600***********************************************************************
040700*
040800      MOVE UNPROT-FSET  TO  MVD-A-PHONE-AREA-CD
040900                            MVD-A-PHONE-1
041000                            MVD-A-PHONE-2
```

Figure 13-4   (Continued)

```
041100                           MVD-A-VENDOR-NAME
041200                           MVD-A-CONTACT
041300                           MVD-A-STREET
041400                           MVD-A-CITY
041500                           MVD-A-STATE-CODE
041600                           MVD-A-ZIP-CODE
041700                           MVD-A-ATTENTION-OF.
041800*
041900 C520-EXIT.
042000     EXIT.
042100*
042200 C530-FORMAT-DETAIL-MAP   SECTION.
042300******************************************************************
042400*            FORMAT DETAIL MAP FOR INITIAL SEND              *
042500*         PERFORMED FROM:  C500-SEND-DETAIL-MAP-AND-DATA     *
042600******************************************************************
042700*
042800* FORMAT VENDOR CODE: A-9999-9   WS- FIELDS ARE AT END OF VENDMAST
042900     MOVE CA-VEND-1       TO   WS-VENDOR-CD-1.
043000     MOVE CA-VEND-2       TO   WS-VENDOR-CD-2.
043100     MOVE CA-VEND-3       TO   WS-VENDOR-CD-3.
043200     MOVE WS-VENDOR-CODE  TO   MVD-D-VENDOR-CODE.
043300*
043400 C530-EXIT.
043500     EXIT.
043600*
043700 C531-GET-STATE-NAME  SECTION.
043800******************************************************************
043900*            LOAD AND SEARCH STATE CODE TABLE                *
044000*         PERFORMED FROM:  E110-EDIT-MAP-FORMAT-VM-RECORD    *
044100******************************************************************
044200*
044300     COPY STPDT037.
044400*
044500 C531-EXIT.
044600     EXIT.
044700*
044800 C600-SEND-CONTROL-MAP-DATAONLY  SECTION.
044900******************************************************************
045000*         SEND CONTROL MAP DATAONLY - SYMBOLIC MAP          *
045100*         PERFORMED FROM:  C000-PROCESS-CONTROL-MAP          *
045200*                SENT FOR INVALID CONDITIONS                 *
045300******************************************************************
045400*
045500     MOVE '1' TO  CA-MAP-CONTROL.
045600     MOVE -1  TO  MVC-L-VEND-CD-1.
045700*
045800     MOVE UNPROT-FSET  TO  MVC-A-VEND-CD-1
045900                           MVC-A-VEND-CD-2
046000                           MVC-A-VEND-CD-3.
046100*
046200     EXEC CICS SEND
046300              MAP      ('MAPPOVC')
046400              MAPSET   ('POVMAD1')
046500              FROM     (VM-CONTROL-MAP)
046600              DATAONLY
046700              CURSOR
046800     END-EXEC.
046900*
047000 C600-EXIT.
047100     EXIT.
047200*
047300 D100-RECEIVE-DETAIL-MAP  SECTION.
047400******************************************************************
047500*          PERFORMED FROM:  E000-ADDITION-PROCESSING         *
047600* ENTER - PROCESSES TRANSACTION         CLEAR - ENDS SESSION *
047700* PF3  - SETS DISPLAY OF CTL MAP       PF5  - RETURNS TO MENU*
047800*           ALL OTHER KEYS ARE INVALID                       *
047900*      STATUS-OF-RECEIVE = 'G'  =  GOOD RECEIVE              *
048000*                          'C'  =  RETURN TO CTL-MAP         *
048100*                          'I'  =  INVALID KEY PRESSED       *
048200******************************************************************
048300*
048400     MOVE LOW-VALUES  TO  VM-DETAIL-MAP.
048500*
048600     IF EIBAID  =  DFHENTER
048700*
048800         EXEC CICS IGNORE CONDITION
048900                  MAPFAIL
049000         END-EXEC
049100*
049200         EXEC CICS RECEIVE
049300                  MAP      ('MAPPOVD')
```

Figure 13-4 (*Continued*)

```
049400                    MAPSET   ('POVMAD2')
049500                    INTO     (VM-DETAIL-MAP)
049600        END-EXEC
049700*
049800        MOVE 'G'  TO  STATUS-OF-RECEIVE
049900     ELSE
050000        IF EIBAID  =  DFHCLEAR
050100           PERFORM C110-END-SESSION
050200        ELSE
050300        IF EIBAID  =  DFHPF3
050400           MOVE 'C'  TO  STATUS-OF-RECEIVE
050500        ELSE
050600        IF EIBAID  =  DFHPF5
050700           PERFORM C120-TRANSFER-XCTL-TO-MENU
050800        ELSE
050900           MOVE 'I'        TO  STATUS-OF-RECEIVE
051000           MOVE 'INVALID KEY PRESSED - PLEASE TRY AGAIN'
051100                           TO  MVD-D-MESSAGE.
051200           MOVE ASKIP-BRT  TO  MVD-A-MESSAGE.
051300*
051400 D100-EXIT.
051500     EXIT.
051600*
051700 D200-SEND-DETAIL-MAP-DATAONLY   SECTION.
051800****************************************************************
051900*        SEND DETAIL MAP DATA ONLY - SYMBOLIC MAP            *
052000*        PERFORMED FROM:  E000-ADDITION-PROCESSING           *
052100*  SENT IF INVALID KEY IS PRESSED ON A RECEIVE OF THE DETAIL MAP *
052200****************************************************************
052300*
052400     MOVE '2'  TO  CA-MAP-CONTROL.
052500*
052600     PERFORM C520-SET-MAP-ATTRIBUTES.
052700*
052800     EXEC CICS SEND
052900                MAP       ('MAPPOVD')
053000                MAPSET    ('POVMAD2')
053100                FROM      (VM-DETAIL-MAP)
053200                DATAONLY
053300                CURSOR
053400        END-EXEC.
053500*
053600 D200-EXIT.
053700     EXIT.
053800*
053900 E000-ADDITION-PROCESSING   SECTION.
054000****************************************************************
054100*        PERFORMED FROM:  AA00-MAINLINE                      *
054200*     DETAIL MAP IS SENT IF AN INVALID KEY WAS PRESSED       *
054300*             OR IF ADD WAS UNSUCCESSFUL                      *
054400****************************************************************
054500*
054600     PERFORM D100-RECEIVE-DETAIL-MAP.
054700*
054800     IF GOOD-RECEIVE
054900        PERFORM E100-ADD-VENDOR-RECORD
055000        IF GOOD-ADD
055100           PERFORM B100-SEND-CONTROL-MAP-AND-DATA
055200        ELSE
055300           PERFORM D200-SEND-DETAIL-MAP-DATAONLY
055400     ELSE
055500        IF RETURN-TO-CTL-MAP
055600           PERFORM B100-SEND-CONTROL-MAP-AND-DATA
055700        ELSE
055800           PERFORM D200-SEND-DETAIL-MAP-DATAONLY.
055900*
056000 E000-EXIT.
056100     EXIT.
056200*
056300 E100-ADD-VENDOR-RECORD SECTION.
056400****************************************************************
056500*        PERFORMED FROM:  E000-ADDITION-PROCESSING           *
056600*     PERFORMS EDITS AND FORMATS VENDOR-MASTER-RECORD        *
056700*          IF GOOD EDIT - ADDS RECORD TO THE FILE            *
056800*  RECORD ALREADY ON FILE MESSAGE COULD ONLY OCCUR IF RECORD WAS *
056900*  ADDED BY ANOTHER TERMINAL SINCE KEYED-IN ON CONTROL SCREEN   *
057000****************************************************************
057100*
057200     MOVE SPACES        TO  VENDOR-MASTER-RECORD.
057300     MOVE CA-VENDOR-CODE TO  VM-VENDOR-CODE.
057400*
057500     MOVE 'E'  TO  STATUS-OF-ADD.
057600*
```

Figure 13-4 *(Continued)*

```
057700      PERFORM E110-EDIT-MAP-FORMAT-VM-RECORD.
057800*
057900      IF GOOD-EDIT
058000          PERFORM E120-WRITE-VENDOR-RECORD
058100          IF GOOD-WRITE
058200              MOVE 'RECORD SUCCESSFULLY ADDED'
058300                              TO  MVC-D-MESSAGE
058400              MOVE ASKIP-BRT  TO  MVC-A-MESSAGE
058500              MOVE 'G' TO STATUS-OF-ADD
058600          ELSE
058700              MOVE 'RECORD TO BE ADDED -ALREADY ON VENDOR FILE'
058800                              TO  MVD-D-MESSAGE
058900              MOVE ASKIP-BRT  TO  MVD-A-MESSAGE.
059000*
059100 E100-EXIT.
059200      EXIT.
059300*
059400 E110-EDIT-MAP-FORMAT-VM-RECORD  SECTION.
059500*************************************************************
059600*      EDIT DETAIL MAP DATA - FORMAT VENDOR MASTER RECORD    *
059700*         PERFORMED FROM:  E100-ADD-VENDOR-RECORD            *
059800*         HIGHLIGHT FIELDS WHICH CONTAIN INCORRECT DATA      *
059900*             OR WHICH ARE MISSING REQUIRED ENTRIES          *
060000*************************************************************
060100*
060200      MOVE 'G'  TO  STATUS-OF-EDIT.
060300*
060400* ASSUME ALL PHONE DIGITS SHOULD BE NUMERIC
060500*
060600      IF MVD-D-PHONE-AREA-CD  IS  NUMERIC
060700         AND
060800         MVD-D-PHONE-1        IS  NUMERIC
060900         AND
061000         MVD-D-PHONE-2        IS  NUMERIC
061100          MOVE MVD-D-PHONE-AREA-CD  TO  VM-AREA-CD
061200          MOVE MVD-D-PHONE-1        TO  VM-PHONE-1-3
061300          MOVE MVD-D-PHONE-2        TO  VM-PHONE-4-7
061400          MOVE ASKIP-NORM           TO  MVD-C-A-PHONE
061500      ELSE
061600          MOVE -1         TO  MVD-L-PHONE-AREA-CD
061700          MOVE ASKIP-BRT  TO  MVD-C-A-PHONE
061800          MOVE 'E'        TO  STATUS-OF-EDIT.
061900*
062000      IF MVD-D-VENDOR-NAME  =  LOW-VALUES  OR  SPACES
062100          MOVE -1         TO  MVD-L-VENDOR-NAME
062200          MOVE ASKIP-BRT  TO  MVD-C-A-VENDOR-NAME
062300          MOVE 'E'        TO  STATUS-OF-EDIT
062400      ELSE
062500          MOVE MVD-D-VENDOR-NAME  TO  VM-VENDOR-NAME
062600          MOVE ASKIP-NORM         TO  MVD-C-A-VENDOR-NAME.
062700*
062800* 'CONTACT' AND 'TO ATTENTION OF' ARE OPTIONAL FIELDS
062900*
063000      IF MVD-L-CONTACT  =  ZERO
063100          MOVE SPACES         TO  VM-CONTACT
063200      ELSE
063300          MOVE MVD-D-CONTACT  TO  VM-CONTACT.
063400*
063500      IF MVD-L-STREET  =  0     OR
063600         MVD-D-STREET  =  SPACES
063700          MOVE -1         TO  MVD-L-STREET
063800          MOVE ASKIP-BRT  TO  MVD-C-A-STREET
063900          MOVE 'E'        TO  STATUS-OF-EDIT
064000      ELSE
064100          MOVE MVD-D-STREET  TO  VM-STREET-ADDRESS
064200          MOVE ASKIP-NORM    TO  MVD-C-A-STREET.
064300*
064400      MOVE ZEROES  TO  VM-DOLLARS-COMMITTED.
064500*
064600      IF MVD-D-CITY  =  LOW-VALUES  OR  SPACES
064700          MOVE -1         TO  MVD-L-CITY
064800          MOVE ASKIP-BRT  TO  MVD-C-A-CITY
064900          MOVE 'E'        TO  STATUS-OF-EDIT
065000      ELSE
065100          MOVE MVD-D-CITY  TO  VM-CITY
065200          MOVE ASKIP-NORM  TO  MVD-C-A-CITY.
065300*
```

Figure 13-4 *(Continued)*

```
065400      MOVE MVD-D-STATE-CODE  TO  WS-STATE-CODE.
065500      PERFORM C531-GET-STATE-NAME.
065600      IF STATE-FOUND
065700          MOVE MVD-D-STATE-CODE  TO  VM-STATE
065800          MOVE WS-STATE-NAME     TO  MVD-D-STATE-NAME
065900          MOVE ASKIP-NORM        TO  MVD-C-A-STATE
066000      ELSE
066100          MOVE ALL '*'    TO  MVD-D-STATE-NAME
066200          MOVE -1         TO  MVD-L-STATE-CODE
066300          MOVE ASKIP-BRT  TO  MVD-C-A-STATE
066400          MOVE 'E'        TO  STATUS-OF-EDIT.
066500*
066600      IF MVD-D-ZIP-CODE  IS  NUMERIC
066700          MOVE MVD-D-ZIP-CODE  TO  VM-ZIP-CODE
066800          MOVE ASKIP-NORM      TO  MVD-C-A-ZIP-CODE
066900      ELSE
067000          MOVE -1         TO  MVD-L-ZIP-CODE
067100          MOVE ASKIP-BRT  TO  MVD-C-A-ZIP-CODE
067200          MOVE 'E'        TO  STATUS-OF-EDIT.
067300*
067400      IF MVD-L-ATTENTION-OF  =  ZERO
067500          MOVE SPACES          TO  VM-TO-ATTN-OF
067600      ELSE
067700          MOVE MVD-D-ATTENTION-OF  TO  VM-TO-ATTN-OF.
067800*
067900      IF STATUS-OF-EDIT  =  'E'
068000          MOVE 'PLEASE CORRECT HIGHLIGHTED FIELDS'
068100                          TO  MVD-D-MESSAGE
068200          MOVE ASKIP-BRT  TO  MVD-A-MESSAGE.
068300*
068400  E110-EXIT.
068500      EXIT.
068600*
068700  E120-WRITE-VENDOR-RECORD  SECTION.
068800***********************************************************
068900*        WRITE VENDOR RECORD - PERFORM JOURNAL POSTING    *
069000*            PERFORMED FROM:  E100-ADD-VENDOR-RECORD       *
069100***********************************************************
069200      MOVE 'E'  TO  STATUS-OF-WRITE.
069300*
069400      EXEC CICS HANDLE CONDITION
069500              DUPREC  (E120-EXIT)
069600      END-EXEC.
069700*
069800      EXEC CICS WRITE
069900              DATASET ('VENDMAST')
070000              FROM    (VENDOR-MASTER-RECORD)
070100              RIDFLD  (CA-VENDOR-CODE)
070200      END-EXEC.
070300*
070400      MOVE 'G'  TO  STATUS-OF-WRITE.
070500*
070600      MOVE 'A'  TO  JR-TYPE.
070700      PERFORM E121-POST-JOURNAL-RECORD.
070800*
070900  E120-EXIT.
071000      EXIT.
071100*
071200  E121-POST-JOURNAL-RECORD  SECTION.
071300***********************************************************
071400*    POST JOURNAL ENTRY - LINK TO JOURNAL PROGRAM 'JRNLPOST'  *
071500*        PERFORMED FROM:  E120-WRITE-VENDOR-RECORD            *
071600***********************************************************
071700*
071800      MOVE 'VM'                  TO  JR-PREFIX.
071900      MOVE VENDOR-MASTER-RECORD  TO  JR-RECORD-DATA.
072000      MOVE SPACES                TO  JR-PASSWORD.
072100*
072200      EXEC CICS LINK
072300              PROGRAM  ('JRNLPOST')
072400              COMMAREA (JOURNAL-RECORD)
072500              LENGTH   (524)
072600      END-EXEC.
072700*
072800  E121-EXIT.
072900      EXIT.
```

2. MOVE −1 TO MVD-L-VENDOR-NAME. Moving a −1 to the symbolic map length field sets the cursor initially at this item.

C520-SET-MAP-ATTRIBUTES. This section turns on the MDT for all data entry fields by moving the UNPROT,FSET attribute to each field prior to the SEND MAP command. The MDT is turned on any time data is keyed into a field. A map could be received after data had been keyed into its fields in order to edit and process the fields. The editing might detect errors in some of the fields and send the map DATAONLY with the field identifiers of the incorrectly entered fields highlighted. The map would be sent with a brightened error message. When FRSET is specified on the BMS map DFHMSD macro, a SEND MAP command turns off all MDTs. This section ensures that all data-entry fields on the map are returned on subsequent receives of the map. There are more sophisticated ways to handle this situation, but this is one of the easier methods. Vendor code is not a data-entry field on the detail map; its BMS map attribute is ASKIP.

C530-FORMAT-DETAIL-MAP. Moves vendor code fields obtained from WS-COMMAREA subfields to the appropriate map locations prior to the send of the detail map. There are no vendor record fields to display since no record exists.

E100-ADD-VENDOR-RECORD. Performs an edit of map data and a format of the vendor record. If the edit and format are successful, a write of the vendor record is performed. The message RECORD SUCCESSFULLY ADDED is normally returned and displayed on the control screen. The message RECORD TO BE ADDED—ALREADY ON VENDOR FILE could only be displayed if an operator at another terminal added the same record you are attempting to add, after you had entered vendor code on the control screen. This program would have previously read the vendor file for the entered vendor code (in section C410-READ-VENDOR-FILE) and determined that it was not online, in order to reach this point. Do not be overly concerned with the possibility of this happening, because it is not a common occurrence. There are techniques, beyond the scope of this book, to control this situation.

E110-EDIT-MAP-FORMAT-VM-RECORD. This section expects that all fields which were entered will be available each time the detail map is received. This will be the case because section C520-SET-MAP-ATTRIBUTES resets the MDTs each time the detail map is sent. There are many different acceptable ways to validate input data received from a screen. This section employs several different methods.

1. A field can be checked for data expected to be numeric such as area code, phone number, and zip code.

2. Fields which contain low-values or spaces may be considered invalid. Using the techniques chosen for the maintenance programs, a field would contain

low-values only if nothing was keyed into the field or if the EOF key was pressed. Spaces would be present in a field only if the operator keyed in at least one space, or if the program moved spaces to a map field prior to a send.

3. Field length could be tested in order to determine if data had been keyed into a field. The field's length would be greater than zero if at least one character had been entered. Be careful how you use the length field because it is sometimes different on the initial receive of a map than it is on subsequent receives of the same map. When an operator enters data, the initial receive of the map returns the actual length keyed in. Subsequent receives of the same map, if the program sets the attribute to FSET and if a field was not rekeyed, will return the full length of the field regardless of how many characters were originally entered.

I have chosen the technique of highlighting (ASKIP,BRT) the field identifiers of items which have been entered incorrectly or for which data has been omitted. I move an error indicator to STATUS-OF-EDIT for invalid fields. On subsequent receives of the same map, the ASKIP,NORM attribute is moved to the field identifier of correctly entered fields. At the end of this section, I check if STATUS-OF-EDIT equals E, and, if so, move the message PLEASE CORRECT HIGHLIGHTED FIELDS to the detail map message field. The detail map is sent DATAONLY in section E000-ADDITION-PROCESSING.

E120-WRITE-VENDOR-RECORD. Write the addition record to the vendor master file. If the record is already on the file, the DUPREC handle condition will be invoked and an E will be returned in STATUS-OF-WRITE. A good write will return a G in STATUS-OF-WRITE. An after (A) journal record posting will be performed; there is no before-record for an add. The DUPREC indicator will be invoked only if an operator at another terminal has already added the same record you are attempting to add.

SUMMARY

This chapter presented an addition program which can be used as a model for most addition programs you will have to write. Several of the commands discussed in preceding chapters were used. The use of attributes was expanded upon, and different techniques for editing data received from the map were discussed. The READ and WRITE file commands were used, and the DUPREC handle condition was coded before the WRITE command was issued.

14

THE CHANGE PROGRAM

After a file has been created, records added to the file, and an inquiry program written to check the status of various fields, it is often necessary to change records in the file. This chapter discusses the change program.

Control and detail maps are used for the change program. The control map shown in Fig. 14-1 requires the terminal operator to key in a vendor code and to press ENTER in order to display the change detail screen. The operator also has the option of transferring control to the vendor file browse, returning to the vendor file maintenance submenu (see Fig. 6-3), or ending the session. The vendor file change program detail map shown in Fig. 2-8 is displayed when the operator keys in an existing vendor code on the control screen and then presses ENTER. The detail map shows all vendor file fields which can be changed on the vendor's record. The detail change screen permits the operator to key in the vendor's new data and then press ENTER in order to update the record. The program will then return to the control screen to allow entry of another vendor's code. The detail screen also permits the operator to return to the change control screen without changing the record, return to the submenu, or to end the session.

BMS Maps

Figures 14-2 and 14-3 show the BMS maps for the control and detail screens, respectively.

BMS Control Map

Only the differences between this map and the BMS control map for the inquiry program (see Fig. 12-1) are shown in Fig. 14-2.

Figure 14-1 Vendor File Changes Control Map.

BMS Detail Map

This map is similar to the addition detail map shown in Fig. 13-3. Only the differences are shown in Fig. 14-3. Keep map fields in similar columns; for related maps, it makes map creation easy.

User-Friendly Symbolic Maps

The user-friendly symbolic maps created to correspond to the generated BMS maps are shown in the copy library (App. B, members MAPVMCTL and MAPVDTL2).

Change Program Source Code

The change program source code, shown in Fig. 14-4, follows the format used in previous examples. I will only discuss the sections which differ from previous examples.

Procedure Division

AA00-MAINLINE. This section is similar to that of the inquiry program in

```
          PRINT NOGEN
POVMCH1   DFHMSD TYPE=MAP,                                              X
              .
              .
              .
          DFHMDF POS=(01,72),                                          X
              ATTRB=ASKIP,                                            X
              LENGTH=07,                                              X
              INITIAL='POVMCH1'
              .
              .
              .
          DFHMDF POS=(02,26),                                          X
              ATTRB=ASKIP,                                            X
              LENGTH=27,                                              X
              INITIAL='VENDOR FILE CHANGES CONTROL'
              .
              .
              .
          DFHMDF POS=(12,19),                                          X
              ATTRB=ASKIP,                                            X
              LENGTH=40,                                              X
              INITIAL='1. TO CHANGE VENDOR RECORD - PRESS ENTER'
```

Figure 14-2 Vendor File Changes BMS Control Map.

Chap. 12, except that perform F000-CHANGE-PROCESSING replaces D000-INQUIRY-PROCESSING and TRANSID POVC replaces POVI.

C400-VERIFY-VENDOR-FILE-STATUS. This section performs a read of the vendor file in order to make sure the vendor record exists. If the vendor is not on the file, an error indicator is set and an error message is returned.

C410-READ-VENDOR-FILE. An E is moved immediately to STATUS-OF-READ prior to executing the READ command for the vendor file. If the record is on the file, it is read into the working-storage area VENDOR-MASTER-RECORD, and a G is moved to STATUS-OF-READ. A vendor record should be on the file for a record which is being changed. A record-not-found condition will be treated as an error in the invoking section.

F100-CHANGE-VENDOR-RECORD. This section reads the change record for update. If the record is not found, an indicative message will be displayed on the detail map. If the record is found, the map's data is edited and the vendor's record is formatted. If the edit and format are successful, a rewrite of the vendor record is performed. The message CHANGE COMPLETED SUCCESSFULLY is normally displayed on the control screen. The message UPDATE VENDOR RECORD—NOT FOUND would only be displayed if an operator at another terminal had deleted the same record you are attempting to read for update, after you had entered the vendor code on the control screen. This program would have previously read the vendor file for the entered vendor code (in section C410-READ-VENDOR-FILE) and determined that it was online in order to reach this point.

```
                     PRINT NOGEN
POVMCH2     DFHMSD TYPE=MAP,                                                X
                     .
                     .
                     .
            DFHMDF POS=(01,72),                                             X
                   ATTRB=ASKIP,                                             X
                   LENGTH=07,                                               X
                   INITIAL='POVMCH2'
                     .
                     .
            DFHMDF POS=(02,30),                                             X
                   ATTRB=ASKIP,                                             X
                   LENGTH=19,                                               X
                   INITIAL='VENDOR FILE CHANGES'
                     .
                     .
            DFHMDF POS=(18,10),                                             X
                   ATTRB=ASKIP,                                             X
                   LENGTH=56,                                               X
                   INITIAL='1. CHANGES, KEY IN NEW DATA             - PRX
                   ESS ENTER'
   *
            DFHMDF POS=(19,10),                                             X
                   ATTRB=ASKIP,                                             X
                   LENGTH=54,                                               X
                   INITIAL='2. RETURN TO CHANGES CONTROL SCREEN     - PRX
                   ESS PF3'
   *
            DFHMDF POS=(20,10),                                             X
                   ATTRB=ASKIP,                                             X
                   LENGTH=54,                                               X
                   INITIAL='3. RETURN TO MENU                       - PRX
                   ESS PF5'
   *
            DFHMDF POS=(21,10),                                             X
                   ATTRB=ASKIP,                                             X
                   LENGTH=56,                                               X
                   INITIAL='4. END OF SESSION                       - PRX
                   ESS CLEAR'
                     .
                     .
                     .
```

Figure 14-3 Vendor File Changes BMS Detail Map.

F110-READ-VENDOR-FOR-UPDATE. This section reads the change vendor record for update. If the record is not on the file, the NOTFND handle condition will be turned on and an E will be returned in STATUS-OF-READ. A good read will return a G in STATUS-OF-READ. A before (B) journal record posting is performed. The after-record will be posted after the rewrite in section F120-REWRITE-VENDOR-RECORD. The NOTFND indicator will only be invoked if an operator at another terminal has deleted the same record you are attempting to change, after you had keyed in vendor code on the control screen.

F120-REWRITE-VENDOR-RECORD. Rewrite the changed vendor record. An after (A) journal record posting will be performed. When the program reaches this point, it has read the vendor record for update and has established exclusive control of the record to be changed.

Figure 14-4 Vendor File Changes Program Source Code.

```
000100 IDENTIFICATION DIVISION.
000200 PROGRAM-ID. POVMADDN.
000300 REMARKS.
000400*******************************************************************
000500*          PURCHASING SYSTEM - VENDOR FILE ADDITIONS           *
000600*   - STARTED BY PURCHASING SYSTEM SUB-MENU PROGRAM 'POVMAINT'  *
000700*          COULD ALSO BE STARTED BY TRANSID 'POVA'             *
000800*******************************************************************
000900 ENVIRONMENT DIVISION.
001000 DATA DIVISION.
001100*
001200 WORKING-STORAGE  SECTION.
001300*
001400 01   WS-PROGRAM-FIELDS.
001500      05  FILLER          PIC X(8)     VALUE 'POVMADDN'.
001600      05  WS-CRT-MESSAGE   PIC X(17)    VALUE 'SESSION COMPLETED'.
001700*
001800*01  VENDOR-MASTER-RECORD
001900                          COPY   VENDMAST.
002000*01  JOURNAL-RECORD
002100                          COPY   JRNLRECD.
002200*01  WS-COMMAREA
002300                          COPY   POWSVMCA.
002400*01  WS-STATUS-FIELDS
002500                          COPY   STWSSTAT.
002600*01  VM-CONTROL-MAP
002700                          COPY   MAPVMCTL.
002800*01  VM-DETAIL-MAP
002900                          COPY   MAPVDTL2.
003000*01  WS-DATE-AND-TIME
003100                          COPY   STWSDTTM.
003200*01  WS-STATE-CODE-SEARCH-ENTRIES
003300                          COPY   STWST037.
003400*01  ATTRIBUTE-LIST
003500                          COPY   STWSATTR.
003600*01  DFHAID
003700                          COPY   DFHAID.
003800*
003900 01  END-OF-WORKING-STORAGE   PIC X(15)   VALUE 'END WS POVMADDN'.
004000*
004100 LINKAGE SECTION.
004200*
004300 01  DFHCOMMAREA                    PIC X(8).
004400*
004500 01  BLL-CELLS.
004600      05  FILLER                   PIC S9(8)   COMP.
004700      05  BLL-CWA-ADDRESS          PIC S9(8)   COMP.
004800      05  BLL-T037-STATE-TABLE-ADDRESS PIC S9(8)  COMP.
004900*
005000*01  CWA-DATA
005100                  COPY   STLNKCWA.
005200*01  T037-STATE-TABLE
005300                  COPY   T037STAT.
005400
005500
005600 PROCEDURE DIVISION.
005700*******************************************************************
005800*      PROGRAM STRUCTURE IS:                                     *
005900*          AA00-MAINLINE                                         *
006000*             B000-INITIAL-ENTRY                                 *
006100*                B100-SEND-CONTROL-MAP-AND-DATA                  *
006200*                   B110-GET-DATE-AND-TIME                       *
006300*                                                               *
006400*             C000-PROCESS-CONTROL-MAP                          *
006500*                C100-RECEIVE-CONTROL-MAP                       *
006600*                   C110-END-SESSION                            *
006700*                   C120-TRANSFER-XCTL-TO-MENU                  *
006800*                   C130-TRANSFER-XCTL-TO-BROWSE                *
006900*                C200-VERIFY-VENDOR-FORMAT                      *
007000*                C400-VERIFY-VENDOR-FILE-STATUS                 *
007100*                   C410-READ-VENDOR-FILE                       *
007200*                C500-SEND-DETAIL-MAP-AND-DATA                  *
007300*                   B110-GET-DATE-AND-TIME                      *
007400*                   C520-SET-MAP-ATTRIBUTES                     *
007500*                   C530-FORMAT-DETAIL-MAP                      *
007600*                      C531-GET-STATE-NAME                      *
007700*                C600-SEND-CONTROL-MAP-DATAONLY                 *
007800*                                                               *
```

Figure 14-4 *(Continued)*

```
007900*               F000-CHANGE-PROCESSING                         *
008000*                 D100-RECEIVE-DETAIL-MAP                      *
008100*                   C110-END-SESSION                           *
008200*                   C120-TRANSFER-XCTL-TO-MENU                 *
008300*                 F100-CHANGE-VENDOR-RECORD                    *
008400*                   F110-READ-VENDOR-FOR-UPDATE                *
008500*                     E121-POST-JOURNAL-RECORD                 *
008600*                   E110-EDIT-MAP-FORMAT-VM-RECORD             *
008700*                     C531-GET-STATE-NAME                      *
008800*                   F120-REWRITE-VENDOR-RECORD                 *
008900*                     E121-POST-JOURNAL-RECORD                 *
009000*                 B100-SEND-CONTROL-MAP-AND-DATA               *
009100*                 D200-SEND-DETAIL-MAP-DATAONLY                *
009200*                 C520-SET-MAP-ATTRIBUTES                      *
009300**********************************************************************
009400*
009500 AA00-MAINLINE  SECTION.
009600*
009700*     SERVICE RELOAD BLL-CELLS.
009800*
009900     MOVE LOW-VALUES  TO  VM-CONTROL-MAP.
010000*
010100     IF EIBCALEN  =  0
010200         PERFORM B000-INITIAL-ENTRY
010300     ELSE
010400         MOVE DFHCOMMAREA  TO  WS-COMMAREA
010500         IF CA-BROWSE
010600             MOVE SPACE       TO  CA-FUNCTION-CODE
010700             MOVE LOW-VALUES  TO  VM-CONTROL-MAP
010800             PERFORM C400-VERIFY-VENDOR-FILE-STATUS
010900             IF GOOD-VERIFY
011000                 PERFORM C500-SEND-DETAIL-MAP-AND-DATA
011100             ELSE
011200                 PERFORM B100-SEND-CONTROL-MAP-AND-DATA
011300         ELSE
0:11400             IF CA-RECEIVE-CTL-MAP
011500                 PERFORM C000-PROCESS-CONTROL-MAP
011600             ELSE
011700                 PERFORM F000-CHANGE-PROCESSING.
011800*
011900     EXEC CICS RETURN
012000             TRANSID  ('POVC')
012100             COMMAREA (WS-COMMAREA)
012200             LENGTH   (8)
012300     END-EXEC.
012400*
012500 B000-INITIAL-ENTRY  SECTION.
012600**********************************************************************
012700*                PERFORMED FROM:   AA00-MAINLINE               *
012800**********************************************************************
012900*
013000     MOVE LOW-VALUES  TO  VM-CONTROL-MAP.
013100     PERFORM B100-SEND-CONTROL-MAP-AND-DATA.
013200*
013300 B000-EXIT.
013400     EXIT.
013500*
013600 B100-SEND-CONTROL-MAP-AND-DATA  SECTION.
013700**********************************************************************
013800*     SEND CONTROL MAP - SYMBOLIC AND PHYSICAL MAPS          *
013900*         PERFORMED FROM:  B000-INITIAL-ENTRY                *
014000*                          F000-CHANGE-PROCESSING            *
014100**********************************************************************
014200*
014300     PERFORM B110-GET-DATE-AND-TIME.
014400     MOVE WS-CURRENT-DATE  TO  MVC-D-DATE.
014500     MOVE WS-MAP-TIME      TO  MVC-D-TIME.
014600*
014700     MOVE -1   TO  MVC-L-VEND-CD-1.
014800     MOVE '1'  TO  CA-MAP-CONTROL.
014900*
015000     EXEC CICS SEND
015100             MAP     ('MAPPOVC')
015200             MAPSET  ('POVMCH1')
015300             FROM    (VM-CONTROL-MAP)
015400             ERASE
015500             CURSOR
015600     END-EXEC.
015700*
015800 B100-EXIT.
015900     EXIT.
016000*
016100 B110-GET-DATE-AND-TIME  SECTION.
```

Figure 14-4 *(Continued)*

```
016200****************************************************************
016300*       STPDDTTM - OBTAIN DATE FROM CWA AND FORMAT TIME       *
016400*       PERFORMED FROM:   B100-SEND-CONTROL-MAP-AND-DATA       *
016500*                         C500-SEND-DETAIL-MAP-AND-DATA        *
016600****************************************************************
016700*
016800      COPY   STPDDTTM.
016900*
017000 B110-EXIT.
017100      EXIT.
017200*
017300 C000-PROCESS-CONTROL-MAP   SECTION.
017400****************************************************************
017500*         PERFORMED FROM:  AA00-MAINLINE                       *
017600*     PROCESS CONTROL MAP - IF VALID SEND DETAIL MAP           *
017700*        ELSE SEND CONTROL MAP WITH INVALID MESSAGE:           *
017800*  1) STATUS-OF-RECEIVE   =  'I'   INVALID KEY PRESSED         *
017900*  2) STATUS-OF-RECEIVE   =  'M'   MAPFAIL - NO DATA ENTERED   *
018000*  3) STATUS-OF-FORMAT    =  'E'   INVALID VENDOR KEYED FORMAT *
018100*  4) STATUS-OF-VERIFY    =  'E'   VENDOR FILE STATUS ERROR    *
018200****************************************************************
018300*
018400      PERFORM C100-RECEIVE-CONTROL-MAP.
018500      IF GOOD-RECEIVE
018600         PERFORM C200-VERIFY-VENDOR-FORMAT
018700         IF VALID-FORMAT
018800            PERFORM C400-VERIFY-VENDOR-FILE-STATUS
018900            IF GOOD-VERIFY
019000               PERFORM C500-SEND-DETAIL-MAP-AND-DATA
019100            ELSE
019200               PERFORM C600-SEND-CONTROL-MAP-DATAONLY
019300         ELSE
019400            PERFORM C600-SEND-CONTROL-MAP-DATAONLY
019500      ELSE
019600         IF MAPFAIL-ON-RECEIVE
019700            MOVE 'VENDOR CODE MUST BE ENTERED - PLEASE KEY-IN'
019800                          TO MVC-D-MESSAGE
019900            MOVE ASKIP-BRT   TO MVC-A-MESSAGE
020000            PERFORM C600-SEND-CONTROL-MAP-DATAONLY
020100         ELSE
020200            PERFORM C600-SEND-CONTROL-MAP-DATAONLY.
020300*
020400 C000-EXIT.
020500      EXIT.
020600*
020700 C100-RECEIVE-CONTROL-MAP   SECTION.
020800****************************************************************
020900*         PERFORMED FROM:  C000-PROCESS-CONTROL-MAP            *
021000*         ENTER IS ONLY VALID DATA ENTRY KEY                   *
021100*  CLEAR KEY - ENDS TERMINAL SESSION      PF5 - RETURNS TO MENU *
021200*                                         PF4 - XCTL TO BROWSE  *
021300*         ALL OTHER AID KEYS ARE INVALID                       *
021400*     STATUS-OF-RECEIVE = 'G'  =  GOOD RECEIVE                  *
021500*                         'M'  =  MAPFAIL                       *
021600*                         'I'  =  INVALID KEY PRESSED           *
021700****************************************************************
021800*
021900      MOVE LOW-VALUES   TO VM-CONTROL-MAP.
022000*
022100      IF EIBAID =  DFHENTER
022200         MOVE 'M'  TO  STATUS-OF-RECEIVE
022300*
022400         EXEC CICS HANDLE CONDITION
022500                   MAPFAIL (C100-EXIT)
022600         END-EXEC
022700*
022800         EXEC CICS RECEIVE
022900                   MAP    ('MAPPOVC')
023000                   MAPSET ('POVMCH1')
023100                   INTO   (VM-CONTROL-MAP)
023200         END-EXEC
023300*
023400         MOVE 'G'  TO  STATUS-OF-RECEIVE
023500      ELSE
023600         IF EIBAID  =  DFHCLEAR
023700            PERFORM C110-END-SESSION
023800         ELSE
023900         IF EIBAID  =  DFHPF5
024000            PERFORM C120-TRANSFER-XCTL-TO-MENU
024100         ELSE
024200         IF EIBAID  =  DFHPF4
024300            PERFORM C130-TRANSFER-XCTL-TO-BROWSE
```

Figure 14-4 *(Continued)*

```
024400           ELSE
024500               MOVE 'I'          TO  STATUS-OF-RECEIVE
024600               MOVE 'INVALID KEY PRESSED - PLEASE TRY AGAIN'
024700                         TO  MVC-D-MESSAGE
024800               MOVE ASKIP-BRT  TO  MVC-A-MESSAGE.
024900*
025000 C100-EXIT.
025100     EXIT.
025200*
025300 C110-END-SESSION  SECTION.
025400*****************************************************************
025500*    CRT OPERATOR PRESSED CLEAR KEY TO END TERMINAL SESSION     *
025600*        PERFORMED FROM:  C100-RECEIVE-CONTROL-MAP              *
025700*                         D100-RECEIVE-DETAIL-MAP               *
025800*****************************************************************
025900*
026000     EXEC CICS SEND
026100             FROM   (WS-CRT-MESSAGE)
026200             LENGTH (17)
026300             ERASE
026400     END-EXEC.
026500*
026600     EXEC CICS RETURN
026700     END-EXEC.
026800*
026900 C110-EXIT.
027000     EXIT.
027100*
027200 C120-TRANSFER-XCTL-TO-MENU  SECTION.
027300*****************************************************************
027400*        OPERATOR PRESSED PF5 TO RETURN TO MENU PROGRAM         *
027500*        PERFORMED FROM:  C100-RECEIVE-CONTROL-MAP              *
027600*                         D100-RECEIVE-DETAIL-MAP               *
027700*****************************************************************
027800*
027900     EXEC CICS XCTL
028000             PROGRAM ('POVMAINT')
028100     END-EXEC.
028200*
028300 C120-EXIT.
028400     EXIT.
028500*
028600 C130-TRANSFER-XCTL-TO-BROWSE  SECTION.
028700*****************************************************************
028800*        OPERATOR PRESSED PF4 TO TRANSFER CONTROL TO BROWSE     *
028900*          PERFORMED FROM:  C100-RECEIVE-CONTROL-MAP            *
029000*****************************************************************
029100*
029200     MOVE LOW-VALUES  TO  WS-COMMAREA.
029300     MOVE 'C'         TO  CA-FUNCTION-CODE.
029400*
029500     EXEC CICS XCTL
029600             PROGRAM  ('POVMBROW')
029700             COMMAREA (WS-COMMAREA)
029800             LENGTH   (8)
029900     END-EXEC.
030000*
030100 C130-EXIT.
030200     EXIT.
030300*
030400 C200-VERIFY-VENDOR-FORMAT  SECTION.
030500*****************************************************************
030600*        VERIFY FORMAT OF VENDOR CODE KEYED-IN = A-9999-9       *
030700*          PERFORMED FROM:  C000-PROCESS-CONTROL-MAP            *
030800*    IF VALID FORMAT - MOVE CODE TO WS-COMMAREA FIELDS (CA- )   *
030900*****************************************************************
031000*
031100     IF (MVC-D-VEND-CD-1  IS  ALPHABETIC
031200               AND
031300      MVC-D-VEND-CD-1  IS NOT =  SPACE)
031400     AND
031500      MVC-D-VEND-CD-2  IS  NUMERIC
031600     AND
031700      MVC-D-VEND-CD-3  IS  NUMERIC
031800         MOVE MVC-D-VEND-CD-1  TO  CA-VEND-1
031900         MOVE MVC-D-VEND-CD-2  TO  CA-VEND-2
032000         MOVE MVC-D-VEND-CD-3  TO  CA-VEND-3
032100         MOVE 'G'          TO  STATUS-OF-FORMAT
032200     ELSE
032300         MOVE 'E'       TO  STATUS-OF-FORMAT
032400         MOVE 'VENDOR CODE FORMAT MUST BE: A-9999-9 - PLEASE RE-EN
032500-            'TER'      TO  MVC-D-MESSAGE
032600         MOVE ASKIP-BRT  TO  MVC-A-MESSAGE.
```

Figure 14-4 *(Continued)*

```
032700*
032800 C200-EXIT.
032900     EXIT.
033000*
033100 C400-VERIFY-VENDOR-FILE-STATUS  SECTION.
033200********************************************************************
033300*            PERFORMED FROM:  C000-PROCESS-CONTROL-MAP          *
033400*              MUST BE A VENDOR RECORD FOR CHANGES              *
033500********************************************************************
033600*
033700     MOVE 'G' TO STATUS-OF-VERIFY.
033800*
033900     PERFORM C410-READ-VENDOR-FILE.
034000*
034100     IF RECORD-NOT-FOUND
034200         MOVE 'E'       TO  STATUS-OF-VERIFY.
034300         MOVE 'VENDOR RECORD NOT ON FILE'
034400                        TO  MVC-D-MESSAGE
034500         MOVE ASKIP-BRT TO  MVC-A-MESSAGE.
034600*
034700 C400-EXIT.
034800     EXIT.
034900*
035000 C410-READ-VENDOR-FILE  SECTION.
035100********************************************************************
035200*        PERFORMED FROM:  C400-VERIFY-VENDOR-FILE-STATUS        *
035300********************************************************************
035400*
035500     MOVE 'E' TO STATUS-OF-READ.
035600*
035700     EXEC CICS HANDLE CONDITION
035800            NOTFND  (C410-EXIT)
035900     END-EXEC.
036000*
036100     EXEC CICS READ
036200            DATASET ('VENDMAST')
036300            INTO    (VENDOR-MASTER-RECORD)
036400            RIDFLD  (CA-VENDOR-CODE)
036500     END-EXEC.
036600*
036700     MOVE 'G' TO STATUS-OF-READ.
036800*
036900 C410-EXIT.
037000     EXIT.
037100*
037200 C500-SEND-DETAIL-MAP-AND-DATA  SECTION.
037300********************************************************************
037400*        SEND DETAIL MAP - PHYSICAL AND SYMBOLIC MAPS           *
037500*            PERFORMED FROM:  C000-PROCESS-CONTROL-MAP          *
037600*  SENT WHEN ALL VALIDATION AND EDIT CONDITIONS HAVE BEEN MET   *
037700********************************************************************
037800*
037900     MOVE LOW-VALUES TO VM-DETAIL-MAP.
038000*
038100     PERFORM B110-GET-DATE-AND-TIME.
038200     MOVE WS-CURRENT-DATE TO MVD-D-DATE.
038300     MOVE WS-MAP-TIME     TO MVD-D-TIME.
038400*
038500     PERFORM C520-SET-MAP-ATTRIBUTES.
038600*
038700     PERFORM C530-FORMAT DETAIL-MAP.
038800*
038900     MOVE -1 TO  MVD-L-VENDOR-NAME.
039000     MOVE '2' TO CA-MAP-CONTROL.
039100*
039200     EXEC CICS SEND
039300            MAP     ('MAPPOVD')
039400            MAPSET  ('POVMCH2')
039500            FROM    (VM-DETAIL-MAP)
039600            ERASE
039700            CURSOR
039800     END-EXEC.
039900*
040000 C500-EXIT.
040100     EXIT.
040200*
040300 C520-SET-MAP-ATTRIBUTES  SECTION.
040400********************************************************************
040500*        PERFORMED FROM:  C500-SEND-DETAIL-MAP-AND-DATA         *
040600*                         D200-SEND-DETAIL-MAP-DATAONLY         *
040700********************************************************************
040800*
040900     MOVE UNPROT-FSET TO  MVD-A-PHONE-AREA-CD
```

Figure 14-4 (*Continued*)

```
041000                              MVD-A-PHONE-1
041100                              MVD-A-PHONE-2
041200                              MVD-A-VENDOR-NAME
041300                              MVD-A-CONTACT
041400                              MVD-A-STREET
041500                              MVD-A-CITY
041600                              MVD-A-STATE-CODE
041700                              MVD-A-ZIP-CODE
041800                              MVD-A-ATTENTION-OF.
041900*
042000 C520-EXIT.
042100     EXIT.
042200*
042300 C530-FORMAT-DETAIL-MAP  SECTION.
042400******************************************************************
042500*       PERFORMED FROM:  C500-SEND-DETAIL-MAP-AND-DATA           *
042600******************************************************************
042700*
042800* FORMAT VENDOR CODE: A-9999-9   WS- FIELDS ARE AT END OF VENDMAST
042900     MOVE CA-VEND-1        TO  WS-VENDOR-CD-1.
043000     MOVE CA-VEND-2        TO  WS-VENDOR-CD-2.
043100     MOVE CA-VEND-3        TO  WS-VENDOR-CD-3.
043200     MOVE WS-VENDOR-CODE   TO  MVD-D-VENDOR-CODE.
043300*
043400     MOVE VM-AREA-CD       TO  MVD-D-PHONE-AREA-CD.
043500     MOVE VM-PHONE-1-3     TO  MVD-D-PHONE-1.
043600     MOVE VM-PHONE-4-7     TO  MVD-D-PHONE-2.
043700     MOVE VM-VENDOR-NAME   TO  MVD-D-VENDOR-NAME.
043800     MOVE VM-CONTACT       TO  MVD-D-CONTACT.
043900     MOVE VM-STREET-ADDRESS TO  MVD-D-STREET.
044000     MOVE VM-CITY          TO  MVD-D-CITY.
044100     MOVE VM-STATE         TO  MVD-D-STATE-CODE.
044200*
044300     MOVE VM-STATE         TO  WS-STATE-CODE.
044400     PERFORM C531-GET-STATE-NAME.
044500     MOVE WS-STATE-NAME    TO  MVD-D-STATE-NAME.
044600*
044700     MOVE VM-ZIP-CODE      TO  MVD-D-ZIP-CODE.
044800     MOVE VM-TO-ATTN-OF    TO  MVD-D-ATTENTION-OF.
044900*
045000 C530-EXIT.
045100     EXIT.
045200*
045300 C531-GET-STATE-NAME  SECTION.
045400******************************************************************
045500*              LOAD AND SEARCH STATE CODE TABLE                  *
045600*          PERFORMED FROM:  C530-SEND-DETAIL-MAP-AND-DATA        *
045700*                           E110-EDIT-MAP-FORMAT-VM-RECORD       *
045800******************************************************************
045900*
046000     COPY   STPDT037.
046100*
046200 C531-EXIT.
046300     EXIT.
046400*
046500 C600-SEND-CONTROL-MAP-DATAONLY  SECTION.
046600******************************************************************
046700*          SEND CONTROL MAP DATAONLY - SYMBOLIC MAP             *
046800*          PERFORMED FROM:  C000-PROCESS-CONTROL-MAP            *
046900*              SENT FOR INVALID CONDITIONS                      *
047000******************************************************************
047100*
047200     MOVE UNPROT-FSET  TO  MVC-A-VEND-CD-1
047300                           MVC-A-VEND-CD-2
047400                           MVC-A-VEND-CD-3.
047500*
047600     MOVE -1  TO  MVC-L-VEND-CD-1.
047700     MOVE '1' TO  CA-MAP-CONTROL.
047800*
047900     EXEC CICS SEND
048000               MAP      ('MAPPOVC')
048100               MAPSET   ('POVMCH1')
048200               FROM     (VM-CONTROL-MAP)
048300               DATAONLY
048400               CURSOR
048500     END-EXEC.
048600*
048700 C600-EXIT.
048800     EXIT.
048900*
049000 D100-RECEIVE-DETAIL-MAP  SECTION.
049100******************************************************************
049200*          PERFORMED FROM:  F000-CHANGE-PROCESSING              *
```

Figure 14-4 *(Continued)*

```
049300*    ENTER - PROCESSES TRANSACTION          CLEAR - ENDS SESSION      *
049400*    PF3    - SET DISPLAY OF CTL MAP         PF5   - RETURNS TO MENU   *
049500*                 ALL OTHER KEYS ARE INVALID                          *
049600*         STATUS-OF-RECEIVE = 'G' =  GOOD RECEIVE                     *
049700*                            'C' =  RETURN TO CTL-MAP                 *
049800*                            'I' =  INVALID KEY PRESSED               *
049900****************************************************************************
050000*
050100     MOVE LOW-VALUES  TO  VM-DETAIL-MAP.
050200*
050300     IF EIBAID  =  DFHENTER
050400*
050500         EXEC CICS IGNORE CONDITION
050600                   MAPFAIL
050700         END-EXEC
050800*
050900         EXEC CICS RECEIVE
051000                   MAP     ('MAPPOVD')
051100                   MAPSET  ('POVMCH2')
051200                   INTO    (VM-DETAIL-MAP)
051300         END-EXEC
051400*
051500         MOVE 'G'  TO  STATUS-OF-RECEIVE
051600     ELSE
051700         IF EIBAID  =  DFHCLEAR
051800             PERFORM C110-END-SESSION
051900         ELSE
052000         IF EIBAID   =  DFHPF3
052100             MOVE 'C'  TO  STATUS-OF-RECEIVE
052200         ELSE
052300         IF EIBAID  =  DFHPF5
052400             PERFORM C120-TRANSFER-XCTL-TO-MENU
052500         ELSE
052600             MOVE 'I'         TO  STATUS-OF-RECEIVE
052700             MOVE 'INVALID KEY PRESSED - PLEASE TRY AGAIN'
052800                              TO  MVD-D-MESSAGE
052900             MOVE ASKIP-BRT  TO  MVD-A-MESSAGE.
053000*
053100 D100-EXIT.
053200     EXIT.
053300*
053400 D200-SEND-DETAIL-MAP-DATAONLY  SECTION.
053500****************************************************************************
053600*        SEND DETAIL MAP DATA ONLY - SYMBOLIC MAP                     *
053700*      PERFORMED FROM:  F000-CHANGE-PROCESSING                        *
053800*  SENT IF INVALID KEY IS PRESSED ON A RECEIVE OF THE DETAIL MAP      *
053900****************************************************************************
054000*
054100     MOVE '2'  TO  CA-MAP-CONTROL.
054200*
054300     PERFORM C520-SET-MAP-ATTRIBUTES.
054400*
054500     EXEC CICS SEND
054600               MAP     ('MAPPOVD')
054700               MAPSET  ('POVMCH2')
054800               FROM    (VM-DETAIL-MAP)
054900               DATAONLY
055000               CURSOR
055100     END-EXEC.
055200*
055300 D200-EXIT.
055400     EXIT.
055500*
055600*
055700 E110-EDIT-MAP-FORMAT-VM-RECORD  SECTION.
055800****************************************************************************
055900*      EDIT DETAIL MAP DATA - FORMAT VENDOR MASTER RECORD            *
056000*         PERFORMED FROM:  F100-CHANGE-VENDOR-RECORD                 *
056100*        HIGHLIGHT FIELDS WHICH CONTAIN INCORRECT DATA               *
056200*           OR WHICH ARE MISSING REQUIRED ENTRIES                    *
056300****************************************************************************
056400*
056500     MOVE 'G'  TO  STATUS-OF-EDIT.
056600*
056700* ASSUME ALL PHONE DIGITS SHOULD BE NUMERIC
056800*
056900     IF MVD-D-PHONE-AREA-CD  IS  NUMERIC
057000        AND
057100        MVD-D-PHONE-1        IS  NUMERIC
057200        AND
057300        MVD-D-PHONE-2       IS  NUMERIC
057400         MOVE MVD-D-PHONE-AREA-CD  TO  VM-AREA-CD
057500         MOVE MVD-D-PHONE-1         TO  VM-PHONE-1-3
```

Figure 14-4 *(Continued)*

```
057600          MOVE MVD-D-PHONE-2              TO   VM-PHONE-4-7
057700          MOVE ASKIP-NORM                TO   MVD-C-A-PHONE
057800      ELSE
057900          MOVE -1          TO   MVD-L-PHONE-AREA-CD
058000          MOVE ASKIP-BRT   TO   MVD-C-A-PHONE
058100          MOVE 'E'         TO   STATUS-OF-EDIT.
058200*
058300      IF MVD-D-VENDOR-NAME  =  LOW-VALUES  OR  SPACES
058400          MOVE -1          TO   MVD-L-VENDOR-NAME
058500          MOVE ASKIP-BRT   TO   MVD-C-A-VENDOR-NAME
058600          MOVE 'E'         TO   STATUS-OF-EDIT
058700      ELSE
058800          MOVE MVD-D-VENDOR-NAME  TO   VM-VENDOR-NAME
058900          MOVE ASKIP-NORM         TO   MVD-C-A-VENDOR-NAME.
059000*
059100* 'CONTACT' AND 'TO ATTENTION OF' ARE OPTIONAL FIELDS
059200*
059300      IF MVD-L-CONTACT  =  ZERO
059400          MOVE SPACES          TO   VM-CONTACT
059500      ELSE
059600          MOVE MVD-D-CONTACT   TO   VM-CONTACT.
059700*
059800      IF MVD-L-STREET  =  0     OR
059900         MVD-D-STREET  =  SPACES
060000          MOVE -1          TO   MVD-L-STREET
060100          MOVE ASKIP-BRT   TO   MVD-C-A-STREET
060200          MOVE 'E'         TO   STATUS-OF-EDIT
060300      ELSE
060400          MOVE MVD-D-STREET   TO   VM-STREET-ADDRESS
060500          MOVE ASKIP-NORM     TO   MVD-C-A-STREET.
060600*
060700      MOVE ZEROES   TO   VM-DOLLARS-COMMITTED.
060800*
060900      IF MVD-D-CITY  =  LOW-VALUES  OR  SPACES
061000          MOVE -1          TO   MVD-L-CITY
061100          MOVE ASKIP-BRT   TO   MVD-C-A-CITY
061200          MOVE 'E'         TO   STATUS-OF-EDIT
061300      ELSE
061400          MOVE MVD-D-CITY   TO   VM-CITY
061500          MOVE ASKIP-NORM   TO   MVD-C-A-CITY.
061600*
061700      MOVE MVD-D-STATE-CODE   TO   WS-STATE-CODE.
061800      PERFORM C531-GET-STATE-NAME.
061900      IF STATE-FOUND
062000          MOVE MVD-D-STATE-CODE   TO   VM-STATE
062100          MOVE WS-STATE-NAME      TO   MVD-D-STATE-NAME
062200          MOVE ASKIP-NORM         TO   MVD-C-A-STATE
062300      ELSE
062400          MOVE ALL '*'     TO   MVD-D-STATE-NAME
062500          MOVE -1          TO   MVD-L-STATE-CODE
062600          MOVE ASKIP-BRT   TO   MVD-C-A-STATE
062700          MOVE 'E'         TO   STATUS-OF-EDIT.
062800*
062900      IF MVD-D-ZIP-CODE  IS  NUMERIC
063000          MOVE MVD-D-ZIP-CODE   TO   VM-ZIP-CODE
063100          MOVE ASKIP-NORM       TO   MVD-C-A-ZIP-CODE
063200      ELSE
063300          MOVE -1          TO   MVD-L-ZIP-CODE
063400          MOVE ASKIP-BRT   TO   MVD-C-A-ZIP-CODE
063500          MOVE 'E'         TO   STATUS-OF-EDIT.
063600*
063700      IF MVD-L-ATTENTION-OF  =  ZERO
063800          MOVE SPACES             TO   VM-TO-ATTN-OF
063900      ELSE
064000          MOVE MVD-D-ATTENTION-OF  TO   VM-TO-ATTN-OF.
064100*
064200      IF STATUS-OF-EDIT  =  'E'
064300          MOVE 'PLEASE CORRECT HIGHLIGHTED FIELDS'
064400                          TO   MVD-D-MESSAGE
064500          MOVE ASKIP-BRT   TO   MVD-A-MESSAGE.
064600*
064700 E110-EXIT.
064800      EXIT.
064900*
065000*
065100 E121-POST-JOURNAL-RECORD   SECTION.
065200***********************************************************
065300*    POST JOURNAL ENTRY - LINK TO JOURNAL PROGRAM 'JRNLPOST'  *
065400*       PERFORMED FROM: F110-READ-VENDOR-FOR-UPDATE           *
065500*                       F120-REWRITE-VENDOR-RECORD            *
065600***********************************************************
065700*
065800      MOVE 'VM'                          TO   JR-PREFIX.
```

Figure 14-4 *(Continued)*

```
065900        MOVE VENDOR-MASTER-RECORD  TO  JR-RECORD-DATA.
066000        MOVE SPACES                TO  JR-PASSWORD.
066100*
066200        EXEC CICS LINK
066300                 PROGRAM   ('JRNLPOST')
066400                 COMMAREA (JOURNAL-RECORD)
066500                 LENGTH   (524)
066600        END-EXEC.
066700*
066800 E121-EXIT.
066900        EXIT.
067000*
067100 F000-CHANGE-PROCESSING  SECTION.
067200****************************************************************
067300*                 PERFORMED FROM:  AA00-MAINLINE              *
067400*        DETAIL MAP IS SENT IF INVALID KEY WAS PRESSED        *
067500*               OR IF CHANGE WAS UNSUCCESSFUL                 *
067600****************************************************************
067700*
067800        PERFORM D100-RECEIVE-DETAIL-MAP.
067900*
068000        IF GOOD-RECEIVE
068100            PERFORM F100-CHANGE-VENDOR-RECORD
068200            IF GOOD-CHANGE
068300                PERFORM B100-SEND-CONTROL-MAP-AND-DATA
068400            ELSE
068500                PERFORM D200-SEND-DETAIL-MAP-DATAONLY
068600        ELSE
068700            IF RETURN-TO-CTL-MAP
068800                PERFORM B100-SEND-CONTROL-MAP-AND-DATA
068900            ELSE
069000                PERFORM D200-SEND-DETAIL-MAP-DATAONLY.
069100*
069200 F000-EXIT.
069300        EXIT.
069400*
069500 F100-CHANGE-VENDOR-RECORD  SECTION.
069600****************************************************************
069700*             PERFORMED FROM:  F000-CHANGE PROCESSING         *
069800*     READ RECORD FOR UPDATE, EDIT MAP DATA AND REWRITE RECORD *
069900* RECORD NOT FOUND COULD NOT OCCUR UNLESS RECORD WAS DELETED   *
070000*   BY ANOTHER TERMINAL SINCE BEING KEYED-IN ON CONTROL SCREEN *
070100****************************************************************
070200*
070300        MOVE 'E'  TO  STATUS-OF-CHANGE.
070400*
070500        PERFORM F110-READ-VENDOR-FOR-UPDATE.
070600*
070700        IF RECORD-NOT-FOUND
070800            MOVE 'UPDATE VENDOR RECORD - NOT FOUND'
070900                          TO  MVD-D-MESSAGE
071000            MOVE ASKIP-BRT  TO  MVD-A-MESSAGE
071100        ELSE
071200            PERFORM E110-EDIT-MAP-FORMAT-VM-RECORD
071300            IF GOOD-EDIT
071400                PERFORM F120-REWRITE-VENDOR-RECORD
071500                MOVE 'CHANGE COMPLETED SUCCESSFULLY'
071600                            TO  MVC-D-MESSAGE
071700                MOVE ASKIP-BRT  TO  MVC-A-MESSAGE
071800                MOVE 'G'        TO  STATUS-OF-CHANGE.
071900*
072000 F100-EXIT.
072100        EXIT.
072200*
072300 F110-READ-VENDOR-FOR-UPDATE  SECTION.
072400****************************************************************
072500*   READ VENDOR RECORD FOR UPDATE - POST BEFORE JOURNAL RECORD *
072600*           PERFORMED FROM:  F100-CHANGE-VENDOR-RECORD         *
072700****************************************************************
072800*
072900        MOVE 'E' TO  STATUS-OF-READ.
073000*
073100        EXEC CICS HANDLE CONDITION
073200                 NOTFND  (F110-EXIT)
073300        END-EXEC.
073400*
073500        EXEC CICS READ
073600                 DATASET ('VENDMAST')
073700                 INTO    (VENDOR-MASTER-RECORD)
073800                 RIDFLD  (CA-VENDOR-CODE)
073900                 UPDATE
074000        END-EXEC.
074100*
```

Figure 14-4   (Continued)

```
074200        MOVE 'G'  TO  STATUS-OF-READ.
074300*
074400        MOVE 'B'  TO  JR-TYPE.
074500        PERFORM E121-POST-JOURNAL-RECORD.
074600*
074700 F110-EXIT.
074800        EXIT.
074900*
075000 F120-REWRITE-VENDOR-RECORD  SECTION.
075100***********************************************************
075200*        REWRITE VENDOR RECORD - POST 'AFTER' JOURNAL RECORD    *
075300*           PERFORMED FROM:  F100-CHANGE-VENDOR-RECORD          *
075400***********************************************************
075500*
075600        EXEC CICS REWRITE
075700               DATASET ('VENDMAST')
075800               FROM    (VENDOR-MASTER-RECORD)
075900        END-EXEC.
076000*
076100        MOVE 'A'  TO  JR-TYPE.
076200        PERFORM E121-POST-JOURNAL-RECORD.
076300*
076400 F120-EXIT.
076500        EXIT.
```

SUMMARY

This chapter presented the change program. It can be used as a model for most change programs you will have to write. Several of the commands discussed in preceding chapters were used. The READ FOR UPDATE and REWRITE file commands were used in the change program.

15

THE DELETE PROGRAM

After a record has been on a file for a period of time, circumstances sometimes require the record to be deleted from the file. This chapter discusses the delete program.

Control and detail maps are used for the delete program. The control map shown in Fig. 15-1 requires the terminal operator to key in a vendor code and to press ENTER in order to display the delete detail screen. The operator also has the option of transferring control to the vendor file browse, returning to the vendor file maintenance submenu (see Fig. 6-3), or ending the session. The vendor file delete program detail map shown in Fig. 2-9 is displayed when the operator enters an existing vendor code on the control screen (Fig. 15-1). The delete detail screen permits the operator to verify the vendor's data in order to make sure the correct record is being deleted. The operator then presses ENTER in order to delete the record. The detail screen also permits the operator to return to the delete control screen without deleting the record, return to the submenu, or to end the session.

BMS Maps

Figures 15-2 and 15-3 show the BMS maps for the control and detail screens, respectively.

BMS Control Map

Only the differences between this map and the BMS control map for the inquiry program (see Fig. 12-1) are shown in Fig. 15-2.

Figure 15-1   Vendor File Deletions Control Map.

BMS Detail Map

This map is similar to the inquiry detail map shown in Fig. 12-2. Only the differences are shown in Fig. 15-3.

User-Friendly Symbolic Maps

The user-friendly symbolic maps which correspond to BMS-generated maps are shown in the copy library (App. B, members MAPVMCTL and MAPVDTL1).

Delete Program Source Code

The delete program source code shown in Fig. 15-4 follows the format used in previous examples. I will only discuss sections which differ from previous examples.

Procedure Division

AA00-MAINLINE. This section is similar to that of the inquiry program in Chap. 12 except that perform G000-DELETE-PROCESSING replaces D000-INQUIRY-PROCESSING and TRANSID POVD replaces POVI.

```
            PRINT NOGEN
POVMDL1     DFHMSD TYPE=MAP,                                                X
                  .
                  .
                  .
            DFHMDF POS=(01,72),                                             X
                  ATTRB=ASKIP,                                             X
                  LENGTH=07,                                               X
                  INITIAL='POVMDL1'
                  .
                  .
                  .
            DFHMDF POS=(02,25),                                             X
                  ATTRB=ASKIP,                                             X
                  LENGTH=29,                                               X
                  INITIAL='VENDOR FILE DELETIONS CONTROL'
                  .
                  .
                  .
            DFHMDF POS=(12,19),                                             X
                  ATTRB=ASKIP,                                             X
                  LENGTH=40,                                               X
                  INITIAL='1. TO DELETE VENDOR RECORD - PRESS ENTER'
                  .
                  .
                  .
```

Figure 15-2   Vendor File Deletions BMS Control Map.

C400-VERIFY-VENDOR-FILE-STATUS.   This section performs a read of the vendor file to make sure the vendor to be deleted is on the file. If the vendor is not on the file, an error indicator is set and an error message returned.

C410-READ-VENDOR-FILE.   A record should be on the file for a vendor which is being deleted. A NOTFND condition will be treated as an error in the invoking section.

F110-READ-VENDOR-FOR-UPDATE.   A before (B) journal record posting is performed. There is no after-record on a delete function.

G100-DELETE-VENDOR-RECORD.   This section reads the delete record for update. If the record is not found, an indicative message will be displayed on the detail map. It would not be necessary to read the record for update prior to deleting if no journal record was being posted. In that case the DELETE command would have to contain the RIDFLD option. A successfully read record is deleted and the message RECORD DELETED SUCCESSFULLY is displayed on the control screen. The message RECORD TO BE DELETED—NOT FOUND would only be displayed if an operator at another terminal deleted the same record you are attempting to delete, after you had entered vendor code on the control screen. The program would have previously read the vendor file for the entered vendor code (in section C410-READ-VENDOR-FILE) and determined that it was online in order to reach this point.

G110-DELETE-VM-RECORD.   Delete the vendor record which was read for update. A before (B) journal record could be posted in this section instead of

```
            PRINT NOGEN
POVMDL2     DFHMSD TYPE=MAP,                                              X
               .
               .
               .
            DFHMDF POS=(01,72),                                           X
                   ATTRB=ASKIP,                                           X
                   LENGTH=07,                                             X
                   INITIAL='POVMDL2'
               .
               .
               .
            DFHMDF POS=(02,30),                                           X
                   ATTRB=ASKIP,                                           X
                   LENGTH=20,                                             X
                   INITIAL='VENDOR FILE DELETION'
               .
               .
               .
            DFHMDF POS=(18,10),                                           X
                   ATTRB=ASKIP,                                           X
                   LENGTH=56,                                             X
                   INITIAL='1. DELETIONS, VERIFY DATA BEFORE DELETING  - PRX
                   ESS ENTER'
    *
            DFHMDF POS=(19,10),                                           X
                   ATTRB=ASKIP,                                           X
                   LENGTH=54,                                             X
                   INITIAL='2. RETURN TO DELETION CONTROL SCREEN       - PRX
                   ESS PF3'
    *
            DFHMDF POS=(20,10),                                           X
                   ATTRB=ASKIP,                                           X
                   LENGTH=54,                                             X
                   INITIAL='3. RETURN TO MENU                          - PRX
                   ESS PF5'
    *
            DFHMDF POS=(21,10),                                           X
                   ATTRB=ASKIP,                                           X
                   LENGTH=56,                                             X
                   INITIAL='4. END OF SESSION                          - PRX
                   ESS CLEAR'
               .
               .
               .
```

Figure 15-3 Vendor File Deletions BMS Detail Map.

in section F110-READ-VENDOR-FOR-UPDATE, in which the logic was performed. When the program reaches this point, it has read the vendor record for
update and has established exclusive control of the record to be deleted.

SUMMARY

This chapter presented the delete program. The program given here can be used
as a model for most delete programs you will have to write. Several of the
commands which were discussed in preceding chapters were used. The READ
FOR UPDATE and DELETE file commands were used in the delete program.

Figure 15-4 Vendor File Deletions Program Source Code.

```
000100 IDENTIFICATION DIVISION.
000200 PROGRAM-ID. POVMDLET.
000300 REMARKS.
000400**************************************************************
000500*          PURCHASING SYSTEM - VENDOR FILE DELETIONS       *
000600*    - STARTED BY PURCHASING SYSTEM SUB-MENU PROGRAM 'POVMAINT'  *
000700*          COULD ALSO BE STARTED BY TRANSID 'POVD'         *
000800**************************************************************
000900 ENVIRONMENT DIVISION.
001000 DATA DIVISION.
001100*
001200 WORKING-STORAGE  SECTION.
001300*
001400 01  WS-PROGRAM-FIELDS.
001500     05  FILLER            PIC X(8)     VALUE 'POVMDLET'.
001600     05  WS-CRT-MESSAGE    PIC X(17)    VALUE 'SESSION COMPLETED'.
001700*
001800*01  VENDOR-MASTER-RECORD
001900                           COPY   VENDMAST.
002000*01  JOURNAL-RECORD
002100                           COPY   JRNLRECD.
002200*01  WS-COMMAREA
002300                           COPY   POWSVMCA.
002400*01  WS-STATUS-FIELDS
002500                           COPY   STWSSTAT.
002600*01  VM-CONTROL-MAP
002700                           COPY   MAPVMCTL.
002800*01  VM-DETAIL-MAP
002900                           COPY   MAPVDTL1.
003000*01  WS-DATE-AND-TIME
003100                           COPY   STWSDTTM.
003200*01  WS-STATE-CODE-SEARCH-ENTRIES
003300                           COPY   STWST037.
003400*01  ATTRIBUTE-LIST
003500                           COPY   STWSATTR.
003600*01  DFHAID
003700                           COPY   DFHAID.
003800*
003900 01  END-OF-WORKING-STORAGE  PIC X(15)   VALUE 'END WS POVMDLET'.
004000*
004100 LINKAGE SECTION.
004200*
004300 01  DFHCOMMAREA                PIC X(8).
004400*
004500 01  BLL-CELLS.
004600     05  FILLER                  PIC S9(8)    COMP.
004700     05  BLL-CWA-ADDRESS         PIC S9(8)    COMP.
004800     05  BLL-T037-STATE-TABLE-ADDRESS  PIC S9(8)    COMP.
004900*
005000*01  CWA-DATA
005100                  COPY   STLNKCWA.
005200*01  T037-STATE-TABLE
005300                  COPY   T037STAT.
005400
005500
005600 PROCEDURE DIVISION.
005700**************************************************************
005800*     PROGRAM STRUCTURE IS:                                *
005900*        AA00-MAINLINE                                     *
006000*           B000-INITIAL-ENTRY                             *
006100*              B100-SEND-CONTROL-MAP-AND-DATA              *
006200*                 B110-GET-DATE-AND-TIME                   *
006300*                                                          *
006400*           C000-PROCESS-CONTROL-MAP                       *
006500*              C100-RECEIVE-CONTROL-MAP                    *
006600*                 C110-END-SESSION                         *
006700*                 C120-TRANSFER-XCTL-TO-MENU               *
006800*                 C130-TRANSFER-XCTL-TO-BROWSE             *
006900*              C200-VERIFY-VENDOR-FORMAT                   *
007000*              C400-VERIFY-VENDOR-FILE-STATUS              *
007100*                 C410-READ-VENDOR-FILE                   *
007200*              C500-SEND-DETAIL-MAP-AND-DATA               *
007300*                 B110-GET-DATE-AND-TIME                   *
007400*                 C530-FORMAT-DETAIL-MAP                   *
007500*                    C531-GET-STATE-NAME                   *
007600*              C600-SEND-CONTROL-MAP-DATAONLY              *
007700*                                                          *
007800*           G000-DELETE-PROCESSING                         *
```

Figure 15-4 *(Continued)*

```
007900*                D100-RECEIVE-DETAIL-MAP                          *
008000*                  C110-END-SESSION                               *
008100*                  C120-TRANSFER-XCTL-TO-MENU                     *
008200*              G100-DELETE-VENDOR-RECORD                          *
008300*                F110-READ-VENDOR-FOR-UPDATE                      *
008400*                  E121-POST-JOURNAL-RECORD                       *
008500*                G110-DELETE-VM-RECORD                            *
008600*            B100-SEND-CONTROL-MAP-AND-DATA                       *
008700*            D200-SEND-DETAIL-MAP-DATAONLY                        *
008800*****************************************************************
008900*
009000 AA00-MAINLINE  SECTION.
009100*
009200*    SERVICE RELOAD BLL-CELLS.
009300*
009400     IF EIBCALEN = 0
009500         PERFORM B000-INITIAL-ENTRY
009600     ELSE
009700         MOVE DFHCOMMAREA  TO  WS-COMMAREA
009800         IF CA-BROWSE
009900             MOVE SPACE        TO  CA-FUNCTION-CODE
010000             MOVE LOW-VALUES   TO  VM-CONTROL-MAP
010100             PERFORM C400-VERIFY-VENDOR-FILE-STATUS
010200             IF GOOD-VERIFY
010300                 PERFORM C500-SEND-DETAIL-MAP-AND-DATA
010400             ELSE
010500                 PERFORM B100-SEND-CONTROL-MAP-AND-DATA
010600         ELSE
010700             IF CA-RECEIVE-CTL-MAP
010800                 PERFORM C000-PROCESS-CONTROL-MAP
010900             ELSE
011000                 PERFORM G000-DELETE-PROCESSING.
011100*
011200     EXEC CICS RETURN
011300           TRANSID  ('POVD')
011400           COMMAREA (WS-COMMAREA)
011500           LENGTH   (8)
011600     END-EXEC.
011700*
011800 B000-INITIAL-ENTRY  SECTION.
011900*****************************************************************
012000*               PERFORMED FROM:  AA00-MAINLINE                 *
012100*****************************************************************
012200*
012300     MOVE LOW-VALUES  TO  VM-CONTROL-MAP.
012400     PERFORM B100-SEND-CONTROL-MAP-AND-DATA.
012500*
012600 B000-EXIT.
012700     EXIT.
012800*
012900 B100-SEND-CONTROL-MAP-AND-DATA  SECTION.
013000*****************************************************************
013100*        SEND CONTROL MAP - SYMBOLIC AND PHYSICAL MAPS         *
013200*             PERFORMED FROM:  B000-INITIAL-ENTRY              *
013300*                              G000-DELETE-PROCESSING          *
013400*****************************************************************
013500*
013600     PERFORM B110-GET-DATE-AND-TIME.
013700     MOVE WS-CURRENT-DATE  TO  MVC-D-DATE.
013800     MOVE WS-MAP-TIME      TO  MVC-D-TIME.
013900*
014000     MOVE -1  TO  MVC-L-VEND-CD-1.
014100     MOVE '1'  TO  CA-MAP-CONTROL.
014200*
014300     EXEC CICS SEND
014400           MAP      ('MAPPOVC')
014500           MAPSET  ('POVMDL1')
014600           FROM    (VM-CONTROL-MAP)
014700           ERASE
014800           CURSOR
014900     END-EXEC.
015000*
015100 B100-EXIT.
015200     EXIT.
015300*
015400 B110-GET-DATE-AND-TIME  SECTION.
015500*****************************************************************
015600*        STPDDTTM - OBTAIN DATE FROM CWA AND FORMAT TIME       *
015700*             PERFORMED FROM:  B100-SEND-CONTROL-MAP-AND-DATA  *
015800*                              C500-SEND-DETAIL-MAP-AND-DATA   *
015900*****************************************************************
016000*
016100     COPY  STPDDTTM.
```

Figure 15-4 *(Continued)*

```
016200*
016300 B110-EXIT.
016400      EXIT.
016500*
016600 C000-PROCESS-CONTROL-MAP  SECTION.
016700***********************************************************************
016800*              PERFORMED FROM:  AA00-MAINLINE                         *
016900*        PROCESS CONTROL MAP - IF VALID SEND DETAIL MAP               *
017000*          ELSE SEND CONTROL MAP WITH INVALID MESSAGE:                *
017100*   1) STATUS-OF-RECEIVE   = 'I'   INVALID KEY PRESSED                *
017200*   2) STATUS-OF-RECEIVE   = 'M'   MAPFAIL - NO DATA ENTERED          *
017300*   3) STATUS-OF-FORMAT    = 'E'   INVALID VENDOR KEYED FORMAT        *
017400*   4) STATUS-OF-VERIFY    = 'E'   VENDOR FILE STATUS ERROR           *
017500***********************************************************************
017600*
017700    PERFORM C100-RECEIVE-CONTROL-MAP.
017800    IF GOOD-RECEIVE
017900       PERFORM C200-VERIFY-VENDOR-FORMAT
018000        IF VALID-FORMAT
018100           PERFORM C400-VERIFY-VENDOR-FILE-STATUS
018200           IF GOOD-VERIFY
018300              PERFORM C500-SEND-DETAIL-MAP-AND-DATA
018400           ELSE
018500              PERFORM C600-SEND-CONTROL-MAP-DATAONLY
018600        ELSE
018700           PERFORM C600-SEND-CONTROL-MAP-DATAONLY
018800    ELSE
018900       IF MAPFAIL-ON-RECEIVE
019000          MOVE 'VENDOR CODE MUST BE ENTERED - PLEASE KEY-IN'
019100                            TO MVC-D-MESSAGE
019200          MOVE ASKIP-BRT  TO MVC-A-MESSAGE
019300          PERFORM C600-SEND-CONTROL-MAP-DATAONLY
019400       ELSE
019500          PERFORM C600-SEND-CONTROL-MAP-DATAONLY.
019600*
019700 C000-EXIT.
019800    EXIT.
019900*
020000 C100-RECEIVE-CONTROL-MAP  SECTION.
020100***********************************************************************
020200*              PERFORMED FROM:  C000-PROCESS-CONTROL-MAP              *
020300*           ENTER IS ONLY VALID DATA ENTRY KEY                        *
020400* CLEAR KEY - ENDS TERMINAL SESSION      PF5 - RETURNS TO MENU        *
020500*                                        PF4 - XCTL TO BROWSE         *
020600*           ALL OTHER AID KEYS ARE INVALID                           *
020700*    STATUS-OF-RECEIVE = 'G' = GOOD RECEIVE                          *
020800*                        'M' = MAPFAIL                               *
020900*                        'I' = INVALID KEY PRESSED                   *
021000***********************************************************************
021100*
021200    MOVE LOW-VALUES  TO  VM-CONTROL-MAP.
021300*
021400    IF EIBAID = DFHENTER
021500       MOVE 'M'  TO  STATUS-OF-RECEIVE
021600*
021700       EXEC CICS HANDLE CONDITION
021800             MAPFAIL (C100-EXIT)
021900       END-EXEC
022000*
022100       EXEC CICS RECEIVE
022200             MAP    ('MAPPOVC')
022300             MAPSET ('POVMDL1')
022400             INTO   (VM-CONTROL-MAP)
022500       END-EXEC
022600*
022700       MOVE 'G'  TO  STATUS-OF-RECEIVE
022800    ELSE
022900       IF EIBAID = DFHCLEAR
023000          PERFORM C110-END-SESSION
023100       ELSE
023200       IF EIBAID = DFHPF5
023300          PERFORM C120-TRANSFER-XCTL-TO-MENU
023400       ELSE
023500       IF EIBAID = DFHPF4
023600          PERFORM C130-TRANSFER-XCTL-TO-BROWSE
023700       ELSE
023800          MOVE 'I'       TO  STATUS-OF-RECEIVE
023900          MOVE 'INVALID KEY PRESSED - PLEASE TRY AGAIN'
024000                         TO  MVC-D-MESSAGE
024100          MOVE ASKIP-BRT TO  MVC-A-MESSAGE.
024200*
024300 C100-EXIT.
024400    EXIT.
```

Figure 15-4 *(Continued)*

```
024500*
024600 C110-END-SESSION  SECTION.
024700*******************************************************************
024800*    CRT OPERATOR PRESSED CLEAR KEY TO END TERMINAL SESSION     *
024900*         PERFORMED FROM:  C100-RECEIVE-CONTROL-MAP             *
025000*                          D100-RECEIVE-DETAIL-MAP              *
025100*******************************************************************
025200*
025300     EXEC CICS SEND
025400              FROM   (WS-CRT-MESSAGE)
025500              LENGTH (17)
025600              ERASE
025700     END-EXEC.
025800*
025900     EXEC CICS RETURN
026000     END-EXEC.
026100*
026200 C110-EXIT.
026300     EXIT.
026400*
026500 C120-TRANSFER-XCTL-TO-MENU  SECTION.
026600*******************************************************************
026700*       OPERATOR PRESSED PF5  TO RETURN TO MENU PROGRAM         *
026800*          PERFORMED FROM:  C100-RECEIVE-CONTROL-MAP            *
026900*                           D100-RECEIVE-DETAIL-MAP             *
027000*******************************************************************
027100*
027200     EXEC CICS XCTL
027300              PROGRAM ('POVMAINT')
027400     END-EXEC.
027500*
027600 C120-EXIT.
027700     EXIT.
027800*
027900 C130-TRANSFER-XCTL-TO-BROWSE  SECTION.
028000*******************************************************************
028100*      OPERATOR PRESSED PF4 TO TRANSFER CONTROL TO BROWSE       *
028200*           PERFORMED FROM:  C100-RECEIVE-CONTROL-MAP           *
028300*******************************************************************
028400*
028500     MOVE LOW-VALUES  TO  WS-COMMAREA.
028600     MOVE 'D'  TO  CA-FUNCTION-CODE.
028700*
028800     EXEC CICS XCTL
028900              PROGRAM  ('POVMBROW')
029000              COMMAREA (WS-COMMAREA)
029100              LENGTH   (8)
029200     END-EXEC.
029300*
029400 C130-EXIT.
029500     EXIT.
029600*
029700 C200-VERIFY-VENDOR-FORMAT  SECTION.
029800*******************************************************************
029900*      VERIFY FORMAT OF VENDOR CODE KEYED-IN = A-9999-9         *
030000*          PERFORMED FROM:  C000-PROCESS-CONTROL-MAP            *
030100*   IF VALID FORMAT - MOVE CODE TO WS-COMMAREA FIELDS (CA- )    *
030200*******************************************************************
030300*
030400     IF (MVC-D-VEND-CD-1  IS  ALPHABETIC
030500                 AND
030600        MVC-D-VEND-CD-1  IS NOT =  SPACE)
030700        AND
030800        MVC-D-VEND-CD-2  IS  NUMERIC
030900        AND
031000        MVC-D-VEND-CD-3  IS  NUMERIC
031100        MOVE MVC-D-VEND-CD-1  TO  CA-VEND-1
031200        MOVE MVC-D-VEND-CD-2  TO  CA-VEND-2
031300        MOVE MVC-D-VEND-CD-3  TO  CA-VEND-3
031400        MOVE 'G'              TO  STATUS-OF-FORMAT
031500     ELSE
031600        MOVE 'E'      TO  STATUS-OF-FORMAT
031700        MOVE 'VENDOR CODE FORMAT MUST BE: A-9999-9 - PLEASE RE-EN
031800-        'TER'        TO  MVC-D-MESSAGE
031900        MOVE ASKIP-BRT  TO  MVC-A-MESSAGE.
032000*
032100 C200-EXIT.
032200     EXIT.
032300*
032400 C400-VERIFY-VENDOR-FILE-STATUS  SECTION.
032500*******************************************************************
032600*          PERFORMED FROM:  C000-PROCESS-CONTROL-MAP            *
032700*          MUST BE A VENDOR RECORD FOR DELETIONS                *
032800*******************************************************************
```

Figure 15-4 *(Continued)*

```
032900*
033000      MOVE 'G'  TO  STATUS-OF-VERIFY.
033100*
033200      PERFORM C410-READ-VENDOR-FILE.
033300*
033400      IF RECORD-NOT-FOUND
033500          MOVE 'E'        TO  STATUS-OF-VERIFY
033600          MOVE 'VENDOR RECORD NOT ON FILE'
033700                          TO  MVC-D-MESSAGE
033800          MOVE ASKIP-BRT  TO  MVC-A-MESSAGE
033900      ELSE
034000          IF VM-DOLLARS-COMMITTED  GREATER THAN  ZERO
034100              MOVE 'E'        TO  STATUS-OF-VERIFY
034200              MOVE 'DOLLARS COMMITTED ARE SIGNIFICANT - CAN
034300-                  ' NOT DELETE'  TO  MVC-D-MESSAGE
034400              MOVE ASKIP-BRT  TO  MVC-A-MESSAGE.
034500*
034600 C400-EXIT.
034700      EXIT.
034800*
034900 C410-READ-VENDOR-FILE  SECTION.
035000*****************************************************************
035100*       PERFORMED FROM:  C400-VERIFY-VENDOR-FILE-STATUS        *
035200*****************************************************************
035300*
035400      MOVE 'E' TO  STATUS-OF-READ.
035500*
035600      EXEC CICS HANDLE CONDITION
035700              NOTFND  (C410-EXIT)
035800      END-EXEC.
035900*
036000      EXEC CICS READ
036100              DATASET ('VENDMAST')
036200              INTO    (VENDOR-MASTER-RECORD)
036300              RIDFLD  (CA-VENDOR-CODE)
036400      END-EXEC.
036500*
036600      MOVE 'G'  TO  STATUS-OF-READ.
036700*
036800 C410-EXIT.
036900      EXIT.
037000*
037100 C500-SEND-DETAIL-MAP-AND-DATA  SECTION.
037200*****************************************************************
037300*        SEND DETAIL MAP - PHYSICAL AND SYMBOLIC MAPS          *
037400*          PERFORMED FROM:  C000-PROCESS-CONTROL-MAP           *
037500*  SENT WHEN ALL VALIDATION AND EDIT CONDITIONS HAVE BEEN MET  *
037600*****************************************************************
037700*
037800      MOVE LOW-VALUES  TO  VM-DETAIL-MAP.
037900*
038000      PERFORM B110-GET-DATE-AND-TIME.
038100      MOVE WS-CURRENT-DATE  TO  MVD-D-DATE.
038200      MOVE WS-MAP-TIME      TO  MVD-D-TIME.
038300*
038400      PERFORM C530-FORMAT-DETAIL-MAP.
038500*
038600      MOVE '2'  TO  CA-MAP-CONTROL.
038700*
038800.     EXEC CICS SEND
038900              MAP     ('MAPPOVD')
039000              MAPSET  ('POVMDL2')
039100              FROM    (VM-DETAIL-MAP)
039200              ERASE
039300      END-EXEC.
039400*
039500 C500-EXIT.
039600      EXIT.
039700*
039800 C530-FORMAT-DETAIL-MAP  SECTION.
039900*****************************************************************
040000*       PERFORMED FROM:  C500-SEND-DETAIL-MAP-AND-DATA         *
040100*****************************************************************
040200*
040300* FORMAT VENDOR CODE: A-9999-9   WS- FIELDS ARE AT END OF VENDMAST
040400      MOVE CA-VEND-1        TO  WS-VENDOR-CD-1.
040500      MOVE CA-VEND-2        TO  WS-VENDOR-CD-2.
040600      MOVE CA-VEND-3        TO  WS-VENDOR-CD-3.
040700      MOVE WS-VENDOR-CODE   TO  MVD-D-VENDOR-CODE.
040800*
040900      MOVE VM-AREA-CD       TO  MVD-D-PHONE-AREA-CD.
041000      MOVE VM-PHONE-1-3     TO  MVD-D-PHONE-1.
041100      MOVE VM-PHONE-4-7     TO  MVD-D-PHONE-2.
041200      MOVE VM-VENDOR-NAME   TO  MVD-D-VENDOR-NAME.
```

Figure 15-4 *(Continued)*

```
041300        MOVE VM-CONTACT              TO  MVD-D-CONTACT.
041400        MOVE VM-STREET-ADDRESS       TO  MVD-D-STREET.
041500        MOVE VM-CITY                 TO  MVD-D-CITY.
041600        MOVE VM-STATE                TO  MVD-D-STATE-CODE.
041700*
041800        MOVE VM-STATE                TO  WS-STATE-CODE.
041900        PERFORM C531-GET-STATE-NAME.
042000        MOVE WS-STATE-NAME           TO  MVD-D-STATE-NAME.
042100*
042200        MOVE VM-ZIP-CODE             TO  MVD-D-ZIP-CODE.
042300        MOVE VM-TO-ATTN-OF           TO  MVD-D-ATTENTION-OF.
042400        MOVE VM-DOLLARS-COMMITTED    TO  MVD-D-DLRS-COMMITTED.
042500*
042600 C530-EXIT.
042700     EXIT.
042800*
042900 C531-GET-STATE-NAME  SECTION.
043000*******************************************************************
043100*              LOAD AND SEARCH STATE CODE TABLE             *
043200*          PERFORMED FROM:  C530-SEND-DETAIL-MAP-AND-DATA   *
043300*******************************************************************
043400*
043500     COPY   STPDT037.
043600*
043700 C531-EXIT.
043800     EXIT.
043900*
044000 C600-SEND-CONTROL-MAP-DATAONLY  SECTION.
044100*******************************************************************
044200*          SEND CONTROL MAP DATAONLY - SYMBOLIC MAP         *
044300*          PERFORMED FROM:  C000-PROCESS-CONTROL-MAP        *
044400*              SENT FOR INVALID CONDITIONS                  *
044500*******************************************************************
044600*
044700     MOVE UNPROT-FSET TO  MVC-A-VEND-CD-1
044800                          MVC-A-VEND-CD-2
044900                          MVC-A-VEND-CD-3.
045000*
045100     MOVE -1   TO  MVC-L-VEND-CD-1.
045200     MOVE '1'  TO  CA-MAP-CONTROL.
045300*
045400     EXEC CICS SEND
045500               MAP      ('MAPPOVC')
045600               MAPSET   ('POVMDL1')
045700               FROM     (VM-CONTROL-MAP)
045800               DATAONLY
045900               CURSOR
046000     END-EXEC.
046100*
046200 C600-EXIT.
046300     EXIT.
046400*
046500 D100-RECEIVE-DETAIL-MAP  SECTION.
046600*******************************************************************
046700*          PERFORMED FROM:  G000-DELETE-PROCESSING          *
046800* ENTER - PROCESSES TRANSACTION       CLEAR - ENDS SESSION  *
046900* PF3   - SETS DISPLAY OF CTL MAP     PF5   - RETURNS TO MENU *
047000*              ALL OTHER KEYS ARE INVALID                   *
047100*      STATUS-OF-RECEIVE  =  'G'  =   GOOD RECEIVE          *
047200*                            'C'  =   RETURN TO CTL-MAP     *
047300*                            'I'  =   INVALID KEY PRESSED   *
047400*******************************************************************
047500*
047600     MOVE LOW-VALUES  TO  VM-DETAIL-MAP.
047700*
047800     IF EIBAID  =  DFHENTER
047900*
048000         EXEC CICS IGNORE CONDITION
048100                   MAPFAIL
048200         END-EXEC
048300*
048400         EXEC CICS RECEIVE
048500                   MAP      ('MAPPOVD')
048600                   MAPSET   ('POVMDL2')
048700                   INTO     (VM-DETAIL-MAP)
048800         END-EXEC
048900*
049000         MOVE 'G' TO  STATUS-OF-RECEIVE
```

Figure 15-4 *(Continued)*

```
049100        ELSE
049200           IF EIBAID = DFHCLEAR
049300              PERFORM C110-END-SESSION
049400           ELSE
049500           IF EIBAID = DFHPF3
049600              MOVE 'C' TO STATUS-OF-RECEIVE
049700           ELSE
049800           IF EIBAID = DFHPF5
049900              PERFORM C120-TRANSFER-XCTL-TO-MENU
050000           ELSE
050100              MOVE 'I'        TO  STATUS-OF-RECEIVE
050200              MOVE 'INVALID KEY PRESSED - PLEASE TRY AGAIN'
050300                              TO  MVD-D-MESSAGE
050400              MOVE ASKIP-BRT  TO  MVD-A-MESSAGE.
050500*
050600 D100-EXIT.
050700     EXIT.
050800*
050900 D200-SEND-DETAIL-MAP-DATAONLY  SECTION.
051000********************************************************************
051100*        SEND DETAIL MAP DATA ONLY - SYMBOLIC MAP              *
051200*     PERFORMED FROM:  G000-DELETE-PROCESSING                  *
051300* SENT IF INVALID KEY IS PRESSED ON A RECEIVE OF THE DETAIL MAP *
051400********************************************************************
051500*
051600     MOVE '2' TO  CA-MAP-CONTROL.
051700*
051800     EXEC CICS SEND
051900               MAP      ('MAPPOVD')
052000               MAPSET   ('POVMOL2')
052100               FROM     (VM-DETAIL-MAP)
052200               DATAONLY
052300     END-EXEC.
052400*
052500 D200-EXIT.
052600     EXIT.
052700*
052800 E121-POST-JOURNAL-RECORD  SECTION.
052900********************************************************************
053000*    POST JOURNAL ENTRY - LINK TO JOURNAL PROGRAM 'JRNLPOST'   *
053100*       PERFORMED FROM:  F110-READ-VENDOR-FOR-UPDATE           *
053200********************************************************************
053300*
053400     MOVE 'VM'                TO  JR-PREFIX.
053500     MOVE VENDOR-MASTER-RECORD TO  JR-RECORD-DATA.
053600     MOVE SPACES              TO  JR-PASSWORD.
053700*
053800     EXEC CICS LINK
053900               PROGRAM  ('JRNLPOST')
054000               COMMAREA (JOURNAL-RECORD)
054100               LENGTH   (524)
054200     END-EXEC.
054300*
054400 E121-EXIT.
054500     EXIT.
054600*
054700 F110-READ-VENDOR-FOR-UPDATE  SECTION.
054800********************************************************************
054900* READ VENDOR RECORD FOR UPDATE - POST BEFORE JOURNAL RECORD   *
055000*          PERFORMED FROM:  G100-DELETE-VENDOR-RECORD          *
055100********************************************************************
055200*
055300     MOVE 'E' TO  STATUS-OF-READ.
055400*
055500     EXEC CICS HANDLE CONDITION
055600               NOTFND  (F110-EXIT)
055700     END-EXEC.
055800*
055900     EXEC CICS READ
056000               DATASET ('VENDMAST')
056100               INTO    (VENDOR-MASTER-RECORD)
056200               RIDFLD  (CA-VENDOR-CODE)
056300               UPDATE
056400     END-EXEC.
056500*
056600     MOVE 'G' TO  STATUS-OF-READ.
056700*
056800     MOVE 'B' TO  JR-TYPE.
```

Figure 15-4 *(Continued)*

```
056900      PERFORM E121-POST-JOURNAL-RECORD.
057000*
057100 F110-EXIT.
057200     EXIT.
057300*
057400 G000-DELETE-PROCESSING  SECTION.
057500***************************************************************
057600*              PERFORMED FROM:  AA00-MAINLINE               *
057700*      DETAIL MAP IS SENT IF AN INVALID KEY WAS PRESSED     *
057800*             OR DELETE RECORD WAS NOT FOUND                *
057900***************************************************************
058000*
058100      PERFORM D100-RECEIVE-DETAIL-MAP.
058200*
058300   IF GOOD-RECEIVE
058400      PERFORM G100-DELETE-VENDOR-RECORD
058500      IF GOOD-DELETE
058600         PERFORM B100-SEND-CONTROL-MAP-AND-DATA
058700      ELSE
058800         PERFORM D200-SEND-DETAIL-MAP-DATAONLY
058900   ELSE
059000      IF RETURN-TO-CTL-MAP
059100         PERFORM B100-SEND-CONTROL-MAP-AND-DATA
059200      ELSE
059300         PERFORM D200-SEND-DETAIL-MAP-DATAONLY.
059400*
059500 G000-EXIT.
059600     EXIT.
059700*
059800 G100-DELETE-VENDOR-RECORD  SECTION.
059900***************************************************************
060000*            PERFORMED FROM:  G000-DELETE-PROCESSING        *
060100*   RECORD NOT FOUND COULD NOT OCCUR UNLESS RECORD WAS DELETED *
060200*   BY ANOTHER TERMINAL SINCE BEING KEYED-IN ON CONTROL SCREEN *
060300***************************************************************
060400*
060500      MOVE 'E'  TO  STATUS-OF-DELETE.
060600*
060700      PERFORM F110-READ-VENDOR-FOR-UPDATE.
060800*
060900   IF RECORD-NOT-FOUND
061000      MOVE 'RECORD TO BE DELETED - NOT FOUND'
061100                       TO  MVD-D-MESSAGE
061200      MOVE ASKIP-BRT  TO  MVD-A-MESSAGE
061300   ELSE
061400      PERFORM G110-DELETE-VM-RECORD
061500      MOVE 'RECORD DELETED SUCCESSFULLY'  TO  MVC-D-MESSAGE
061600      MOVE ASKIP-BRT                      TO  MVC-A-MESSAGE
061700      MOVE 'G'                            TO  STATUS-OF-DELETE.
061800*
061900 G100-EXIT.
062000     EXIT.
062100*
062200 G110-DELETE-VM-RECORD  SECTION.
062300***************************************************************
062400*     DELETE VENDOR RECORD - POST 'BEFORE' JOURNAL RECORD   *
062500*           PERFORMED FROM:  G100-DELETE-VENDOR-RECORD       *
062600***************************************************************
062700*
062800      EXEC CICS DELETE
062900              DATASET ('VENDMAST')
063000      END-EXEC.
063100*
063200 G110-EXIT.
063300     EXIT.
```

16

TEMPORARY-STORAGE CONTROL

Temporary-storage control, like the use of field attributes, seems to cause application programmers some difficulty. The use of a single temporary storage record does not seem to pose any special problems, but the employment of multiple queue records in a browse program's paging logic often causes much difficulty. I will first discuss temporary-storage control commands and then the use of single queue records in this chapter. I will then cover several techniques used for paging logic which employ multiple temporary-storage (TS) queue records. Chapter 17 will present a complete browse program detailing one of the paging methods presented in this chapter.

A TS queue created by one program or task can be used in the same or different program or task. TS queues may be created in either main storage or auxiliary storage. Main-storage queues are not used very often, and the browse program in the next chapter will use auxiliary storage. COMMAREA can be used to supplement or replace TS queues in many situations. These queues are available from the time they are created until they are deleted by a program or by the startup of the CICS system. They do not require that any predefined CICS table entries be made.

Relating TS Queues to VSAM Files

TS auxiliary queues can be likened to VSAM files. The key to a queue consists of up to eight characters which are defined in the creating and using programs. It is common practice to use an eight-character queue name. These queues can be used by many different programs which are executing at different terminals. It is advisable to make a TS queue unique to the terminal at which the task is being executed; otherwise, a program running at another terminal could unknowingly delete your queue. This is generally accomplished by using the EIB field EIBTRMID as the first four positions of the queue name. The next four positions should be characters which are meaningful to the program or system such as MAP1, BROW, or PAGE. If only one queue is being used in a program, EIBTRNID may be used for the second four characters of the queue name. It is the responsibility of the application programmer to delete TS queues when they are no longer needed. TS is a finite resource and could become full if queues which were no longer needed were not deleted. In addition to the eight-position key, these queues have an item number attached to the queue record. It is easier to understand TS queues if you consider the item number as part of the queue's key. For instance, if EIBTRMID is TERM and the transaction code is POVB, a queue of three records can be visualized as having keys of TERMPOVB/1, TERMPOVB/2, and TERMPOVB/3.

TS control commands include:

1. WRITEQ TS—Writes a new or additional TS queue record.

2. WRITEQ TS REWRITE—Updates a TS queue record.

3. READQ TS—Reads a TS queue record which has been previously created.

4. DELETEQ TS—Deletes a TS queue which is no longer needed.

Required Working-Storage Fields

Prior to using TS queues, it is necessary to define several fields in working storage: the queue name, the data portion of the queue, the length of the queue, and an item number. Length and item can be hard-coded if they are not variable. The names used in the command descriptions are

```
01 TS-QUEUE.
   05 TS-TERMID          PIC X(4).
   05 TS-QUEUE-NAME      PIC X(4).

01 TS-DATA.
   05 TS-FIELD-1         . . .
   05 TS-FIELD-2         . . .
      .
      .
      .
01 TS-LENGTH             PIC S9999  COMP  VALUE ZEROES.
01 TS-ITEM               PIC S9999  COMP  VALUE ZEROES.
```

The terminal identifier EIBTRMID will be moved into TS-TERMID, and the transaction code EIBTRNID, or a programmer-defined suffix, will be moved into TS-QUEUE-NAME. Queue length, TS-LENGTH, can be defined as a constant or can have length moved to it prior to executing a TS command. Item number, TS-ITEM, can be a constant or can have a value moved to it, added to it, or subtracted from it. Both TS-LENGTH and TS-ITEM must be defined as halfword binary values. For example,

```
MOVE EIBTRMID   TO   TS-TERMID.
MOVE EIBTRNID   TO   TS-QUEUE-NAME.
MOVE 1          TO   TS-ITEM.
MOVE 100        TO   TS-LENGTH.
```

Write a TS Queue

It is necessary to create or write a TS queue before it can be accessed. TS queue WRITE command format is

```
EXEC CICS WRITEQ TS
          QUEUE  (TS-QUEUE)
          FROM   (TS-DATA)
          LENGTH (TS-LENGTH)
          ITEM   (TS-ITEM)
END-EXEC.
```

The letters TS following the WRITEQ command are optional but are customarily included. The queue name is TS-QUEUE, and the data written is in the working-storage field TS-DATA. Working-storage fields TS-LENGTH and TS-ITEM, defined as binary halfwords, are set prior to the write. The system will assign a sequential item number starting from 1 when a queue is written. I have found that fewer problems occur when the item is set by the program prior to the write. All examples will move a value to the working-storage field used to hold the value of ITEM, prior to issuing a write.

• Handle Conditions—It is normally not necessary to check for any handle conditions prior to writing a TS queue.

Rewrite a TS Queue

TS queues are updated by including a REWRITE option. The format of the TS queue REWRITE option is similar to that of the WRITEQ TS command with the REWRITE option added as follows:

```
EXEC CICS WRITEQ  TS
           QUEUE   (TS-QUEUE)
           FROM    (TS-DATA)
           LENGTH  (TS-LENGTH)
           ITEM    (TS-ITEM)
           REWRITE
END-EXEC.
```

The queue name is TS-QUEUE, and the data rewritten is located in the working-storage field TS-DATA. Working-storage fields TS-LENGTH and TS-ITEM, defined in working storage as binary halfwords, are set prior to the write. A TS record which is to be changed must be read prior to issuing a REWRITE.

- Handle Conditions—It is normally not necessary to check for any handle conditions prior to rewriting a queue. Conditions which might occur during testing include: QIDERR (queue not found) and ITEMERR (the queue exists but the item specified was not found).

Read a TS Queue

The READQ TS command format is similar to that of the write queue. READQ TS and INTO (TS-DATA) replace WRITEQ TS and the FROM option. A previously written queue is read by setting the item number to the proper value before reading the queue INTO (TS-DATA). READQ TS command format is

```
EXEC CICS READQ   TS
           QUEUE   (TS-QUEUE)
           INTO    (TS-DATA)
           LENGTH  (TS-LENGTH)
           ITEM    (TS-ITEM)
END-EXEC.
```

ITEM could be omitted, in which case the next TS queue record would be retrieved. Always include ITEM on all applicable TS commands because there is less chance of errors occurring when a program directly controls item number. TS queue records can be read either sequentially or randomly by specifying the appropriate ITEM number. They can be read in reverse sequence by decreasing ITEM.

- Handle Conditions—It is normally not necessary to check for any handle conditions prior to reading a TS queue. Conditions which could occur during testing include QIDERR and ITEMERR.

Delete a TS Queue

The TS delete queue command format requires only the queue name. The entire queue must be deleted; it is not possible to delete individual items. DELETEQ TS command format is

```
EXEC CICS DELETEQ TS
              QUEUE   (TS-QUEUE)
END-EXEC.
```

- Handle Conditions—It is normally advisable to check for the QIDERR handle condition before deleting a queue. QIDERR occurs because programs using queues often delete the queue, if it exists, at the beginning of a program and should delete it prior to exiting the program, if it is no longer required.
- Ignore Condition—QIDERR is often handled by ignoring the condition if it occurs. If the program attempts to delete the queue and it does not exist, no ABEND will occur.

Using Single Queue Records

The use of single queue records is rather simple. One program writes a TS queue record and that record will be read and rewritten in other programs. The queue would probably be deleted only in the program which creates the queue. A single queue might be used to hold keys of records which are passed from program to program. When many programs in a system are interrelated, it sometimes simplifies a system if a TS queue is used. Passing record keys from program to program or from task to task in the COMMAREA in a multiprogram system can sometimes become complicated if different-size COMMAREAs are used.

TS Paging Logic Techniques

You may be wondering how you would send previously displayed screens when using the file control browse commands described in Chap. 11. TS queues are often employed for paging logic (scrolling) in browse programs. Paging refers to the sequential scrolling forward or backward through a list of sequential records, such as a vendor code and name list. A selection is often made from this list and passed to another program. Chapter 17 will detail one technique for performing this logic.

Paging done using temporary storage is usually controlled *in* a program by item number and *externally* by the use of PF keys. It is customary to use PF1 for forward scrolling and PF2 for backward paging. Program logic could be included to start a browse at the first or last map written to the queue. Logic must be included in all paging routines to prevent scrolling beyond the limits of the item numbers which have been created.

Your data processing installation may have standard scrolling routines already defined which you can incorporate into your programs. Many different approaches may be taken to paging logic depending on the situation and file being accessed. Most of the techniques employing temporary storage and used to write paging logic routines fall into one of the following categories:

1. Write the entire symbolic map out to temporary storage and retrieve records as necessary.

2. Write only significant map data to temporary storage. The items can be retrieved as needed and the symbolic map formatted with significant data which was saved.

3. Write only record keys to temporary storage. This method requires rereading records when paging backward.

4. Read all records before displaying any maps.

Write the Entire Symbolic Map to Temporary Storage

As each map is displayed during a browse function, the symbolic map is written out to a TS queue and the item number is incremented by one. Displaying the prior map requires decreasing the item number by 1 and reading the queue which contains the last symbolic map displayed. The queue record is read into the symbolic map's working-storage area, and the map is displayed. Each time the item number is incremented, its highest value must be saved. This is done so that when backward paging is performed, followed by forward paging, the program will know when to stop paging forward or to start creating additional TS records. Logic would have to be employed to prevent decrementing the item number below 1 when paging backward.

Write Only Significant Map Data to Temporary Storage

This technique is similar to writing the entire symbolic map to temporary storage, but only significant map data is saved in working storage and written to a queue. When a program pages backward or forward, it reconstructs the symbolic map from the data which was saved in the queue record. This method has the advantage of creating smaller queues, but it requires more program code. You should develop your techniques in accordance with company standards or, if none exist, establish standards for your installation.

Write Only Record Keys to Temporary Storage

The key of the first or last record displayed on each map can be saved in a TS queue. As the terminal operator scrolls backward or forward, the program can reread records starting with keys which are equal to or greater than the saved keys. Each map can be reformatted as it was the first time the map was displayed. This method requires the least amount of temporary storage and is the technique used for the browse program in Chap. 17. A disadvantage of this method is that records will have to be reread when paging takes place in order to format the map.

Read All Records Before Displaying Any Maps

This is perhaps the simplest scrolling method to work with. All maps to be displayed as part of a browse are written to temporary storage before any map is displayed. When all the maps for a given browse have been written to the queue, the program starts the display from the first map written. Forward and backward scrolling is permitted. This method differs from the first scrolling method discussed in that the latter writes maps to temporary storage only when they are initially displayed, whereas this method writes all maps to temporary storage before any map is displayed. The drawback to using this method for long browses is that many more records would have to be read and their maps saved even if they did not need to be displayed.

Paging Logic Techniques Without Using Temporary Storage

Paging logic can be accomplished without using TS queues. Two methods which are sometimes employed are

1. Save the first and last key displayed on a map in the COMMAREA. Then, depending on the AID key pressed, issue a READNEXT or READPREV command. This logic can get complicated. For instance, when paging backward, the READPREV command is executed and a map is formatted from bottom to top. If 15 items are displayed per page and you page backward and only 10 records are read, the first five lines of the screen's multiple data would contain spaces and have to be adjusted.

2. The COMMAREA could be used to store the code of the first or last item on each page. These codes could be indexed through and records reread in order to affect paging logic. This is a good method if key size is small and you can limit the number of pages to be browsed.

TS Random Access Methods

As mentioned previously, your understanding of TS queues will be enhanced if you can relate queues to VSAM files. If the terminal at which a program was being executed had an ID of TERM and the TRANSID was POVB, symbolic map data saved could be conceptualized as follows:

KEY Queue Name	Item	First or Last Key	or	Symbolic Map Data
TERMPOVB	1	Map 1 key		Map 1 data
"	2	" 2 "		" 2 "
"	3	" 3 "		" 3 "

When a program sends the first map, it writes out a TS queue with a key of TEMPPOVB/1. The program increments item number as the program pages forward by adding one to the working-storage item field. It creates queue records with keys of TEMPPOVB/2, TEMPPOVB/3, etc. An alternate approach would be to save the first or last record key displayed on the map. The map could be reconstructed as paging takes place, instead of saving the entire map in temporary storage.

Backward scrolling is accomplished by subtracting 1 from item number each time the program scrolls backward. Item number must be defined in the working-storage COMMAREA when scrolling, since it changes with forward or backward paging. You would also save the item number of the last map which was displayed in COMMAREA. Routines can be written to skip to the first or last record which was displayed, after scrolling forward or backward several pages.

SUMMARY

I found the use of a TS queue valuable in a case where a database file was loaded in ascending date sequence and the user wanted a display in descending date order. This database did not permit backward reading through the use of a command such as READPREV. I was able to simulate the use of STARTBR and READPREV commands by employing a TS queue. The technique required reading each of the required records which were in ascending date sequence and writing a TS queue ITEM for each record. The records were then accessed in descending date sequence by reading the TS queue items in reverse order by subtracting 1 from ITEM number as each queue item was retrieved. The TS queue was read in reverse order until ITEM was decremented to zero. This use of a TS queue worked well because the number of date records was small and the transaction was not used frequently. The technique employed would be inefficient if there were numerous date records and the display was a high-use transaction. It is inefficient to read, write, and then reread each record. You are, in effect, sorting a segment of the file into a different sequence. The use of a SORT is not permitted in an online system. It is important when online files are created that their records be loaded in the sequence which corresponds to the order in which records will most commonly be read.

TS queues can aid a designer/programmer in many situations, and their use is limited only by the creativity of the programmer in accordance with good design principles. Since there are inefficiencies involved when TS queues are used, you should consider the use of the COMMAREA in their place whenever practical.

The intent of this chapter was to familiarize you with TS queues. TS commands are easy to understand but sometimes difficult to use for paging logic. The commands discussed were WRITEQ TS, WRITEQ TS REWRITE, READQ TS, and DELETEQ TS. Single-record TS queues were discussed, as were multiple queue records which are used for paging logic. Some practical applications of TS queues were discussed. Creative application programmers will find many uses for TS queues. Some installations have developed standards for paging techniques. Chapter 17 will illustrate the use of some TS commands in the browse program.

This chapter attempted to convey ideas for the use of TS queues. Once you understand the concept and the commands, you will be able to implement design ideas which may, at first, have seemed difficult to perform. Consider alternate approaches to the solution of a problem before deciding on the method to be employed. For instance, the use of the COMMAREA may be more efficient than is the use of a TS queue. An understanding of various techniques for solving a problem will make you more effective in your design and programming.

17

THE BROWSE PROGRAM

Several paging techniques were discussed in Chap. 16. The technique of writing only a record's key to temporary storage, as a map is displayed, is employed for the browse program in this chapter. This example covers most of the functions you will be required to perform in a browse program.

Only one map (see Fig. 2-10) is used for the browse program. The terminal operator can key in the TRANSID POVB and press ENTER in order to display the browse map. The browse can also be invoked by a transfer of control from another program. The operator has the option of returning to the vendor file maintenance submenu (see Fig. 6-3) or ending the session. The screen displays up to 15 vendor file records from which the terminal operator can make a selection and pass the selected vendor code to an invoking program. The operator can page forward if the required vendor is not displayed and can page backward in order to view a previously displayed screen. This example does not permit backward paging beyond the vendor used as a starting point for the browse.

The operator can reset the browse starting point during any point of the display by entering a new code on the screen and pressing a designated PF key. When the browse starting point is reset, the operator can scroll forward and then backward from that point. You would reset the browse after displaying a map and finding that the desired record was far from the record shown on the screen. The RESET BROWSE option encourages an operator to limit the scope of a browse.

BMS Browse Map

Figure 17-1 contains the BMS map corresponding to the browse map shown in Fig. 2-10. All browse map field attributes are defined as ASKIP, except for the SELECTION and RESET VENDOR CODE fields. The SELECTION field

Figure 17-1   Vendor File Browse BMS Map.

```
            PRINT NOGEN
POVMBR1     DFHMSD TYPE=MAP,                                          X
                   CTRL=(FREEKB,FRSET),                               X
                   LANG=COBOL,                                        X
                   MODE=INOUT,                                        X
                   TERM=3270,                                         X
                   TIOAPFX=YES
*
MAPPOVC     DFHMDI LINE=01,                                           X
                   COLUMN=01,                                         X
                   SIZE=(24,80)
*
            DFHMDF POS=(01,01),                                       X
                   ATTRB=ASKIP,                                       X
                   LENGTH=05,                                         X
                   INITIAL='DATE: '
*
MCDATE      DFHMDF POS=(01,07),                                       X
                   ATTRB=ASKIP,                                       X
                   LENGTH=08
*
            DFHMDF POS=(01,27),                                       X
                   ATTRB=ASKIP,                                       X
                   LENGTH=25,                                         X
                   INITIAL='ABC MANUFACTURING COMPANY'
*
            DFHMDF POS=(01,72),                                       X
                   ATTRB=ASKIP,                                       X
                   LENGTH=07,                                         X
                   INITIAL='POVMBR1'
*
            DFHMDF POS=(02,01),                                       X
                   ATTRB=ASKIP,                                       X
                   LENGTH=05,                                         X
                   INITIAL='TIME: '
*
MCTIME      DFHMDF POS=(02,07),                                       X
                   ATTRB=ASKIP,                                       X
                   LENGTH=08
*
            DFHMDF POS=(02,30),                                       X
                   ATTRB=ASKIP,                                       X
                   LENGTH=18,                                         X
                   INITIAL='VENDOR FILE BROWSE'
*
            DFHMDF POS=(03,03),                                       X
                   ATTRB=ASKIP,                                       X
                   LENGTH=21,                                         X
                   INITIAL='VENDOR CD VENDOR NAME'
*
            DFHMDF POS=(03,39),                                       X
                   ATTRB=ASKIP,                                       X
                   LENGTH=06,                                         X
                   INITIAL='STREET'
*
```

attribute is defined as IC,NUM, which makes the field UNPROT and inserts the cursor at this field when the map is sent. The RESET VENDOR CODE field attribute is set to UNPROT. The DFHMDF macro labeled MCOCCUR shows how the OCCURS clause can be used to generate 15 lines of map data, each of which contains 79 characters plus an attribute.

User-Friendly Symbolic Maps

The user-friendly symbolic map is unique to the vendor browse and is hard-coded in the program.

Figure 17-1 *(Continued)*

```
            DFHMDF POS=(03,60),                                      X
                   ATTRB=ASKIP,                                      X
                   LENGTH=12,                                        X
                   INITIAL='CITY / STATE'
*
MCOCCUR     DFHMDF POS=(04,01),                                      X
                   ATTRB=ASKIP,                                      X
                   LENGTH=79,                                        X
                   OCCURS=15
*
MCSELEC     DFHMDF POS=(19,01),                                      X
                   ATTRB=(IC,NUM),                                   X
                   LENGTH=02
*
            DFHMDF POS=(19,04),                                      X
                   ATTRB=ASKIP,                                      X
                   LENGTH=11,                                        X
                   INITIAL=': SELECTION'
*
            DFHMDF POS=(20,06),                                      X
                   ATTRB=ASKIP,                                      X
                   LENGTH=18,                                        X
                   INITIAL='RESET VENDOR CODE:
*
MCRVCOD     DFHMDF POS=(20,25),                                      X
                   ATTRB=(UNPROT),                                   X
                   LENGTH=06
*
            DFHMDF POS=(20,32),                                      X
                   ATTRB=ASKIP,                                      X
                   LENGTH=01
*
            DFHMDF POS=(21,01),                                      X
                   ATTRB=ASKIP,                                      Y
                   LENGTH=51,                                        X
                   INITIAL='1. FWD  - PF1        4. KEY IN SELECTION   -X
                   PF6'
*
            DFHMDF POS=(22,01),                                      X
                   ATTRB=ASKIP,                                      X
                   LENGTH=51,                                        X
                   INITIAL='2. BWD  - PF2        5. KEY IN RESET VENDOR -X
                   PF7'
*
            DFHMDF POS=(23,01),                                      X
                   ATTRB=ASKIP,                                      X
                   LENGTH=53,                                        Y
                   INITIAL='3. MENU - PF5        6. END OF SESSION     -X
                   CLEAR'
*
MCMESSG     DFHMDF POS=(24,01),                                      X
                   ATTRB=ASKIP,                                      X
                   LENGTH=79
*
            DFHMSD TYPE=FINAL
            END
```

Browse Program Source Code

The browse program's source code is shown in Fig. 17-2. The program's initial
entry logic is shown following the main processing logic which is executed much
more frequently than is initial entry in a browse program. This technique is often
employed in online programming in order to minimize paging requirements.

Procedure Division

AA00-MAINLINE. If this program was started by a TRANSID, the program will
move low-values to WS-COMMAREA and will start its browse at the beginning

Figure 17-2 Vendor File Browse Program Source Code.

```
000100 IDENTIFICATION DIVISION.
000200 PROGRAM-ID. POVMBROW.
000300 REMARKS.
000400****************************************************************
000500*            PURCHASING SYSTEM - VENDOR FILE BROWSE           *
000600*      - STARTED BY PURCHASING SYSTEM MAINTENANCE PROGRAMS    *
000700*            OR DIRECTLY BY ENTERING  TRANSID 'POVB'          *
000800*      PF1 - PAGE FORWARD          PF6 - RETURN WITH SELECTION*
000900*      PF2 - PAGE BACKWARD         PF7 - RESET BROWSE KEY     *
001000****************************************************************
001100 ENVIRONMENT DIVISION.
001200 DATA DIVISION.
001300*
001400 WORKING-STORAGE  SECTION.
001500*
001600 01  WS-PROGRAM-FIELDS.
001700     05  FILLER            PIC X(8)      VALUE 'POVMBROW'.
001800     05  WS-CRT-MESSAGE    PIC X(17)     VALUE 'SESSION COMPLETED'
001900     05  SUB               PIC S9999     COMP  VALUE ZEROES.
002000     05  WS-SELECTION      PIC 99              VALUE ZEROES.
002100     05  WS-XCTL-PROGRAM   PIC X(8)            VALUE SPACES.
002200*
002300 01  WS-DISPLAY-DATA.
002400     05  WS-SELECT             PIC 99.
002500     05  FILLER               PIC X.
002600     05  WS-VM-KEY            PIC X(8).
002700     05  FILLER               PIC X.
002800     05  WS-VENDOR-NAME       PIC X(25).
002900     05  FILLER               PIC X.
003000     05  WS-STREET-ADDRESS    PIC X(20).
003100     05  FILLER               PIC X.
003200     05  WS-CITY-STATE        PIC X(20).
003300*
003400 01  TEMPORARY-STORAGE-FIELDS.
003500     05  TS-QUEUE.
003600         10  TS-EIBTRMID      PIC X(4).
003700         10  TS-QUEUE-NAME    PIC X(4).
003800     05  TS-LENGTH            PIC S9999     CQMP  VALUE +6.
003900     05  TS-RECORD.
004000         10  TS-VENDOR-CD     PIC X(6).
004100     05  TS-SUB              PIC S9999     COMP  VALUE ZEROES.
004200*
004300 01  WS-COMMAREA.
004400     05  CA-FUNCTION-CODE     PIC X.
004500         88  CA-INQUIRY                   VALUE 'I'.
004600         88  CA-ADDITION                  VALUE 'A'.
004700         88  CA-CHANGE                    VALUE 'C'.
004800         88  CA-DELETE                    VALUE 'D'.
004900         88  CA-BROWSE                    VALUE 'B'.
005000     05  CA-MAP-CONTROL       PIC X.
005100     05  CA-VENDOR-CODE.
005200         10  CA-VEND-1        PIC X.
005300         10  CA-VEND-2        PIC X(4).
005400         10  CA-VEND-3        PIC X.
005500     05  CA-LAST-KEY          PIC X(6).
005600     05  CA-TS-ITEM           PIC S9999     COMP.
005700     05  CA-TS-MAXIMUM        PIC S9999     COMP.
005800     05  CA-TS-EOF-SWITCH     PIC X.
005900
006000 01  VM-BROWSE-MAP.
006100     05  FILLER               PIC X(12).
006200*
006300     05  MVC-L-DATE           PIC S9(4)     COMP.
006400     05  MVC-A-DATE           PIC X.
006500     05  MVC-D-DATE           PIC X(8).
006600*
006700     05  MVC-L-TIME           PIC S9(4)     COMP.
006800     05  MVC-A-TIME           PIC X.
006900     05  MVC-D-TIME           PIC X(8).
007000*
007100     05  MVC-OCCURS    OCCURS  15 TIMES.
007200         10  MVC-L-OCCURS     PIC S9(4)     COMP.
007300         10  MVC-A-OCCURS     PIC X.
007400         10  MVC-D-OCCURS     PIC X(79).
007500*
007600     05  MVC-L-SELECTION      PIC S9(4)     COMP.
007700     05  MVC-A-SELECTION      PIC X.
007800     05  MVC-D-SELECTION      PIC 99.
007900*
008000     05  MVC-L-RESET-CODE     PIC S9(4)     COMP.
008100     05  MVC-A-RESET-CODE     PIC X.
008200     05  MVC-D-RESET-CODE     PIC X(6).
008300*
```

Figure 17-2 *(Continued)*

```
008400      05  MVC-L-MESSAGE              PIC S9(4)    COMP.
008500      05  MVC-A-MESSAGE              PIC X.
008600      05  MVC-D-MESSAGE              PIC X(79).
008700*
008800*01· VENDOR-MASTER-RECORD
008900                             COPY    VENDMAST.
009000*01  WS-STATUS-FIELDS
009100                             COPY    STWSSTAT.
009200*01  WS-DATE-AND-TIME
009300                             COPY    STWSDTTM.
009400*01  ATTRIBUTE-LIST
009500                             COPY    STWSATTR.
009600*01  DFHAID
009700                             COPY    DFHAID.
009800*
009900 01  END-OF-WORKING-STORAGE  PIC X(15)   VALUE 'END WS POVMBROW'.
010000*
010100 LINKAGE SECTION.
010200*
010300 01  DFHCOMMAREA                      PIC X(19).
010400*
010500 01  BLL-CELLS.
010600      05  FILLER                      PIC S9(8)   COMP.
010700      05  BLL-CWA-ADDRESS             PIC S9(8)   COMP.
010800*
010900*01  CWA-DATA
011000                 COPY    STLNKCWA.
011100
011200
011300 PROCEDURE DIVISION.
011400*****************************************************************
011500*      PROGRAM STRUCTURE IS:                                    *
011600*          AA00-MAINLINE                                        *
011700*            B000-PROCESS-MAP                                   *
011800*              B100-PAGE-FORWARD                                *
011900*                B110-SEND-MAP-DATAONLY                         *
012000*                  B111-RESET-OCCURS-ATTRIBUTES                 *
012100*                B120-RETURN-TO-CICS                            *
012200*                B130-READ-TS                                   *
012300*                B140-START-BROWSE                              *
012400*                B150-BROWSE-PROCESSING                         *
012500*                  B151-FORMAT-OCCURS                           *
012600*                  B152-FORMAT-MAP                              *
012700*                  B153-WRITE-TS-RECORD                         *
012800*                B110-SEND-MAP-DATAONLY                         *
012900*                  B111-RESET-OCCURS-ATTRIBUTES                 *
013000*              B200-PAGE-BACKWARD                               *
013100*                B110-SEND-MAP-DATAONLY                         *
013200*                  B111-RESET-OCCURS-ATTRIBUTES                 *
013300*                B120-RETURN-TO-CICS                            *
013400*                B130-READ-TS                                   *
013500*                B140-START-BROWSE                              *
013600*                B150-BROWSE-PROCESSING                         *
013700*                  B151-FORMAT-OCCURS                           *
013800*                  B152-FORMAT-MAP                              *
013900*                  B153-WRITE-TS-RECORD                         *
014000*              B300-TRANSFER-XCTL-TO-MENU                       *
014100*                B310-INITIALIZE-AND-DELETEQ                    *
014200*              B400-RETURN-WITH-SELECTION                       *
014300*                B310-INITIALIZE-AND-DELETEQ                    *
014400*                B410-XCTL-TO-INVOKING-PROGRAM                  *
014500*                B110-SEND-MAP-DATAONLY                         *
014600*                  B111-RESET-OCCURS-ATTRIBUTES                 *
014700*                B120-RETURN-TO-CICS                            *
014800*              B500-RESET-KEY                                   *
014900*                B310-INITIALIZE-AND-DELETEQ                    *
015000*                B140-START-BROWSE                              *
015100*                B150-BROWSE-PROCESSING                         *
015200*                  B151-FORMAT-OCCURS                           *
015300*                  B152-FORMAT-MAP                              *
015400*·                 B153-WRITE-TS-RECORD                         *
015500*                B110-SEND-MAP-DATAONLY                         *
015600*                  B111-RESET-OCCURS-ATTRIBUTES                 *
015700*                B120-RETURN-TO-CICS                            *
015800*              B600-END-SESSION                                 *
015900*                B310-INITIALIZE-AND-DELETEQ                    *
016000*                                                              *
016100*          C000-INITIAL-ENTRY                                   *
016200*            B310-INITIALIZE-AND-DELETEQ                        *
016300*            B140-START-BROWSE                                  *
016400*            B150-BROWSE-PROCESSING                             *
016500*              B151-FORMAT-OCCURS                               *
016600*              B152-FORMAT-MAP                                  *
```

Figure 17-2 (Continued)

```
016700*                        B153-WRITE-TS-RECORD                       *
016800*                 C100-SEND-MAP-AND-DATA                            *
016900*                    C110-GET-DATE-AND-TIME                         *
017000*                 B111-RESET-OCCURS-ATTRIBUTES                      *
017100*************************************************************************
017200
017300 AA00-MAINLINE  SECTION.
017400
017500*    SERVICE RELOAD BLL-CELLS.
017600
017700     IF EIBCALEN  =  0
017800         MOVE LOW-VALUES  TO  WS-COMMAREA
017900         PERFORM C000-INITIAL-ENTRY
018000     ELSE
018100         MOVE DFHCOMMAREA  TO  WS-COMMAREA
018200         IF EIBTRNID  =  'POVB'
018300             PERFORM B000-PROCESS-MAP
018400         ELSE
018500             PERFORM C000-INITIAL-ENTRY.
018600*
018700     EXEC CICS RETURN
018800             TRANSID  ('POVB')
018900             COMMAREA (WS-COMMAREA)
019000             LENGTH   (19)
019100     END-EXEC.
019200*
019300*
019400 B000-PROCESS-MAP  SECTION.
019500*************************************************************************
019600*               PERFORMED FROM:  AA00-MAINLINE                      *
019700*************************************************************************
019800*
019900     MOVE LOW-VALUES  TO  VM-BROWSE-MAP.
020000*
020100     EXEC CICS HANDLE AID
020200             PF1    (B100-PAGE-FORWARD)
020300             PF2    (B200-PAGE-BACKWARD)
020400             PF5    (B300-TRANSFER-XCTL-TO-MENU)
020500             PF6    (B400-RETURN-WITH-SELECTION)
020600             PF7    (B500-RESET-KEY)
020700             CLEAR  (B600-END-SESSION)
020800             ANYKEY (B000-INVALID-KEY)
020900     END-EXEC.
021000*
021100     EXEC CICS IGNORE CONDITION
021200             MAPFAIL
021300     END-EXEC.
021400*
021500     EXEC CICS RECEIVE
021600             MAP    ('MAPPOVC')
021700             MAPSET ('POVMBR1')
021800             INTO   (VM-BROWSE-MAP)
021900     END-EXEC.
022000*
022100*  ENTER IS AN INVALID KEY
022200*
022300 B000-INVALID-KEY.
022400     MOVE 'I'          TO  STATUS-OF-RECEIVE.
022500     MOVE 'INVALID KEY PRESSED - PLEASE TRY AGAIN'
022600                       TO  MVC-D-MESSAGE.
022700     MOVE ASKIP-BRT  TO  MVC-A-MESSAGE.
022800     MOVE -1           TO  MVC-L-SELECTION.
022900     PERFORM B110-SEND-MAP-DATAONLY.
023000*
023100 B000-EXIT.
023200     EXIT.
023300 B100-PAGE-FORWARD  SECTION.
023400*************************************************************************
023500*        INVOKED BY HANDLE AID FROM:  B000-PROCESS-MAP              *
023600*************************************************************************
023700*
023800     ADD 1  TO  CA-TS-ITEM.
023900*
024000     IF CA-TS-ITEM  IS GREATER THAN  CA-TS-MAXIMUM
024100         IF CA-LAST-KEY  =  HIGH-VALUES
024200             SUBTRACT 1  FROM  CA-TS-ITEM
024300             MOVE 'CURRENT PAGE IS LAST PAGE'
024400                       TO   MVC-D-MESSAGE
024500             MOVE ASKIP-BRT  TO  MVC-A-MESSAGE
024600             MOVE -1           TO  MVC-L-SELECTION
024700             PERFORM B110-SEND-MAP-DATAONLY
024800             PERFORM B120-RETURN-TO-CICS
024900         ELSE
```

Figure 17-2 *(Continued)*

```
025000                MOVE CA-LAST-KEY  TO  CA-VENDOR-CODE
025100*
025200******************************************************************
025300* CA-LAST-KEY CONTAINS THE KEY OF THE LAST VENDOR DISPLAYED  *
025400* ON THE PREVIOUS PAGE.  THE START BROWSE WILL, AS THE LOGIC *
025500* IS WRITTEN, DISPLAY THIS ITEM AGAIN AT THE TOP OF THE NEXT *
025600* PAGE.  YOU CAN GET AROUND THIS IN ONE OF TWO WAYS:         *
025700*    1) IF YOUR KEY IS NUMERIC, ADD 1 TO CA-VENDOR-CODE      *
025800*    2) ISSUE AN ADDITIONAL READNEXT AFTER THE STARTBR       *
025900******************************************************************
026000*
026100     ELSE
026200         PERFORM B130-READ-TS
026300         MOVE TS-VENDOR-CD  TO  CA-VENDOR-CODE.
026400*
026500     PERFORM B140-START-BROWSE.
026600     IF GOOD-STARTBR
026700         PERFORM B150-BROWSE-PROCESSING
026800         MOVE -1 TO  MVC-L-SELECTION
026900     ELSE
027000         MOVE 'START BROWSE KEY BEYOND END OF FILE'
027100                         TO  MVC-D-MESSAGE
027200         MOVE ASKIP-BRT  TO  MVC-A-MESSAGE
027300         MOVE -1         TO  MVC-L-RESET-CODE.
027400*
027500     PERFORM B110-SEND-MAP-DATAONLY.
027600     PERFORM B120-RETURN-TO-CICS.
027700*
027800 B100-EXIT.
027900     EXIT.
028000 B110-SEND-MAP-DATAONLY  SECTION.
028200*
028300******************************************************************
028400*     PERFORMED FROM:  B000-PROCESS-MAP                    *
028500*                      B100-PAGE-FORWARD                   *
028600*                      B200-PAGE-BACKWARD                  *
028700*                      B400-RETURN-WITH-SELECTION          *
028800*                      B500-RESET-KEY                      *
028900******************************************************************
029000*
029100     PERFORM B111-RESET-OCCURS-ATTRIBUTES
029200             VARYING SUB  FROM  1 BY 1  UNTIL  SUB  =  16.
029300*
029400     MOVE UNPROT-NUM-FSET  TO  MVC-A-SELECTION.
029500     MOVE UNPROT-FSET      TO  MVC-A-RESET-CODE.
029600*
029700     EXEC CICS SEND
029800             MAP     ('MAPPOVC')
029900             MAPSET  ('POVMBR1')
030000             FROM    (VM-BROWSE-MAP)
030100             DATAONLY
030200             CURSOR
030300     END-EXEC.
030400*
030500 B110-EXIT.
030600     EXIT.
030700*
030800 B111-RESET-OCCURS-ATTRIBUTES  SECTION.
030900******************************************************************
031000*             PERFORMED FROM:  B110-SEND-MAP-DATAONLY      *
031100*                              C100-SEND-MAP-AND-DATA      *
031200******************************************************************
031300*
031400     MOVE ASKIP-FSET  TO  MVC-A-OCCURS (SUB).
031500*
031600 B111-EXIT.
031700     EXIT.
031800 B120-RETURN-TO-CICS  SECTION.
032000******************************************************************
032100*             PERFORMED FROM:  B100-PAGE-FORWARD           *
032200*                              B200-PAGE-BACKWARD          *
032300*                              B400-RETURN-WITH-SELECTION  *
032400*                              B500-RESET-KEY              *
032500******************************************************************
032600*
032700     EXEC CICS RETURN
032800             TRANSID  ('POVB')
032900             COMMAREA (WS-COMMAREA)
033000             LENGTH   (19)
033100     END-EXEC.
033200*
```

Figure 17-2 *(Continued)*

```
033300 B120-EXIT.
033400     EXIT.
033500*
033600 B130-READ-TS   SECTION.
033700****************************************************************
033800*               PERFORMED FROM:  B100-PAGE-FORWARD           *
033900*                                B200-PAGE-BACKWARD          *
034000****************************************************************
034100*
034200     MOVE EIBTRMID  TO   TS-EIBTRMID.
034300     MOVE 'POVB'    TO   TS-QUEUE-NAME.
034400*
034500     EXEC CICS READQ TS
034600          QUEUE  (TS-QUEUE)
034700          INTO   (TS-RECORD)
034800          LENGTH (TS-LENGTH)
034900          ITEM   (CA-TS-ITEM)
035000     END-EXEC.
035100*
035200 B130-EXIT.
035300     EXIT.
035400 B140-START-BROWSE   SECTION.
035500****************************************************************
035600*               PERFORMED FROM:  B100-PAGE-FORWARD           *
035700*                                B200-PAGE-BACKWARD          *
035800*                                B500-RESET-KEY              *
035900*                                C000-INITIAL-ENTRY          *
036000****************************************************************
036100*
036200     EXEC CICS HANDLE CONDITION
036300               NOTFND (B140-EXIT)
036400     END-EXEC.
036500*
036600     MOVE 'E'  TO  STATUS-OF-BROWSE.
036700*
036800     EXEC CICS STARTBR
036900          DATASET ('VENDMAST')
037000          RIDFLD  (CA-VENDOR-CODE)
037100          GTEQ
037200     END-EXEC.
037300*
037400     MOVE 'G'  TO  STATUS-OF-BROWSE.
037500*
037600 B140-EXIT.
037700     EXIT.
037800*
037900 B150-BROWSE-PROCESSING   SECTION.
038000****************************************************************
038100*               PERFORMED FROM:  B100-PAGE-FORWARD           *
038200*                                B200-PAGE-BACKWARD          *
038300*                                B500-RESET-KEY              *
038400*                                C000-INITIAL-ENTRY          *
038500****************************************************************
038600*
038700     MOVE LOW-VALUES  TO  VM-BROWSE-MAP.
038800*
038900     PERFORM B151-FORMAT-OCCURS
039000             VARYING SUB FROM 1 BY 1  UNTIL  SUB  GREATER  15.
039100*
039200     PERFORM B152-FORMAT-MAP  UNTIL   TS-SUB  GREATER  14
039300                              OR   STATUS-OF-READ  =  'F'.
039400*
039500 B150-ENDBR.
039600     EXEC CICS ENDBR
039700          DATASET ('VENDMAST')
039800     END-EXEC.
039900*
040000     IF END-OF-FILE
040100         MOVE HIGH-VALUES  TO  CA-LAST-KEY
040200         MOVE 'CURRENT PAGE IS LAST PAGE'
040300                           TO  MVC-D-MESSAGE
040400         MOVE ASKIP-BRT  TO  MVC-A-MESSAGE
040500     ELSE
040600         MOVE ASKIP-DRK  TO  MVC-A-MESSAGE.
040700     IF CA-TS-EOF-SWITCH  =  'E'
040800         NEXT SENTENCE
040900     ELSE
041000         IF CA-TS-ITEM  IS GREATER THAN  CA-TS-MAXIMUM
```

Figure 17-2 *(Continued)*

```
041100              PERFORM B153-WRITE-TS-RECORD.
041200*
041300 B150-EXIT.
041400     EXIT.
041500*
041600 B151-FORMAT-OCCURS  SECTION.
041700*
041800*******************************************************************
041900*           PERFORMED FROM:  B150-BROWSE-PROCESSING          *
042000*******************************************************************
042100*
042200     MOVE SPACES  TO  MVC-D-OCCURS (SUB).
042300*
042400 B151-EXIT.
042500     EXIT.
042600*
042700 B152-FORMAT-MAP  SECTION.
042800*******************************************************************
042900*           PERFORMED FROM:  B150-BROWSE-PROCESSING          *
043000*******************************************************************
043100*
043200     MOVE 'G'  TO  STATUS-OF-READ.
043300*
043400     EXEC CICS HANDLE CONDITION
043500              ENDFILE (B152-ENDBR)
043600     END-EXEC.
043700*
043800     EXEC CICS READNEXT
043900              DATASET ('VENDMAST')
044000              INTO    (VENDOR-MASTER-RECORD)
044100              RIDFLD  (CA-VENDOR-CODE)
044200     END-EXEC.
044300*
044400     ADD 1  TO  TS-SUB.
044500*
044600     IF TS-SUB  =  1
044700        MOVE CA-VENDOR-CODE  TO  TS-VENDOR-CD.
044800     IF CA-TS-ITEM  IS GREATER THAN  CA-TS-MAXIMUM
044900        MOVE CA-VENDOR-CODE  TO  CA-LAST-KEY.
045000*
045100     MOVE SPACES           TO  WS-DISPLAY-DATA.
045200     MOVE TS-SUB           TO  WS-SELECT.
045300*
045400     MOVE CA-VEND-1        TO  WS-VENDOR-CD-1.
045500     MOVE CA-VEND-2        TO  WS-VENDOR-CD-2.
045600     MOVE CA-VEND-3        TO  WS-VENDOR-CD-3.
045700     MOVE WS-VENDOR-CODE   TO  WS-VM-KEY.
045800*
045900     MOVE VM-VENDOR-NAME   TO  WS-VENDOR-NAME.
046000     MOVE VM-STREET-ADDRESS TO WS-STREET-ADDRESS.
046100     MOVE VM-CITY-STATE    TO  WS-CITY-STATE.
046200*
046300     MOVE WS-DISPLAY-DATA  TO  MVC-D-OCCURS (TS-SUB).
046400*
046500     GO TO  B152-EXIT.
046600*
046700 B152-ENDBR.
046800     MOVE 'F'  TO  STATUS-OF-READ.
046900*
047000 B152-EXIT.
047100     EXIT.
047200*
047300 B153-WRITE-TS-RECORD  SECTION.
047400*******************************************************************
047500*           PERFORMED FROM:  B150-BROWSE-PROCESSING          *
047600*******************************************************************
047700*
047800     IF END-OF-FILE
047900        MOVE 'E'  TO  CA-TS-EOF-SWITCH.
048000*
048100     ADD 1 TO CA-TS-MAXIMUM.
048200*
048300     MOVE EIBTRMID  TO  TS-EIBTRMID.
048400     MOVE 'POVB'    TO  TS-QUEUE-NAME.
048500*
048600     EXEC CICS WRITEQ TS
048700              QUEUE (TS-QUEUE)
048800              FROM  (TS-RECORD)
```

Figure 17-2 (*Continued*)

```
048900                    LENGTH  (TS-LENGTH)
049000                    ITEM    (CA-TS-ITEM)
049100      END-EXEC.
049200*
049300 B153-EXIT.
049400      EXIT.
049500*
049600 B200-PAGE-BACKWARD  SECTION.
049700*************************************************************
049800*          INVOKED BY HANDLE AID FROM:  B000-PROCESS-MAP    *
049900*************************************************************
050000*
050100      SUBTRACT 1  FROM  CA-TS-ITEM.
050200*
050300      IF CA-TS-ITEM  IS LESS THAN  1
050400          ADD 1  TO  CA-TS-ITEM
050500          MOVE 'CURRENT PAGE IS FIRST PAGE TO BE DISPLAYED'
050600                        TO  MVC-D-MESSAGE
050700          MOVE ASKIP-BRT  TO  MVC-A-MESSAGE
050800          MOVE -1         TO  MVC-L-SELECTION
050900          PERFORM B110-SEND-MAP-DATAONLY
051000          PERFORM B120-RETURN-TO-CICS.
051100
051200      PERFORM B130-READ-TS.
051300      MOVE TS-VENDOR-CD  TO  CA-VENDOR-CODE.
051400      PERFORM B140-START-BROWSE.
051500      IF GOOD-STARTBR
051600          PERFORM B150-BROWSE-PROCESSING
051700          MOVE -1  TO  MVC-L-SELECTION
051800      ELSE
051900          MOVE 'START BROWSE KEY BEYOND END OF FILE'
052000                        TO  MVC-D-MESSAGE
052100          MOVE ASKIP-BRT  TO  MVC-A-MESSAGE
052200          MOVE -1         TO  MVC-L-RESET-CODE.
052300*
052400      PERFORM B110-SEND-MAP-DATAONLY.
052500      PERFORM B120-RETURN-TO-CICS.
052600*
052700 B200-EXIT.
052800      EXIT.
052900*
053000 B300-TRANSFER-XCTL-TO-MENU  SECTION.
053100*************************************************************
053200*          PERFORMED FROM:  B000-PROCESS-MAP               *
053300*************************************************************
053400*
053500      PERFORM B310-INITIALIZE-AND-DELETEQ.
053600*
053700      EXEC CICS XCTL
053800              PROGRAM ('POVMAINT')
053900      END-EXEC.
054000*
054100 B300-EXIT.
054200      EXIT.
054300*
054400 B310-INITIALIZE-AND-DELETEQ  SECTION.
054500*
054600*************************************************************
054700*          PERFORMED FROM:  B300-TRANSFER-XCTL-TO-MENU     *
054800*                           B400-RETURN-WITH-SELECTION     *
054900*                           B500-RESET-KEY                 *
055000*                           B600-END-SESSION               *
055100*                           C000-INITIAL-ENTRY             *
055200*************************************************************
055300*
055400      MOVE 1          TO  CA-TS-ITEM.
055500      MOVE ZEROES     TO  CA-TS-MAXIMUM.
055600      MOVE LOW-VALUES TO  CA-LAST-KEY.
055700      MOVE SPACES     TO  CA-TS-EOF-SWITCH.
055800*
055900      EXEC CICS IGNORE CONDITION
056000              QIDERR
056100      END-EXEC.
056200*
056300      MOVE EIBTRMID  TO  TS-EIBTRMID.
056400      MOVE 'POVB'    TO  TS-QUEUE-NAME.
056500*
056600      EXEC CICS DELETEQ TS
```

Figure 17-2 *(Continued)*

```
056700                 QUEUE (TS-QUEUE)
056800     END-EXEC.
056900*
057000 B310-EXIT.
057100     EXIT.
057200*
057300 B400-RETURN-WITH-SELECTION  SECTION.
057400*******************************************************************
057500*        INVOKED BY HANDLE AID FROM:  B000-PROCESS-MAP          *
057600*******************************************************************
057700*
057800     IF (MVC-D-SELECTION  IS GREATER THAN   0)   AND
057900        (MVC-D-SELECTION  IS LESS THAN    16)
058000         MOVE MVC-D-SELECTION  TO  WS-SELECTION
058100         MOVE MVC-D-OCCURS (WS-SELECTION)  TO  WS-DISPLAY-DATA
058200         IF WS-SELECT = WS-SELECTION
058300             PERFORM B310-INITIALIZE-AND-DELETEQ
058400             MOVE WS-VM-KEY        TO  WS-VENDOR-CODE
058500             MOVE WS-VENDOR-CD-1  TO  CA-VEND-1
058600             MOVE WS-VENDOR-CD-2  TO  CA-VEND-2
058700             MOVE WS-VENDOR-CD-3  TO  CA-VEND-3
058800             PERFORM B410-XCTL-TO-INVOKING-PROGRAM.
058900*
059000     MOVE 'INVALID SELECTION - PLEASE RE-ENTER SELECTION'
059100                     TO   MVC-D-MESSAGE.
059200     MOVE ASKIP-BRT   TO  MVC-A-MESSAGE.
059300*
059400     MOVE -1         TO  MVC-L-SELECTION.
059500*
059600     PERFORM B110-SEND-MAP-DATAONLY.
059700     PERFORM B120-RETURN-TO-CICS.
059800*
059900 B400-EXIT.
060000     EXIT.
060100*
060200 B410-XCTL-TO-INVOKING-PROGRAM  SECTION.
060300*******************************************************************
060400*        PERFORMED FROM:  B400-RETURN-WITH-SELECTION           *
060500*******************************************************************
060600*
060700     IF CA-ADDITION      MOVE 'POVMADDN' TO  WS-XCTL-PROGRAM
060800     ELSE  IF CA-CHANGE  MOVE 'POVMCHGE' TO  WS-XCTL-PROGRAM
060900     ELSE  IF CA-DELETE  MOVE 'POVMDLET' TO  WS-XCTL-PROGRAM
061000     ELSE                MOVE 'POVMINQY' TO  WS-XCTL-PROGRAM.
061100*
061200     MOVE 'B' TO  CA-FUNCTION-CODE.
061300*
061400     EXEC CICS XCTL
061500             PROGRAM  (WS-XCTL-PROGRAM)
061600             COMMAREA (WS-COMMAREA)
061700             LENGTH   (8)
061800     END-EXEC.
061900*
062000 B410-EXIT.
062100     EXIT.
062200*
062300 B500-RESET-KEY  SECTION.
062400*******************************************************************
062500*        INVOKED BY HANDLE AID FROM:  B000-PROCESS-MAP          *
062600*******************************************************************
062700*
062800     MOVE MVC-D-RESET-CODE  TO  CA-VENDOR-CODE.
062900     MOVE SPACES            TO  MVC-D-RESET-CODE.
063000*
063100     PERFORM B310-INITIALIZE-AND-DELETEQ.
063200     PERFORM B140-START-BROWSE.
063300     IF GOOD-STARTBR
063400         PERFORM B150-BROWSE-PROCESSING
063500         MOVE -1  TO  MVC-L-SELECTION
063600     ELSE
063700         MOVE 'START BROWSE KEY IS BEYOND END OF FILE - PLEASE RE-
063800-             'ENTER KEY'  TO  MVC-D-MESSAGE
063900             MOVE ASKIP-BRT  TO  MVC-A-MESSAGE
064000             MOVE -1         TO  MVC-L-RESET-CODE.
064100*
064200     PERFORM B110-SEND-MAP-DATAONLY.
064300     PERFORM B120-RETURN-TO-CICS.
064400*
```

Figure 17-2 *(Continued)*

```
064500 B500-EXIT.
064600     EXIT.
064700*
064800 B600-END-SESSION  SECTION.
064900*****************************************************************
065000*               INVOKED BY :  B000-PROCESS-MAP                  *
065100*****************************************************************
065200*
065300     PERFORM B310-INITIALIZE-AND-DELETEQ.
065400*
065500     EXEC CICS SEND
065600               FROM   (WS-CRT-MESSAGE)
065700               LENGTH (17)
065800               ERASE
065900     END-EXEC.
066000*
066100     EXEC CICS RETURN
066200     END-EXEC.
066300*
066400 B600-EXIT.
066500     EXIT.
066600*
066700 C000-INITIAL-ENTRY  SECTION.
066800*****************************************************************
066900*             PERFORMED FROM:  AA00-MAINLINE                    *
067000*****************************************************************
067100*
067200     MOVE LOW-VALUES  TO  VM-BROWSE-MAP.
067300     PERFORM B310-INITIALIZE-AND-DELETEQ.
067400     PERFORM B140-START-BROWSE.
067500     IF GOOD-STARTBR
067600         PERFORM B150-BROWSE-PROCESSING
067700     ELSE
067800         MOVE 'START BROWSE KEY BEYOND END OF FILE'
067900                     TO  MVC-D-MESSAGE
068000         MOVE ASKIP-BRT  TO  MVC-A-MESSAGE.
068100     PERFORM C100-SEND-MAP-AND-DATA.
068200*
068300 C000-EXIT.
068400     EXIT.
068500*
068600 C100-SEND-MAP-AND-DATA  SECTION.
068700*****************************************************************
068800*             PERFORMED FROM:  C000-INITIAL-ENTRY               *
068900*****************************************************************
069000*
069100*    PERFORM C110-GET-DATE-AND-TIME.
069200     PERFORM B111-RESET-OCCURS-ATTRIBUTES
069300               VARYING SUB  FROM  1 BY 1  UNTIL  SUB  =  16.
069400*
069500     MOVE WS-CURRENT-DATE  TO  MVC-D-DATE.
069600     MOVE WS-MAP-TIME      TO  MVC-D-TIME.
069700*
069800     MOVE -1             TO  MVC-L-SELECTION.
069900     MOVE UNPROT-NUM-FSET  TO  MVC-A-SELECTION.
070000     MOVE UNPROT-FSET    TO  MVC-A-RESET-CODE.
070100*
070200     EXEC CICS SEND
070300               MAP    ('MAPPOVC')
070400               MAPSET ('POVMBR1')
070500               FROM   (VM-BROWSE-MAP)
070600               ERASE
070700               CURSOR
070800     END-EXEC.
070900*
071000 C100-EXIT.
071100     EXIT.
071200*
071300 C110-GET-DATE-AND-TIME  SECTION.
071400*****************************************************************
071500*             PERFORMED FROM:  C100-SEND-MAP-AND-DATA           *
071600*****************************************************************
071700*
071800     COPY   STPDDTTM.
071900*
072000 C110-EXIT.
072100     EXIT.
```

of the file. This is done to keep the program as simple as possible. If EIBCALEN is greater than 0, then this program was either started by another program or is returning to itself in the pseudoconversational mode. The EIB field EIBTRNID contains the transaction identifier of the current task. For instance, if this program was started by the inquiry program, EIBTRNID would equal POVI. When this program issues a RETURN command with a TRANSID, a new task will be started and EIBTRNID will equal POVB.

B000-PROCESS-MAP. This section employs the CICS HANDLE AID command. EIBAID could have been tested as done with previous RECEIVE MAP commands, but I want to illustrate how HANDLE AID functions. HANDLE AID is invoked upon an execution of a RECEIVE MAP command. Control would pass to section B100-PAGE-FORWARD if PF1 was pressed. Pressing PF2 would transfer control to section B200-PAGE-BACKWARD, etc. ANYKEY transfers control to B000-INVALID-KEY for any key which is not specified; it does not include the ENTER key. In this example, if ENTER is pressed, control will pass to the statement following the RECEIVE MAP command, paragraph B000-INVALID-KEY.

B100-PAGE-FORWARD. Forward paging is accomplished by adding 1 to the COMMAREA field CA-TS-ITEM and if CA-TS-ITEM is greater than CA-TS-MAXIMUM

1. If CA-LAST-KEY = HIGH-VALUES, this indicates that the end of file had been reached on a previous entry into the program; if so an appropriate message is displayed.

2. If end of file has not been reached, then the CA-LAST-KEY, the last key read during a previous entry into the program, is moved to CA-VENDOR-CODE to initialize the browse starting key. As pointed out in the program comments, CA-LAST-KEY contains the key of the last vendor displayed on the previous page. The STARTBR command will start the browse with the last record from the previous page displayed at the top of the new page. This can be prevented by:

   a. Adding 1 to the key, if it is numeric.

   b. If the key is not numeric, issuing an additional READNEXT command after the STARTBR command.

If CA-TS-ITEM is equal to or less than CA-TS-MAXIMUM, the program has paged backward and is now paging forward. CA-TS-ITEM would be used to read the TS queue. Then the vendor record key obtained, TS-VENDOR-CD, would be moved to CA-VENDOR-CODE to initialize the browse starting point.

B110-SEND-MAP-DATAONLY. Prior to the SEND MAP command, all OCCURS attributes are set by B111-RESET-OCCURS-ATTRIBUTES to ASKIP,FSET. This results in the data which is displayed in the 15 occurrence fields being returned to the program when the RECEIVE MAP command is executed. This is necessary if a selection is entered on the screen and PF6 is pressed. UNPROT,FSET is moved to attributes in order to make sure fields are returned to the program on a receive. On a subsequent RECEIVE MAP command, only fields which were keyed in immediately prior to the receive will be returned to the program, unless they have been FSET.

B130-READ-TS. This section sets the TS queue name and reads the record which corresponds to the specified item number. All queue names in this program are the same. They contain eight characters and consist of the four-character terminal ID and the four-character transaction code POVB. The EIB field EIBTRNID should not be substituted for the constant POVB because if this program was started by another program, EIBTRNID would not equal POVB upon initial entry. If your program contains more than one TS queue, it will always be necessary to use unique names for the last four positions of queue name.

B140-START-BROWSE. If CA-VENDOR-CODE is greater than the last key on the file then the NOTFND handle condition will be invoked and an E will be returned in STATUS-OF-BROWSE. The STARTBR command will set the starting position in the file at the vendor master file (VENDMAST) vendor code which is greater than or equal to (GTEQ) the code in CA-VENDOR-CODE.

B150-BROWSE-PROCESSING. The OCCURS fields on the symbolic map are initialized to spaces by performing B151-FORMAT-OCCURS. This is necessary when the program is near the end of the file because low-values in a map field are not transmitted on a receive or send of a map. If the last page to be displayed contained only 5 vendors, the data from the last 10 vendors of the previous page would be present at the bottom of the screen. A send which contained low-values in the occurrence fields would not erase the last 10 occurrences. Moving spaces to the occurrence fields prior to the send does erase the unwanted information from the screen because spaces are transmitted.

If the end of file is reached in the routine B152-FORMAT-MAP, control will pass to B150-ENDBR and STATUS-OF-READ will contain an F, which signals END-OF-FILE. A HANDLE CONDITION command can be placed at any point in a program. It is activated when the condition occurs. After a browse is complete, it is good practice to terminate the browse by issuing the ENDBR command. If CA-TS-EOF-SWITCH equals E, this indicates that the end of a file had been reached on a previous entry into the program and the final TS queue has been written. If CA-TS-ITEM is greater than CA-TS-MAXIMUM, the program is paging forward and displaying data for the first time; therefore, a queue record must be written. If CA-TS-ITEM is not greater than CA-TS-MAXIMUM, the program is paging forward after having performed backward paging and the queue record key has already been written to temporary storage.

B120-RETURN-TO-CICS. This section returns control to CICS with a COMM-AREA which contains several fields which are needed for the paging routines. The new fields will be discussed as encountered.

B152-FORMAT-MAP. The READNEXT command is executed 15 times or until the end of file is reached. The first vendor code of each map is saved in the TS field TS-VENDOR-CD. The first time a new screen is formatted, the last key on the screen is saved in CA-LAST-KEY. This key is used in the page-forward routine. The occurrence fields are formatted and moved to the map.

B153-WRITE-TS-RECORD. This section sets the queue name and writes a TS queue which contains the key of the last record displayed on the map. The queue record is written *from* the TS-RECORD in working storage. CA-TS-MAXIMUM is incremented each time a TS queue record is written. It is used as an upper limit when the program pages backward and then forward again. CA-TS-EOF-SWITCH will contain an E when the end of file has been reached. This is a signal that the final TS queue record has been written.

B200-PAGE-BACKWARD. Backward paging is accomplished by subtracting 1 from CA-TS-ITEM. If the result is not less than the first item written to temporary storage, the appropriate queue is retrieved and its data, TS-VENDOR-CD, is used to start the browse.

B300-TRANSFER-XCTL-TO-MENU. This section transfers control back to the submenu program POVMAINT (see map in Fig. 6-3). It is good practice to delete TS queues which are no longer required before exiting a program.

B310-INITIALIZE-AND-DELETEQ. WS-COMMAREA fields which are required for paging logic are initialized and the TS queue is deleted. This program allows the browse starting point to be reset; therefore, it may be necessary to reinitialize certain fields. CA-TS-ITEM is used by paging logic to keep track of the last page displayed. It is added to or subtracted from in forward and backward paging routines. CA-TS-MAXIMUM holds the item number of the last map written to temporary storage. CA-LAST-KEY will hold the key of the last browse record read. CA-TS-EOF-SWITCH signals that the end of file has been reached on a READNEXT command.

Another use for the IGNORE CONDITION command previously discussed is shown. The IGNORE command directs the program to ignore the QIDERR condition if it occurs. The QIDERR condition occurs when a queue to be deleted does not exist. If the program did not provide for this condition, the task would ABEND if the condition occurred. The HANDLE CONDITION command could also be used in this situation:

```
EXEC CICS HANDLE CONDITION
          QIDERR  (B310-EXIT)
END-EXEC.
```

This queue should not normally exist when the program is first entered but might be present if a previous execution of the program had ABENDed. Application programs which use TS queues should always delete the queue when it is no longer required because a queue consumes system resources.

B400-RETURN-WITH-SELECTION. The range of the selected vendor is validated. If the selection is within the allowable range, 1 through 15, the map selection is used as a subscript in order to move the appropriate map occurrence to WS-DISPLAY-DATA. The map received returns only FSET fields. The WS-DISPLAY-DATA field WS-SELECT is compared to WS-SELECTION. The map selection entry could be in the range of 1 through 15, but the last map displayed might have fewer than 15 entries. Once it has been determined that a valid selection has been made, the TS queue is deleted. The vendor code is then moved to WS-COMMAREA subfields and a perform issued to transfer control to the appropriate program.

B410-XCTL-TO-INVOKING-PROGRAM. This section assumes that another program transferred control to this program and passed a COMMAREA function code for the inquiry or maintenance function. The appropriate program name is moved to the field WS-XCTL-PROGRAM; a B is moved to CA-FUNCTION-CODE and control is transferred to the designated program. Section AA00-MAINLINE of the invoking inquiry or maintenance program would have to be modified in order to accept the vendor code which was being transferred. For example,

```
IF EIBCALEN = 0
      PERFORM B000-INITIAL-ENTRY
ELSE
      MOVE DFHCOMMAREA TO WS-COMMAREA
      IF CA-BROWSE
            MOVE SPACE          TO CA-FUNCTION-CODE
            MOVE LOW-VALUES TO VM-CONTROL-MAP
            PERFORM C400-VERIFY-VENDOR-FILE-STATUS
            IF GOOD-VERIFY
                  PERFORM C500-SEND-DETAIL-MAP-AND-DATA
            ELSE
                  PERFORM B100-SEND-CONTROL-MAP-AND-DATA
      ELSE
            IF CA-RECEIVE-CTL-MAP
                  PERFORM C000-PROCESS-CONTROL-MAP
            ELSE
                  PERFORM . . .
```

B500-RESET-KEY. The browse starting key is reset when the terminal operator enters a key into the RESET VENDOR CODE field and presses PF7. A start browse is performed and, if successful, the map is formatted and displayed. If the RESET key is beyond the end of the file, the cursor is positioned at the start of the RESET field and an appropriate message is displayed.

B600-END-SESSION. The TS queue should be deleted before control is returned to CICS.

C000-INITIAL-ENTRY. The TS queue is deleted and related fields are initialized. The STARTBR command will set the starting point at the beginning of the file because CA-VENDOR-CODE will contain low-values. This approach was taken to keep the browse, inquiry, and maintenance programs as simple as possible. B150-BROWSE-PROCESSING will format the screen with the first 15 vendors in the file. If an inquiry or maintenance program had passed a vendor code to this program in COMMAREA, then the first vendor displayed would be equal to or greater than that code.

SUMMARY

DELETEQ, WRITEQ, and READQ TS commands were used in the browse program as were the STARTBR and READNEXT file control commands. The HANDLE AID command was used in place of the EIBAID technique used in previous examples. Routines for forward and backward paging were explained. A method which can be used to return a selected code to an invoking program was covered, and it was shown how a browse starting point could be reset.

Paging logic sometimes presents programming difficulties but is made easier once you understand the basic principles involved. The technique of paging demonstrated is a good way to learn the basics of browse logic. Once you have an understanding of how paging works, you can use this program as a guide to develop more sophisticated browse programs.

18

CICS DEBUGGING AND TESTING

Debugging and testing CICS programs is easier in an online environment than it is for batch systems. Debugging refers to the process of removing obvious errors such as ABENDs from a program, while testing refers to proving that a program functions as specified. Many interactive aids exist which make it easy for the CICS programmer to determine and correct the cause of program errors. Some of the aids available include execution diagnostic facility (EDF), interactive testing tools, CICS ABEND determination aids, and CICS dumps. A programmer familiar with some of these tools can usually diagnose and correct online program problems faster than can be done in a batch environment. Testing may be easier and faster in an online environment, but it must be more thorough than in a batch system. Batch program errors often occur without a user being aware that a problem ever existed. Online program errors may be visible to users at many different locations across the country and can trigger concerned phone calls to data center representatives. It is better to overtest a system and its programs, even if it means a delay in implementation, than to rush a system into production and correct errors as they occur. The best designed and tested systems will contain some oversights and errors, but it is important to minimize their occurrence. The credibility and reputation of a data processing installation is not enhanced when there are numerous ABENDs while a user is working with an on online system in a production environment.

Execution Diagnostic Facility

EDF is often the only tool an online programmer will need in order to debug and test a CICS program. It should only be used for testing command-level CICS programs. The execution of CICS programs is intercepted every time a CICS command is encountered and at other points during the execution of the program. Each command is displayed before execution, and most are displayed after execution is complete. When the commands are displayed, the applications programmer is given the ability to make changes to commands and conditions, display and alter working storage, display the EIB, and bypass the display of undesired CICS commands. During execution of the program, the programmer can force the program to be ABENDed, with or without a CICS dump. EDF can be terminated after the desired point in the program execution has been reached. The last map displayed can be brought back to the screen at each point at which the program stops to display a command. When a program ABEND occurs, the programmer can use EDF to determine and temporarily correct the error condition.

EDF Initiation

EDF is run as a CICS transaction and can be initiated on the terminal being used by entering a TRANSID of CEDF on a cleared screen and pressing ENTER. EDF can be invoked on a different terminal by clearing the screen and entering the ID of the other terminal, after keying in CEDF plus a space (i.e., CEDF T023). When EDF is run on a single terminal, program maps will be displayed interspersed between the display of EDF screens. When two terminals are used to run EDF, one screen will display a program's map while a second terminal will display and monitor EDF screens. EDF is most often run on one terminal, and I will present a typical EDF session as it would be run using this approach. If you run EDF on two adjacent terminals, the technique used will be basically the same.

EDF can be invoked for the browse program discussed in the last chapter as follows:

1. Clear the screen.

2. Key in CEDF and press ENTER.

3. THIS TERMINAL: EDF MODE ON will be displayed.

4. Clear the screen.

5. Key in the TRANSID POVB and press ENTER.

6. The program initiation screen shown in Fig. 18-1 will be displayed.

Program Initiation Screen

The program initiation screen shown in Fig. 18-1 displays the EIB as it exists upon initial entry into the program. Line 1 of the screen is basically the same for all EDF displays and contains:

1. TRANSACTION: POVB—This is the TRANSID associated with the task. For this screen, it is the TRANSID entered to initiate the browse program. If the browse had been invoked from the inquiry program, the TRANSID of

```
TRANSACTION: POVB    PROGRAM: POVMBROW    TASK NUMBER 0000402    DISPLAY:  00
STATUS:   PROGRAM INITIATION

       EIBTIME    = +0112215
       EIBDATE    = +0086023
       EIBTRNID   = 'POVB'
       EIBTASKN   = +0000402
       EIBTRMID   = 'T022'
       EIBCPOSN   = +00004
       EIBCALEN   = +00000
       EIBAID     = X'7D'                          AT X'0014477B'
       EIBFN      = X'0000'                        AT X'0014477C'
       EIBRCODE   = X'000000000000'                AT X'0014477E'
       EIBDS      = '........'
       EIBREQID   = '........'
    +  EIBRSRCE   = '              '



ENTER:  CONTINUE
PF1 : UNDEFINED            PF2 : SWITCH HEX/CHAR      PF3 : END EDF SESSION
PF4 : SUPPRESS DISPLAYS    PF5 : WORKING STORAGE      PF6 : USER DISPLAY
PF7 : SCROLL BACK          PF8 : SCROLL FORWARD       PF9 : STOP CONDITIONS
PF10: PREVIOUS DISPLAY     PF11: UNDEFINED            PF12: UNDEFINED
```

Figure 18-1 EDF Program Initiation Screen.

the inquiry program (POVI) would be displayed on this line until the program executed a return with a TRANSID of POVB. Look at the displayed EIB fields and note that the EIB field EIBTRNID contains the same TRANSID displayed on line 1.

2. PROGRAM: POVMBROW—This is the program name associated with the browse program.

3. TASK NUMBER 0000402—This is a sequential task number assigned by the system. This task number remains the same until the program executes a return. A return terminates the current task, and, if the return contains a TRANSID, a new task is initiated and assigned the next available sequential number. Note that the EIB field EIBTASKN contains this same task number.

4. DISPLAY: 00—This reflects the current screen being displayed. As succeeding screens are displayed, it is possible to view previous displays. The number displayed next to DISPLAY would be decremented by one for each prior screen displayed, i.e., -01, -02, etc.

Line 2 contains the status of the EDF screen being displayed. The status of this first screen is PROGRAM INITIATION. The status will change as different EDF screens are displayed.

Line 3 for this display is blank but would display the COMMAREA, if one existed, as shown in Fig. 18-8.

The remaining EIB fields commonly referenced are

1. EIBTIME and EIBDATE—These contain the time and date at which the transaction was initiated.

2. EIBTRMID—The terminal at which the transaction is running.

3. EIBCPOSN—The position of the cursor. We initiated the transaction by entering a four-position TRANSID; therefore, the cursor ends up in screen position 4.

4. EIBCALEN—The COMMAREA length. This length is always equal to zero when a transaction is initiated by keying a TRANSID on the screen and pressing ENTER. If a program is invoked by another program which passes a COMMAREA or if it is returned to with a TRANSID and a COMMAREA, then EIBCALEN will equal the length of that COMMAREA.

5. EIBAID—This contains the hexadecimal code associated with the AID key which was last pressed. X'7D' is the code associated with the ENTER key. See App. A-3 for a list of the decimal values associated with the AID keys.

The PF keys at the bottom of the screen change for some EDF screens, but a given function is always associated with the same PF key. I will discuss the more important PF keys in succeeding EDF screen examples. ENTER: CONTINUE is displayed, above the PF key instructions. EDF progresses by pressing the ENTER key. You could keep pressing ENTER until you came to the EDF screen displayed in Fig. 18-2. Since EDF stops at every CICS command, a few intervening screens would be displayed for the ASSIGN and ADDRESS commands contained in the date and time routine shown in App. B for copy library member STPDDTTM.

ABOUT-TO-EXECUTE Command Screen

EDF displays a screen prior to the execution of a CICS command. This is illustrated by the highlighted status field on line 2 of Fig. 18-2. The highlighted CICS command about to be executed is shown on line 3. The command EXEC CICS SEND is followed on succeeding lines by its options and arguments.

```
 TRANSACTION: POVB    PROGRAM: POVMBROW    TASK NUMBER 0000402    DISPLAY:   00
 STATUS:   ABOUT TO EXECUTE COMMAND
 EXEC CICS SEND
   MAP('MAPPOVC')
   FROM('...............01/23/86...11.22.15................................ ...)
   MAPSET('POVMBR1')
   TERMINAL
   ERASE




   OFFSET:X'00132C'      LINE:   00268       EIBFN=X'1804'


 ENTER:   CONTINUE
 PF1 : UNDEFINED            PF2 : SWITCH HEX/CHAR      PF3 : UNDEFINED
 PF4 : SUPPRESS DISPLAYS    PF5 : WORKING STORAGE      PF6 : USER DISPLAY
 PF7 : SCROLL BACK          PF8 : SCROLL FORWARD       PF9 : STOP CONDITIONS
 PF10: PREVIOUS DISPLAY     PF11: UNDEFINED            PF12: ABEND USER TASK
```

Figure 18-2 EDF About-to-Execute Command Screen.

EDF sometimes displays a default option, such as TERMINAL, which was not coded in the program's CICS command. The programmer can overtype any EDF display at which the cursor stops next to when the TAB key is pressed. A command can be negated by overtyping the command function with either NOP or NOOP. The arguments for options such as MAP, MAPSET, and FROM can be altered by overtyping the existing data. The programmer can overtype in character format or can press PF2 to switch to a hexadecimal display and make the change in hex. If an argument displays a period, it is best to switch to hex if a change must be made to that field.

At the bottom of the screen above the instructions, two or three fields may be displayed:

1. OFFSET: X'00132C'—This is the program CLIST offset and may be used to locate the CICS command about to execute.

2. LINE: 0268—This is the line number corresponding to the translator printout of the CICS program. LINE will only be displayed if the program was translated using the DEBUG option. The DEBUG option generates larger program load modules because the translator line numbers must be saved in order to be displayed.

3. EIBFN='X'1804'—This is an EIB function code which is updated when a CICS command has been executed. X'1804' represents the SEND MAP command.

Program Map Display Screen

Press the ENTER key to continue the EDF session. The next screen displayed will be the program map being sent. It will be similar to the screen shown in Fig. 1-11. Data can be entered on this display of the map or you can wait until the next display of the same map. Data entered on this map will be remembered and need not be entered again on the next display of the map.

Command Execution Complete Screen

A command execution complete screen similar to that shown in Fig. 18-3 will be displayed at the completion of most CICS commands. ABEND, RE-TURN, and XCTL do not display a command execution complete screen. The EDF map displays two new fields—the response field and EIBRCODE. The response field shows RESPONSE: NORMAL. Response will usually be NORMAL unless a handle condition has been invoked, in which case the invoked condition will be displayed in the response field. A programmer can use the response field to test various conditions by overtyping the contents of the response field. A program will then follow the logic path which would have occurred if the condition had actually happened. The EIB field EIBRCODE is generally not used by an applications programmer. This field contains the response code and is usually handled in the program by the HANDLE CONDITION command. The programmer can end

```
TRANSACTION: POVB    PROGRAM: POVMBROW    TASK NUMBER 0000402    DISPLAY:  00
STATUS:  COMMAND EXECUTION COMPLETE
EXEC CICS SEND
  MAP('MAPPOVC')
  FROM('.............01/23/86...11.22.15............................'...)
  MAPSET('POVMBR1')
  TERMINAL
  ERASE




  OFFSET:X'00132C'     LINE:   00268     EIBFN=X'1804'
  RESPONSE: NORMAL                        EIBRCODE=X'000000000000'

  ENTER:   CONTINUE
  PF1 : UNDEFINED             PF2 : SWITCH HEX/CHAR      PF3 : END EDF SESSION
  PF4 : SUPPRESS DISPLAYS     PF5 : WORKING STORAGE      PF6 : USER DISPLAY
  PF7 : SCROLL BACK           PF8 : SCROLL FORWARD       PF9 : STOP CONDITIONS
  PF10: PREVIOUS DISPLAY      PF11: UNDEFINED            PF12: ABEND USER TASK
```

Figure 18-3   EDF Command Execution Complete Screen.

the EDF session at any screen that displays the instruction PF3 : END EDF
SESSION.

Working-Storage Display Screen

A working-storage screen similar to Fig. 18-4 would be displayed if the programmer pressed the PF5 key while Fig. 18-3 was displayed. The working-storage screen displays the highlighted starting address of main storage, followed on succeeding lines by a column of main-storage addresses, working-storage offsets, four columns of hexadecimal data, and the corresponding 16 bytes of data in

```
TRANSACTION: POVB    PROGRAM: POVMBROW    TASK NUMBER 0000402    DISPLAY:  00
  ADDRESS: 0010060C                       WORKING STORAGE
00100600   000000                                  D7D6E5D4    ............POVM
00100610   000004  C2D9D6E6 E2C5E2E2 C9D6D540 C3D6D4D7    BROWSESSION COMP
00100620   000014  D3C5E3C5 C4000000 00404040 40404040    LETED..........
00100630   000024  40000000 00000000 00000000 00000000    ................
00100640   000034  00000000 00000000 00000000 00000000    ................
00100650   000044  00000000 00000000 00000000 00000000    ................
00100660   000054  00000000 00000000 00000000 00000000    ................
00100670   000064  00000000 00000000 00000000 00000000    ................
00100680   000074  00000000 00000000 00000000 00000000    ................
00100990   000084  00000000 00000000 00000000 00000000    ................
001009A0   000094  00000000 00000000 00000000 00000000    ................
001009B0   0000A4  00000000 00000000 00000000 00000000    ................
001009C0   0000B4  00000000 00000000 00000000 00000000    ................
001009D0   0000C4  00000000 00000000 00000000 00000000    ................
001009E0   0000D4  00000000 00000000 00000000 00000000    ................
001009F0   0000E4  00000000 00000000 00000000 00000000    ................

  ENTER:   CURRENT DISPLAY
  PF1 : UNDEFINED             PF2 : UNDEFINED            PF3 : UNDEFINED
  PF4 : EIB DISPLAY           PF5 : WORKING STORAGE      PF6 : USER DISPLAY
  PF7 : SCROLL BACK HALF      PF8 : SCROLL FORWARD HALF  PF9 : UNDEFINED
  PF10: SCROLL BACK FULL      PF11: SCROLL FORWARD FULL  PF12: REMEMBER DISPLAY
```

Figure 18-4   EDF Working-Storage Screen.

character format. Any data in the program's working storage can be changed by overtyping either the hexadecimal data or the character data and pressing the ENTER key. Working storage may be scrolled through in a forward or backward direction depending on the PF key used. The programmer-defined working-storage literal END WS PROGNAME will signal the end of working storage. The EIB can be displayed from the working-storage screen by pressing PF4. The user map last displayed can be redisplayed by pressing PF6 : USER DISPLAY. Normally up to the last 10 CICS command screens are saved for possible redisplay. The working-storage screen or any EDF display which has PF12 : REMEMBER DISPLAY allows you to press this key in order to save the current screen for future display. The highlighted main-storage address at the top of the screen can be overtyped with the address of any area of main storage which is in the region or partition. Only the program's working storage can be altered; other main storage is display only. Press the ENTER key to get out of the working-storage display and to return to the current display, Fig. 18-3 for this example.

RETURN EDF Screen

Press ENTER to continue and the EDF display will move to Fig. 18-5, the return screen. The return EDF screen will only display an about-to-execute screen. As mentioned previously, there is no command execution complete screen for RETURN, ABEND, and XCTL commands. The arguments of TRANSID and COMMAREA could be overtyped if this would assist in testing.

Program Termination Screen

The program termination screen shown in Fig. 18-6 would be displayed when you press ENTER while the return screen is displayed.

```
 TRANSACTION: POVB   PROGRAM: POVMBROW   TASK NUMBER 0000402   DISPLAY:  00
 STATUS:  ABOUT TO EXECUTE COMMAND
 EXEC CICS RETURN
   TRANSID('POVB')
   COMMAREA(' 1..........')
   LENGTH(+00012)




    OFFSET:X'0012C4'    LINE:   00231      EIBFN=X'0E08'

 ENTER:  CONTINUE
 PF1 : UNDEFINED            PF2 : SWITCH HEX/CHAR     PF3 : UNDEFINED
 PF4 : SUPPRESS DISPLAYS    PF5 : WORKING STORAGE     PF6 : USER DISPLAY
 PF7 : SCROLL BACK          PF8 : SCROLL FORWARD      PF9 : STOP CONDITIONS
 PF10: PREVIOUS DISPLAY     PF11: UNDEFINED           PF12: ABEND USER TASK
```

Figure 18-5 Return EDF Screen.

```
TRANSACTION: POVB   PROGRAM: POVMBROW   TASK NUMBER 0000402   DISPLAY:   00
STATUS:  PROGRAM TERMINATION




                                    .

ENTER:   CONTINUE
PF1 :  UNDEFINED            PF2 :  SWITCH HEX/CHAR      PF3 :  END EDF SESSION
PF4 :  SUPPRESS DISPLAYS    PF5 :  WORKING STORAGE      PF6 :  USER DISPLAY
PF7 :  SCROLL BACK          PF8 :  SCROLL FORWARD       PF9 :  STOP CONDITIONS
PF10:  PREVIOUS DISPLAY     PF11:  UNDEFINED            PF12:  ABEND USER TASK
```

Figure 18-6 EDF Program Termination Screen.

Task Termination Screen

The task termination screen shown in Fig. 18-7 is displayed next when the ENTER key is pressed. The programmer has the option at this point to continue or to end the EDF session. Overtype the NO next to REPLY with YES in order to continue the EDF session or just press the ENTER key with NO displayed to end the session. The browse screen shown in Fig. 1-11 will be redisplayed whether or not the session is continued and a new task will be initiated when an AID key is pressed.

```
TRANSACTION: POVB                       TASK NUMBER 0000402   DISPLAY:   00
STATUS:   TASK TERMINATION





TO CONTINUE EDF SESSION REPLY YES                              REPLY: NO
ENTER:   CONTINUE
PF1 :  UNDEFINED            PF2 :  SWITCH HEX/CHAR      PF3 :  END EDF SESSION
PF4 :  SUPPRESS DISPLAYS    PF5 :  WORKING STORAGE      PF6 :  USER DISPLAY
PF7 :  SCROLL BACK          PF8 :  SCROLL FORWARD       PF9 :  STOP CONDITIONS
PF10:  PREVIOUS DISPLAY     PF11:  UNDEFINED            PF12:  UNDEFINED
```

Figure 18-7 EDF Task Termination Screen.

```
TRANSACTION: PQVB    PROGRAM: POVMBROW    TASK NUMBER 0000416    DISPLAY:    00
STATUS:   PROGRAM INITIATION
        COMMAREA      = ' 1..........'
        EIBTIME       = +0112327
        EIBDATE       = +0086023
        EIBTRNID      = 'POVB'
        EIBTASKN      = +0000416
        EIBTRMID      = 'T022'
        EIBCPOSN      = +01441
        EIBCALEN      = +00019
        EIBAID        = X'7D'                              AT X'0013263A'
        EIBFN         = X'0000'                            AT X'0013263B'
        EIBRCODE      = X'000000000000'                    AT X'0013263D'
        EIBDS         = '........'
        EIBREQID      = '........'
   +    EIBRSRCE    , = '        '


ENTER:   CONTINUE
PF1 : UNDEFINED              PF2 : SWITCH HEX/CHAR      PF3 : END EDF SESSION
PF4 : SUPPRESS DISPLAYS      PF5 : WORKING STORAGE      PF6 : USER DISPLAY
PF7 : SCROLL BACK            PF8 : SCROLL FORWARD       PF9 : STOP CONDITIONS
PF10: PREVIOUS DISPLAY       PF11: UNDEFINED            PF12: UNDEFINED
```

Figure 18-8   EDF Succeeding Entry Program Initiation Screen.

Program Initiation Redisplayed

The program initiation screen shown in Fig. 18-8 will be displayed if you overtyped YES on the task termination screen in Fig. 18-7 and pressed ENTER in order to continue the EDF session. This program initiation screen is similar to the screen displayed in Fig. 18-1; however, I want to point out a few significant changes. Note that the task number at the top of the screen and in EIBTASKN has changed from 402 to 416. The COMMAREA is now displayed on line 3, and its length is shown in the COMMAREA length field EIBCALEN. The cursor position (EIBCPOSN) reflects the position of the cursor on the screen before an AID key was pressed.

EDF Stop Conditions Screen

The display on condition screen shown in Fig. 18-9 will be displayed if you press PF9 on any EDF screen which lists PF9 : STOP CONDITIONS. This screen allows you to suppress the display of EDF screens you do not want to view in order to stop only at specified commands or upon encountering specific conditions. You could suppress displays of the EDF screens presented in the sample EDF session until the return screen was displayed. Just enter RETURN next to EXEC CICS in Fig. 18-9 and press the PF4 key as indicated in the instructions in order to suppress displays and continue processing. This screen allows you to enter a handle condition you wish to stop at, next to CICS EXCEPTIONAL CONDITION. You could enter conditions such as NOTFND and PGMIDERR next to this field identifier and press PF4 until one of the indicated conditions is encountered. You could continue pressing PF4 to suppress displays on any EDF screen which contained the PF4 : SUPPRESS DISPLAYS instruction.

```
TRANSACTION: POVB   PROGRAM: POVMBROW   TASK NUMBER 0000402   DISPLAY:   00
DISPLAY ON CONDITION:-

       COMMAND:              EXEC CICS
       OFFSET:                   X'.......'
       LINE NUMBER:              ........
       CICS EXCEPTIONAL CONDITION:
       ANY CICS ERROR CONDITION      YES
       TRANSACTION ABEND             YES
       NORMAL TASK TERMINATION       YES
       ABNORMAL TASK TERMINATION     YES




ENTER:   CURRENT DISPLAY
PF1  : UNDEFINED           PF2  : UNDEFINED          PF3  : UNDEFINED
PF4  : SUPPRESS DISPLAYS   PF5  : WORKING STORAGE    PF6  : USER DISPLAY
PF7  : UNDEFINED           PF8  : UNDEFINED          PF9  : UNDEFINED
PF10: UNDEFINED            PF11: UNDEFINED           PF12: REMEMBER DISPLAY
```

Figure 18-9 EDF Stop Conditions Screen.

You could stop at specific line numbers if the program was translated with the DEBUG option which generated line numbers. The line number would be the translator listing line number and must contain six digits. It is the line number at which a command starts. The program offset corresponding to the command could also be entered.

Generally this screen is used to bypass the display of undesired EDF screens by entering a command beyond those you wish to suppress. For instance, in a browse program you would have to press the ENTER key numerous times in order to get past a series of READNEXT commands in an EDF session. You could find the command following the READNEXT command in your program and set a stop condition in order to suppress all displays until that command was reached.

Program ABEND Display

A screen similar to that shown in Fig. 18-10 will be displayed when an ABEND occurs. A common program ABEND is the ASRA, a four-character code which is displayed on the screen, denoting that a program data exception has occurred. This is generally the result of nonnumeric data's being present in a numeric field which is used in a program calculation. Normally an ASRA occurs between two CICS commands and it is difficult to determine which instruction caused the ABEND. One of two CICS commands is sometimes included in a test version of a program in order to determine where the ASRA occurred: ASKTIME and/or ENTER. Remember to remove such commands and any test data placed in working storage from a program before compiling its production version. The ASKTIME command was discussed in Chap. 10. The format of the ENTER command is

```
            EXEC CICS ENTER
                      TRACEID   (nnn)
            END-EXEC.
```

This command results in an entry to a CICS trace table and will not affect the execution of your program, but it can help you to narrow in on a program ASRA. The TRACEID entry (nnn) can be any number between 000 and 199, and it will be displayed when EDF stops at the ENTER command.

The ASKTIME and ENTER commands can be placed between other CICS commands and, unless suppressed, will display on an EDF screen as other CICS commands do. If several ASKTIME commands are placed in a program, the programmer has to keep track of which one is being executed. This may be done manually or by placing an indicative field at the beginning of working storage to signal which ASKTIME command is being executed. You can then press PF5 in order to display working storage and visually check this field. The ENTER command has an advantage over ASKTIME in that you can assign a sequence number to TRACEID which displays on the EDF screen and enables you to determine which of multiple commands is being executed. You can also move suspected data fields to the beginning of working storage in order to make them easier to find and examine when working storage is displayed.

ABEND a CICS Task

A CICS task can be ABENDed from any screen which displays PF12 : ABEND USER TASK. Pressing PF12 prompts you to ENTER ABEND CODE AND REQUEST ABEND AGAIN. You can ABEND the task with or without a

```
 TRANSACTION: POVB    PROGRAM: POVMBROW   TASK NUMBER 0000402   DISPLAY:   00
 STATUS:   AN ABEND HAS OCCURRED

       EIBTIME     = +0112215
       EIBDATE     = +0086023
       EIBTRNID    = 'POVB'
       EIBTASKN    = +0000402
       EIBTRMID    = 'T022'
       EIBCPOSN    = +00004
       EIBCALEN    = +00000
       EIBAID      = X'7D'                             AT X'0014477B'
       EIBFN       = X'0000'                           AT X'0014477C'
       EIBRCODE    = X'000000000000'                   AT X'0014477E'
       EIBDS       = '........'
       EIBREQID    = '........'
  +    EIBRSRCE    = '        '
                                    INTERRUPT: DATA EXCEPTION
   ABEND :   ASRA                   PSW: X'087C0008D013292A'

 ENTER:  CONTINUE
 PF1  : UNDEFINED           PF2  : SWITCH HEX/CHAR     PF3  : END EDF SESSION
 PF4  : SUPPRESS DISPLAYS   PF5  : WORKING STORAGE     PF6  : USER DISPLAY
 PF7  : SCROLL BACK         PF8  : SCROLL FORWARD      PF9  : STOP CONDITIONS
 PF10: PREVIOUS DISPLAY     PF11: UNDEFINED            PF12: ABEND USER TASK
```

Figure 18-10 EDF ABEND Screen.

dump. If a dump is desired, you enter the desired ABEND code you want to show up on the dump next to REPLY: which will be displayed. If no dump is needed, just enter NO and press PF12 again to ABEND the task.

Interactive Testing Tools

There are excellent interactive testing tools available which can significantly decrease the time required to test and debug CICS programs. EDF has limitations which are overcome by some of the interactive testing tools. One of the tools I have worked with does not require you to modify your program in order to stop between CICS commands. Your program can be stopped at any section or paragraph name or at various statement numbers. You can display and change most EIB and working-storage fields by reference to their symbolic names. The point at which a program is to be stopped can be altered at various break points as the execution of a program progresses and the flow of a program's logic can be altered. I use EDF along with this tool and find that they complement one another. I use EDF to trace the basic flow of a program and resort to an interactive testing tool in order to diagnose more difficult problems.

CICS Dumps

CICS dumps are often used in order to determine the cause of an ABEND which occurred in a production environment. CICS dumps are similar to batch dumps and their discussion is beyond the scope of this book.

CICS ABEND Determination Aids

There are CICS ABEND determination aids which, when available, practically eliminate the need for CICS dumps. One of these aids I have worked with allows you to display online a menu listing all ABENDS which have occurred in the test and production system. You can select the ABEND which occurred in your program and display the information and data unique to it. There is no need to wait until a dump is printed and then search through a series of dumps to find the one that is yours. The information is displayed in a user-friendly fashion and it is easy for the programmer to determine the cause of the ABEND. The online ABEND determination aid is much easier to work with and master than is the dump reading.

CICS Testing Techniques

Although it is always desirable to have files defined before testing begins, occasionally there may be a time lag between the times when a program is written and when the needed files are available. I recommend testing programs as soon as possible after they are written. Programs often contain numerous details which can be forgotten with the passing of time. If no test data is available, create some in the test version of your program. Instead of performing a section which reads a file, perform a special section written for testing which moves constant data to the fields of the required record layout. When the required file becomes available, remove the test data from your program. The program may later encounter some errors when the live file's data is used, but you will have eliminated most other errors and the program flow should be running smoothly.

SUMMARY

This chapter covered several debugging and testing techniques which I hope will be helpful as you start writing your own CICS programs. The chapter concentrated on EDF, which is a good tool available to most CICS installations. The determination and correction of program errors encountered in online systems is easier than it is in a batch environment. Several interactive testing tools and debugging aids are available. They are being enhanced, and new tools are being developed in order to make the task of online testing and debugging simpler.

19

COLOR AND REVERSE-VIDEO ATTRIBUTE EXTENSIONS

The use of color attributes and reverse video in CICS applications that are developed for microcomputers should eventually become commonplace. This will be due to the widespread availability of color monitors. The use of these attributes on microcomputers is identical to their use on mainframe CICS and is similar to the use of attributes described in Chaps. 5 and 6. Essentially all that is required to use these features is to include an additional entry in the DFHMSD macro and one or two extra entries in the DFHMDF macro when defining the BMS map. The generated symbolic map will include four additional single-character fields. These fields, which are handled in a fashion similar to other attributes, must be provided for when creating user-friendly symbolic maps. Prior to testing all programs presented in this book, it was convenient to write a "front-end" program to initiate the DEMO system. The CWA which was used in many of the purchase order system's programs is given initial values by this program. CWA specific logic can be easily commented out if your microcomputer CICS software does not support this feature. That program, named SYSETCWA, can be found in App. H; it is initiated by entering a TRANSID of DEMO. The display of the program's map, PODEMO1, is shown in Fig. 19-1.

Figure 19-2 shows the complete BMS map which defines this screen. Asterisks have been inserted in column 1, between macros, to increase readability. The map is used in this chapter to demonstrate the use of the color and highlighting features of CICS.

Extended Attributes

The use of extended attributes requires supporting entries on the DFHMSD and DFHMDF macros of the BMS map. The DFHMSD entry defines whether extended attributes are supported, while the DFHMDF entries define attributes such as color and reverse video.

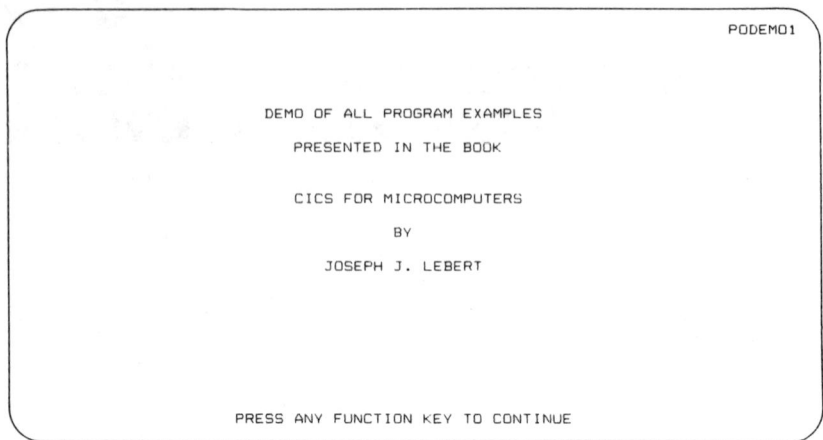

```
                                                              PODEMO1



                       DEMO OF ALL PROGRAM EXAMPLES

                       PRESENTED IN THE BOOK

                       CICS FOR MICROCOMPUTERS

                                  BY

                       JOSEPH J. LEBERT




                    PRESS ANY FUNCTION KEY TO CONTINUE
```

Figure 19-1   DEMO System Initial Screen.

EXTATT Operand and Parameters

The following excerpt from Fig. 19-2 shows the format of the DFHMSD macro that supports extended attributes.

```
PODEMO1    DFHMSD  TYPE=MAP,                    X
                   TIOAPFX=YES,                 X
                   CTRL=(FRSET,FREEKB),         X
                   TERM=3270,                   X
                   LANG=COBOL,                  X
                   EXTATT=YES,                  X
                   MODE=INOUT
```

Note that this macro is similar to the other DFHMSD macros that were defined and used in prior BMS maps. The only additional entry, EXTATT=YES, is required to support extended attributes. The permissable parameters for the EXTATT operand and their meanings are as follows:

$$
EXTATT = \begin{cases} NO \\ YES \\ MAPONLY \end{cases}
$$

• NO — This parameter, which is the default, indicates that extended attributes **are** *not* used by the BMS map.

Figure 19-2 DEMO System Initiation Screen BMS Map.

```
PODEMO1   DFHMSD TYPE=MAP,                                          X
                 TIOAPFX=YES,                                       X
                 CTRL=(FRSET,FREEKB),                               X
                 TERM=3270,                                         X
                 LANG=COBOL,                                        X
                 EXTATT=YES,                                        X
                 MODE=INOUT
*
MAPDEMO   DFHMDI SIZE=(24,80),                                      X
                 COLUMN=0001,                                       X
                 LINE=0001
*
          DFHMDF POS=(01,72),                                       X
                 LENGTH=07,                                         X
                 ATTRB=(ASKIP),                                     X
                 INITIAL='PODEMO1'
*
          DFHMDF POS=(06,25),                                       X
                 LENGTH=28,                                         X
                 ATTRB=(ASKIP),                                     X
                 COLOR=YELLOW,                                      X
                 INITIAL='DEMO OF ALL PROGRAM EXAMPLES'
*
          DFHMDF POS=(08,28),                                       X
                 LENGTH=22,                                         X
                 ATTRB=(ASKIP),                                     X
                 COLOR=TURQUOISE,                                   X
                 INITIAL='PRESENTED IN THE BOOK:'
*
          DFHMDF POS=(10,25),                                       X
                 LENGTH=24,                                         X
                 ATTRB=(ASKIP),                                     X
                 COLOR=RED,                                         X
                 HILIGHT=REVERSE,                                   X
                 INITIAL='
*
          DFHMDF POS=(11,25),                                       X
                 LENGTH=24,                                         X
                 ATTRB=(ASKIP),                                     X
                 COLOR=RED,                                         X
                 HILIGHT=REVERSE,                                   X
                 INITIAL='CICS FOR MICROCOMPUTERS'
*
          DFHMDF POS=(12,25),                                       X
                 LENGTH=24,                                         X
                 ATTRB=(ASKIP),                                     X
                 COLOR=RED,                                         X
                 HILIGHT=REVERSE,                                   X
                 INITIAL='
*
          DFHMDF POS=(13,25),                                       X
                 LENGTH=24,                                         X
                 ATTRB=(ASKIP),                                     X
                 COLOR=RED,                                         X
                 HILIGHT=REVERSE,                                   X
                 INITIAL='          BY            '
*
          DFHMDF POS=(14,25),                                       X
                 LENGTH=24,                                         X
                 ATTRB=(ASKIP),                                     X
                 COLOR=RED,                                         X
                 HILIGHT=REVERSE,                                   X
                 INITIAL='                        '
*
          DFHMDF POS=(15,25),                                       X
                 LENGTH=24,                                         X
                 ATTRB=(ASKIP),                                     X
                 COLOR=RED,                                         X
                 HILIGHT=REVERSE,                                   X
                 INITIAL='    JOSEPH J. LEBERT    '
*
          DFHMDF POS=(16,25),                                       X
                 LENGTH=24,                                         X
                 ATTRB=(ASKIP),                                     X
                 COLOR=RED,                                         X
                 HILIGHT=REVERSE,                                   X
                 INITIAL='
*
```

Figure 19-2 *(Continued)*

```
MAPMESG   DFHMDF POS=(24,01),                                                 X
              LENGTH=79,                                                      X
              ATTRB=(ASKIP),                                                  X
              COLOR=GREEN,                                                    X
              HILIGHT=REVERSE,                                                X
              INITIAL='                    PRESS ANY FUNCTION KEY TO CX
          ONTINUE

          DFHMSD TYPE=FINAL
              END
```

- YES — The inclusion of this parameter indicates that extended attributes are to be used with the BMS map and that supporting entries are to be generated as part of the symbolic map.

- MAPONLY — This parameter is used to indicate that extended attributes will be used by the physical map but not by the symbolic map. The symbolic map entries which support extended attributes will *not* be generated. A SEND MAP which includes the physical map will display the terminal's default colors.

The COLOR Operand

The following DFHMDF entry, taken from Fig. 19-2, is typical of those which support color attributes.

```
DFHMDF POS=(06,25),                                       X
    LENGTH=28,                                            X
    ATTRB=(ASKIP),                                        X
    COLOR=YELLOW,                                         X
    INITIAL='DEMO OF ALL PROGRAM EXAMPLES'
```

This macro is similar to other DFHMDF macros that were defined and used in prior BMS maps. The only new entry, COLOR=YELLOW, is included to indicate that the value DEMO OF ALL PROGRAM EXAMPLES is to be displayed in yellow. The permissable parameters for the COLOR operand are as follows:

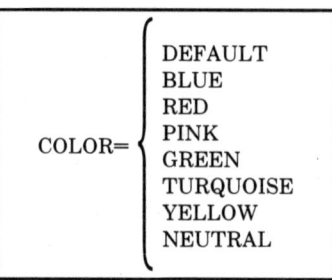

The HILIGHT Operand

The following DFHMDF entries, taken from Fig. 19-2, are typical of those which support HILIGHT attributes.

```
        DFHMDF POS=(10,25),                      X
               LENGTH=24,                        X
               ATTRB=(ASKIP),                    X
               COLOR=RED,                        X
               HILIGHT=REVERSE,                  X
               INITIAL='                 '

        DFHMDF POS=(11,25),                      X
               LENGTH=24,                        X
               ATTRB=(ASKIP),                    X
               COLOR=RED,                        X
               HILIGHT=REVERSE,                  X
               INITIAL='CICS FOR MICROCOMPUTERS'
```

The only new entry used is the HILIGHT operand which indicates that the lines are to be displayed in reverse video. Line 10 shows how a line can be displayed in reverse video and in a selected color. Line 11 shows how to display a field that contains an initial value in reverse video. Reverse video indicates that the foreground and background colors are to be reversed on the screen. For example, a light color which is normally displayed on a dark background will be displayed as a dark color on a light background. For line 11, the value CICS FOR MICROCOMPUTERS will display as dark letters on a red background.

The permissable parameters for the HILIGHT operand depend on the terminal used. The possible entries are

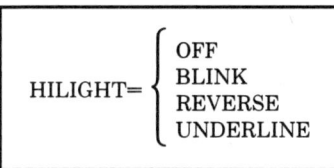

- OFF — This parameter is the default; it indicates that highlighting is *not* used.

- BLINK — BLINK indicates that a field is to be alternately displayed and not displayed. This blinking effect causes irritation to many viewers, and its use is generally not recommended.

- REVERSE — This parameter is included to indicate that the foreground and background colors of a field are to be reversed.

- UNDERLINE — A field for which this parameter is indicated will be displayed with underscore characters.

Extended Attribute Symbolic Maps

Symbolic map entries are generated for all BMS map DFHMDF macros which contain a label. For example, the BMS map in Fig. 19-2, which contains only one label, will generate the following symbolic map:

```
        01    MAPDEMOI.
              02    FILLER                          PIC X(12).
              02    MAPMESGL                        PIC S9(4) COMP.
              02    MAPMESGF                        PIC X.
              02    FILLER REDEFINES MAPMESGF.
                    03    MAPMESGA                  PIC X.
              02    FILLER                          PIC X(4).
              02    MAPMESGI                        PIC X(79).
   *
        01    MAPDEMOO REDEFINES MAPDEMOI.
              02    FILLER                          PIC X(12).
              02    FILLER                          PIC X(3).
              02    MAPMESGC                        PIC X.
              02    MAPMESGP                        PIC X.
              02    MAPMESGH                        PIC X.
              02    MAPMESGV                        PIC X.
              02    MAPMESGO                        PIC X(79).
```

This symbolic map contains four new output map entry "types" which were not present in previously discussed symbolic maps. The entries are MAPMESGC, MAPMESGP, MAPMESGH, and MAPMESGV. Note the suffixes C, P, H, and V used for these entries. Four additional entries, which contain these suffixes, are generated for each BMS map DFHMDF field that contains a label. The fields are always generated in the indicated sequence and must be provided for if you create your own user-friendly symbolic maps. The field suffixes are defined as follows:

```
        C = Color
        P = Program symbol
        H = Highlight
        V = Validation
```

The only entries from the above list that are discussed in this text are the color and highlight attributes. The color and highlight characteristics of a field may be altered in the symbolic map prior to issuing a SEND MAP command which contains the symbolic map. The character used to modify the color and highlight attributes may be taken from the DFHBMSCA copy member, or you can add entries to the standard attribute list copy member, STWSATTR, which is defined in App. B. The DFHBMSCA entries are as follows:

```
   05   DFHDFCOL      PIC X   VALUE   ' '.
   05   DFHBLUE       PIC X   VALUE   '1'.
   05   DFHRED        PIC X   VALUE   '2'.
   05   DFHPINK       PIC X   VALUE   '3'.
   05   DFHGREEN      PIC X   VALUE   '4'.
   05   DFHTURQ       PIC X   VALUE   '5'.
   05   DFHYELLO      PIC X   VALUE   '6'.
   05   DFHNEUTR      PIC X   VALUE   '7'.

   05   DFHDFHI       PIC X   VALUE   ' '.
   05   DFHBLINK      PIC X   VALUE   '1'.
   05   DFHREVRS      PIC X   VALUE   '2'.
   05   DFHUNDLN      PIC X   VALUE   '4'.
```

Suggested names for an expansion of the copy member STWSATTR are

```
   05   COL-DEFAULT      PIC X   VALUE   ' '.
   05   BLUE             PIC X   VALUE   '1'.
   05   RED              PIC X   VALUE   '2'.
   05   PINK             PIC X   VALUE   '3'.
   05   GREEN            PIC X   VALUE   '4'.
   05   TURQUOISE        PIC X   VALUE   '5'.
   05   YELLOW           PIC X   VALUE   '6'.
   05   NEUTRAL          PIC X   VALUE   '7'.

   05   HLT-DEFAULT      PIC X   VALUE   ' '.
   05   BLINK            PIC X   VALUE   '1'.
   05   REVERSE-VIDEO    PIC X   VALUE   '2'.
   05   UNDERLINE        PIC X   VALUE   '4'.
```

The color of the message field could be changed from green (the BMS-map-defined color) to yellow, and the highlighting changed from reverse video to normal display by executing the following moves prior to issuing a SEND MAP command:

```
   MOVE DFHYELLO        TO   MAPMESGC.
   MOVE DFHDFHI         TO   MAPMESGH.
                or
   MOVE YELLOW          TO   MAPMESGC.
   MOVE HLT-DEFAULT     TO   MAPMESGH.
```

SUMMARY

The use of color attributes and extended highlighting should become common in microcomputer applications; these attributes are handled in a fashion similar to those discussed in previous chapters. This chapter discussed the BMS map additions to the DFHMSD and DFHMDF macros required to activate these attributes. The permissable parameters of the DFHMSD macro's EXTATT operand were discussed, as were the COLOR and HILIGHT operands of the DFHMDF macro. New entries that are generated in the symbolic map to support extended highlighting and color attributes were explained.

20

MISCELLANEOUS CICS COMMANDS AND NUMERIC EDITING

This chapter is intended to be a brief introduction to CICS commands and techniques that are less frequently used than the commands discussed in preceding chapters. It is possible to design and write most CICS applications and programs using only the CICS commands discussed up to this point. Commands that are currently supported by one or more microcomputer software implementations of CICS are discussed. Some of these commands may not support all the options and HANDLE CONDITIONs available with mainframe CICS. However, they function well enough to enable you to develop and test most microcomputer programs in which they are used. As multitasking capabilities are added to the operating system and software, additional mainframe CICS commands should become available to microcomputer users of CICS.

The numeric editing of input data seems not to have any general industrywide standard. Most data processing installations have standards that apply to their companies, and many have standard modules that are commonly used for editing. These modules may take the form of copy members or linked-to programs or may just be copied from one program to another. This chapter discusses numeric editing considerations and includes a copy member routine that should satisfy most of your editing requirements.

CICS Commands

ABEND

The ABEND is used to abort a program when an error is detected rather than have CICS perform the termination. The specification of ABCODE will result in the display of the specified code when the program is terminated. ABCODE's four-character abend code can be either defined in working storage or may be hard-coded by enclosing the code in quotes. The ABEND command has the following format:

```
EXEC CICS ABEND
        [ABCODE ('ABCD')
                    / (WS-ABCODE)]
END-EXEC.
```

BIF DEEDIT

This CICS built-in function is used to remove unwanted characters from an input field; it is most often used for numeric editing. BIF DEEDIT can be used to remove special characters such as commas, decimals, and plus and minus signs that are keyed into an input field. The resulting field will be right-justified, and its high-order positions will be zero-filled. BIF DEEDIT has the following format:

```
EXEC CICS BIF DEEDIT
            FIELD (WS-DATA)
            LENGTH (nn)
        END-EXEC.
```

The following examples and comments should help to clarify the use of BIF DEEDIT. The length of the input field is eleven (11).

WS-DATA before	WS-DATA after	Comments
121,201.00	00012120100	Commas and decimals are removed
200	00000000200	High-order positions are zero-filled
2.00	00000000200	Note that 'after' field is same as above
555-55-5555	00555555555	Special characters removed
$9,876.54	00000987654	Same as above
12/25/99	00000122599	Same as above
123.45−	00000012345	Non-low-order '-' is stripped
123.45−	0000001234N	Low-order '-' results in signed low-order
−123.45	00000012345	High-order sign is stripped
+123.45	00000012345	Same as above
123.45+	00000012345	Low-order '+' is removed or ignored
1234M	00000012345	Non-low-order sign is stripped
1234M	0000001234M	Low-order letter or sign remains
123.45CR	00000012345	Non-low-order 'CR' is stripped
123.45CR	0000001234N	Low-order 'CR' results in minus sign
123.45DR	0000012345R	'DR' treated as are other letters
123 456 789	00000000123	Characters following a space are ignored
1A2B3C4D5EF	0000012345F	All but low-order letters are removed
123_____	00000000123	Underline characters are removed

BIF DEEDIT appears to be a very powerful editing tool, but in practice its use is limited. As seen in the preceding examples, 2.00 and 200 both translate into 200. If decimal places are to be entered into a field, they must always be entered even if the decimal field is all zeros. For example, if a field is to be defined as having two decimal places, then 200 must be entered as 200.00. Also, invalid characters are removed without notification of incorrect entry. For example, a field entered as 1,23,456,7890,,0 would not be detected as being erroneous; the commas would just be removed. The numeric editing that is commonly required is discussed later in this chapter under "Numeric Editing."

CANCEL

The CANCEL command is used to cancel a transaction that has been initiated by the issuance of a START command. This command is not commonly used because a transaction cannot be canceled once it has begun executing. The CANCEL command has the following format:

```
EXEC CICS CANCEL
           TRANSID ('TRID')
END-EXEC.
```

DELETEQ TD

The DELETEQ TD command is used to delete all records from a transient data queue. It has the following format:

```
EXEC CICS DELETEQ TD
           QUEUE (TD-QUEUE)
END-EXEC.
```

FORMATTIME

The FORMATTIME command is used to set the time and date in various formats in programmer-defined fields. This command requires an input field that is passed by using the ABSTIME option. ABSTIME is defined as the elapsed time in milliseconds since zero hours on January 1, 1900. It can be calculated or derived for the current date and time by including the ABSTIME option on the ASKTIME command as follows:

```
EXEC CICS ASKTIME
           ABSTIME (FO-ABSTIME)
END-EXEC.
```

FO-ABSTIME must be defined as a doubleword (8 bytes). Its contents can be stored in a record as part of a key field or as a data element. EIBTIME, which is sometimes used as part of a record's key for time-stamping audit records, may not always change between file writes because of the computer's speed of processing. This can result in a duplicate key condition and may require additional logic to reexecute ASKTIME and to again process the write. The use of ABSTIME should break time down to a fine enough interval so that this problem is eliminated. The options of FORMATTIME most likely to be used in a microcomputer environment along with representative working-storage fields are as follows:

```
05   FO-ABSTIME        PIC S9(16)   COMP    VALUE ZEROS.
05   FO-TIME           PIC X(8)     VALUE SPACES.
05   FO-TIMESEP        PIC X        VALUE '.'.
05   FO-DATESEP        PIC X        VALUE '-'.
05   FO-YYDDD          PIC X(6)     VALUE SPACES.
05   FO-YYMMDD         PIC X(8)     VALUE SPACES.
05   FO-YYDDMM         PIC X(8)     VALUE SPACES.
05   FO-MMDDYY         PIC X(8)     VALUE SPACES.
05   FO-DDMMYY         PIC X(8)     VALUE SPACES.
05   FO-DAYCOUNT       PIC S9(8)    COMP    VALUE ZEROS.
05   FO-DAYOFWEEK      PIC S9(8)    COMP    VALUE ZEROS.
05   FO-DAYOFMONTH     PIC S9(8)    COMP    VALUE ZEROS.
05   FO-MONTHOFYEAR    PIC S9(8)    COMP    VALUE ZEROS.
05   FO-YEAR           PIC S9(8)    COMP    VALUE ZEROS.

EXEC CICS FORMATTIME
          ABSTIME         (FO-ABSTIME)
          TIME            (FO-TIME)
          TIMESEP         (FO-TIMESEP)
          DATESEP         (FO-DATESEP)
          YYDDD           (FO-YYDDD)
          YYMMDD          (FO-YYMMDD)
          YYDDMM          (FO-YYDDMM)
          MMDDYY          (FO-MMDDYY)
          DDMMYY          (FO-DDMMYY)
          DAYCOUNT        (FO-DAYCOUNT)
          DAYOFWEEK       (FO-DAYOFWEEK)
          DAYOFMONTH      (FO-DAYOFMONTH)
          MONTHOFYEAR     (FO-MONTHOFYEAR)
          YEAR            (FO-YEAR)
END-EXEC.
```

Only the desired options need be specified on the FORMATTIME command, and the results of the execution will be found in the appropriate working-storage fields. The options of FORMATTIME are

• ABSTIME — The argument of this required entry may be derived from the execution of the ASKTIME command, may have been saved in a data record, or may be calculated as discussed below. It must be defined as a doubleword (8 bytes).

ABSTIME Calculation Logic: If you know or calculate the Julian date for a future or past date, a routine can be coded to determine the number of days that have elapsed since January 1, 1900, for example.

1. Divide 4 into the Julian year to determine the number of leap years.
2. Compute non-leap years = Julian year − number of leap years.
3. Compute days to beginning of year = (365 × number of non-leap years) + (366 × number of leap years).
4. Days since 1/1/00 = days to beginning of year + Julian days. *Adjustments to this logic have to be made at the year 2000.*

ABSTIME can be calculated (zero time) by multiplying days since 1/1/00 × 86,400 s/day × 1000 ms/s.

- TIME — An eight-character field in hh:mm:ss format depending on the separator defined by TIMESEP.

- TIMESEP — A separator character that will be used to split time into hh.mm.ss format. If this option is specified without an argument, then the default separator is a colon (:). A six-character field without separators will be returned if this option is omitted.

- DATESEP — A separator character that will be used to split the date into an appropriate format. If this option is specified without an argument, then the default separator is a slash (/). A field without separators will be returned if this option is omitted.

- YYDDD — The date will be returned to a six-character working-storage field for this option in Julian date format, with or without separator characters, depending on whether DATESEP is specified.

- YYMMDD, YYDDMM, MMDDYY, and DDMMYY — The date will be returned to an eight-character working-storage field for these options in the indicated format, with or without separator characters, depending on whether DATESEP is specified.

- DAYCOUNT — The argument to this option will receive the number of days since January 1, 1900. This option should be helpful in determining the number of days between two dates. The receiving field should be specified as a binary fullword.

- DAYOFWEEK — The argument to this option will receive a relative number that represents the day of the week: Sunday = 0, Saturday = 6. The receiving field should be specified as a binary fullword.

- DAYOFMONTH — The argument to this option will receive the day of the month. The receiving field should be specified as a binary fullword.

- MONTHOFYEAR — The argument to this option will receive the month of the year. The receiving field should be specified as a binary fullword.

- YEAR — The year will be returned to working storage as a four-digit year. The receiving field should be defined as a binary fullword.

FREEMAIN

The FREEMAIN command is used to release storage that has been acquired by the GETMAIN command. This command is not used often because acquired storage is released automatically when a task ends. The DATA option reference is to the linkage section data pointed to by a BLL cell. The FREEMAIN command has the following format:

```
EXEC CICS FREEMAIN
           DATA (LS-DATA)
END-EXEC.
```

GETMAIN

The GETMAIN command is used to acquire main storage for use in the linkage section when the locate mode rather than the move mode of processing is used. It is necessary to acquire storage for output type operations only when storage has not been automatically acquired by an input operation. For instance, if a write command is not preceded by a read command, then storage must be acquired. Read commands that use the SET option acquire their own storage. GETMAIN uses the SET option to establish addressability using BLL cells which were discussed in Chap. 10. LENGTH must have its data value specified as a halfword binary value (PIC S9999 COMP) when the value is defined in working storage. The storage acquired can be initialized to a given value, generally low-values, by defining a 1-byte value in working storage and including the INITIMG option. The GET-MAIN command has the following format:

```
EXEC CICS GETMAIN
           SET        (BLL-pointer)
           LENGTH     (WS-LENGTH) / (nn)
           [INITIMG   (WS-INITIAL)]
END-EXEC.
```

HANDLE ABEND

The HANDLE ABEND command is used to direct control to a program, section, or paragraph if an abend occurs. The abend program or routine can contain logic for any desired abend processing. The PROGRAM option designates the program that is to receive control if an abend occurs, while the LABEL option directs control to the specified section or paragraph name. The CANCEL option deactivates a HANDLE ABEND command, while RESET reactivates the condition. HANDLE ABEND has the following format:

```
        EXEC CICS HANDLE ABEND
            [PROGRAM (WS-PROGRAM) / ('PROGNAME')]
               [LABEL   (X000-SECTION-PARAGRAPH)]
               [CANCEL]
               [RESET]
        END-EXEC.
```

POP

The POP command is used to restore the status of HANDLE CONDITIONs that were suspended by the issuance of a PUSH command. The PUSH and POP commands would generally be used in standard subroutines that issue HANDLE CONDITION commands of their own. The POP command has the following format:

```
        EXEC CICS POP HANDLE
        END-EXEC.
```

PUSH

The PUSH command suspends all active HANDLE CONDITIONs. This command could be executed by a standard subroutine that uses HANDLE CONDITIONs of its own. Existing HANDLE CONDITIONs are saved and can be restored to their status prior to entering the subroutine by issuing the POP command before exiting the subroutine. The PUSH command has the following format:

```
        EXEC CICS PUSH HANDLE
        END-EXEC.
```

READ

The use of the READ command when the locate mode is employed is similar to its use when the move mode of processing is employed. The difference is that the SET option is used instead of the INTO option. Refer to Chap. 11 for further information on the READ command. It has the following format:

```
EXEC CICS READ
          DATASET   (FCT entry)
          SET       (BLL-RECORD-I-O-pointer)
          RIDFLD    (WS-RECORD-KEY)
END-EXEC.
```

READNEXT

The use of the READNEXT command when the locate mode is employed is similar to its use when the move mode of processing is employed. The difference is that the SET option is used instead of the INTO option. Refer to Chap. 11 for further information on the READNEXT command. It has the following format:

```
EXEC CICS READNEXT
          DATASET   (FCT entry)
          SET       (BLL-RECORD-I-O-pointer)
          RIDFLD    (WS-RECORD-KEY)
END-EXEC.
```

READPREV

The use of the READPREV command when the locate mode is employed is similar to its use when the move mode of processing is employed. The difference is that the SET option is used instead of the INTO option. Refer to Chap. 11 for further information on the READPREV command. It has the following format:

```
EXEC CICS READPREV
          DATASET   (FCT entry)
          SET       (BLL-RECORD-I-O-pointer)
          RIDFLD    (WS-RECORD-KEY)
END-EXEC.
```

READQ TD

The READQ TD command provides for the retrieval of transient data queue records that were written by a WRITEQ TD command. The QUEUE option designates a one- to four-character queue name that must be defined in a CICS system table called the destination control table (DCT). The INTO or SET options may be used to direct the queue's input into either a working-storage or linkage section input area. The handle condition QZERO is used to test if a transient data queue is empty. The LENGTH option's data area must be specified as a halfword binary value (PIC S9999 COMP) and prior to the issuance of the read must be defined as the length of the largest record that is to be read. The actual length of the record that is read is stored in the LENGTH field's data area at the completion of the read. READQ TD may have the following format:

```
EXEC CICS READQ TD
          QUEUE     (TD-QUEUE)
          [INTO     (TD-DATA)
          / SET     (BLL-TD-DATA-pointer)]
          LENGTH    (TD-LENGTH)
END-EXEC.
```

READQ TS

The use of the READQ TS command when the locate mode is employed is similar to its use when the move mode of processing is employed. The difference is that the SET option is used instead of the INTO option. The LENGTH option 's data area must be specified as a halfword binary value (PIC S9999   COMP) and prior to the issuance of the read must be defined as the length of the largest record that is to be read. It has the following format:

```
EXEC CICS READQ TS
          QUEUE     (TS-QUEUE)
          SET       (BLL-TS-DATA-pointer)
          LENGTH    (TS-LENGTH)
          ITEM      (TS-ITEM)
END-EXEC.
```

RECEIVE MAP

The use of the RECEIVE MAP when the locate mode is employed is similar to its use when the move mode of processing is employed. The difference is that the SET option is used instead of the INTO option. It has the following format:

```
EXEC CICS RECEIVE
          MAP       (mapname)
          MAPSET    (mapset)
          SET       (BLL-map-pointer)
END-EXEC.
```

RETRIEVE

Data passed to a program that was initiated by issuing a START command can be accessed in the running program by issuing the RETRIEVE command. The data is retrieved and stored in the field specified by the INTO or SET option. The LENGTH option's length field specifies the expected size of the passed data before it is retrieved and its actual length after the RETRIEVE command is executed. The LENGTH's data area must be specified as a halfword binary value (PIC S9999 COMP). The ENDDATA and NOTFND handle conditions may be tested when using the RETRIEVE command which has the following format:

```
EXEC CICS RETRIEVE
            INTO     (WS-DATA)
            / SET      (BLL-pointer)
            LENGTH (WS-LENGTH)
END-EXEC.
```

SEND TEXT

The SEND TEXT command is commonly used interchangeably with the SEND command that was discussed in Chap. 5. SEND TEXT has the following format:

```
EXEC CICS SEND TEXT
            FROM    (WS-MESSAGE)
            LENGTH (nn)
            [ERASE]
END-EXEC.
```

START

The START command is issued to initiate another transaction while the current task continues. The TRANSID option specifies the name of the transaction code that was used to initiate the new program. The running program terminates its execution by executing a return to CICS without a TRANSID. Data may optionally be passed to the initiated program by including the FROM and LENGTH options. The LENGTH's data area must be specified as a halfword binary value (PIC S9999 COMP). This data may be accessed in the new program by the issuance of the RETRIEVE command. The START command has the following format:

```
EXEC CICS START
            TRANSID ('TRID')
            [FROM    (WS-DATA)]
            [LENGTH (WS-LENGTH)]
END-EXEC.
```

WRITEQ TD

The WRITEQ TD command is used to write data to a transient data queue. The QUEUE option specifies the name of the queue which must be defined in the DCT. The FROM option specifies the name of the output data area, while LENGTH, which is defined as a binary halfword (PIC S9999   COMP), gives the length of the output record. WRITEQ TD has the following format:

```
EXEC CICS WRITEQ TD
          QUEUE     (TD-QUEUE)
          FROM      (TD-DATA)
          LENGTH    (TD-LENGTH)
END-EXEC.
```

NUMERIC EDITING

It was mentioned in the introduction to this chapter that the numeric editing of input data seems not to have any general industrywide standard. Users often want to have the ability to enter data into a field in its edited format and expect the system to notify them of any input format errors. Most data processing installations have standards that apply to their departments, and many have standard modules that are commonly used for editing. These modules may take the form of copy members, linked-to programs, or may just be copied from one program to another. This section discusses numeric editing considerations and includes a copy member module that should satisfy most of your editing requirements. This module was written for ease of understanding and modification and should be easy enough to follow and customize for your own unique data-entry requirements. Other data-entry techniques were discussed in Chap. 2 and were illustrated in Fig. 2-5. Some programs enter whole numbers and decimal digits into two separate map fields. This technique is awkward in that it requires tabbing to the decimal portion of a numeric field when the whole number portion is not completely filled with data.

As mentioned earlier, BIF DEEDIT has limited uses since it basically removes nonnumeric data, right-justifies, and zero-fills high-order positions. The following examples and comments show how data edited using the module in this section will appear on the screen after being edited. The edit mask used for the examples is ---------9.99, although any valid numeric edit mask could be used. Contrast the first part of this example with corresponding data edited by BIF DEEDIT in the example presented earlier in this chapter.

Screen before	Screen after	Comments
121,201.00	121201.00	Commas are removed
200	200.00	Field is decimal-aligned
2.00	2.00	This field is different than that above
555-55-5555	555-55-5555	Error — embedded or excess signs
$9,876.54	$9,876.54	Error — dollar sign not permitted
12/25/99	12/25/99	Error — slash (/) not permitted
123.45−	−123.45	Signs can be entered in high- or low-order position of field
−123.45	−123.45	High-order sign is OK
+123.45	123.45	High-order '+' is removed or ignored
123.45+	123.45	Low-order '+' is removed or ignored
1234M	1234M	Error — alpha is invalid
123.45CR	123.45CR	Error — alpha is invalid
123.45DR	123.45DR	Same as above
123 456 789	123 456 789	Error — embedded characters are invalid
1A2B3C4D5EF	1A2B3C4D5EF	Error — alpha is invalid
123_____	123	Underline characters are removed
10.+	10.00	Sign can immediately precede or follow a decimal point
−.10	−0.10	Same as above
− .10	− .10	Error — no embedded spaces before a sign
10. −	10. −	Error — no embedded spaces after a sign
−10.2−	−10.2−	Error — only one sign is permitted
10-23	10-23	Error — no embedded sign is allowed
10 23	10 23	Error — no embedded spaces are permitted
1234,567	1234567	Valid — routine allows any number of digits *before* first comma
1,2345,678	1,2345,678	Error — three digits must follow every comma
123.45,6	123.45,6	Error — comma cannot occur after a decimal is entered
,123.56	,123.56	Error — cannot have a leading comma
123.456.789	123.456.789	Error — only one decimal point permitted
123_456_789	123_456_789	Error — only trailing underline allowed
.		Error — no digits or decimal number
0	0.00	Zeros will be returned if zeros, spaces, or low-values are passed

The examples above illustrate some of the requirements of a good numeric edit module. The features of the edit module in this chapter can be summarized as follows:

1. Only specified characters are permitted. The copy module in this chapter allows the entry of only the digits 0 through 9, one sign, one decimal, commas, and underline characters. All other characters are flagged as errors.

2. Only one optional leading or trailing plus (+) or minus (−) sign is permitted; *plus* is the default entry.

3. No embedded blanks are permitted; this includes blanks immediately following a leading sign or preceding a trailing sign.

4. Only one optional decimal point followed by up to 6 decimal digits is permitted. Excess decimal digits are flagged as errors. The number of decimal places specified can vary from field to field.

5. Up to 12 whole number digits separated by commas in appropriate groups of three are permitted. Any number of digits can precede the first comma. Excess whole number digits are flagged as errors, as is improper comma usage. Commas need not be entered; however, if they are used, they must be followed by three digits.

6. All error conditions are recorded by moving a two-character status code to a working-storage status field named NUMED-STATUS. This code can be tested by the program, and an appoprate error message can be displayed. This routine moves a descriptive message to the working storage field NUMED-MESSAGE if errors are detected.

7. Trailing underline characters are removed, while any other underline characters result in an input field being detected as being invalid.

8. The routine can be customized during program execution for designated characters. Moving low-values to any of the fields NUMED-COMMA, NUMED-DECIMAL, NUMED-MINUS, NUMED-PLUS, and/or NUMED-UNDER-LINE prior to performing the routine Z99Y-NUMERIC-EDIT will result in those fields being treated as invalid input. Each field is restored to its initial value by the routine before the routine is exited.

9. The edit module should be easy to use. The module in this chapter requires the inclusion of one copy member in the working storage section (STWSNUME) and one in the procedure division (STPDNUME). The routine is invoked as follows:

```
            MOVE mapfldI    TO    WS-NUMEDT-INPUT.
            MOVE nn         TO    WS-NUMEDT-DIGITS.
            MOVE d          TO    WS-NUMEDT-DECIMALS.

            PERFORM Z99Y-NUMERIC-EDIT.
            IF NUMEDT-STATUS    =    SPACES
                MOVE WS-NUMEDT-OUTPUT    TO    xx
                MOVE WS-NUMEDT-OUTPUT    TO    edit field
                MOVE edit field          TO    mapfldO
            ELSE
                PERFORM bad edit logic.

        where mapfldI = map input field to be edited. Define in
                        map as PIC X (map field size)
              nn = maximum number of whole numbers
                   permitted. 00 is the minimum; 12 is
                   maximum. This can be adjusted for each
                   field
```

(Continued)

(Continued)

d = maximum number of decimal digits
    permitted. 0 is the minimum; 6 is
    maximum. This can be adjusted for each
    field

xx = working storage, COMMAREA, file,
    linkage section field, etc.

edit field = the edit mask that is used to define the
    map output display field

mapfldO = map output field, either edited or original
    field if errors. The map's output field can
    be defined with an edit mask, but the
    input field must be defined as X's.

bad edit logic = can perform routines that will highlight
    an erroneous field and position the cursor
    at the field, set an error indicator switch,
    display the error message stored in
    NUMED-MESSAGE, etc.

Figure 20-1 shows numeric edit's WORKING-STORAGE SECTION copy member (STWSNUME). Numeric edit's PROCEDURE DIVISION copy member (STPDNUME) is shown in Fig. 20-2. This routine contains numerous comments that will enable you to modify the edit module if necessary; they should also make it easier for you to understand the module.

SUMMARY

This chapter presented a brief introduction to CICS commands that are less frequently used than are those presented in earlier chapters. All commands are now available on one or more microcomputer implementations of CICS. The bibliography at the end of the appendixes should provide you with suitable reference material if you require additional information on some of the commands presented in this chapter. The numeric edit module should provide you with a working model that can be used unchanged on your microcomputer or mainframe or that can be customized for your particular editing needs.

You now have the knowledge and tools necessary to write and maintain most CICS programs and systems in both a microcomputer and mainframe environment. Your mastery of CICS will come with study and practice. No single book contains all the information you need to know about CICS; start a collection of books on CICS and other data processing–related subjects. CICS, like many other subjects, is easy once you learn and master the fundamentals.

Figure 20-1 Working-Storage Copy Member (STWSNUME) for Numeric Editing.

```
000100***********************************************************************
000200*    'STWSNUME'   WORKING STORAGE FOR NUMERIC EDIT ROUTINE        *
000300*    COPY 'STPDNUME' INTO PROCEDURE DIVISION FOR NUMERIC EDIT     *
000400***********************************************************************
000500*
000600 01   NUMED-FIELDS.
000700      05   NUMED-INPUT.
000800           10   NUMED-IN         PIC X      OCCURS 24 TIMES.
000900*
001000      05   NUMED-OUT.
001100           10   NUMED-OUTPUT     PIC S9(12)V9(6)   VALUE ZEROES.
001200*
001300      05   NUMED-MESSAGE            PIC X(79)      VALUE SPACES.
001400      05   NUMED-DIGITS            PIC 99          VALUE ZEROES.
001500      05   NUMED-DECIMALS          PIC 9           VALUE ZEROES.
001600      05   NUMED-DIGIT-COUNT       PIC 99          VALUE ZEROES.
001700      05   NUMED-DEC-NUM-COUNT     PIC 9           VALUE ZEROES.
001800      05   NUMED-DEC-PT-COUNT      PIC 9.          VALUE ZEROES.
001900      05   NUMED-SIGN-COUNT        PIC 9           VALUE ZEROES.
002000      05   NUMED-NUM-AFTER-COMMA-COUNT    PIC 99   VALUE ZEROES.
002100      05   NUMED-NUM-AFTER-COMMA-SWITCH   PIC X    VALUE 'N'.
002200      05   NUMED-NEG-SIGN                 PIC X    VALUE 'N'.
002300*
002400 01   NUMED-BUILD.
002500      05   NUMED-B-DIGITS.
002600           10   NUMED-B-DIG      PIC X      OCCURS 12 TIMES.
002700      05   NUMED-B-DECIMALS.
002800           10   NUMED-B-DEC      PIC X      OCCURS  6 TIMES.
002900*
003000* THE FOLLOWING CAN BE DEACTIVATED BY MOVING LOW-VALUES TO FIELD
003100* IMMEDIATELY PRIOR TO EACH PERFORM OF Z99Y-NUMERIC-EDIT.  THE
003200* ROUTINE RESTORES FIELDS TO THEIR INITIAL STATUS PRIOR TO EXITING
003300*
003400 01   NUMED-CUSTOMIZE.
003500      05   NUMED-COMMA        PIC X            VALUE ','.
003600      05   NUMED-DECIMAL      PIC X            VALUE '.'.
003700      05   NUMED-MINUS        PIC X            VALUE '-'.
003800      05   NUMED-PLUS         PIC X            VALUE '+'.
003900      05   NUMED-UNDERLINE    PIC X            VALUE '_'.
004000*
004100 01   NUMED-SUBSCRIPTS.
004200      05   NES1             PIC S9(4)   COMP   VALUE ZEROES.
004300      05   NES2             PIC S9(4)   COMP   VALUE ZEROES.
004400      05   NESBEG           PIC S9(4)   COMP   VALUE ZEROES.
004500      05   NESEND           PIC S9(4)   COMP   VALUE ZEROES.
004600      05   NESDEC           PIC S9(4)   COMP   VALUE ZEROES.
004700*
004800      05   NUMED-STATUS     PIC XX             VALUE SPACES.
004900           88   NUMED-GOOD-EDIT                VALUE '  '.
005000           88   INVALID-DIGIT-DEC-PASSED       VALUE 'IP'.
005100           88   EXCESS-SIGNS                   VALUE 'ES'.
005200           88   EXCESS-DECIMAL-POINTS          VALUE 'EP'.
005300           88   EXCESS-WHOLE-NUMBERS           VALUE 'EN'.
005400           88   EXCESS-DECIMAL-DIGITS          VALUE 'ED'.
005500           88   INVALID-CHAR-INCL-IMBED-BLANKS VALUE 'IC'.
005600           88   INVALID-FORMAT                 VALUE 'IF'.
005700           88   COMMA-AFTER-DECIMAL            VALUE 'CD'.
005800           88   NO-DIGITS-ENTERED              VALUE 'ND'.
005900           88   NOT-3-DIGITS-AFTER-COMMA       VALUE 'N3'.
```

Figure 20-2   Procedure Division Copy Member (STPDNUME) for Numeric Editing.

```
000100 Z99Y-NUMERIC-EDIT  SECTION.
000200*
000300****************************************************************
000400*    'STPDNUME'  NUMERIC EDIT ROUTINE - PROCEDURE DIVISION      *
000500*                                                               *
000600*  GOOD EDIT:    SPACES ARE RETURNED IN NUMED-STATUS            *
000700*                OUTPUT IS RETURNED IN NUMED-OUTPUT             *
000800*  INPUT ERROR: 2-CHAR ERROR CODE IS RETURNED IN NUMED-STATUS   *
000900*                ZEROES ARE RETURNED IN NUMED-OUTPUT            *
001000*                ERROR MESSAGE IS RETURNED IN NUMED-MESSAGE      *
001100****************************************************************
001200*
001300     MOVE SPACES  TO   NUMED-STATUS.
001400     MOVE ZEROES  TO   NUMED-OUTPUT.
001500     MOVE ZEROES  TO   NUMED-BUILD.
001600     MOVE ZEROES  TO   NUMED-DEC-PT-COUNT.
001700     MOVE ZEROES  TO   NUMED-SIGN-COUNT.
001800     MOVE ZEROES  TO   NUMED-DIGIT-COUNT.
001900     MOVE ZEROES  TO   NUMED-DEC-NUM-COUNT.
002000     MOVE 3       TO   NUMED-NUM-AFTER-COMMA-COUNT.
002100     MOVE 'N'     TO   NUMED-NUM-AFTER-COMMA-SWITCH.
002200     MOVE 'N'     TO   NUMED-NEG-SIGN.
002300     MOVE SPACES  TO   NUMED-MESSAGE.
002400*
002500* PASSED DIGIT AND DECIMAL COUNT REQUIREMENTS:
002600*   1) MUST BE NUMERIC
002700*   2) DIGITS CANNOT EXCEED 12
002800*   3) DECIMALS CANNOT EXCEED 6
002900*   4) BOTH CANNOT BE ZEROES
003000*
003100     IF (NUMED-DIGITS    IS  NUMERIC   AND
003200         NUMED-DIGITS    IS  LESS THAN  13)
003300        AND
003400        (NUMED-DECIMALS  IS  NUMERIC   AND
003500         NUMED-DECIMALS  IS  LESS THAN   7)
003600           NEXT SENTENCE
003700     ELSE
003800         MOVE 'IP' TO  NUMED-STATUS
003900         GO TO  Z99Y-RESTORE-NUMED-FIELDS.
004000*
004100     IF NUMED-DIGITS   = 0  AND
004200        NUMED-DECIMALS = 0
004300        MOVE 'IP' TO  NUMED-STATUS
004400        GO TO  Z99Y-RESTORE-NUMED-FIELDS.
004500*
004600* ZEROES WILL BE RETURNED IN NUMED-OUTPUT IF SPACES,
004700*   LOW-VALUES. OR ZEROES ARE PASSED IN NUMED-INPUT
004800*
004900     IF NUMED-INPUT = SPACES OR LOW-VALUES OR  ZEROES
005000        GO TO  Z99Y-RESTORE-NUMED-FIELDS.
005100*
005200     MOVE ZEROES  TO  NESBEG.
005300     PERFORM Z99Y-FIND-1ST-SIGNIF-CHAR
005400          VARYING NES1   FROM  1  BY  1
005500             UNTIL NESBEG IS GREATER THAN  ZEROES.
005600*
005700     GO TO  Z99Y-LOCATE-END-OF-FIELD.
005800*
005900 Z99Y-FIND-1ST-SIGNIF-CHAR.
006000     IF NUMED-IN (NES1)  NOT = SPACE
006100        MOVE NES1 TO  NESBEG.
006200*
006300 Z99Y-LOCATE-END-OF-FIELD.
006400     MOVE ZEROES  TO  NESEND.
006500     PERFORM Z99Y-FIND-LAST-SIGNIF-CHAR
006600          VARYING NES1   FROM  24  BY  -1
006700             UNTIL NESEND  IS GREATER THAN  ZEROES
006800                OR NES1    IS EQUAL TO       ZEROES.
006900*
007000* NES1 WOULD ONLY = 0 IF THE ONLY CHARACTERS IN A FIELD
007100* WERE UNDERLINE CHARACTERS
007200*
007300     IF NESEND  = 0
007400        MOVE 'ND' TO  NUMED-STATUS
007500        GO TO  Z99Y-RESTORE-NUMED-FIELDS
007600     ELSE
007700        GO TO  Z99Y-INITIATE-EDITING.
007800*
```

Figure 20-2 *(Continued)*

```
007900 Z99Y-FIND-LAST-SIGNIF-CHAR.
008000*
008100* TRAILING UNDERLINE CHARACTERS ARE ELIMINATED
008200*   OTHERS WILL BE FLAGGED AS ERRORS DURING EDITING
008300*
008400     IF NUMED-IN (NES1)  =  NUMED-UNDERLINE
008500        MOVE SPACE  TO  NUMED-IN (NES1).
008600*
008700     IF NUMED-IN (NES1)  NOT =  SPACE
008800        MOVE NES1  TO  NESEND.
008900*
009000 Z99Y-INITIATE-EDITING.
009100     MOVE ZEROES  TO  NESDEC.
009200     PERFORM Z99Z-EDIT-PASS
009300        VARYING NES1 FROM  NESBEG  BY  1
009400           UNTIL NES1  IS GREATER THAN  NESEND
009500              OR NUMED-STATUS  IS NOT =  SPACES.
009600*
009700     IF NUMED-STATUS  IS NOT =  SPACES
009800        GO TO  Z99Y-RESTORE-NUMED-FIELDS.
009900*
010000* AT THIS POINT NUMED-DEC-PT-COUNT = 0 OR 1 AND NO ERRORS HAVE
010100*   BEEN FOUND IN INPUT DATA
010200*
010300     IF NUMED-DEC-PT-COUNT  =  1
010400        MOVE ZEROES  TO  NES2
010500        PERFORM Z99Y-NE-SET-DECIMALS
010600           VARYING NES1  FROM  NESDEC  BY  1
010700              UNTIL NES1  IS GREATER THAN  NESEND
010800     ELSE
010900        MOVE NESEND  TO  NESDEC.
011000*
011100     GO TO  Z99Y-FORMAT-WHOLE-NUMBER.
011200*
011300 Z99Y-NE-SET-DECIMALS.
011400*
011500* STARTING AT DECIMAL POINT, STORE ALL DECIMAL DIGITS UNTIL
011600*   THE END OF THE FIELD IS ENCOUNTERED
011700*
011800     IF NUMED-IN (NES1)  IS NUMERIC
011900        ADD 1                 TO  NES2
012000        MOVE NUMED-IN (NES1)  TO  NUMED-B-DEC (NES2).
012100*
012200 Z99Y-FORMAT-WHOLE-NUMBER.
012300*
012400     MOVE 12  TO NES2.
012500     PERFORM Z99Y-NE-SET-WHOLE-NUMBER
012600        VARYING NES1  FROM  NESDEC  BY  -1
012700           UNTIL NES1  IS EQUAL TO  0
012800              OR NES2  IS EQUAL TO  0.
012900*
013000     GO TO  Z99Y-MOVE-BUILT-NUM-TO-OUTPUT.
013100*
013200 Z99Y-NE-SET-WHOLE-NUMBER.
013300*
013400* STORE ALL WHOLE NUMBER DIGITS FROM RIGHT TO LEFT OF WHOLE
013500*   NUMBER PORTION OF THE FIELD.  DECIMAL AND COMMAS, IF ANY,
013600*   ARE BYPASSED.
013700*
013800     IF NUMED-IN (NES1)  IS NUMERIC
013900        MOVE NUMED-IN (NES1)  TO   NUMED-B-DIG (NES2)
014000        SUBTRACT 1            FROM  NES2.
014100*
014200 Z99Y-MOVE-BUILT-NUM-TO-OUTPUT.
014300     MOVE NUMED-BUILD  TO  NUMED-OUT.
014400*
014500     IF NUMED-NEG-SIGN  =  'Y'
014600        MULTIPLY -1  BY  NUMED-OUTPUT.
014700*
014800 Z99Y-RESTORE-NUMED-FIELDS.
014900*
015000* RESTORE FIELDS THAT MAY HAVE BEEN NEGATED BY BEING SET TO
015100*   LOW-VALUES BEFORE PERFORMING Z99Y-NUMERIC-EDIT
015200*
015300     MOVE ','  TO  NUMED-COMMA.
015400     MOVE '.'  TO  NUMED-DECIMAL.
015500     MOVE '-'  TO  NUMED-MINUS.
015600     MOVE '+'  TO  NUMED-PLUS.
```

Figure 20-2 *(Continued)*

```
015700      MOVE '_' TO  NUMED-UNDERLINE.
015800
015900      IF NUMED-STATUS  =  SPACES
016000          MOVE SPACES                       TO  NUMED-MESSAGE
016100      ELSE
016200      IF NUMED-STATUS  =  'IP'
016300          MOVE 'INVALID NUMBER OF DIGITS OR DECIMALS PASSED'
016400                                            TO  NUMED-MESSAGE
016500      ELSE
016600      IF NUMED-STATUS  =  'ES'
016700          MOVE 'EXCESS SIGNS'               TO  NUMED-MESSAGE
016800      ELSE
016900      IF NUMED-STATUS  =  'EP'
017000          MOVE 'EXCESS DECIMAL POINTS'  TO  NUMED-MESSAGE
017100      ELSE
017200      IF NUMED-STATUS  =  'EN'
017300          MOVE 'EXCESS WHOLE NUMBERS'   TO  NUMED-MESSAGE
017400      ELSE
017500      IF NUMED-STATUS  =  'ED'
017600          MOVE 'EXCESS DECIMAL DIGITS'  TO  NUMED-MESSAGE
017700      ELSE
017800      IF NUMED-STATUS  =  'IC'
017900          MOVE 'INVALID CHARACTER'      TO  NUMED-MESSAGE
018000      ELSE
018100      IF NUMED-STATUS  =  'IF'
018200          MOVE 'INVALID FORMAT'         TO  NUMED-MESSAGE
018300      ELSE
018400      IF NUMED-STATUS  =  'CD'
018500          MOVE 'COMMA AFTER DECIMAL'    TO  NUMED-MESSAGE
018600      ELSE
018700      IF NUMED-STATUS  =  'ND'
018800          MOVE 'NO DIGITS ENTERED'      TO  NUMED-MESSAGE
018900      ELSE
019000      IF NUMED-STATUS  =  'N3'
019100          MOVE 'NOT 3 DIGITS FOLLOWING A COMMA'
019200              TO  NUMED-MESSAGE
019300      ELSE
019400          MOVE 'UNSPECIFIED ERROR'      TO  NUMED-MESSAGE.
019500*
019600 Z99Y-EXIT.
019700      EXIT.
019800*
019900*
020000 Z99Z-EDIT-PASS  SECTION.
020100*****************************************************************
020200*           PERFORMED FROM:  Z99Y-NUMERIC-EDIT              *
020300*****************************************************************
020400*
020500* THE ONLY VALID CHARACTERS ARE: THE DIGITS 0 THROUGH 9,
020600*    A SINGLE SIGN (- OR +), COMMAS, OR A SINGLE DECIMAL POINT
020700*    IMBEDDED SPACES ARE NOT PERMITTED
020800* ANY 'VALID' CHARACTERS MAY BE DEACTIVATED BY MOVING LOW-VALUES
020900*    TO THE CHARACTER'S WORKING STORAGE FIELD BEFORE PERFORMING
021000*    Z99Y-NUMERIC-EDIT,  FIELDS ARE RESET AT END OF ROUTINE.
021100*
021200      IF  NUMED-IN (NES1)  IS NUMERIC
021300          OR
021400          (NUMED-IN (NES1)  =    NUMED-DECIMAL  OR  NUMED-COMMA
021500                         OR  NUMED-MINUS   OR  NUMED-PLUS)
021600          NEXT SENTENCE
021700      ELSE
021800          MOVE 'IC' TO  NUMED-STATUS
021900          GO TO Z99Z-EXIT.
022000*
022100* MAY BE A MAXIMUM OF 1 SIGN THAT, IF PRESENT, MUST BE AT THE
022200*    START OR END OF A FIELD.
022300*
022400      IF NUMED-IN (NES1)  =  '-'  OR  '+'
022500          ADD 1 TO  NUMED-SIGN-COUNT
022600          IF NUMED-SIGN-COUNT  IS GREATER THAN  1
022700              MOVE 'ES' TO  NUMED-STATUS
022800              GO TO  Z99Z-EXIT.
022900          ELSE
023000              IF NES1 = NESBEG  OR  NESEND
023100                  NEXT SENTENCE
023200              ELSE
023300              MOVE 'IF' TO  NUMED-STATUS
023400              GO TO  Z99Z-EXIT.
```

Figure 20-2 *(Continued)*

```
023500*
023600* SET NEGATIVE SIGN INDICATOR
023700*
023800     IF NUMED-IN (NES1)  =  '-'
023900        MOVE 'Y'  TO  NUMED-NEG-SIGN.
024000*
024100* SAVE LOCATION OF DECIMAL POINT, IF ANY, IN NESDEC
024200*   MAY BE A MAXIMUM OF 1 DECIMAL POINT
024300*
024400     IF NUMED-IN (NES1)  =  '.'
024500        MOVE NES1  TO  NESDEC
024600        ADD 1      TO  NUMED-DEC-PT-COUNT
024700        IF NUMED-DEC-PT-COUNT  IS GREATER THAN  1
024800           MOVE 'EP'  TO  NUMED-STATUS
024900           GO TO  Z99Z-EXIT.
025000*
025100* TEST THAT COUNT OF WHOLE NUMBERS IN INPUT FIELD DOES NOT EXCEED
025200*   THE MAXIMUM NUMBER OF DIGITS PASSED TO THE ROUTINE
025300* NESDEC = ZERO UNTIL A DECIMAL POINT HAS BEEN ENCOUNTERED
025400*
025500     IF NESDEC  =  0
025600        IF NUMED-IN (NES1)  IS NUMERIC
025700           ADD 1  TO  NUMED-DIGIT-COUNT
025800           IF NUMED-DIGIT-COUNT  >  NUMED-DIGITS
025900              MOVE 'EN'  TO  NUMED-STATUS
026000              GO TO  Z99Z-EXIT.
026100*
026200* NESDEC IS GREATER THAN ZERO WHEN A DECIMAL POINT HAS BEEN
026300*   ENCOUNTERED AND ITS POSITION SAVED IN NESDEC
026400* COMMA MUST NOT FOLLOW DECIMAL POINT
026500* TEST THAT COUNT OF DECIMAL POS. IN INPUT FIELD DOES NOT EXCEED
026600*   THE MAXIMUM NUMBER OF DIGITS PASSED TO THE ROUTINE
026700*
026800     IF NESDEC  IS GREATER THAN  0
026900        IF NUMED-IN (NES1)  =  ','
027000           MOVE 'CD'  TO  NUMED-STATUS
027100           GO TO  Z99Z-EXIT
027200        ELSE
027300           IF NUMED-IN (NES1)  IS NUMERIC
027400              ADD 1  TO  NUMED-DEC-NUM-COUNT
027500              IF NUMED-DEC-NUM-COUNT  >  NUMED-DECIMALS
027600                 MOVE 'ED'  TO  NUMED-STATUS
027700                 GO TO  Z99Z-EXIT.
027800*
027900* CHECK THAT AT LEAST ONE WHOLE NUMBER OR ONE DECIMAL DIGIT
028000*   WAS ENTERED
028100*
028200     IF NES1  =  NESEND
028300        IF NUMED-DIGIT-COUNT    IS GREATER THAN  0
028400        OR
028500           NUMED-DEC-NUM-COUNT  IS GREATER THAN  0
028600           NEXT SENTENCE
028700        ELSE
028800           MOVE 'ND'  TO  NUMED-STATUS
028900           GO TO  Z99Z-EXIT.
029000*
029100*
029200* CHECK FOR TWO CONSECUTIVE NON-NUMERIC CHARACTERS
029300*   ONLY VALID COMBINATIONS OF TWO NON-NUMERIC CHARACTERS
029400*   ARE: +.  -.  .+  .-
029500*
029600     IF NES1  NOT =  NESEND
029700        MOVE NES1  TO  NES2
029800        ADD 1  TO  NES2
029900        IF NUMED-IN (NES1)    IS  NUMERIC
030000           NEXT SENTENCE
030100        ELSE
030200           IF NUMED-IN (NES2)  IS  NUMERIC
030300              NEXT SENTENCE
030400           ELSE
030500              IF ((NUMED-IN (NES1)  =  '-'  OR  '+')  AND
030600                   NES1  =  NESBEG                     AND
030700                   NUMED-IN (NES2)  =  '.')
030800              OR
030900                 ((NUMED-IN (NES2)  =  '-'  OR  '+')  AND
031000                   NES2  =  NESEND                     AND
031100                   NUMED-IN (NES1)  =  '.')
031200                 NEXT SENTENCE
```

Figure 20-2 *(Continued)*

```
031300                    ELSE
031400                         MOVE 'IF'  TO  NUMED-STATUS
031500                         GO TO  Z99Z-EXIT.
031600*
031700* ANY NUMBER OF HIGH ORDER DIGITS MAY PRECEDE THE 'FIRST' COMMA.
031800* LEADING COMMAS ARE FLAGGED AS ERRORS.
031900* IF NUMED-NUM-AFTER-COMMA-COUNT IS GREATER THAN O WHEN A COMMA,
032000*   DECIMAL, OR THE END OF INPUT DATA IS REACHED, THEN
032100*   LESS THAN 3 DIGITS FOLLOWED A COMMA
032200*
032300     IF NUMED-IN (NES1) =  ','
032400          IF NUMED-DIGIT-COUNT  =  O
032500              MOVE 'IF'  TO  NUMED-STATUS
032600              GO TO  Z99Z-EXIT.
032700*
032800* EXACTLY 3 DIGITS MUST FOLLOW AN OPTIONAL COMMA.
032900* NUMED-NUM-AFTER-COMMA-COUNT IS INITIALLY SET TO 3
033000*
033100     IF NUMF  IN (NES1)  =  ','
033200        IF NUMED-NUM-AFTER-COMMA-COUNT  =  3
033300           MOVE 'Y'   TO  NUMED-NUM-AFTER-COMMA-SWITCH
033400           MOVE ZERO  TO  NUMED-NUM-AFTER-COMMA-COUNT
033500        ELSE
033600           MOVE 'N3' TO  NUMED-STATUS
033700           GO TO  Z99Z-EXIT.
033800*
033900* COUNT DIGITS FOLLOWING A COMMA
034000*
034100     IF NUMED-IN (NES1) IS NUMERIC
034200        IF NUMED-NUM-AFTER-COMMA-SWITCH  =  'Y'
034300           ADD 1  TO  NUMED-NUM-AFTER-COMMA-COUNT.
034400*
034500     IF NES1  =  NESDEC  OR  NESEND
034600        IF NUMED-NUM-AFTER-COMMA-SWITCH    =  'Y'
034700           IF NUMED-NUM-AFTER-COMMA-COUNT  =   3
034800              MOVE 'N'  TO  NUMED-NUM-AFTER-COMMA-SWITCH
034900           ELSE
035000              MOVE 'N3' TO  NUMED-STATUS
035100              GO TO  Z99Z-EXIT.
035200*
035300 Z99Z-EXIT.
035400     EXIT.
```

CONTENTS

Appendix A consists of the execute interface block (EIB), a description of commonly referenced EIB fields, and the attention identifier fields (DFHAID). DFHAID fields can be copied into working storage, and a program can compare the appropriate field against the EIB field EIBAID in order to determine which AID key was pressed.

APPENDIX A-1:
EXECUTE INTERFACE BLOCK (EIB)

The EIB COPY statement is generated by the CICS translator and copied into a program's linkage section at compile time. The EIB contains fields similar to the following:

```
Ø1  DFHEIBLK COPY DFHEIBLK.
*    EIBLK EXEC INTERFACE BLOCK
*
Ø1  DFHEIBLK.
*         EIBTIME     TIME IN ØHHMMSS FORMAT
    Ø2  EIBTIME     PIC S9(7)     COMP-3.
*
*         EIBDATE     DATE IN ØØYYDDD FORMAT
    Ø2  EIBDATE     PIC S9(7)     COMP-3.
*
*         EIBTRNID    TRANSACTION IDENTIFIER
    Ø2  EIBTRNID    PIC X(4).
*
*         EIBTASKN    TASK NUMBER
    Ø2  EIBTASKN    PIC S9(7)     COMP-3.
*
*         EIBTRMID    TERMINAL IDENTIFIER
    Ø2  EIBTRMID    PIC X(4).
*
*         DFHEIGDI    RESERVED
    Ø2  DFHEIGDI    PIC S9(4)     COMP.
*
*         EIBCPOSN    CURSOR POSITION
    Ø2  EIBCPOSN    PIC S9(4)     COMP.
*
*         EIBCALEN    COMMAREA LENGTH
    Ø2  EIBCALEN    PIC S9(4)     COMP.
*
*         EIBAID      ATTENTION IDENTIFIER
    Ø2  EIBAID      PIC X.
*
*         EIBFN       FUNCTION CODE
    Ø2  EIBFN       PIC XX.
*
*         EIBRCODE    RESPONSE CODE
    Ø2  EIBRCODE    PIC X(6).
*
*         EIBDS       DATASET NAME
    Ø2  EIBDS       PIC X(8).
*
*         EIBREQID    REQUEST IDENTIFIER
    Ø2  EIBREQID    PIC X(8).
```

APPENDIX A-2:
COMMONLY REFERENCED EIB FIELDS

EIBTIME   – Time that the task was initiated.

EIBDATE   – Date the task was started.

EIBTRNID – Transaction Identifier (TRANSID).

EIBTASKN – contains the task number assigned by CICS.

EIBTRMID – Terminal Identifier.

EIBCPOSN – position of the cursor on the screen before a
Receive Map Command is executed.

EIBCALEN – length of the COMMAREA – determined by the size of
the LENGTH ( ) field in a RETURN or XCTL command.

EIBAID   – Attention Identifier, contents are determined by
the AID key pressed

APPENDIX A-3:
ATTENTION IDENTIFIER FIELDS (DFHAID)

A DFHAID field can be compared against the EIB field EIBAID, in order to determine which AID key was pressed by a terminal operator. DFHAID consists of fields which are similar to the following:

```
01   DFHAID    COPY   DFHAID.
01   DFHAID.
       02   DFHNULL        PIC X   VALUE ' '.
       02   DFHENTER       PIC X   VALUE QUOTE.
       02   DFHCLEAR       PIC X   VALUE ' '.
       02   DFHPEN         PIC X   VALUE '='.
       02   DFHOPID        PIC X   VALUE 'W'.
       02   DFHPA1         PIC X   VALUE '('.
       02   DFHPA2         PIC X   VALUE ' '.
       02   DFHPA3         PIC X   VALUE ','.
       02   DFHPF1         PIC X   VALUE '1'.
       02   DFHPF2         PIC X   VALUE '2'.
       02   DFHPF3         PIC X   VALUE '3'.
       02   DFHPF4         PIC X   VALUE '4'.
       02   DFHPF5         PIC X   VALUE '5'.
       02   DFHPF6         PIC X   VALUE '6'.
       02   DFHPF7         PIC X   VALUE '7'.
       02   DFHPF8         PIC X   VALUE '8'.
       02   DFHPF9         PIC X   VALUE '9'.
       02   DFHPF10        PIC X   VALUE ' '.
       02   DFHPF11        PIC X   VALUE '='.
       02   DFHPF12        PIC X   VALUE ''''.
       02   DFHPF13        PIC X   VALUE 'A'.
       02   DFHPF14        PIC X   VALUE 'B'.
       02   DFHPF15        PIC X   VALUE 'C'.
       02   DFHPF16        PIC X   VALUE 'D'.
       02   DFHPF17        PIC X   VALUE 'E'.
       02   DFHPF18        PIC X   VALUE 'F'.
       02   DFHPF19        PIC X   VALUE 'G'.
       02   DFHPF20        PIC X   VALUE 'H'.
       02   DFHPF21    .   PIC X   VALUE 'I'.
       02   DFHPF22        PIC X   VALUE ' '.
       02   DFHPF23        PIC X   VALUE '.'.
       02   DFHPF24        PIC X   VALUE ')'.
```

CONTENTS

Appendix B consists of copy library members common to more than one text program. It is good practice to develop copy library members for any data items or routines which are expected to be used in more than one program or system. Note the consistency of prefix usage among most data-item copy members. Similar prefixes associate data items with a particular library member.

COPY LIBRARY

The copy library entries are arranged alphabetically for ease of locating as follows:

APPENDIX B-1

```
000100***********************************************************************
000200*    'JRNLRECD'        JOURNAL RECORD          524 BYTES LONG        *
000300*    MANY PROGRAMS FORMAT A 'BEFORE' AND 'AFTER' RECORD WHEN         *
000400*    MAINTENANCE IS PERFORMED AGAINST THE FOLLOWING FILES:          *
000500*         VENDOR-MASTER-FILE        ITEM-MASTER-FILE                 *
000600*                   PURCHASE-ORDER-MASTER-FILE                       *
000700***********************************************************************
000800*
000900 01  JOURNAL-RECORD.
001000     05  JR-KEY.
001100         10  JR-EIBDATE          PIC S9(7)   COMP-3.
001200         10  JR-EIBTIME          PIC S9(7)   COMP-3.
001300         10  JR-SEQUENCE-NUMBER  PIC S9(5)   COMP-3.
001400     05  JR-TYPE                 PIC X.
001500         88  JR-BEFORE-IMAGE                         VALUE 'B'.
001600         88  JR-AFTER-IMAGE                          VALUE 'A'.
001700     05  JR-PREFIX               PIC XX.
001800         88  JR-VENDOR-MASTER                        VALUE 'VM'.
001900         88  JR-PURCHASE-ORDER-MASTER                VALUE 'PO'.
002000         88  JR-ITEM-MASTER                          VALUE 'IM'.
002100     05  JR-EIBTRMID             PIC X(4).
002200     05  JR-PASSWORD             PIC X(6).
002300     05  JR-RECORD-DATA          PIC X(500).
```

APPENDIX B-2

```
000100****************************************************************
000200*    'MAPVDTL1'    VENDOR INQUIRY & DELETE DETAIL - SYMBOLIC MAP    *
000300****************************************************************
000400*
000500 01  VM-DETAIL-MAP.
000600     05  FILLER                 PIC X(12).
000700*
000800     05  MVD-L-DATE             PIC S9(4)    COMP.
000900     05  MVD-A-DATE             PIC X.
001000     05  MVD-D-DATE             PIC X(8).
001100*
001200     05  MVD-L-TIME             PIC S9(4)    COMP.
001300     05  MVD-A-TIME             PIC X.
001400     05  MVD-D-TIME             PIC X(8).
001500*
001600     05  MVD-L-VENDOR-CODE      PIC S9(4)    COMP.
001700     05  MVD-A-VENDOR-CODE      PIC X.
001800     05  MVD-D-VENDOR-CODE      PIC X(8).
001900*
002000     05  MVD-L-VENDOR-NAME      PIC S9(4)    COMP.
002100     05  MVD-A-VENDOR-NAME      PIC X.
002200     05  MVD-D-VENDOR-NAME      PIC X(25).
002300*
002400     05  MVD-L-PHONE-AREA-CD    PIC S9(4)    COMP.
002500     05  MVD-A-PHONE-AREA-CD    PIC X.
002600     05  MVD-D-PHONE-AREA-CD    PIC XXX.
002700*
002800     05  MVD-L-PHONE-1          PIC S9(4)    COMP.
002900     05  MVD-A-PHONE-1          PIC X.
003000     05  MVD-D-PHONE-1          PIC XXX.
003100*
003200     05  MVD-L-PHONE-2          PIC S9(4)    COMP.
003300     05  MVD-A-PHONE-2          PIC X.
003400     05  MVD-D-PHONE-2          PIC X(4).
003500*
003600     05  MVD-L-CONTACT          PIC S9(4)    COMP.
003700     05  MVD-A-CONTACT          PIC X.
003800     05  MVD-D-CONTACT          PIC X(25).
003900*
004000     05  MVD-L-STREET           PIC S9(4)    COMP.
004100     05  MVD-A-STREET           PIC X.
004200     05  MVD-D-STREET           PIC X(20).
004300*
004400     05  MVD-L-DLRS-COMMITTED   PIC S9(4)    COMP.
004500     05  MVD-A-DLRS-COMMITTED   PIC X.
004600     05  MVD-D-DLRS-COMMITTED   PIC $$,$$$,$$$.99CR.
004700*
004800     05  MVD-L-CITY             PIC S9(4)    COMP.
004900     05  MVD-A-CITY             PIC X.
005000     05  MVD-D-CITY             PIC X(18).
005100*
005200     05  MVD-L-STATE-CODE       PIC S9(4)    COMP.
005300     05  MVD-A-STATE-CODE       PIC X.
005400     05  MVD-D-STATE-CODE       PIC XX.
005500*
005600     05  MVD-L-STATE-NAME       PIC S9(4)    COMP.
005700     05  MVD-A-STATE-NAME       PIC X.
005800     05  MVD-D-STATE-NAME       PIC X(14).
005900*
006000     05  MVD-L-ZIP-CODE         PIC S9(4)    COMP.
006100     05  MVD-A-ZIP-CODE         PIC X.
006200     05  MVD-D-ZIP-CODE         PIC X(5).
006300*
006400     05  MVD-L-ATTENTION-OF     PIC S9(4)    COMP.
006500     05  MVD-A-ATTENTION-OF     PIC X.
006600     05  MVD-D-ATTENTION-OF     PIC X(20).
006700*
006800     05  MVD-L-MESSAGE          PIC S9(4)    COMP.
006900     05  MVD-A-MESSAGE          PIC X.
007000     05  MVD-D-MESSAGE          PIC X(79).
```

APPENDIX B-3

```
000100***********************************************************************
000200*     'MAPVDTL2'   VENDOR ADD & CHANGE DETAIL - SYMBOLIC MAP     *
000300***********************************************************************
000400*
000500 01  VM-DETAIL-MAP.
000600     05  FILLER                   PIC X(12).
000700*
000800     05  MVD-L-DATE               PIC S9(4)    COMP.
000900     05  MVD-A-DATE               PIC X.
001000     05  MVD-D-DATE               PIC X(8).
001100*
001200     05  MVD-L-TIME               PIC S9(4)    COMP.
001300     05  MVD-A-TIME               PIC X.
001400     05  MVD-D-TIME               PIC X(8).
001500*
001600     05  MVD-L-VENDOR-CODE        PIC S9(4)    COMP.
001700     05  MVD-A-VENDOR-CODE        PIC X.
001800     05  MVD-D-VENDOR-CODE        PIC X(8).
001900*
002000     05  MVD-C-L-VENDOR-NAME      PIC S9(4)    COMP.
002100     05  MVD-C-A-VENDOR-NAME      PIC X.
002200     05  MVD-C-D-VENDOR-NAME      PIC X(5).
002300*
002400     05  MVD-L-VENDOR-NAME        PIC S9(4)    COMP.
002500     05  MVD-A-VENDOR-NAME        PIC X.
002600     05  MVD-D-VENDOR-NAME        PIC X(25).
002700*
002800     05  MVD-C-L-PHONE            PIC S9(4)    COMP.
002900     05  MVD-C-A-PHONE            PIC X.
003000     05  MVD-C-D-PHONE            PIC X(6).
003100*
003200     05  MVD-L-PHONE-AREA-CD      PIC S9(4)    COMP.
003300     05  MVD-A-PHONE-AREA-CD      PIC X.
003400     05  MVD-D-PHONE-AREA-CD      PIC XXX.
003500*
003600     05  MVD-L-PHONE-1            PIC S9(4)    COMP.
003700     05  MVD-A-PHONE-1            PIC X.
003800     05  MVD-D-PHONE-1            PIC XXX.
003900*
004000     05  MVD-L-PHONE-2            PIC S9(4)    COMP.
004100     05  MVD-A-PHONE-2            PIC X.
004200     05  MVD-D-PHONE-2            PIC X(4).
004300*
004400     05  MVD-L-CONTACT            PIC S9(4)    COMP.
004500     05  MVD-A-CONTACT            PIC X.
004600     05  MVD-D-CONTACT            PIC X(25).
004700*
004800     05  MVD-C-L-STREET           PIC S9(4)    COMP.
004900     05  MVD-C-A-STREET           PIC X.
005000     05  MVD-C-D-STREET           PIC X(17).
005100*
005200     05  MVD-L-STREET             PIC S9(4)    COMP.
005300     05  MVD-A-STREET             PIC X.
005400     05  MVD-D-STREET             PIC X(20).
005500
005600     05  MVD-C-L-CITY             PIC S9(4)    COMP.
005700     05  MVD-C-A-CITY             PIC X.
005800     05  MVD-C-D-CITY             PIC X(5).
005900*
006000     05  MVD-L-CITY               PIC S9(4)    COMP.
006100     05  MVD-A-CITY               PIC X.
006200     05  MVD-D-CITY               PIC X(18).
006300*
006400     05  MVD-C-L-STATE            PIC S9(4)    COMP.
006500     05  MVD-C-A-STATE            PIC X.
006600     05  MVD-C-D-STATE            PIC X(6).
006700*
```

APPENDIX B-3 *(Continued)*

```
006800    05   MVD-L-STATE-CODE        PIC S9(4)    COMP.
006900    05   MVD-A-STATE-CODE        PIC X.
007000    05   MVD-D-STATE-CODE        PIC XX.
007100*
007200    05   MVD-L-STATE-NAME        PIC S9(4)    COMP.
007300    05   MVD-A-STATE-NAME        PIC X.
007400    05   MVD-D-STATE-NAME        PIC X(14).
007500*
007600    05   MVD-C-L-ZIP-CODE        PIC S9(4)    COMP.
007700    05   MVD-C-A-ZIP-CODE        PIC X.
007800    05   MVD-C-D-ZIP-CODE        PIC X(4).
007900*
008000    05   MVD-L-ZIP-CODE          PIC S9(4)    COMP.
008100    05   MVD-A-ZIP-CODE          PIC X.
008200    05   MVD-D-ZIP-CODE          PIC X(5).
008300*
008400    05   MVD-L-ATTENTION-OF      PIC S9(4)    COMP.
008500    05   MVD-A-ATTENTION-OF      PIC X.
008600    05   MVD-D-ATTENTION-OF      PIC X(20).
008700*
008800    05   MVD-L-MESSAGE           PIC S9(4)    COMP.
008900    05   MVD-A-MESSAGE           PIC X.
009000    05   MVD-D-MESSAGE           PIC X(79).
```

APPENDIX B-4

```
000100****************************************************************
000200*   'MAPVMCTL'   VENDOR MAINTENANCE CONTROL - SYMBOLIC MAP    *
000300****************************************************************
000400*
000500 01  VM-CONTROL-MAP.
000600     05  FILLER                PIC X(12).
000700*
000800     05  MVC-L-DATE            PIC S9(4)   COMP.
000900     05  MVC-A-DATE            PIC X.
001000     05  MVC-D-DATE            PIC X(8).
001100*
001200     05  MVC-L-TIME            PIC S9(4)   COMP.
001300     05  MVC-A-TIME            PIC X.
001400     05  MVC-D-TIME            PIC X(8).
001500*
001600     05  MVC-L-VEND-CD-1       PIC S9(4)   COMP.
001700     05  MVC-A-VEND-CD-1       PIC X.
001800     05  MVC-D-VEND-CD-1       PIC X.
001900*
002000     05  MVC-L-VEND-CD-2       PIC S9(4)   COMP.
002100     05  MVC-A-VEND-CD-2       PIC X.
002200     05  MVC-D-VEND-CD-2       PIC X(4).
002300*
002400     05  MVC-L-VEND-CD-3       PIC S9(4)   COMP.
002500     05  MVC-A-VEND-CD-3       PIC X.
002600     05  MVC-D-VEND-CD-3       PIC X.
002700*
002800     05  MVC-L-MESSAGE         PIC S9(4)   COMP.
002900     05  MVC-A-MESSAGE         PIC X.
003000     05  MVC-D-MESSAGE         PIC X(79).
```

```
000100**********************************************************************
000200*         'POWSVMCA'  PURCHASING SYSTEM - VENDOR COMMAREA         *
000300**********************************************************************
000400*
000500 01  WS-COMMAREA.
000600     05  CA-FUNCTION-CODE          PIC X           VALUE SPACE.
000700         88  CA-INQUIRY                            VALUE 'I'.
000800         88  CA-ADDITION                           VALUE 'A'.
000900         88  CA-CHANGE                             VALUE 'C'.
001000         88  CA-DELETE                             VALUE 'D'.
001100         88  CA-BROWSE                             VALUE 'B'.
001200*
001300     05  CA-MAP-CONTROL            PIC X           VALUE SPACE.
001400         88  CA-RECEIVE-CTL-MAP                    VALUE '1'.
001500         88  CA-RECEIVE-DTL-MAP                    VALUE '2'.
001600*
001700     05  CA-VENDOR-CODE.
001800         10  CA-VEND-1             PIC X           VALUE LOW-VALUES.
001900         10  CA-VEND-2             PIC X(4)        VALUE LOW-VALUES.
002000         10  CA-VEND-3             PIC X           VALUE LOW-VALUES.
```

APPENDIX B-6

```
000100***********************************************************************
000200* 'STLNKCWA'  - COMMON WORK AREA (CWA)  - LINKAGE SECTION ENTRY *
000300*     GENERALLY USED WITH:  'STWSDTTM' AND 'STPDDTTM' COPIES    *
000400***********************************************************************
000500*
000600 01  CWA-DATA.
000700     05  CWA-CURRENT-DATE       PIC X(8).
000800*         MM/DD/YY
000900     05  CWA-ALPHA-DATA         PIC X(18).
001000*         E.G.  SEPTEMBER 10, 1985
001100     05  CWA-DATE-MMDDYY        PIC X(6).
001200     05  CWA-DATE-YYMMDD        PIC X(6).
001300     05  CWA-COMPANY-NAME       PIC X(25).
```

APPENDIX B-7

```
000100*************************************************************
000200*        'STPDDTTM'  - COMMON DATE/TIME FORMATTING ROUTINE    *
000300*  RETRIEVE CURRENT DATE FROM CWA - FORMAT EIBTIME TO 'HH.MM.SS' *
000400*  COPY 'STWSDTTM' INTO WORKING STORAGE FOR REQUIRED WS- FIELDS *
000500*  COPY 'STLNKCWA' INTO LINKAGE SECTION UNDER BLL-CELLS        *
000600*                  DEFINE:  BLL-CWA-ADDRESS                    *
000700*************************************************************
000800*
000900     EXEC CICS ASSIGN
001000               CWALENG (WS-CWA-LENGTH)
001100     END-EXEC.
001200*
001300     IF WS-CWA-LENGTH  IS GREATER THAN  ZERO
001400         EXEC CICS ADDRESS
001500               CWA (BLL-CWA-ADDRESS)
001600         END-EXEC
001700*
001800*        SERVICE RELOAD CWA-DATA
001900*
002000         MOVE CWA-CURRENT-DATE  TO  WS-CURRENT-DATE
002100     ELSE
002200         MOVE 'ERRORCWA'          TO  WS-CURRENT-DATE.
002300*
002400* FORMAT TIME TO 'HH.MM.SS'
002500     MOVE EIBTIME     TO  WS-EIB-TIME.
002600     MOVE WS-EIB-HH  TO  WS-MAP-HH.
002700     MOVE WS-EIB-MM  TO  WS-MAP-MM.
002800     MOVE WS-EIB-SS  TO  WS-MAP-SS.
```

APPENDIX B-8

```
000100***********************************************************************
000200*        'STPDT037'   LOAD AND SEARCH STATE CODE TABLE          *
000300*     GOOD HIT:   STATE NAME IS RETURNED IN WS-STATE-NAME        *
000400*                  WS-STATE-SEARCH-STATUS = 'G'                  *
000500*     NOT FOUND:  ALL  '*'  ARE RETURNED IN WS-STATE-NAME        *
000600*                  WS-STATE-SEARCH-STATUS = 'E'                  *
000700*  COPY 'STWST037' INTO WORKING STORAGE FOR REQUIRED FIELDS      *
000800*  COPY 'T037STAT' INTO LINKAGE SECTION FOR STATE TABLE          *
000900*              DEFINE:  BLL-T037-STATE-TABLE-ADDRESS             *
001000***********************************************************************
001100*
001200     EXEC CICS LOAD
001300             PROGRAM ('T037LOAD')
001400             SET     (BLL-T037-STATE-TABLE-ADDRESS)
001500.    END-EXEC.
001600*
001700*    SERVICE RELOAD T037-STATE-TABLE.
001800*
001900     SET T037-INDEX  TO  1.
002000     SEARCH T037-STATE-ENTRIES
002100        AT END
002200            MOVE 'E'    TO  WS-STATE-SEARCH-STATUS
002300            MOVE ALL '*' TO  WS-STATE-NAME
002400        WHEN
002500          WS-STATE-CODE  =  T037-STATE-CODE (T037-INDEX)
002600            MOVE 'G'     TO  WS-STATE-SEARCH-STATUS
002700            MOVE T037-STATE-NAME (T037-INDEX)  TO  WS-STATE-NAME.
002800*
002900     EXEC CICS RELEASE
003000             PROGRAM ('T037LOAD')
003100     END-EXEC.
```

APPENDIX B-9

```
000100******************************************************************
000200* 'STWSATTR'   STANDARD ATTRIBUTE LIST USED BY THIS INSTALLATION *
000300******************************************************************
000400*
000500 01  ATTRIBUTE-LIST.
000600     05  UNPROT-NORM            PIC X      VALUE SPACE.
000700     05  UNPROT-FSET            PIC X      VALUE 'A'.
000800     05  UNPROT-BRT             PIC X      VALUE 'H'.
000900     05  UNPROT-BRT-FSET        PIC X      VALUE 'I'.
001000     05  UNPROT-DRK             PIC X      VALUE '<'.
001100     05  UNPROT-DRK-FSET        PIC X      VALUE '('.
001200     05  UNPROT-NUM             PIC X      VALUE '&'.
001300     05  UNPROT-NUM-FSET        PIC X      VALUE 'J'.
001400     05  UNPROT-BRT-NUM         PIC X      VALUE 'Q'.
001500     05  UNPROT-BRT-NUM-FSET    PIC X      VALUE 'R'.
001600     05  UNPROT-DRK-NUM         PIC X      VALUE '*'.
001700     05  UNPROT-DRK-NUM-FSET    PIC X      VALUE ')'.
001800     05  ASKIP-NORM             PIC X      VALUE '0'.
001900     05  ASKIP-FSET             PIC X      VALUE '1'.
002000     05  ASKIP-BRT              PIC X      VALUE '8'.
002100     05  ASKIP-BRT-FSET         PIC X      VALUE '9'.
002200     05  ASKIP-DRK              PIC X      VALUE '@'.
002300     05  ASKIP-DRK-FSET         PIC X      VALUE QUOTE.
```

APPENDIX B-10

```
000100******************************************************************
000200*        'STWSDTTM'  WORKING STORAGE FOR:  DATE/TIME EDITING       *
000300*        DATE IS RETRIEVED FROM THE CWA AND TIME FROM EIBTIME      *
000400*   COPY 'STPDDTTM' INTO PROCEDURE DIVISION FOR FORMATTING LOGIC'  *
000500*   COPY 'STLNKCWA' INTO LINKAGE SECTION FOR CWA AREA              *
000600******************************************************************
000700*
000800 01  WS-DATE-AND-TIME.
000900     05  WS-CURRENT-DATE          PIC X(8)             VALUE SPACES.
001000*
001100     05  WS-MAP-TIME.
001200         10  WS-MAP-HH            PIC XX               VALUE 'HH'.
001300         10  FILLER              PIC X                VALUE '.'.
001400         10  WS-MAP-MM            PIC XX               VALUE 'MM'.
001500         10  FILLER              PIC X                VALUE '.'.
001600         10  WS-MAP-SS            PIC XX               VALUE 'SS'.
001700*
001800     05  WS-EIB-TIME              PIC 9(6)             VALUE ZEROES.
001900     05 FILLER    REDEFINES   WS-EIB-TIME.
002000         10  WS-EIB-HH            PIC XX.
002100         10  WS-EIB-MM            PIC XX.
002200         10  WS-EIB-SS            PIC XX.
002300*
002400 01  WS-CWA-LENGTH               PIC S9(4)    COMP    VALUE ZEROES.
```

APPENDIX B-11

```
000100*********************************************************************
000200*          'STWSSTAT'  COMMON PROGRAM STATUS FIELDS              *
000300*********************************************************************
000400*
000500 01  WS-STATUS-FIELDS.
000600     05  STATUS-OF-RECEIVE        PIC X              VALUE SPACE.
000700         88  GOOD-RECEIVE                            VALUE 'G'.
000800         88  RETURN-TO-CTL-MAP                       VALUE 'C'.
000900         88  INVALID-KEY-PRESSED                     VALUE 'I'.
001000         88  MAPFAIL-ON-RECEIVE                      VALUE 'M'.
001100*
001200     05  STATUS-OF-SELECTION      PIC X              VALUE SPACE.
001300         88  VALID-SELECTION                         VALUE 'G'.
001400         88  INVALID-SELECTION                       VALUE 'E'.
001500*
001600     05  STATUS-OF-FORMAT         PIC X              VALUE SPACE.
001700         88  VALID-FORMAT                            VALUE 'G'.
001800         88  INVALID-FORMAT                          VALUE 'E'.
001900*
002000     05  STATUS-OF-READ           PIC X              VALUE SPACE.
002100         88  RECORD-RETRIEVED                        VALUE 'G'.
002200         88  RECORD-NOT-FOUND                        VALUE 'E'.
002300         88  END-OF-FILE                             VALUE 'F'.
002400*
002500     05  STATUS-OF-VERIFY         PIC X              VALUE SPACE.
002600         88  GOOD-VERIFY                             VALUE 'G'.
002700         88  VERIFY-ERROR                            VALUE 'E'.
002800*
002900     05  STATUS-OF-DELETE         PIC X              VALUE SPACE.
003000         88  GOOD-DELETE                             VALUE 'G'.
003100         88  RECORD-NOT-DELETED                      VALUE 'E'.
003200*
003300     05  STATUS-OF-CHANGE         PIC X              VALUE SPACE.
003400         88  GOOD-CHANGE                             VALUE 'G'.
003500         88  RECORD-NOT-CHANGED                      VALUE 'E'.
003600*
003700     05  STATUS-OF-EDIT           PIC X              VALUE SPACE.
003800         88  GOOD-EDIT                               VALUE 'G'.
003900         88  ERROR-ON-EDIT                           VALUE 'E'.
004000*
004100     05  STATUS-OF-WRITE          PIC X              VALUE SPACE.
004200         88  GOOD-WRITE                              VALUE 'G'.
004300         88  DUPLICATE-RECORD                        VALUE 'E'.
004400*
004500     05  STATUS-OF-ADD            PIC X              VALUE SPACE.
004600         88  GOOD-ADD                                VALUE 'G'.
004700         88  RECORD-NOT-ADDED                        VALUE 'E'.
004800*
004900     05  STATUS-OF-BROWSE         PIC X              VALUE SPACE.
005000         88  GOOD-STARTBR                            VALUE 'G'.
005100         88  BROWSE-NOTFND                           VALUE 'E'.
```

APPENDIX B-12

```
000100***********************************************************************
000200*    'STWST037'   STATE CODE AND NAME WORKING STORAGE ENTRIES     *
000300*       COPY 'T037STAT' INTO LINKAGE SECTION FOR STATE TABLE      *
000400*       COPY 'STPDT037' INTO PROCEDURE DIVISION FOR SEARCH LOGIC  *
000500***********************************************************************
000600*
000700 01  WS-STATE-CODE-SEARCH-ENTRIES.
000800     05  WS-STATE-CODE           PIC XX.
000900     05  WS-STATE-NAME           PIC X(14).
001000     05  WS-STATE-SEARCH-STATUS  PIC X          VALUE SPACE.
001100         88  STATE-FOUND                        VALUE 'G'.
001200         88  STATE-NOT-FOUND                    VALUE 'E'.
```

APPENDIX B-13

```
000100**********************************************************************
000200* 'T037STAT' - STATE CODE AND NAME TABLE - LINKAGE SECTION ENTRY *
000300*  COPY 'STWST037' INTO WORKING STORAGE FOR REQUIRED WS- FIELDS  *
000400*  COPY 'STPDT037' INTO PROCEDURE DIVISION FOR SEARCH LOGIC      *
000500**********************************************************************
000600*
000700 01   T037-STATE-TABLE.
000800      05   T037-STATE-ENTRIES
000900           OCCURS 50 TIMES
001000           INDEXED BY   T037-INDEX.
001100           10   T037-STATE-CODE     PIC XX.
001200           10   T037-STATE-NAME     PIC X(14).
```

APPENDIX B-14

```
000100******************************************************************
000200*    'VENDMAST'   VENDOR MASTER RECORD   -   169 BYTES LONG        *
000300******************************************************************
000400*
000500 01  VENDOR-MASTER-RECORD.
000600     05  VM-VENDOR-CODE.
000700         10  VM-VEND-CD-1        PIC X.
000800         10  VM-VEND-CD-2        PIC X(4).
000900         10  VM-VEND-CD-3        PIC X.
001000     05  VM-VENDOR-NAME          PIC X(25).
001100     05  VM-STREET-ADDRESS       PIC X(20).
001200     05  VM-CITY-STATE-ZIP.
001300         10  VM-CITY-STATE.
001400             15  VM-CITY         PIC X(18).
001500             15  VM-STATE        PIC XX.
001600         10  VM-ZIP-CODE         PIC X(5).
001700     05  VM-TO-ATTN-OF           PIC X(20).
001800     05  VM-PHONE-NO.
001900         10  VM-AREA-CD          PIC XXX.
002000         10  VM-PHONE-1-3        PIC XXX.
002100         10  VM-PHONE-4-7        PIC X(4).
002200     05  VM-CONTACT              PIC X(25).
002300     05  VM-DOLLARS-COMMITTED    PIC S9(7)V99    COMP-3.
002400     05  FILLER                  PIC X(33).
002500*
002600******************************************************************
002700*    WORKING STORAGE FIELDS USED FOR EDITING OF VENDOR CODE      *
002800******************************************************************
002900*
003000 01  WS-VENDOR-CODE.
003100     05  WS-VENDOR-CD-1          PIC X           VALUE SPACE.
003200     05  FILLER                  PIC X           VALUE '-'.
003300     05  WS-VENDOR-CD-2          PIC X(4)        VALUE SPACES.
003400     05  FILLER                  PIC X           VALUE '-'.
003500     05  WS-VENDOR-CD-3          PIC X           VALUE SPACE.
```

DOS BATCH FILES AND COMMANDS

Appendix C is intended for readers who use DOS but are not familiar with batch files. The following overview may prove helpful when you are ready to use CICS software on a microcomputer. A batch file is similar to a mainframe's DOS or OS job stream in that it permits several steps (commands) to be executed through the submission of a single job (batch file). The name of a batch file follows the conventions of other DOS files; it consists of from one to eight alphanumeric characters. The extension of a batch file must be BAT. For example,

```
xxxxxxxx.BAT
```

DOS commands can be included in a batch file; refer to your DOS manual for a detailed reference of DOS commands and batch files. Several DOS commands and controlling statements that are commonly used in a batch file are included in the file EXAMPLE.BAT which follows.

```
REM %1 AND %2 ARE VARIABLES
ECHO OFF
IF NOT EXIST  %1.FIL  GOTO  ERROR1
IF EXIST  %1.FIL  ERASE %1.FIL
IF NOT EXIST  %2.FIL  GOTO  ERROR2
ERASE %2.FIL
GOTO END
:ERROR1
ECHO ON
ECHO FILE %1.FIL DOES NOT EXIST
GOTO END
:ERROR2
ECHO ON
ECHO FILE %2.FIL DOES NOT EXIST IN %0 > %2.ERR
:END
```

The batch file EXAMPLE.BAT can be executed by entering EXAMPLE on the DOS command line, without the BAT extension. An explanation of the commands used in this batch file follows.

- REM — The inclusion of a remark (REM) command in a batch file results in a display of the message that follows the REM command when the batch file is executed. This message is generally used for documentation purposes, and its display can be suppressed by ECHO OFF which is discussed below.

• ECHO — The ECHO command has several forms.

```
ECHO
ECHO OFF
ECHO ON
ECHO [message]
```

ECHO — Shows the current status of ECHO.

ECHO OFF — Suppresses the display of DOS batch file commands which are by default listed prior to execution.

ECHO ON — Restores the display of batch file commands that had been suppressed by a previous ECHO OFF command.

ECHO [message] — A message that follows the ECHO command will be displayed whether ECHO is ON or OFF.

• IF [NOT] — The IF command can be used to test for the absence or existence of a file as follows:

```
IF NOT EXIST file   GOTO   ERROR1
IF EXIST file   ERASE file
```

The first command directs that control pass to the batch file's label ERROR1 if the *file* does *not* exist. The second command directs that if the *file* does exist, then it should be erased. The test for EXIST is not required in this case because if the file does not exist, the previous IF NOT EXIST would pass control to ERROR1. Batch file labels to which control is to be passed are identified by a colon which precedes the label such as :ERROR1, :ERROR2, and :END in the batch file EXAMPLE.BAT.

• GOTO label — This command causes control to pass to the label that follows the GOTO.

• ERASE file — The ERASE command will erase the specified file.

• %n Replaceable parameters — Any parameters that follow the batch file's name when it is entered on the DOS command line are referred to as replaceable parameters. They are substituted for parameters within the batch file that are preceded by a percent sign (%). The first parameter that follows the batch file's name on the DOS command line is substituted for the batch file's %1 parameter. The second parameter that follows the batch file's name is substituted for the batch file's %2 parameter, etc. The digits 0 through 9 can be used as part of replaceable parameters. The name of the batch file itself is represented by %0. For example, if the following is entered on the DOS command line,

```
C>example work1 work2
```

then the batch file will be executed as follows:

```
REM work1 AND work2 ARE VARIABLES
ECHO OFF
IF NOT EXIST   work1.FIL   GOTO   ERROR1
IF EXIST   work1.FIL   ERASE work1.FIL
IF NOT EXIST   work2.FIL   GOTO   ERROR2
ERASE work2.FIL
GOTO END
:ERROR1
ECHO ON
ECHO FILE work1.FIL DOES NOT EXIST
GOTO END
:ERROR2
ECHO ON
ECHO FILE work2.FIL DOES NOT EXIST IN example > work2.ERR
:END
```

Redirecting Output

Output which would by default be displayed on the screen can be redirected to the printer or to a disk file. The greater than symbol (>) is used to indicate that output is to be redirected. For example, in the batch file EXAMPLE.BAT the messages that follow the ECHO commands would display on the screen by default. The second ECHO's message is redirected to a file that has an extension of ERR; it is named work2.ERR in the preceding batch file example. The message could be redirected to the printer by coding PRN immediately following the greater than symbol and eliminating the output file's name. For example,

```
ECHO message > PRN
```

If output is redirected to a file which already exists, that file is replaced by the redirected output. Redirected output can be *added* to an existing file by using a double greater than (>>) sign instead of a single greater than sign. For example,

```
ECHO message >> %2.ERR
```

Redirecting Input

The default device for the entry of input is the terminal's keyboard. Input may be redirected to be received from a file by preceding the file with a less than (<) sign. For example,

```
program < file.EXT
```

This would result in input being received into the *program* from file.EXT instead of from the keyboard.

Miscellaneous DOS Commands and Options

Other commands and options that you may encounter in batch files are described below.

• IF command—additional options.

```
IF [NOT] ERRORLEVEL n DOS command
```

This option of the IF command directs that the DOS command be executed if the previously executed program returned an exit code number of n or greater.

```
IF %1 = = file1    GOTO LABEL1
```

This string condition would be true if the parameter entered on the DOS command line for replaceable parameter %1 was equal to the string "file1."

• LINK program—The LINK program combines two or more object files into a single file. It is commonly used to combine prewritten and compiled I/O routines with a program that uses those routines.

• PAUSE [message]—The pause command is similar to the ECHO command in that it will display a message on the console. The message will only be displayed if ECHO is *on*. The difference is that the PAUSE command will suspend execution of the batch file until a keyboard key is pressed. This enables an operator to take required action such as mounting a floppy disk before continuing or to cancel further execution.

CICS TABLE ENTRIES FOR EXAMPLES IN THIS TEXT

Appendix D contains all CICS table PCT, PPT, and FCT entries required to support the purchase order system examples in this text. The macros used for these tables contain some operands and parameters which were not mentioned in the basic discussion of these tables in this text. The discussion in this appendix contains only the entries that you will need to get your system up and running with the examples presented in this text. For a more complete discussion of CICS tables you should refer to IBM's *CICS Resource Definition Guide* and to David Lee's *CICS/VS Online System Design and Implementation Techniques*. These are listed in the Bibliography. Extended file table (XFT) entries, which are unique to Realia's RealCICS, relate FCT entries to the microcomputer. The discussion of these entries should provide you with a background that will be helpful if your microcomputer's software requires you to code them.

PCT Entries

The PCT entries used are as follows:

```
DFHPCT TYPE=ENTRY,TRANSID=DEMO,TWASIZE=0,PROGRAM=SYSETCWA
DFHPCT TYPE=ENTRY,TRANSID=POVM,TWASIZE=0,PROGRAM=POVMAINT
DFHPCT TYPE=ENTRY,TRANSID=POVI, TWASIZE=0,PROGRAM=POVMINQY
DFHPCT TYPE=ENTRY,TRANSID=POVC, TWASIZE=0,PROGRAM=POVMCHGE
DFHPCT TYPE=ENTRY,TRANSID=POVA, TWASIZE=0,PROGRAM=POVMADDN
DFHPCT TYPE=ENTRY,TRANSID=POVD, TWASIZE=0,PROGRAM=POVMDLET
DFHPCT TYPE=ENTRY,TRANSID=POVB, TWASIZE=0,PROGRAM=POVMBROW
```

- DFHPCT — Macro which defines the PCT.
- TYPE=ENTRY — Specifies that a PCT entry is to be generated.
- TRANSID=xxxx — A one- to four-character transaction identifier code.
- TWASIZE=0 — The transaction work area (TWA) size. The TWA, not commonly employed in command level CICS programs, is not used in this text.
- PROGRAM=xxxxxxxx — This one- to eight-character program name is used to associate the TRANSID to a specific program.

The PPT entries used are as follows:

PPT entries for programs:
DFHPPT TYPE=ENTRY,PROGRAM=SYSETCWA,PGMLANG=COBOL
DFHPPT TYPE=ENTRY,PROGRAM=POVMAINT,PGMLANG=COBOL,RES=YES
DFHPPT TYPE=ENTRY,PROGRAM=JRNLPOST,PGMLANG=COBOL,RES=YES
DFHPPT TYPE=ENTRY,PROGRAM=POVMINQY,PGMLANG=COBOL
DFHPPT TYPE=ENTRY,PROGRAM=POVMCHGE,PGMLANG=COBOL
DFHPPT TYPE=ENTRY,PROGRAM=POVMADDN,PGMLANG=COBOL
DFHPPT TYPE=ENTRY,PROGRAM=POVMDLET,PGMLANG=COBOL
DFHPPT TYPE=ENTRY,PROGRAM=POVMBROW,PGMLANG=COBOL

PPT entries for mapsets:
DFHPPT TYPE=ENTRY,MAPSET=POVMNT1,RES=YES
DFHPPT TYPE=ENTRY,MAPSET=POVMIQ1
DFHPPT TYPE=ENTRY,MAPSET=POVMIQ2
DFHPPT TYPE=ENTRY,MAPSET=POVMCH1
DFHPPT TYPE=ENTRY,MAPSET=POVMCH2
DFHPPT TYPE=ENTRY,MAPSET=POVMAD1
DFHPPT TYPE=ENTRY,MAPSET=POVMAD2
DFHPPT TYPE=ENTRY,MAPSET=POVMDL1
DFHPPT TYPE=ENTRY,MAPSET=POVMDL2
DFHPPT TYPE=ENTRY,MAPSET=POVMBR1
DFHPPT TYPE=ENTRY,MAPSET=PODEMO1

PPT entries for tables:
DFHPPT TYPE=ENTRY,PROGRAM=TO37LOAD,RES=YES
DFHPPT TYPE=ENTRY,PROGRAM=TO53JRSQ,RES=YES

- DFHPPT — Macro which defines the PPT.
- TYPE=ENTRY — Specifies that a PPT entry is to be generated.
- PROGRAM=xxxxxxxx — A one- to eight-character program or table name.
- PGMLANG=COBOL — The program language of the source program. If no entry is specified, the default is PGMLANG=ASSEMBLER. This entry must be omitted for BMS maps.
- RES=YES — Specifies that a program is to be resident in memory; the default is RES=NO. Frequently accessed programs and mapsets are usually defined as resident in order to eliminate the system overhead required to reload a program.
- MAPSET — A one- to seven-character mapset name.

The FCT entries used are as follows:

```
Vendor master file:
DFHFCT TYPE=DATASET,DATASET=VENDMAST,ACCMETH=KSDS,      C
       SERVREQ=(UPDATE,BROWSE,DELETE,NEWREC)

Journal file:
DFHFCT TYPE=DATASET,DATASET=JOURNAL1,ACCMETH=KSDS,      C
       SERVREQ=(UPDATE,DELETE,NEWREC)
```

- DFHFCT — Macro which defines the FCT.
- TYPE=DATASET — Defines this as a data set entry.
- DATASET=xxxxxxxx — A one- to eight-character data set name. This is the entry used with DATASET for file control commands.
- ACCMETH=KSDS — This entry defines the data set to be accessed as a key-sequenced data set (KSDS). An entry-sequenced data set (ESDS) would be coded as ACCMETH=ESDS.
- SERVREQ — This entry defines the type of service requests which can be processed against a file as follows:
  BROWSE — The file may be browsed through by accessing records sequentially.
  DELETE — Records can be deleted from the file.
  NEWREC — Records can be added to the file.
  UPDATE — Records can be read and updated on the file.

The XFT entries used are as follows:

```
            Vendor master file:
            DFHXFT TYPE=FILE,                     C
                   FILENAME='VENDMAST.VSM',       C
                   DATASET=VENDMAST,              C
                   KEY=(6,0),                     C
                   ACCMETH=KSDS,                  C
                   RECLEN=169

            Journal file:
            DFHXFT TYPE=FILE,                     C
                   FILENAME='JOURNAL1.VSM',       C
                   DATASET=JOURNAL1,              C
                   KEY=(11,0),                    C
                   ACCMETH=KSDS,                  C
                   RECLEN=524
```

- DFHXFT — A macro, unique to RealCICS, which defines the XFT.
- TYPE=FILE — Defines this as a RealCICS file.
- FILENAME='xxxxxxxx.ext' — This is the DOS file name and follows DOS naming conventions.
- DATASET=xxxxxxxx — This one- to eight-character data set name must correspond to the DATASET entry in the FCT.
- KEY=(length,offset) — This entry specifies the length and offset of a record's key. Position 1 of a record is considered offset 0.
- ACCMETH=KSDS — This entry defines the data set to be accessed as a key-sequenced data set (KSDS). An entry-sequenced data set (ESDS) would be coded as ACCMETH=ESDS.
- RECLEN=999 — This entry specifies the length of records in the file.

REALIA'S REALCICS
SOFTWARE HIGHLIGHTS

Realia's RealCICS was used to test and debug all program examples in this text. This software is highly compatible with mainframe CICS, and all programs ran exactly as intended; *no* changes were required due to RealCICS. The use of DFHEIBLK, DFHAID, and DFHBMSCA by RealCICS is similar to their use with mainframe CICS. RealCICS generates its own code for the DFHEIVAR calls required by its translator. Realia's MAPEDIT module was used to create and modify all BMS maps discussed in this text, while its BMS module was used to generate the symbolic maps, along with the physical maps, in a microcomputer-compatible form. The generated symbolic maps are identical to those produced by mainframe CICS. A resource definition table (RDT) module was used to convert CICS table macros for PCT, PPT, and FCT entries to a microcomputer-compatible format. The entries for these tables plus the extended file table (XFT), a table unique to Realia's microcomputer implementation of CICS, can be found in App. D.

Realia's Development and Operating Environment

Realia's RealCICS consists of a development system and an operating environment. The development system facilitates the design and coding of BMS maps and command-level CICS programs. A utility program is provided for the creation of a null key-sequenced data set (KSDS) that can be used as a CICS program's VSAM file. Realia provides a skeleton Cobol program that enables a programmer to create microcomputer-compatible code that simulates an assembler code table. The table can then be accessed by the LOAD command that was discussed in Chap. 8. A state code-and-name table and a journal table were created for use in testing the programs in this text, using an easy-to-modify skeleton program provided by Realia. The operating environment facilitates the testing, debugging, and execution of programs by emulating the running of CICS on a microcomputer.

Using MAPEDIT

MAPEDIT is a map generator and editor which enables a screen designer to easily and quickly create and test new BMS maps or to alter and test existing BMS maps. It is menu-driven and enables a map designer to add or delete parameters quickly and easily for the following BMS macros: DFHMSD, DFHMDI, and DFHMDF.

Macro parameters can be added or deleted by placing the cursor on a keyword and pressing a designated keyboard function key to toggle an entry to an active or inactive status. This feature is especially appealing when designing maps that contain color attributes. The location of a field on a map or the result of a change in color or initial value can be checked immediately by displaying the altered screen. The generation of code to handle an OCCURS worked properly. The need to create the user-friendly symbolic maps discussed in Chap. 6 to redefine the BMS map's seven-character field names is eliminated. MAPEDIT permits up to 30-character labels including the generated suffix. Commonly used map fields can be stored in a template and inserted into a map by pressing a defined keyboard function key. Map fields can be easily copied or moved, blank lines can be added, and existing lines can be deleted. This tool makes it easy to design several versions of a map to present to users for evaluation before programming begins. The PPT entry for a map is not required by MAPEDIT; it must be added before a program that uses the map is executed. The screens in Figs. E-1 to E-4 are used by the MAPEDIT map generator.

Realia's BMS Processor

Realia's BMS processor is used to convert the BMS macros created by MAPEDIT or a text editor into a symbolic map's copy member and to create a physical map that is microcomputer-compatible. The source BMS code file (.BMS extension) created or updated by MAPEDIT is input to this module which creates two DOS files that have the following suffixes:

- $.EXE — Contains code for the functions of the physical map in microcomputer format

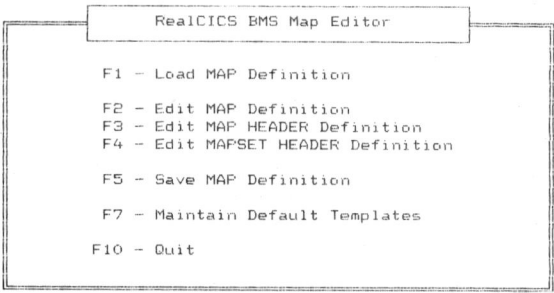

Figure E-1 RealCICS BMS Map Editor.

```
 ┌──── Mapset Header Definition - DFHMSD ├────────────────────────────────┐
 │                                       ──────── MAPSET NAME=POVMNT1      │
 │          TYPE=&SYSPARM                                                  │
 │      STORAGE=Auto|BASE=                                                 │
 │         LANG=(Cobol|Asm|PLI|RPG)     MODE=(In|Out|Inout)               │
 │         CTRL=(Frset,Freekb,Alarm,Print,   )                            │
 │      EXTATT=(No|Maponly|Yes)                                            │
 │        COLOR=(Blue|Red|Pink|Green|Turquoise|Yellow|Neutral|Default)    │
 │      HILIGHT=(Off|Blink|Reverse|Underline)                             │
 │           PS=(Base,   )                                                 │
 │       VALIDN=(Mustenter,Mustfill,Trigger)                              │
 │         TERM=3270      SUFFIX=                                          │
 │      TIOAPFX=(Yes|No)                                                   │
 │        PARTN=(  ,Activate)    LDC=                                      │
 │        OBFMT=(Yes|No)         DATA=(Field|Block)                       │
 │         HTAB=                                                           │
 │         VTAB=                                                           │
 ├────────────────────────────────────────────────────────────────────────┤
 │ TAB, Shift-TAB, and Arrow Keys move the cursor.  Bright keywords are active; │
 │ dim ones are inactive.  Press F1 to activate/deactivate a keyword.     │
 │ Pressing a letter acts as a TAB to the next word starting with that letter. │
 │ Press RETURN for next operand; F3 for previous operand.                │
 └────────────────────────────────────────────────────────────────────────┘
Press F9 when complete, ESC to cancel, Alt-H for Help
```

Figure E-2   Mapset Header Definition — DFHMSD.

- .COB — Contains the symbolic map's copy code which is identical in format to that generated on the mainframe

An operating environment transaction, CMAP, can be executed to display and test the entry of data fields on a map. This transaction functions similarly to the CECI transaction for a SEND of a map that was described in Chap. 6.

```
 ┌──── Map Header Definition - DFHMDI ├──────────────────────────────────┐
 │                                     ──────── MAP NAME=MAPPOVM           │
 │         SIZE=(24,80)                                                    │
 │         CTRL=(Frset,Freekb,Alarm,Print,                                │
 │       EXTATT=(No|Maponly|Yes)                                          │
 │        COLOR=(Blue|Red|Pink|Green|Turquoise|Yellow|Neutral|Default)    │
 │           PS=(Base|    )                                               │
 │      HILIGHT=(Off|Blink|Reverse|Underline)                             │
 │       VALIDN=(Mustenter,Mustfill,Trigger)                              │
 │       COLUMN=(   1|Next|Same)                                          │
 │         LINE=(   1|Next|Same)                                          │
 │       FIELDS=No                                                         │
 │        PARTN=(  ,Activate)     OBFMT=(Yes|No)                          │
 │      TIOAPFX=(Yes|No)          HEADER=Yes                              │
 │         DATA=(Field|Block)     TRAILER=Yes                             │
 │      JUSTIFY=(Left,Right|First,Last)                                   │
 ├────────────────────────────────────────────────────────────────────────┤
 │ TAB, Shift-TAB, and Arrow Keys move the cursor.  Bright keywords are active; │
 │ dim ones are inactive.  Press F1 to activate/deactivate a keyword.     │
 │ Pressing a letter acts as a TAB to the next word starting with that letter. │
 │ Press RETURN for next operand; F3 for previous operand.                │
 └────────────────────────────────────────────────────────────────────────┘
Press F9 when complete, ESC to cancel, Alt-H for Help
```

Figure E-3   Mapset Header Definition — DFHMDI.

```
┌─ DFHMDF - BMS Field Definition ─┐
        POS=( 1 ,27 )
      LABEL=
      LENGTH=25      Maximum length  44
  TERMINATOR=(None|Stop|Askip)
        ATTRB=(Askip|Prot|Unprot,Num,Brt|Norm|Dark,Det,Ic,Fset)
     INITIAL=(Char,Hex) ABC MANUFACTURING COMPANY
       PICIN=
      PICOUT=
       COLOR=(Blue|Red|Pink|Green|Turquoise|Yellow|Neutral|Default)
     HILIGHT=(Off|Blink|Reverse|Underline)
     JUSTIFY=(Left,Right|Blank,Zero fill)
      VALIDN=(Mustenter,Mustfill,Trigger)
          PS=(Base,
       GROUP=            OCCURS=

  TAB, Shift-TAB, and Arrow Keys move the cursor.  Bright keywords are active;
  dim ones are inactive.  Press F1 to activate/deactivate a keyword.
  Pressing a letter acts as a TAB to the next word starting with that letter.
  Press RETURN for next operand; F3 for previous operand.

Press F9 When Complete, ESC To Cancel Alt-H FOR Help
```

Figure E-4 **BMS Field Definition — DFHMDF.**

Realia's Translator

Realia's translator preprocesses command-level CICS statements and generates Cobol code that can be compiled, linked, and executed in the RealCICS's operating environment. A member that is to be included in a program's procedure division by using a copy statement must have been preprocessed by the translator if it contains any CICS commands. The new preprocessed member is the one copied into the program when it is compiled.

RDT Processor

The RDT processor converts CICS table macros such as the PPT, PCT, FCT, and XFT entries to a form that is microcomputer-compatible. These tables can be established as individual members or combined into one member. An executable DOS file is created for each of the tables when they are passed through the RDT processor. Each table can contain a SUFFIX=xx entry that becomes the suffix of the generated executable file. For instance, the purchase order system defined the entry SUFFIX=PO for all tables. This resulted in the creation of the following executable files: DFHPPTPO.EXE, DFHPCTPO.EXE, DFHFCTPO.EXE, and DFHXFTPO.EXE. Entries included in these tables for the purchasing system are defined in App. D. The advantage of using a suffix for tables common to an individual application is that all entries for an application can be stored together and loaded when the operating environment is initiated. An operating environment override file can be defined that will use the requested suffix entries. This file is Realia's version of the mainframe's system initiation table (SIT).

Creating Null KSDS Files

Realia provides a utility named REALCOPY that can create a null key-sequenced data set (KSDS). CICS programs can add records to this file as well as delete or change records. The text's vendor master file VENDMAST and journal file JOURNAL1 were created using this utility as follows:

REALCOPY NUL VENDMAST.VSM[X169]
REALCOPY NUL JOURNAL1.VSM[X524]

Here X designates an indexed file, and 169 and 524 are the record lengths.

REALDBUG

The use of Realia's REALDBUG makes the testing of CICS programs easy and should increase productivity. REALDBUG highlights the Cobol statement about to be executed as a program is advanced one step at a time. A programmer can also set a breakpoint at which the program will stop execution. The viewing and altering of data fields is easy while a program is being stepped through or while it is stopped at a break point. The cursor can be moved onto a field if you wish to view its contents, and its value can be altered if desired. The screen in Fig. E-5 is typical of REALDBUG displays.

```
Realia REALDBUG V2.00 POVMADDN Enter next command
  1141 *
  1142      USING DFHEIBLK DFHCOMMAREA.
  1143 DFHO-MAINLINE SECTION.
  1144 DFHO-MAINLINE-PARAG.
  1145      PERFORM DFHO-INIT.
  1146 AA00-MAINLINE SECTION.
  1147 *
  1148 *    SERVICE RELOAD BLL-CELLS.
  1149 *
  1150      IF EIBCALEN = 0
  1151           PERFORM B000-INITIAL-ENTRY
  1152      ELSE
  1153           MOVE DFHCOMMAREA TO WS-COMMAREA
  1154           IF CA-RECEIVE-CTL-MAP
  1155                PERFORM C000-PROCESS-CONTROL-MAP
  1156           ELSE

  Advance      Breakpoint   Examine      Find defn   Goto next   Jump back
  Look value   Next range   Program set  Quit or F2  Range set   Step ranges
  Trace        Unset range  View value   Where defn  eXecute set
Ctrl Tab Home CR    SCROLL: PgDn PgUp + -    HELP: F1 Alt-A/Z  ||
```

Figure E-5   Typical REALDBUG Display.

Software RealCICS's CWA Support

RealCICS supports the CWA and the use of BLL cells. I wrote a simple program called SYSETCWA that is triggered by a TRANSID named DEMO. That program is listed in App. H; its BMS map which illustrates the definition of color attributes can be found in Chap. 19.

REALMENU

RealCICS provides a user-friendly interface that makes it easy to generate, compile, and link RDT and BMS files. This menu can be used in place of the batch files supplied with the software to initiate translate, compile, and link CICS programs. It can initiate the BMS map editor and run CICS programs and the RealCICS debug facility as well as other functions. The screen in Fig. E-6 shows some of the REALMENU options.

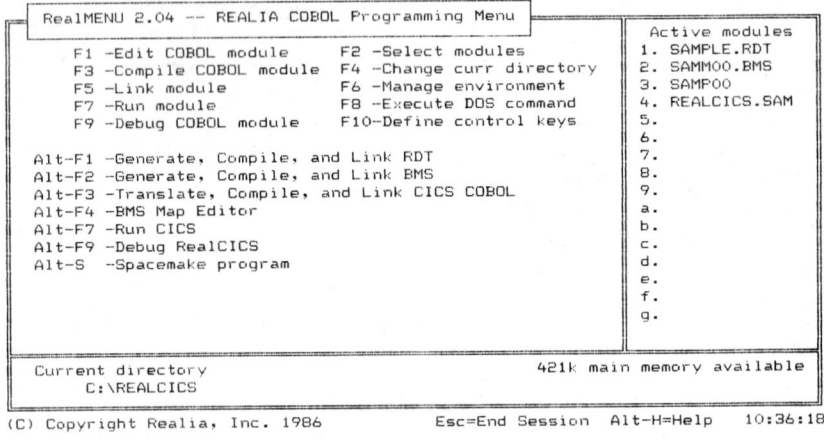

```
RealMENU 2.04 -- REALIA COBOL Programming Menu
                                                    Active modules
     F1 -Edit COBOL module     F2 -Select modules    1. SAMPLE.RDT
     F3 -Compile COBOL module  F4 -Change curr directory  2. SAMM00.BMS
     F5 -Link module           F6 -Manage environment  3. SAMP00
     F7 -Run module            F8 -Execute DOS command  4. REALCICS.SAM
     F9 -Debug COBOL module    F10-Define control keys  5.
                                                        6.
   Alt-F1 -Generate, Compile, and Link RDT             7.
   Alt-F2 -Generate, Compile, and Link BMS             8.
   Alt-F3 -Translate, Compile, and Link CICS COBOL     9.
   Alt-F4 -BMS Map Editor                              a.
   Alt-F7 -Run CICS                                    b.
   Alt-F9 -Debug RealCICS                              c.
   Alt-S  -Spacemake program                           d.
                                                        e.
                                                        f.
                                                        g.

   Current directory                   421k main memory available
        C:\REALCICS

(C) Copyright Realia, Inc. 1986      Esc=End Session  Alt-H=Help    10:36:18
```

Figure E-6   RealMENU Options.

MICRO FOCUS'S PC-CICS
SOFTWARE HIGHLIGHTS

Micro Focus's PC-CICS was used to test all programs in this text. This software is highly compatible with mainframe CICS, and all programs ran exactly as intended with only minor *design* changes required. The use of DFHEIBLK, DFHAID, and DFHBMSCA by PC-CICS is similar to their use with mainframe CICS. PC-CICS generates its own code to support DFHEIVAR translator functions. A system of easy-to-use menus is employed to create and modify BMS maps and to generate symbolic maps, along with physical maps, in a microcomputer-compatible form. The generated symbolic maps are identical to those produced by mainframe CICS. A system of user-friendly menus facilitates creation and maintenance of required PCT and FCT entries. EXEC CICS commands are preprocessed, and programs are syntax-checked in a fashion that permits a user, during testing, to view the source code as it was coded. The Micro Focus ANIMATOR test facility does not display translator-generated calls, which are of no interest to an applications programmer, during program animation.

Micro Focus's Development and
Operating Environment

Micro Focus's PC-CICS development environment is menu-driven. A series of easy-to-use menus are used to assemble maps and to preprocess, syntax-check, and compile command-level CICS programs. This environment supports the addition and maintenance of PCT and FCT entries. The addition of a FCT entry defines a null key-sequenced data set (KSDS) that can be used as a CICS program's VSAM file. The operating environment facilitates the testing, debugging, and execution of programs by emulating the running of CICS on a microcomputer.

Screen Development Facility

The screen development facility provides easy-to-use menus that prompt a user through the creation and maintenance of BMS maps. The FREE FORM SCREEN PAINT option permits the initial design of screens and future maintenance of BMS macros. BMS macros can be transferred, unchanged, in both directions between mainframes and micros. Macros are converted to a Micro Focus–compatible format, and COBOL copy statements are generated. User-friendly symbolic maps, discussed in Chap. 6, can be generated because the one- to seven-character BMS field names may optionally be replaced with descriptive Cobol names. These names can contain up to 30 characters including a generated suffix.

A test definition can be generated that produces code which emulates the function of a physical map. Parameters for DFHMSD, DFHMDI, and DFHMDF macros can be easily added, changed, or deleted using a series of self-prompting menus. Map lines can be deleted or inserted by positioning the cursor on the appropriate line and pressing a designated function key. This ease of creation and modification of maps facilitates the prototyping of different versions of a screen for user approval. The result of field or color changes can be viewed immediately—before programming is started. PC-CICS does not require PPT entries for BMS maps. The screens in Figs. F-1 to F-3 are representative of those used by the PC-CICS Screen Development System.

Micro Focus's Map Assembler

PC-CICS employs a series of user-friendly menus to create new BMS maps or to alter existing maps. The BMS maps are input to the creation of a physical map which is microcomputer-compatible and a symbolic map that is identical in format to the copy member created by mainframe CICS. The source BMS file (.BMS extension) is input to this module which creates two DOS files that have the following suffixes:

- .MST—Contains code for the functions of the physical map in a microcomputer format
- .CPY—Contains the symbolic map's copy code which is identical in format to that generated on the mainframe

An operating environment transaction CMAP can be executed to display and

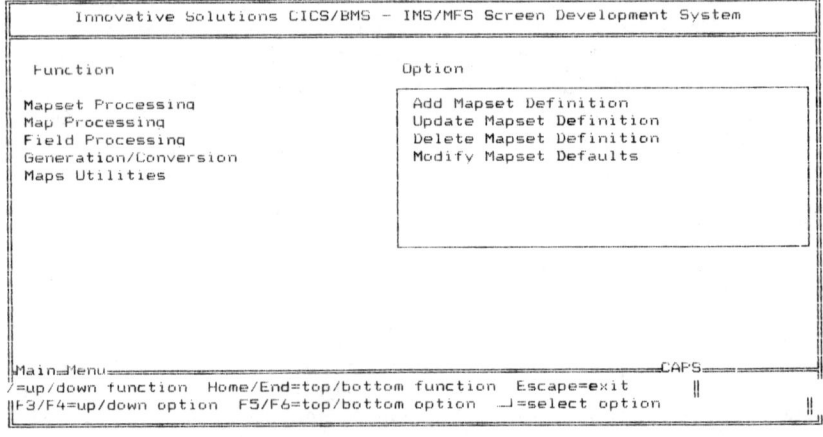

Figure F-1 Innovative Solutions CICS/BMS—IMS/MFS Screen Development System.

```
Basic Mapping Support/Message Format Services Screen Development System
                         Field
01,07 MDDATE
01,27          ABC MANUFACTURING COMPANY
01,72          POVMAD2
02,01          TIME:
02,07 MDTIME
02,30          VENDOR FILE ADDITION
04,01          VENDOR CODE:
04,14 MDVNDCD
05,08 MDCVMNM
05,14 MDVNDNM
05,40
05,45 MDCPHON
05,54          (
05,56 MDAREAC
05,60          )

Field=Update=POVMAD2=MAPPOVD================================CAPS=====
/=up/down list  HOME/END=top/bottom list  Escape=exit
PgDn=next page  Ctrl&Home=beginning of list  ◄┘=select field
```

Figure F-2 BMS/Message Format Services Screen Development System — Field Update.

test the entry of data fields on a map. This transaction is similar to the CECI transaction for a SEND of a map that was described in Chap. 6.

Micro Focus's Translator

PC-CICS's program translation is initiated by a menu, and code is created that can be used with the Micro Focus ANIMATOR debugging tool. The program can be compiled when all known bugs are removed. The translator preprocesses com-

```
Basic Mapping Support/Message Format Service Screens Development System

Options                                Value of Options
  NAME --------- MDDATE
  COLOR --------              Default
  ATTR --------- ASKIP        Blue
  HILIGHT ------              Red
  JUSTIFY ------              Pink
  OCCURS -------              Green
  PS -----------              Turquoise
  VALIDN -------              Yellow
  PICIN --------              Neutral
  PICOUT -------
  GRPNAME ------
  COBOL NAME --
  INITIAL ------

Field=Definition=Update=POVMAD2=MAPPOVD==================CAPS=====
F1=help  F2=clear value F3/F4=up/down value   F5/F6=top/bottom value   F10=view
/=up/down option  Escape
```

Figure F-3 BMS/Message Format Services Screen Development System — Field Definition Update.

mand-level CICS commands and generates code that can be executed using the PC-CICS animate or run facility.

System Parameters Facility

PC-CICS employs easy-to-use menus and screens for the entry and maintenance of PCT and FCT entries. These table entries generate the resources that are required to support the appropriate transactions, programs, and files. A one- to four-character TRANSID and an associated program name is defined using the PCT option. Entry of a KSDS file in the FCT automatically establishes a key-sequenced data set as a null file and makes it available to the system. File I/O modules are generated when using the FCT option. That option facilitates the entry of data set name, record length, key location, and primary or alternate key designation. The screens in Figs. F-4 and F-5 are representative of those used by the System Parameters Facility.

ANIMATOR

ANIMATOR, an interactive debugging tool supplied with PC-CICS, should make the testing of programs easy and increase programmers' productivity. ANIMATOR displays source code and highlights the Cobol statement that is to be executed next as a program is advanced one step at a time. A programmer can set unconditional or conditional breakpoints at which a program will pause in its execution. The viewing and altering of data fields is easy as a program is being stepped through or while it is stopped at a breakpoint. A new Cobol statement can be entered during animation and executed immediately. The cursor can be moved

```
╔══════════════════════════════════════════════════════════════════════╗
║      Innovative Solutions CICS Cobol Command Level Development System   ║
╠══════════════════════════════════════════════════════════════════════╣
║      Tran ID      Program Name      Request Status                      ║
║      DEMO         SYSETCWA                                              ║
║      PUVA         PUVMADDN                                              ║
║      PUVB         PUVMBROW                                              ║
║      PUVC         POVMCHGE                                              ║
║      PUVD         PUVMDLET                                              ║
║      PUVI         POVMINQY                                              ║
║      PUVM         POVMAINT                                              ║
║───────────────────────────END-OF-FILE───────────────────────────────── ║
║                                                                        ║
║                                                                        ║
║                                                                        ║
║                                                                        ║
║                                                                        ║
║                                                                        ║
║                                                                        ║
║PCT Entry Maintenance══════════════════════════════════════CAPS════════ ║
║/=up/down tran id  PgDn=next page  Ctrl&Home=beginning  Escape          ║
║F3=change program  F4=add tran id  F10=delete tran id                   ║
╚══════════════════════════════════════════════════════════════════════╝
```

Figure F-4 Innovative Solutions CICS Cobol Command-Level Development System—PCT Entry Maintenance.

```
┌─────────────────────────────────────────────────────────────────────────┐
│         Innovative Solutions CICS Cobol Command Level Development System   │
│ ═══════════════════════════════════════════════════════════════════════ │
│  File Control Options                                                      │
│   File Name ─────────────────────── VENDMAST                              │
│   Primary or Alternate (P or A) ───── P                                   │
│   Record Length ──────────────────     169                                │
│   Key Location ─────────────────────     1                                │
│   Key Length ───────────────────────     6                                │
│   Associated File ID ──────────────                                       │
│                                                                           │
│                                                                           │
│                                                                           │
│                                                                           │
│                                                                           │
│                                                                           │
│                                                                           │
│ ┴CT┴File┴Maintenance════════════════════════════════════════CAPS══════   │
│ /=up/down option  F7=save  Escape         ‖                               │
└─────────────────────────────────────────────────────────────────────────┘
```

Figure F-5 Innovative Solutions CICS Cobol Command-Level Development System — FCT File Maintenance.

onto a field in order to view its contents, and the field's value can be altered. A designated function key can be pressed at any point during program animation in order to view the user screen. The screen in Fig. F-6 is representative of those used by the ANIMATOR facility.

SPF Interface

A micro/SPF program editor which is highly compatible with the Interactive System Productivity Facility (ISPF) used with IBM mainframe systems can be

```
605*******************************************************************
606*           PERFORMED FROM:   B150-BROWSE-PROCESSING        *
607*******************************************************************
608*
609      MOVE 'G'  TO  STATUS-OF-READ.
610*
611      EXEC CICS HANDLE CONDITION
612               ENDFILE (B152-ENDBR)
613      END-EXEC.
614*
615      EXEC CICS READNEXT
616               DATASET ('VENDMAST')
617               INTO    (VENDOR-MASTER-RECORD)
618               RIDFLD  (CA-VENDOR-CODE)
619      END-EXEC.
620*
621      ADD 1  TO  TS-SUB.
622*
623      IF TS-SUB  =  1
624         MOVE CA-VENDOR-CODE  TO  TS-VENDOR-CD.
625      IF CA-TS-ITEM  IS GREATER THAN  CA-TS-MAXIMUM
Animate───PGVMBROW──────────────────────Level=04─Speed=3─Caps─Num─Scroll
F1=help F2=view F3=align F4=exchange F5=where F6=look-up  F9/F10=word-</> Escape
Step Go Zoom next-If Perform Reset Break Env Query Find Locate Text Do 0-9=speed
```

Figure F-6 ANIMATOR Screen.

```
----------------------  micro/SPF PRIMARY OPTION MENU  ------------------  ENTER SELECTION
OPTION  ===>
                                                             USERID   - MICROSPF
    O   ISPF PARMS  - Specify user parameters                TIME     - 00:38:30
    1   BROWSE      - Display source data or output listings TERMINAL - IBM P.C.
    2   EDIT        - Create or change source data           PF KEYS  - 24
    3   UTILITIES   - Perform utility functions
    4   FOREGROUND  - Invoke language processors in foreground
    6   COMMAND     - Enter DOS command
    C   CHANGES     - Display summary of changes for this release
    N   NCF         - Network Copy Facility
    T   TUTORIAL    - Display information about micro/SPF
    V   VDAM        - Invoke VDAM Express menu
    X   EXIT        - Terminate micro/SPF

Enter END command to terminate micro/SPF



    ----------------------------------------------------------------------------
    | micro/SPF                                                   Version 3.2  |
    | Copyright (c) 1983,1984,1985                          All Rights Reserved|
    | Serial No. SAPC320985001520                          Phaser Systems, Inc.|
    ----------------------------------------------------------------------------
    06/01/87 00:38 CD>C:\PCCICS                                       CAPS
```

Figure F-7 Micro/SPF Primary Option Menu.

initiated directly from the PC-CICS main menu. Micro/SPF, in addition to being almost identical to ISPF's browse and edit functions, has the ability to handle very large source programs as a result of its virtual paging technology. The micro/SPF screen in Fig. F-7 should look familiar to mainframe programmers who have worked with ISPF.

TRIANGLE'S CICS/PC
SOFTWARE HIGHLIGHTS

Triangle's CICS/pc was used to test all programs in this text. This software is highly compatible with mainframe CICS, and all programs ran exactly as intended with only minor *design* changes required. The use of DFHEIBLK, DFHAID, DFHBMSCA, and DFHEIVAR by CICS/pc is similar to their use with mainframe CICS. CICS/pc is unique in that it can be used with several different Cobol compilers including Realia's 2.0W or later versions and Micro Focus's COBOL/2. CICS/pc supports both Realia's REALDBUG and Micro Focus's Xilerator, a native code debugging tool. These debugging tools in addition to CICS/pc's Execution Diagnostic Facility (EDF), which is similar to the mainframe's EDF, give programmers a variety of debugging options. CICS/pc's BMS module was used to generate all the text's symbolic maps, along with physical maps in a microcomputer-compatible form. The generated symbolic maps are identical to those produced by mainframe CICS. All CICS tables for the PCT, PPT, and FCT were maintained by CEDA, an easy-to-use CICS transaction. CICS/pc's translator and operating environment as well as the CEDF transaction, the EDF transaction, and the FILE transaction were used for testing.

Triangle's Development and
Operating Environment

Triangle's CICS/pc consists of a development and operating environment. CICS development consists of DOS files that are used for the assembly of BMS maps and the translation and compilation of command-level CICS programs. The operating environment facilitates the testing, debugging, and execution of programs by emulating the running of CICS on a microcomputer. This environment supports the addition and maintenance of CICS tables using the CEDA transaction. New PCT, PPT, FCT, and destination control table (DCT) entries can be added to these tables. The addition of a FCT entry in effect creates a null key-sequenced data set (KSDS) that can be used as a CICS program's VSAM file.

Triangle's BMSASM File

Triangle supplies BMSASM, an executable DOS file, which uses BMS macros as input to create a symbolic map's copy member and a physical map that is microcomputer-compatible. The source BMS code file (.ASM extension) is input to this program which creates two DOS files that have the following suffixes:

- .BMS — Contains code for the functions of the physical map in a microcomputer format
- .COB — Contains the symbolic map's copy code which is identical in format to that generated on the mainframe

An operating environment transaction CEDM can be executed to display and test the entry of data fields on a map. This transaction is similar to the CECI transaction for a SEND of a map which was described in Chap. 6.

Triangle's Translator

Triangle's translator is part of a batch file that is unique to the Cobol compiler being used. It preprocesses command-level CICS commands and generates Cobol code that can be compiled, linked, and executed in the CICS/pc operating environment.

CEDA Transaction

The CEDA transaction displays user-friendly screens that prompt the user for PCT, PPT, DCT, and FCT entries. Table entries can be added, changed, or deleted, and inquiries can be made against these tables. These entries generate the resources that are required to support the appropriate transactions, programs, and files. Entry of a KSDS file in the FCT automatically establishes a key-sequenced data set as a null file and makes it available to the system. The screens in Figs. G-1 to G-4 show the entries required by these tables.

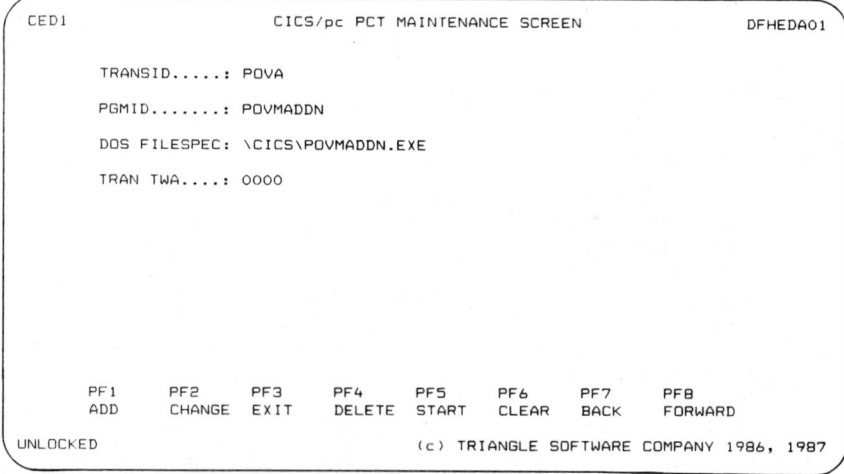

```
CED1                    CICS/pc PCT MAINTENANCE SCREEN              DFHEDAO1


        TRANSID.....: POVA

        PGMID.......: POVMADDN

        DOS FILESPEC: \CICS\POVMADDN.EXE

        TRAN TWA....: 0000






        PF1      PF2      PF3      PF4      PF5      PF6      PF7      PF8
        ADD      CHANGE   EXIT     DELETE   START    CLEAR    BACK     FORWARD

UNLOCKED                             (c) TRIANGLE SOFTWARE COMPANY 1986, 1987
```

Figure G-1 CICS/pc PCT Maintenance Screen — CED1.

```
CED2                    CICS/pc PCT MAINTENANCE SCREEN              DFHEDA02



         PGMID.......: POVMAD1

         DOS FILESPEC: \CICS\POVMAD1.BMS

         USAGE.......: M      P=PROGRAM, M=MAP







         PF1      PF2      PF3      PF4      PF5      PF6      PF7      PF8
         ADD      CHANGE   EXIT     DELETE   START    CLEAR    BACK     FORWARD
UNLOCKED                             (c) TRIANGLE SOFTWARE COMPANY 1986, 1987
```

Figure G-2   **CICS/pc PCT Maintenance Screen — CED2.**

CEDF Transaction

Triangle's CEDF transaction has many similarities to IBM mainframe computer's CEDF transaction. The user is given an initial screen that functions similarly to the EDF stop conditions screen described in Chap. 18. CICS/pc's initial screen looks different but serves a similar purpose; it permits users to define all CICS

```
CED3                    CICS/pc DCT MAINTENANCE SCREEN              DFHEDA03



         DEST NAME...: FLAT

         TYPE........: E

         REC LENGTH..: 00169

         DOS PATH....: C:\CICS\FLAT.VSM







         PF1      PF2      PF3      PF4      PF5      PF6      PF7      PF8
         ADD      CHANGE   EXIT     DELETE   START    CLEAR    BACK     FORWARD
UNLOCKED                             (c) TRIANGLE SOFTWARE COMPANY 1986, 1987
```

Figure G-3   **CICS/pc DCT Maintenance Screen.**

```
 CED4                   CICS/pc FCT MAINTENANCE SCREEN              DFHEDA04

        FILE NAME---> VENDMAST                   DSORG K (E,K,R)

        DOS PATH----> \CICS

        MAX LRECL---> 00169 MIN LRECL 00169 KEYLEN 006 KEYPOS 00000

    OPTIONS: READ: Y WRITE: Y DELETE: Y UPDATE: Y BROWSE: Y


       AIX NAME  KL    KP DUPS                 AIX NAME  KL    KP DUPS




       PF1      PF2      PF3      PF4      PF5      PF6      PF7    PF8
       ADD      CHANGE   EXIT     DELETE   START    CLEAR    BACK   FORWARD
 UNLOCKED                            (c) TRIANGLE SOFTWARE COMPANY 1986, 1987
```

Figure G-4 CICS/pc FCT Maintenance Screen.

commands at which program execution is to stop. Other screens function in a manner similar to that which mainframe programmers are accustomed. Chapter 18 should provide a background which will make the use of CICS/pc's CEDF easy. The screens in Figs. G-5 to G-7 are representative of those used by the CICS/pc CEDF function.

```
 CEDF               CICS/pc  Diagnostic Action Menu

 PLACE A NON-BLANK CHARACTER NEXT TO THE COMMANDS THAT CEDF SHOULD MONITOR
        NOTE:     ANY COMMAND NOT SELECTED WILL NOT BE DISPLAYED BY CEDF


    ABEND              ADDRESS            ASSIGN            ASKTIME
    BIF DEEDIT         BMS RECEIVE        BMS SEND          BMS SEND CNTL
    BMS SEND TEXT      CONVERSE           DELETE            DELETEQ TD
    DELETEQ TS         END BROWSE         FORMATTIME        FREEMAIN
    GETMAIN            HANDLE ABEND       HANDLE AID        HANDLE COND
    IGNORE COND        ISSUE ERASEAUP     LINK              LOAD
    POP                PUSH               READ              READ NEXT
    READ PREV          READQ TD           READQ TS          RELEASE
    RESET BROWSE       RETURN             REWRITE           START BROWSE
    TC RECEIVE         TC SEND            UNLOCK            WRITE
    WRITEQ TD          WRITEQ TS          XCTL

    UNSUPPORTED COMMANDS                  ALL COMMANDS



 ENTER KEY-MAKE SELECTION   PF1-CLEAR ALL SELECTIONS  CLEAR-SELECTION COMPLETE
 UNLOCKED                             (c) TRIANGLE SOFTWARE COMPANY 1986, 1987
```

Figure G-5 CICS/pc Diagnostic Action Menu.

```
                  TRANSACTION: POVM       PROGRAM: POVMAINT
         STATUS: PROGRAM INITIATION

               EIBTIME      = 0063944
               EIBDATE      = 0087152
               EIBTRNID     = 'POVM'
               EIBTASKN     = 0000016
               EIBTRMID     = '3278'
               EIBCPOSN     = 00004
               EIBCALEN     = 00000
               EIBAID       = X'27'
               EIBFN        = X'0E08' RETURN
               EIBRCODE     = X'000000000000'
               EIBDS        =
               EIBRESP      = 0000




         PF2: SWITCH HEX/CHAR       ENTER: CONTINUE
         PF3: END EDF SESSION       PF12: ABORT TRANS
         PF6: SHOW USER DISPLAY


                UNLOCKED            (c) TRIANGLE SOFTWARE COMPANY  1986
```

Figure G-6 **Program Initiation Screen.**

Other Debugging Aids

Triangle's CICS/pc enables users, in addition to CEDF, to use the debugging facilities that are available with your Cobol compiler. Tools such as Realia's REALDBUG and Micro Focus's Xilerator can be used. These tools enable a program to highlight the source code statement that is about to be executed as a

```
                  TRANSACTION: POVM       PROGRAM: POVMAINT
         STATUS: ABOUT TO EXECUTE COMMAND
         EXEC CICS BMS SEND
              MAP('MAPPOVM ')
              MAPSET('POVMNT1 ')
              MAPONLY
              ERASE




         RESPONSE:

         EIBFN=X'1804' BMS SEND



         PF2: SWITCH HEX/CHAR       ENTER: CONTINUE
         PF3: END EDF SESSION       PF12: ABORT TRANS
         PF6: SHOW USER DISPLAY


                UNLOCKED            (c) TRIANGLE SOFTWARE COMPANY  1986
```

Figure G-7 **Command Execute Screen.**

program is advanced one step at a time. The viewing and altering of data fields is easy as a program is being stepped through or when it is stopped at a break point.

FILE Transaction

CICS/pc's FILE transaction provides file browse and update capabilities for use with VSAM files, temporary storage, and transient data queues. The "CICS/pc File Edit/Display" screen in Fig. G-8 shows the basic layout of the FILE transaction's screen.

Data types and functions supported by the FILE transaction are:

- DATATYPE defines the type of data to be entered.
  FC—File control, the default, is used for VSAM files.
  TS—Temporary storage.
  TD—Transient data.
- FUNC is the function to be performed. Supported functions are:
  BEGB—Begin a browse.
  NEXT—Display the next record during browse processing.
  PREV—Display the previous record during browse processing.
  ENDB—End a browse.
  GET—Get and display the record entered next to the record identification field (RCID).
  GETU—Get the record for update that was entered next to RCID.
  ADDN—Add a new record. The RCID and DATA fields must be entered.
  CHGE—Change a record. The RCID and DATA fields must be entered.

```
 FILE                         CICS/pc File Edit/Display              DFHM005
 DATATYPE FC  FUNC NEXT FILEID VENDMAST SRCHTYP GKGE SIZE 00000
   RCID A01001
   DATA
   MESG FBP00081 - BROWSE STARTED

 LOC
 0000 4130313030314141-20494E4455535452 *A01001AA INDUSTR* MODE      = BROWSE
 0010 49414C2053555050-4C49455320202035 *IAL SUPPLIES   5* DSNAME    = VENDMAST
 0020 35358204855445534F-4E20535452454554 *55 HUDSON STREET* ORG     = KSDS
 0030 2020204E45574152-4B20202020202020 *     NEWARK      * MIN RECSZ= 169
 0040 2020202020202030-37313032525041554C *         07102PAUL* MAX RECSZ= 169
 0050 20414E444552534F-4E20202020202020 * ANDERSON        * KEY LEN  = 6
 0060 333031353535353130-30304A4F484E2053 *3015551000JOHN S* KEY POS  = 0
 0070 494D50534F4E204F-52204D2E204A4F4E *IMPSON OR M. JON*
 0080 4553200000000000C-2020202020202020 *ES .....        *
 0090 2020202020202020-2020202020202020 *                *
 00A0 2020202020202020-20             *                *




 PF1-FORWARD    PF2-BACKWARD    PF10-HEX/CHAR    CLEAR-END
 UNLOCKED                               (c) TRIANGLE SOFTWARE COMPANY 1986, 1987
```

Figure G-8 CICS/pc File Edit/Display Screen.

```
  IMEX                         FILE IMPORT/EXPORT

           IMPORT OR EXPORT? (I OR E) -->'E

           FLAT FILE (TD DESTID) -------> FLAT

           VSAM FILE (FCT DS ID) -------> VENDMAST

           NUMBER OF RECORDS COPIED ----> 17






  UNLOCKED                          (c) TRIANGLE SOFTWARE COMPANY 1986, 1987
```

Figure G-9 File Import-Export Screen

DEL — Delete the record that was entered next to RCID.

FILL — Fill a record with additional data. The RCID and DATA fields must be entered.

RSET — Reset a TS queue.

RWRT — Rewrite a TS queue.

IMEX Transaction

CICS/pc provides an import-export (IMEX) transaction that permits the transfer of data between PC-DOS and VSAM files. Data can be downloaded from the mainframe to PC-DOS files and then imported to create VSAM files for CICS/pc microcomputer applications. Likewise, VSAM files that have been updated by CICS/pc applications can be extracted to PC-DOS files for uploading to a mainframe computer. IMEX includes a file utility that properly handles the conversion of mainframe EBCDIC code to microcomputer ASCII code or reverses the conversion as required. Packed-decimal and binary file data are handled by this utility. The CICS/pc screen used by IMEX is shown in Fig. G-9.

THE DEMO INITIATION PROGRAM'S SOURCE CODE

Appendix H contains the DEMO initiation program, SYSETCWA (Fig. H-1). This short program was written to illustrate the display of color attributes on the system initiation screen that was defined as PODEMO1 in Chap. 18. It was also used to initiate the CWA with the current date which is used in several purchase order system programs in this text. The appropriate logic can be commented out if your microcomputer CICS software does not support the CWA. SYSETCWA is initiated by entering the TRANSID DEMO that was defined in the PCT table in App. D.

Figure H-1   DEMO Initiation Program.

```
000100 IDENTIFICATION DIVISION.
000200 PROGRAM-ID. SYSETCWA.
000300*
000400*                    DISPLAY INITIAL DEMO SCREEN
000500*      SET DIFFERENT FORMATS OF DATE IN THE COMMON WORK AREA (CWA).
000600*
000700 ENVIRONMENT DIVISION.
000800 DATA DIVISION.
000900*
001000 WORKING-STORAGE SECTION.
001100*
001200 01  WS-PROGRAM-FIELDS.
001300     05  FILLER                PIC  X(8)     VALUE 'SYSETCWA'.
001400*
001500     05  WS-CWA-LENGTH         PIC  S9(4)    COMP  VALUE ZEROES.
001600*
001700     05  WS-DATE-YYMMDD.
001800         10  WS-YY-1           PIC XX.
001900         10  WS-MM-1           PIC 99.
002000         10  WS-DD-1           PIC XX.
002100*
002200     05  WS-DATE-MMDDYY.
002300         10  WS-MM-2           PIC 99.
002400         10  WS-DD-2           PIC XX.
002500         10  WS-YY-2           PIC XX.
002600*
002700     05  WS-CURRENT-DATE.
002800         10  WS-CUR-MM         PIC 99.
002900         10  FILLER            PIC X         VALUE '/'.
003000         10  WS-CUR-DD         PIC XX.
003100         10  FILLER            PIC X         VALUE '/'.
003200         10  WS-CUR-YY         PIC XX.
003300*
003400 01  WS-COMMAREA               PIC X.
003700*
003800* COPY BMS SYMBOLIC MAP
003900     COPY PODEMO1.
004000*
004100*
004200 LINKAGE SECTION.
004300*
004400 01  BLL-CELLS.
004500     02  FILLER                PIC  S9(8) COMP.
004600     02  BLL-CWA-ADDRESS       PIC  S9(8) COMP.
004700*
004800*01 CWA-DATA
004900              COPY STLNKCWA.
005000*
005100*
005200 PROCEDURE DIVISION.
005300*
005400 AA00-MAINLINE  SECTION.
005500*
005600*    SERVICE RELOAD BLL-CELLS.
005700*
005800     IF EIBCALEN = ZERO
005900        EXEC CICS SEND
006000              MAP     ('MAPDEMO')
006100              MAPSET ('PODEMO1')
006200              ERASE
006300        END-EXEC
006400*
006500        EXEC CICS RETURN
006600              TRANSID ('DEMO')
006700              COMMAREA (WS-COMMAREA)
006800              LENGTH  (1)
006900        END-EXEC.
007000*
007100*
007200     PERFORM B000-FORMAT-DATE.
007300*
007400     PERFORM C000-FORMAT-CWA.
007500*
007600* TRANSFER CONTROL TO MAIN MENU
007700*
007800     EXEC CICS XCTL
007900              PROGRAM ('POVMAINT')
```

Figure H-1 *(Continued)*

```
008000      END-EXEC.
008100*
008200*
008300 B000-FORMAT-DATE  SECTION.
008400*
008500      MOVE CURRENT-DATE  TO  WS-CURRENT-DATE.
008600*
008700* SET WS-DATE-MMDDYY
008800      MOVE WS-CUR-MM     TO   WS-MM-1.
008900      MOVE WS-CUR-DD     TO   WS-DD-1.
009000      MOVE WS-CUR-YY     TO   WS-YY-1.
009100*
009200* SET WS-DATE-YYMMDD
009300      MOVE WS-CUR-MM     TO   WS-MM-2.
009400      MOVE WS-CUR-DD     TO   WS-DD-2.
009500      MOVE WS-CUR-YY     TO   WS-YY-2.
009600*
009700 B000-EXIT.
009800      EXIT.
009900*
010000*
010100 C000-FORMAT-CWA  SECTION.
010200*
010300      EXEC CICS ASSIGN
010400           CWALENG (WS-CWA-LENGTH)
010500      END-EXEC.
010600
010700      IF WS-CWA-LENGTH  IS GREATER THAN  ZERO
010800          NEXT SENTENCE
010900      ELSE
011000          GO TO  C000-EXIT.
011100
011200      EXEC CICS ADDRESS
011300           CWA (BLL-CWA-ADDRESS)
011400      END-EXEC.
011500*
011600*     SERVICE RELOAD CWA-DATA.
011700*
011800      MOVE SPACES                  TO  CWA-DATA.
011900*
012000      MOVE WS-CURRENT-DATE         TO  CWA-CURRENT-DATE.
012100*
012200      MOVE WS-DATE-MMDDYY          TO  CWA-DATE-MMDDYY.
012300*
012400      MOVE WS-DATE-YYMMDD          TO  CWA-DATE-YYMMDD.
012500*
012600      MOVE 'ABC MANUFACTURING COMPANY'  TO  CWA-COMPANY-NAME.
012700*
012800 C000-EXIT.
012900      EXIT.
```

COMPLETE BMS MAPS FOR TEXT'S PROGRAMS

Appendix I presents complete BMS maps for those programs which included an abbreviated version of the BMS map.

The following BMS maps were included in the text in their entirety; the chapter in which they are found is noted.

BMS map name	Chapter
POVMNT1	6
POVMIQ1	12
POVMIQ2	12
POVMAD2	13
POVMBR1	17
PODEMO1	19

The next group of BMS maps were included in the text in an abbreviated form. They are presented in this appendix in their entirety; the chapter in which they are used is noted.

BMS map name	Chapter	Reference
POVMAD1	13	App. I-1
POVMCH1	14	App. I-2
POVMCH2	14	App. I-3
POVMDL1	15	App. I-4
POVMDL2	15	App. I-5

```
POVMAD1   DFHMSD TYPE=MAP,                                          X
                 TIOAPFX=YES,                                       X
                 CTRL=(FRSET,FREEKB),                               X
                 TERM=3270,                                         X
                 LANG=COBOL,                                        X
                 MODE=INOUT
*
MAPPOVC   DFHMDI SIZE=(24,80),                                      X
                 COLUMN=0001,                                       X
                 LINE=0001
*
          DFHMDF POS=(01,01),                                       X
                 LENGTH=05,                                         X
                 ATTRB=(ASKIP),                                     X
                 INITIAL='DATE:'
*
MCDATE DFHMDF POS=(01,07),                                          X
                 LENGTH=08,                                         X
                 ATTRB=(ASKIP)
*
          DFHMDF POS=(01,27),                                       X
                 LENGTH=25,                                         X
                 ATTRB=(ASKIP),                                     X
                 INITIAL='ABC MANUFACTURING COMPANY'
*
          DFHMDF POS=.01,72),                                       X
                 LENGTH=07,                                         X
                 ATTRB=(ASKIP),                                     X
                 INITIAL='POVMAD1'
*
          DFHMDF POS=(02,01),                                       X
                 LENGTH=05,                                         X
                 ATTRB=(ASKIP),                                     X
                 INITIAL='TIME:'
*
MCTIME DFHMDF POS=(02,07),                                          X
                 LENGTH=08,                                         X
                 ATTRB=(ASKIP)
*
          DFHMDF POS=(02,25),                                       X
                 LENGTH=29,                                         X
                 ATTRB=(ASKIP),                                     X
                 INITIAL='VENDOR FILE ADDITIONS CONTROL'
*
          DFHMDF POS=(07,25),                                       X
                 LENGTH=12,                                         X
                 ATTRB=(ASKIP),                                     X
                 INITIAL='VENDOR CODE:'
*
MCVCOD1 DFHMDF POS=(07,38),                                         X
                 LENGTH=01,                                         X
                 ATTRB=(UNPROT,IC)
*
          DFHMDF POS=(07,40),                                       X
                 LENGTH=01,                                         X
                 ATTRB=(ASKIP),                                     X
                 INITIAL='-'
*
MCVCOD2 DFHMDF POS=(07,42),                                         X
                 LENGTH=04,                                         X
                 ATTRB=(UNPROT)
*
```

Figure APPENDIX I-1 *(Continued)*

```
          DFHMDF POS=(07,47),                              X
                 LENGTH=01,                                X
                 ATTRB=(ASKIP),                            X
                 INITIAL='-'
*
MCVCOD3 DFHMDF POS=(07,49),                                X
                 LENGTH=01,                                X
                 ATTRB=(UNPROT)
*
          DFHMDF POS=(07,51),                              X
                 LENGTH=01,                                X
                 ATTRB=(ASKIP)
*
          DFHMDF POS=(12,19),                              X
                 LENGTH=40,                                X
                 ATTRB=(ASKIP),                            X
                 INITIAL='1. TO ADD VENDOR RECORD    - PRESS ENTER'
*
          DFHMDF POS=(14,19),                              X
                 LENGTH=38,                                X
                 ATTRB=(ASKIP),                            X
                 INITIAL='2. TO BROWSE VENDOR FILE   - PRESS PF4'
*
          DFHMDF POS=(16,19),                              X
                 LENGTH=38,                                X
                 ATTRB=(ASKIP),                            X
                 INITIAL='3. TO RETURN TO MENU       - PRESS PF5'
*
          DFHMDF POS=(18,19),                              X
                 LENGTH=40,                                X
                 ATTRB=(ASKIP),                            X
                 INITIAL='4. TO END SESSION          - PRESS CLEAR'
*
MAPMESG DFHMDF POS=(24,01),                                X
                 LENGTH=79,                                X
                 ATTRB=(ASKIP)
*
          DFHMSD TYPE=FINAL
                 END
```

```
POVMCH1   DFHMSD TYPE=MAP,                                          X
          TIOAPFX=YES,                                             X
          CTRL=(FRSET,FREEKB),                                     X
          TERM=3270,                                               X
          LANG=COBOL,                                              X
          MODE=INOUT
*
MAPPOVC   DFHMDI SIZE=(24,80),                                     X
          COLUMN=0001,                                             X
          LINE=0001
*
          DFHMDF POS=(01,01),                                      X
          LENGTH=05,                                               X
          ATTRB=(ASKIP),                                           X
          INITIAL='DATE:'
*
MCDATE DFHMDF POS=(01,07),                                         X
          LENGTH=08,                                               X
          ATTRB=(ASKIP)
*
          DFHMDF POS=(01,27),                                      X
          LENGTH=25,                                               X
          ATTRB=(ASKIP),                                           X
          INITIAL='ABC MANUFACTURING COMPANY'
*
          DFHMDF POS=(01,72),                                      X
          LENGTH=07,                                               X
          ATTRB=(ASKIP),                                           X
          INITIAL='POVMCH1'
*
          DFHMDF POS=(02,01),                                      X
          LENGTH=05,                                               X
          ATTRB=(ASKIP),                                           X
          INITIAL='TIME:'
*
MCTIME DFHMDF POS=(02,07),                                         X
          LENGTH=08,                                               X
          ATTRB=(ASKIP)
*
          DFHMDF POS=(02,26),                                      X
          LENGTH=27,                                               X
          ATTRB=(ASKIP),                                           X
          INITIAL='VENDOR FILE CHANGES CONTROL'
*
          DFHMDF POS=(07,25),                                      X
          LENGTH=12,                                               X
          ATTRB=(ASKIP),                                           X
          INITIAL='VENDOR CODE:'
*
MCVCOD1 DFHMDF POS=(07,38),                                        X
          LENGTH=01,                                               X
          ATTRB=(UNPROT,IC)
*
          DFHMDF POS=(07,40),                                      X
          LENGTH=01,                                               X
          ATTRB=(ASKIP),                                           X
          INITIAL='-'
*
MCVCOD2 DFHMDF POS=(07,42),                                        X
          LENGTH=04,                                               X
          ATTRB=(UNPROT)
*
```

Figure APPENDIX I-2 *(Continued)*

```
          DFHMDF POS=(07,47),                                          X
                 LENGTH=01,                                            X
                 ATTRB=(ASKIP),                                        X
                 INITIAL='-'
*
MCVCOD3 DFHMDF POS=(07,49),                                            X
                 LENGTH=01,                                            X
                 ATTRB=(UNPROT)
*
          DFHMDF POS=(07,51),                                          X
                 LENGTH=01,                                            X
                 ATTRB=(ASKIP)
*
          DFHMDF POS=(12,19),                                          X
                 LENGTH=40,                                            X
                 ATTRB=(ASKIP),                                        X
                 INITIAL='1. TO CHANGE VENDOR RECORD - PRESS ENTER'
*
          DFHMDF POS=(14,19),                                          X
                 LENGTH=38,                                            X
                 ATTRB=(ASKIP),                                        X
                 INITIAL='2. TO BROWSE VENDOR FILE   - PRESS PF4'
*
          DFHMDF POS=(16,19),                                          X
                 LENGTH=38,                                            X
                 ATTRB=(ASKIP),                                        X
                 INITIAL='3. TO RETURN TO MENU       - PRESS PF5'
*
          DFHMDF POS=(18,19),                                          X
                 LENGTH=40,                                            X
                 ATTRB=(ASKIP),                                        X
                 INITIAL='4. TO END SESSION          - PRESS CLEAR'
*
MAPMESG DFHMDF POS=(24,01),                                            X
                 LENGTH=79,                                            X
                 ATTRB=(ASKIP)
*
          DFHMSD TYPE=FINAL
                 END
```

```
POVMCH2   DFHMSD TYPE                                                   X
              TIO',                                                     X
              C'RL                                                      X
              TERM=3270,                                                X
              LANG=COBOL,                                               X
              MODE=INOUT
*
MAPPOVD   DFHMDI SIZE=(24,80),                                          X
              COLUMN=0001,                                              X
              LINE=0001
*
          DFHMDF POS=(01,01),                                          X
              LENGTH=05,                                                X
              ATTRB=(ASKIP),                                            X
              INITIAL='DATE:'
*
MDDATE    DFHMDF POS=(01,07),                                          X
              LENGTH=08,                                                X
              ATTRB=(ASKIP)
*
          DFHMDF     01,27),                                           X
              LENGTH=25,                                                X
              ATTRB=(ASKIP),                                            X
              INITIAL='ABC MANUFACTURING COMPANY'
*
          DFHMDF POS=(01,72),                                          X
              LENGTH=07,                                                X
              ATTRB=(ASKIP),                                            X
              INITIAL='POVMCH2'
*
          DFHMDF POS=(02,01),                                          X
              LENGTH=05,                                                X
              ATTRB=(ASKIP),                                            X
              INITIAL='TIME:'
*
MDTIME    DFHMDF POS=(02,07),                                          X
              LENGTH=08,                                                X
              ATTRB=(ASKIP)
*
          DFHMDF POS=(02,30),                                          X
              LENGTH=19,                                                X
              ATTRB=(ASKIP),                                            X
              INITIAL='VENDOR FILE CHANGES'
*
          DFHMDF POS=(04,01),                                          X
              LENGTH=12,                                                X
              ATTRB=(ASKIP),                                            X
              INITIAL='VENDOR CODE:'
*
MDVNDCD   DFHMDF POS=(04,14),                                          X
              LENGTH=08
*
MDCVMNM   DFHMDF POS=(05,08),                                          X
              LENGTH=05,                                                X
              ATTRB=(ASKIP),                                            X
              INITIAL='NAME:'
*
MDVNDNM   DFHMDF POS=(05,14),                                          X
              LENGTH=25,                                                X
              ATTRB=(UNPROT,IC)
*
          DFHMDF POS=(05,40),                                          X
              LENGTH=01,                                                X
              ATTRB=(ASKIP)
*
```

Figure APPENDIX I-3 *(Continued)*

```
MDCPHON  DFHMDF POS=(05,45),                                    X
                LENGTH=06,                                      X
                ATTRB=(ASKIP),                                  X
                INITIAL='PHONE:'
*
         DFHMDF POS=(05,54),                                    X
                LENGTH=01,                                      X
                ATTRB=(ASKIP),                                  X
                INITIAL='('
*
MDAREAC  DFHMDF POS=(05,56),                                    X
                LENGTH=03,                                      X
                ATTRB=(UNPROT)
*
         DFHMDF POS=(05,60),                                    X
                LENGTH=01,                                      X
                ATTRB=(ASKIP),                                  X
                INITIAL=')'
*
MDPHON1  DFHMDF POS=(05,62),                                    X
                LENGTH=03,                                      X
                ATTRB=(UNPROT)
*
         DFHMDF POS=(05,66),                                    X
                LENGTH=01,                                      X
                ATTRB=(ASKIP),                                  X
                INITIAL='-'
*
MDPHON2  DFHMDF POS=(05,68),                                    X
                LENGTH=04,                                      X
                ATTRB=(UNPROT)
*
         DFHMDF POS=(05,73),                                    X
                LENGTH=01,                                      X
                ATTRB=(ASKIP)
*
         DFHMDF POS=(06,45),                                    X
                LENGTH=08,                                      X
                ATTRB=(ASKIP),                                  X
                INITIAL='CONTACT:'
*
MDCONTA  DFHMDF POS=(06,54),                                    X
                LENGTH=25,                                      X
                ATTRB=(UNPROT)
*
         DFHMDF POS=(06,80),                                    X
                LENGTH=01,                                      X
                ATTRB=(ASKIP,DRK)
*
MDCSTRT  DFHMDF POS=(08,01),                                    X
                LENGTH=17,                                      X
                ATTRB=(ASKIP),                                  X
                INITIAL='ADDRESS - STREET:'
*
MDSTRET  DFHMDF POS=(08,19),                                    X
                LENGTH=20,                                      X
                ATTRB=(UNPROT)
*
         DFHMDF POS=(08,40),                                    X
                LENGTH=01,                                      X
                ATTRB=(ASKIP)
*
MDCCITY  DFHMDF POS=(09,13),                                    X
                LENGTH=05,                                      X
                ATTRB=(ASKIP),                                  X
                INITIAL='CITY:'
*
MDCITY   DFHMDF POS=(09,19),                                    X
                LENGTH=18,                                      X
                ATTRB=(UNPROT)
*
         DFHMDF POS=(09,38),                                    X
                LENGTH=01,                                      X
                ATTRB=(ASKIP)
*
```

Figure APPENDIX I-3 *(Continued)*

```
MDCSTAT  DFHMDF POS=(10,12),                                         X
                LENGTH=06,                                           X
                ATTRB=(ASKIP),                                       X
                INITIAL='STATE:'
*
MDSTATE  DFHMDF POS=(10,19),                                         X
                LENGTH=02,                                           X
                ATTRB=(UNPROT)
*
MDSTANM  DFHMDF POS=(10,22),                                         X
                LENGTH=14,                                           X
                ATTRB=(ASKIP)
*
MDCZIP   DFHMDF POS=(11,14),                                         X
                LENGTH=04,                                           X
                ATTRB=(ASKIP),                                       X
                INITIAL='ZIP:'
*
MDZIP    DFHMDF POS=(11,19),                                         X
                LENGTH=05,                                           X
                ATTRB=(UNPROT)
*
         DFHMDF POS=(11,25),                                         X
                LENGTH=01,                                           X
                ATTRB=(ASKIP)
*
         DFHMDF POS=(13,02),                                         X
                LENGTH=16,                                           X
                ATTRB=(ASKIP),                                       X
                INITIAL='TO ATTENTION OF:'
*
MDATTOF  DFHMDF POS=(13,19),                                         X
                LENGTH=20,                                           X
                ATTRB=(UNPROT)
*
         DFHMDF POS=(13,40),                                         X
                LENGTH=01,                                           X
                ATTRB=(ASKIP)
*
         DFHMDF POS=(18,10),                                         X
                LENGTH=56,                                           X
                ATTRB=(ASKIP),                                       X
                INITIAL='1. CHANGES, KEY IN NEW DATA        - PRX
                ESS ENTER'
*
         DFHMDF POS=(19,10),                                         X
                LENGTH=54,                                           X
                ATTRB=(ASKIP),                                       X
                INITIAL='2. RETURN TO CHANGES CONTROL SCREEN - PRX
                ESS PF3'
*
         DFHMDF POS=(20,10),                                         X
                LENGTH=54,                                           X
                ATTRB=(ASKIP),                                       X
                INITIAL='3. RETURN TO MENU                  - PRX
                ESS PF5'
*
         DFHMDF POS=(21,10),                                         X
                LENGTH=56,                                           X
                ATTRB=(ASKIP),                                       X
                INITIAL='4. END OF SESSION                  - PRX
                ESS CLEAR'
*
MAPMESG  DFHMDF POS=(24,01),                                         X
                LENGTH=79,                                           X
                ATTRB=(ASKIP)
*
         DFHMSD TYPE=FINAL
                END
```

APPENDIX I-4

```
POVMDL1   DFHMSD TYPE=MAP,                                           X
                 TIOAPFX=YES,                                        X
                 CTRL=(FRSET,FREEKB),                                X
                 TERM=3270,                                          X
                 LANG=COBOL,                                         X
                 MODE=INOUT
*
MAPPOVC   DFHMDI SIZE=(24,80),                                       X
                 COLUMN=0001,                                        X
                 LINE=0001
*
          DFHMDF POS=(01,01),                                        X
                 LENGTH=05,                                          X
                 ATTRB=(ASKIP),                                      X
                 INITIAL='DATE:'
*
MCDATE    DFHMDF POS=(01,07),                                        X
                 LENGTH=08,                                          X
                 ATTRB=(ASKIP)
*
          DFHMDF POS=(01,27),                                        X
                 LENGTH=25,                                          X
                 ATTRB=(ASKIP),                                      X
                 INITIAL='ABC MANUFACTURING COMPANY'
*
          DFHMDF POS=(01,72),                                        X
                 LENGTH=07,                                          X
                 ATTRB=(ASKIP),                                      X
                 INITIAL='POVMDL1'
*
          DFHMDF POS=(02,01),                                        X
                 LENGTH=05,                                          X
                 ATTRB=(ASKIP),                                      X
                 INITIAL='TIME:'
*
MCTIME    DFHMDF POS=(02,07),                                        X
                 LENGTH=08,                                          X
                 ATTRB=(ASKIP)
*
          DFHMDF POS=(02,25),                                        X
                 LENGTH=29,                                          X
                 ATTRB=(ASKIP),                                      X
                 INITIAL='VENDOR FILE DELETIONS CONTROL'
*
          DFHMDF POS=(07,25),                                        X
                 LENGTH=12,                                          X
                 ATTRB=(ASKIP),                                      X
                 INITIAL='VENDOR CODE:'
*
MCVCOD1   DFHMDF POS=(07,38),                                        X
                 LENGTH=01,                                          X
                 ATTRB=(UNPROT,IC)
*
          DFHMDF POS=(07,40),                                        X
                 LENGTH=01,                                          X
                 ATTRB=(ASKIP),                                      X
                 INITIAL='-'
*
MCVCOD2   DFHMDF POS=(07,42),                                        X
                 LENGTH=04,                                          X
                 ATTRB=(UNPROT)
*
```

Figure APPENDIX I-4 *(Continued)*

```
            DFHMDF POS=(07,47),                                    X
                   LENGTH=01,                                      X
                   ATTRB=(ASKIP),                                  X
                   INITIAL='-'
*
MCVCOD3     DFHMDF POS=(07,49),                                    X
                   LENGTH=01,                                      X
                   ATTRB=(UNPROT)
*
            DFHMDF POS=(07,51),                                    X
                   LENGTH=01,                                      X
                   ATTRB=(ASKIP)
*
            DFHMDF POS=(12,19),                                    X
                   LENGTH=40,                                      X
                   ATTRB=(ASKIP),                                  X
                   INITIAL='1. TO DELETE VENDOR RECORD - PRESS ENTER'
*
            DFHMDF POS=(14,19),                                    X
                   LENGTH=38,                                      X
                   ATTRB=(ASKIP),                                  X
                   INITIAL='2. TO BROWSE VENDOR FILE   - PRESS PF4'
*
            DFHMDF POS=(16,19),                                    X
                   LENGTH=38,                                      X
                   ATTRB=(ASKIP),                                  X
                   INITIAL='3. TO RETURN TO MENU       - PRESS PF5'
*
            DFHMDF POS=(18,19),                                    X
                   LENGTH=40,                                      X
                   ATTRB=(ASKIP),                                  X
                   INITIAL='4. TO END SESSION          - PRESS CLEAR'
*
MAPMESG     DFHMDF POS=(24,01),                                    X
                   LENGTH=79,                                      X
                   ATTRB=(ASKIP)
*
            DFHMSD TYPE=FINAL
                   END
```

```
POVMDL2   DFHMSD TYPE=MAP,
                 TIOAPFX=YES,                                      X
                 CTRL=(FRSET,FREEKB),                              X
                 TERM=3270,                                        X
                 LANG=COBOL,                                       X
                 MODE=INOUT                                        X
*
MAPPOVD   DFHMDI SIZE=(24,80),
                 COLUMN=0001,                                      X
                 LINE=0001                                         X
*
          DFHMDF POS=(01,01),
                 LENGTH=05,                                        X
                 ATTRB=(ASKIP),                                    X
                 INITIAL='DATE:'                                   X
*
MDDATE    DFHMDF POS=(01,07),
                 LENGTH=08,                                        X
                 ATTRB=(ASKIP)                                     X
*
          DFHMDF POS=(01,27),
                 LENGTH=25,                                        X
                 ATTRB=(ASKIP),                                    X
                 INITIAL='ABC MANUFACTURING COMPANY'               X
*
          DFHMDF POS=(01,72),
                 LENGTH=07,                                        X
                 ATTRB=(ASKIP),                                    X
                 INITIAL='POVMDL2'                                 X
*
          DFHMDF POS=(02,01),
                 LENGTH=05,                                        X
                 ATTRB=(ASKIP),                                    X
                 INITIAL='TIME:'                                   X
*
MDTIME    DFHMDF POS=(02,07),
                 LENGTH=08,                                        X
                 ATTRB=(ASKIP)                                     X
*
          DFHMDF POS=(02,30),
                 LENGTH=20,                                        X
                 ATTRB=(ASKIP),                                    X
                 INITIAL='VENDOR FILE DELETION'                    X
*
          DFHMDF POS=(04,01),
                 LENGTH=12,                                        X
                 ATTRB=(ASKIP),                                    X
                 INITIAL='VENDOR CODE:'                            X
*
MDVNDCD   DFHMDF POS=(04,14),
                 LENGTH=08,                                        X
                 ATTRB=(ASKIP)                                     X
*
          DFHMDF POS=(05,08),
                 LENGTH=05,                                        X
                 ATTRB=(ASKIP),                                    X
                 INITIAL='NAME:'                                   X
*
MDVNDNM   DFHMDF POS=(05,14),
                 LENGTH=25,                                        X
                 ATTRB=(ASKIP)                                     X
*
```

Figure APPENDIX I-5 *(Continued)*

```
            DFHMDF POS=(05,45),                              X
                   LENGTH=06,                                X
                   ATTRB=(ASKIP),                            X
                   INITIAL='PHONE:'
*
            DFHMDF POS=(05,54),                              X
                   LENGTH=01,                                X
                   ATTRB=(ASKIP),                            X
                   INITIAL='('
*
MDAREAC     DFHMDF POS=(05,56),                              X
                   LENGTH=03,                                X
                   ATTRB=(ASKIP)
*
            DFHMDF POS=(05,60),                              X
                   LENGTH=01,                                X
                   ATTRB=(ASKIP),                            X
                   INITIAL=')'
*
MDPHON1     DFHMDF POS=(05,62),                              X
                   LENGTH=03,                                X
                   ATTRB=(ASKIP)
*
            DFHMDF POS=(05,66),                              X
                   LENGTH=01,                                X
                   ATTRB=(ASKIP),                            X
                   INITIAL='-'
*
MDPHON2     DFHMDF POS=(05,68),                              X
                   LENGTH=04,                                X
                   ATTRB=(ASKIP)
*
            DFHMDF POS=(06,45),                              X
                   LENGTH=08,                                X
                   ATTRB=(ASKIP),                            X
                   INITIAL='CONTACT:'
*
MDCONTA     DFHMDF POS=(06,54),                              X
                   LENGTH=25,                                X
                   ATTRB=(ASKIP)
*
            DFHMDF POS=(08,01),                              X
                   LENGTH=17,                                X
                   ATTRB=(ASKIP),                            X
                   INITIAL='ADDRESS - STREET:'
*
MDSTRET     DFHMDF POS=(08,19),                              X
                   LENGTH=20,                                X
                   ATTRB=(ASKIP)
*
            DFHMDF POS=(08,45),                              X
                   LENGTH=18,                                X
                   ATTRB=(ASKIP),                            X
                   INITIAL='DOLLARS COMMITTED:'
*
MDDLRSC     DFHMDF POS=(08,64),                              X
                   LENGTH=15,                                X
                   ATTRB=(ASKIP),                            X
                   PICOUT='$$,$$$,$$$.99CR'
*
            DFHMDF POS=(09,13),                              X
                   LENGTH=05,                                X
                   ATTRB=(ASKIP),                            X
                   INITIAL='CITY:'
*
MDCITY      DFHMDF POS=(09,19),                              X
                   LENGTH=18,                                X
                   ATTRB=(ASKIP)
*
            DFHMDF POS=(10,12),                              X
                   LENGTH=06,                                X
                   ATTRB=(ASKIP),                            X
                   INITIAL='STATE:'
*
MDSTATE     DFHMDF POS=(10,19),                              X
                   LENGTH=02,                                X
                   ATTRB=(ASKIP)
*
```

Figure APPENDIX I-5 *(Continued)*

```
MDSTANM   DFHMDF POS=(10,22),                                           X
                LENGTH=14,                                              X
                ATTRB=(ASKIP)
*
          DFHMDF POS=(11,14),                                           X
                LENGTH=04,                                              X
                ATTRB=(ASKIP),                                          X
                INITIAL='ZIP:'
*
MDZIP     DFHMDF POS=(11,19),                                           X
                LENGTH=05,                                              X
                ATTRB=(ASKIP)
*
          DFHMDF POS=(13,02),                                           X
                LENGTH=16,                                              X
                ATTRB=(ASKIP),                                          X
                INITIAL='TO ATTENTION OF:'
*
MDATTOF   DFHMDF POS=(13,19),                                           X
                LENGTH=20,                                              X
                ATTRB=(ASKIP)
*
          DFHMDF POS=(18,10),                                           X
                LENGTH=56,                                              X
                ATTRB=(ASKIP),                                          X
                INITIAL='1. DELETIONS, VERIFY DATA BEFORE DELETING  - PRX
                ESS ENTER'
*
          DFHMDF POS=(19,10),                                           X
                LENGTH=54,                                              X
                ATTRB=(ASKIP),                                          X
                INITIAL='2. RETURN TO DELETION CONTROL SCREEN      - PRX
                ESS PF3'
*
          DFHMDF POS=(20,10),                                           X
                LENGTH=54,                                              X
                ATTRB=(ASKIP),                                          X
                INITIAL='2. RETURN TO MENU                          - PRX
                ESS PF5'
*
          DFHMDF POS=(21,10),                                           X
                LENGTH=56,                                              X
                ATTRB=(ASKIP),                                          X
                INITIAL='3. END OF SESSION                          - PRX
                ESS CLEAR'
*
MAPMESG   DFHMDF POS=(24,01),                                           X
                LENGTH=79,                                              X
                ATTRB=(ASKIP)
*
          DFHMSD TYPE=FINAL
                END
```

CICS COMMAND REFERENCE

Appendix J is intended to be a reference to CICS commands that you may wish to look up for a quick format check. The commands are listed alphabetically for convenience, and, following in parentheses, a reference is made to the chapter(s) in which the command is discussed. The box below each entry gives the format for that command. The commands listed in this appendix are currently supported by one or more microcomputer software implementations of CICS. Additional CICS commands should become available to microcomputer users of CICS as multitasking capabilities are added to the operating system and software.

ABEND. (Chap. 20)

```
EXEC CICS ABEND
        [ABCODE ('ABCD')
                / (WS-ABCODE)]
        END-EXEC.
```

ADDRESS. (Chap. 12)

```
EXEC CICS ADDRESS
        CWA (BLL-CWA-ADDRESS)
        END-EXEC.
```

ASKTIME. (Chaps. 10 and 20)

```
EXEC CICS ASKTIME
        [ABSTIME (FO-TIME)]
        END-EXEC.
```

ASSIGN. (Chap. 12)

```
EXEC CICS ASSIGN
        CWALENG (WS-CWA-LENGTH)
        END-EXEC.
```

BIF DEEDIT.   (Chap. 20)

```
EXEC CICS BIF DEEDIT
              FIELD      (WS-DATA)
              LENGTH    (nn)
END-EXEC.
```

CANCEL.   (Chap. 20)

```
EXEC CICS CANCEL
              TRANSID ('TRID')
END-EXEC.
```

DELETE.   (Chap. 11)

```
EXEC CICS DELETE
              DATASET    (FCT entry)
              [RIDFLD    (WS-RECORD-KEY)]
END-EXEC.
```

DELETEQ TD.   (Chap. 20)

```
EXEC CICS DELETEQ TD
              QUEUE (TD-QUEUE)
END-EXEC.
```

DELETEQ TS.   (Chap. 16)

```
EXEC CICS DELETEQ TS
              QUEUE (TS-QUEUE)
END-EXEC.
```

ENDBR.   (Chap. 11)

```
EXEC CICS ENDBR
              DATASET (FCT entry)
END-EXEC.
```

FORMATTIME. (Chap. 20)

```
EXEC CICS FORMATTIME
        ABSTIME        (FO-ABSTIME)
        TIME           (FO-TIME)
        TIMESEP        (FO-TIMESEP)
        DATESEP        (FO-DATESEP)
        YYDDD          (FO-YYDDD)
        YYMMDD         (FO-YYMMDD)
        YYDDMM         (FO-YYDDMM)
        MMDDYY         (FO-MMDDYY)
        DDMMYY         (FO-DDMMYY)
        DAYCOUNT       (FO-DAYCOUNT)
        DAYOFWEEK      (FO-DAYOFWEEK)
        DAYOFMONTH     (FO-DAYOFMONTH)
        MONTHOFYEAR    (FO-MONTHOFYEAR)
        YEAR           (FO-YEAR)
END-EXEC.
```

FREEMAIN. (Chap. 20)

```
EXEC CICS FREEMAIN
          DATA (LS-DATA)
END-EXEC.
```

GETMAIN. (Chap. 20)

```
EXEC CICS GETMAIN
        SET (BLL-pointer)
        LENGTH (WS-LENGTH) / (nn)
        [INITIMG (WS-INITIAL)]
END-EXEC.
```

HANDLE ABEND. (Chap. 20)

```
EXEC CICS HANDLE ABEND
        [PROGRAM (WS-PROGRAM) / ('PROGNAME')]
        [LABEL   (X000-SECTION-PARAGRAPH)]
        [CANCEL]
        [RESET]
END-EXEC.
```

HANDLE AID.   (Chap. 7)

```
EXEC CICS HANDLE AID
          AID KEY (section/paragraph)
          . . .
END-EXEC.
```

HANDLE CONDITION.   (Chap. 5)

```
EXEC CICS HANDLE CONDITION
          condition-name (section/paragraph)
          . . .
END-EXEC.
```

IGNORE CONDITION.   (Chap. 7)

```
EXEC CICS IGNORE CONDITION
          condition-name
          . . .
END-EXEC.
```

LINK.   (Chap. 8)

```
EXEC CICS LINK
          PROGRAM (WS-PROGRAM-NAME)
          / ('PROGNAME')
          [COMMAREA (WS-COMMAREA)]
          [LENGTH    (WS-CA-LENGTH)]
END-EXEC.
```

LOAD.   (Chap. 8)

```
EXEC CICS LOAD
          PROGRAM    (WS-PROGRAM-NAME)
          SET        (BLL-pointer)
          HOLD
END-EXEC.
```

POP. (Chap. 20)

```
EXEC CICS POP HANDLE
END-EXEC.
```

PUSH. (Chap. 20)

```
EXEC CICS PUSH HANDLE
END-EXEC.
```

READ. (Chaps. 11 and 20)

```
EXEC CICS READ
          DATASET    (FCT entry)
          INTO       (WS-RECORD-I-O-AREA)
        / SET        (BLL-pointer)
          RIDFLD     (WS-RECORD-KEY)
          [UPDATE]
END-EXEC.
```

READNEXT. (Chaps. 11 and 20)

```
EXEC CICS READNEXT
          DATASET    (FCT entry)
          INTO       (WS-RECORD-I-O-AREA)
        / SET        (BLL-pointer)
          RIDFLD     (WS-RECORD-KEY)
END-EXEC.
```

READPREV. (Chaps. 11 and 20)

```
EXEC CICS READPREV
          DATASET    (FCT entry)
          INTO       (WS-RECORD-I-O-AREA)
        / SET        (BLL-pointer)
          RIDFLD     (WS-RECORD-KEY)
END-EXEC.
```

READQ TD. (Chap. 20)

```
EXEC CICS READQ TD
        QUEUE    (TD-QUEUE)
        INTO     (TD-DATA)
      / SET      (BLL-pointer)
        LENGTH   (TD-LENGTH)
END-EXEC.
```

READQ TS. (Chaps. 16 and 20)

```
EXEC CICS READQ TS
        QUEUE    (TS-QUEUE)
        INTO     (TS-DATA)
      / SET      (BLL-pointer)
        LENGTH   (TS-LENGTH)
        ITEM     (TS-ITEM)
END-EXEC.
```

RECEIVE. (Chap. 5)

```
EXEC CICS RECEIVE
        INTO     (WS-INPUT)
        LENGTH   (WS-LENGTH)
END-EXEC.
```

RECEIVE MAP. (Chaps. 7 and 20)

```
EXEC CICS RECEIVE
        MAP      (mapname)
        MAPSET   (mapset)
        [INTO    (WS-MAP-AREA)
      / SET      (BLL-pointer)]
END-EXEC.
```

RELEASE. (Chap. 8)

```
EXEC CICS RELEASE
        PROGRAM (name)
END-EXEC.
```

RESETBR. (Chap. 11)

```
EXEC CICS RESETBR
          DATASET   (FCT entry)
          RIDFLD    (WS-RECORD-KEY)
          GTEQ
END-EXEC.
```

RETRIEVE. (Chap. 20)

```
EXEC CICS RETRIEVE
          INTO      (WS-DATA)
        / SET       (BLL-pointer)
          LENGTH    (WS-LENGTH)
END-EXEC.
```

RETURN. (Chap. 5)

```
EXEC CICS RETURN
END-EXEC.
```

REWRITE. (Chap. 11)

```
EXEC CICS REWRITE
          DATASET   (FCT entry)
          FROM      (WS-RECORD-I-O-AREA)
END-EXEC.
```

SEND. (Chap. 5)

```
EXEC CICS SEND
          FROM      (WS-MESSAGE)
          LENGTH    (nn)
          [ERASE]
END-EXEC.
```

SEND MAP. (Chap. 7)

```
EXEC CICS SEND
        MAP      (mapname)
        MAPSET   (mapset)
        FROM     (WS-MAP-AREA)
        [MAPONLY / DATAONLY]
        [ERASE / ERASEAUP]
        [CURSOR]
        [FREEKB]
        [FRSET]
        [ALARM]
END-EXEC.
```

SEND TEXT. (Chap. 20)

```
EXEC CICS SEND TEXT
        FROM     (WS-MESSAGE)
        LENGTH   (nn)
        [ERASE]
END-EXEC.
```

START. (Chap. 20)

```
EXEC CICS START
        TRANSID  ('TRID')
        [FROM     (WS-DATA)]
        [LENGTH   (WS-LENGTH)]
END-EXEC.
```

STARTBR. (Chap. 11)

```
EXEC CICS STARTBR
        DATASET      (FCT entry)
        RIDFLD       (WS-RECORD-KEY)
        GTEQ
        KEYLENGTH    (GENERIC-KEY-LENGTH)
        GENERIC
END-EXEC.
```

UNLOCK. (Chap. 11)

```
            EXEC CICS UNLOCK
                      DATASET (FCT entry)
            END-EXEC.
```

WRITE. (Chap. 11)

```
      EXEC CICS WRITE
                DATASET   (FCT entry)
                FROM      (WS-RECORD-I-O-AREA)
                RIDFLD    (WS-RECORD-KEY)
      END-EXEC.
```

WRITEQ TD. (Chap. 20)

```
            EXEC CICS WRITEQ TD
                      QUEUE    (TD-QUEUE)
                      FROM     (TD-DATA)
                      LENGTH   (TD-LENGTH)
            END-EXEC.
```

WRITEQ TS. (Chap. 16)

```
            EXEC CICS WRITEQ TS
                      QUEUE    (TS-QUEUE)
                      FROM     (TS-DATA)
                      LENGTH   (TS-LENGTH)
                      ITEM     (TS-ITEM)
                      [REWRITE]
            END-EXEC.
```

XCTL. (Chap. 8)

```
            EXEC CICS XCTL
                      PROGRAM      (WS-PROGRAM-NAME)
                            /  ('PROGNAME')
                      [COMMAREA  (WS-COMMAREA)]
                      [LENGTH     (WS-CA-LENGTH)]
            END-EXEC.
```

BIBLIOGRAPHY

Bruno, W., and L. Bosland: *CICS Mastering Command Level Coding using COBOL*, Prentice-Hall, Englewood Cliffs, N.J., 1984.

International Business Machines Corporation Publications. (Check with IBM for latest version, release, and order number because they change periodically.) *CICS Resource Definition Guide, Customer Information Control System/Virtual Storage (CICS/VS) Application Programmer's Reference Manual (Command Level),* and the *VSAM Primer and Reference.*

Jatich, Alida: *CICS Command Level Programming,* Wiley, New York, 1985.

Le Bert, Joseph J.: *CICS Made Easy,* McGraw-Hill Book Company, New York, 1986.

Le Bert, Joseph J., and James B. Massoni: *Advanced Interactive Cobol for Micros: A Practical Approach,* Prentice Hall, Englewood Cliffs, N.J., 1988.

Lee, S. David: *CICS/VS Online System Design and Implementation Techniques,* CCD ONLINE Systems, Dallas, Tex., 1986.

Lee, S. David: *CICS/VS Command Level Programming with COBOL Examples,* CCD ONLINE Systems, Dallas, Tex., 1983.

Lim, Pacifico A.: *CICS/VS Command Level with ANS COBOL Examples.* Van Nostrand Reinhold, New York, 1982.

Lowe, Doug: *CICS for the COBOL Programmer Part 1: An Introductory Course,* Mike Murach & Associates, Fresno, Calif., 1984.

Lowe, Doug: *VSAM for the COBOL Programmer,* Mike Murach & Associates, Fresno, Calif., 1982.

Noll, Paul, and M. Murach: *The COBOL Programmer's Handbook.* Mike Murach & Associates, Fresno, Calif., 1985.

Noll, Paul, and M. Murach: *How to Design and Develop COBOL Programs,* Mike Murach & Associates, Fresno, Calif., 1985.

Wipfler, Arlene: *CICS Application Development and Programming,* Macmillan Publishing Company, New York, 1987.

Wolverton, Van: *Running MS DOS,* Microsoft Press, Bellevue, Wash., 1984.

CICS Software Vendors

Micro Focus, 2465 East Bayshore Road, Suite 400, Palo Alto, Calif., 94303.

Realia Inc., 10 South Riverside Plaza, Chicago, Ill., 60606.

Triangle Software Company, 4340 Stevens Creek Blvd., Suite 275, San Jose, Calif., 95129.

Index

About the Author

Joseph J. Le Bert has played a major role in the development, programming, and maintenance of numerous online and batch systems while functioning as a consultant, project leader, and senior programmer analyst at several companies. He predicts that the use of online interactive systems will grow rapidly, replacing many obsolete batch systems. He is the author of *CICS MADE EASY,* published by McGraw-Hill in 1986, and coauthor with James B. Massoni of *Advanced Interactive Cobol for Micros: A Practical Approach* published by Prentice-Hall in 1988.